I0796725

Rorke's Drift Revisited

Rorke's Drift Revisited

A New Account of the Most Famous Battle of the Anglo-Zulu War

Adrian Greaves

Pen & Sword
MILITARY

First published in Great Britain in 2025 by
Pen & Sword Military
An imprint of Pen & Sword Books Limited
Yorkshire – Philadelphia

ISBN 978 1 03612 215 7

A CIP catalogue record for this book is available from the British Library.

Typeset by Mac Style
Printed in the UK by CPI Group (UK) Ltd, Croydon, CR0 4YY.

The Publisher's authorised representative in the EU for product safety is Authorised Rep Compliance Ltd., Ground Floor, 71 Lower Baggot Street, Dublin D02 P593, Ireland.
www.arccompliance.com

For a complete list of Pen & Sword titles please contact

PEN & SWORD BOOKS LIMITED
47 Church Street, Barnsley, South Yorkshire, S70 2AS, England
E-mail: enquiries@pen-and-sword.co.uk
Website: www.pen-and-sword.co.uk
or
PEN AND SWORD BOOKS
1950 Lawrence Road, Havertown, PA 19083, USA
E-mail: uspen-and-sword@casematepublishers.com
Website: www.penandswordbooks.com

Contents

About the Author

Dr Adrian Greaves, a distinguished author, historian and former 1960s Welch Regiment army officer, has updated and clarified the history of Rorke's Drift by using previously unseen material to both solve a number of mysteries and explain little known facts.

On retirement from the police service in 1989 he went to Rorke's Drift. His visit was mainly out of curiosity having seen the film *Zulu*, but he found scant evidence to support much of the film. At nearby Fugitives' Drift he met and was befriended by David Rattray who was preparing the ground for his lodge. For the next thirty years he used David Rattray's ever-increasingly famous Fugitives' Drift Lodge as his base to research and reassess various aspects of the Anglo-Zulu war. The results of his initial research and many of his subsequent discoveries about Rorke's Drift were the subject of his successful 2002 PhD thesis. This academic work and subsequent meticulous research, and discovery of previously unknown accounts, gives the modern reader a fresh in-depth reassessment of Rorke's Drift.

Greaves' dedicated research in the UK, Europe and South Africa coincided with his role as journal editor of the prestigious *Anglo Zulu War Historical Society* (*AZWHS*). In 2002 he spent many months researching and exploring the Rorke's Drift battlefield with David Rattray while the pair prepared their enduring *Guidebook to the Battlefields of Zululand*. From the Rattrays' lodge overlooking the battlefields they examined many aspects of the war, along with the consequences of that day for both Britain and the world. This latest work uses original sources, including previously unknown material such as the Harford papers which he and Dr David Payne discovered, the diaries and paintings of the Rorke's Drift nurse, Sister Janet Wells, the validity of the alleged Chard reports, and investigates the truthfulness of a clutch of dubious Rorke's Drift accounts.

Foreword

Dr David Payne. *AZWHS* researcher and author of *Harford*

Military victories have long been defining moments in our nation's history and Rorke's Drift is a classic example which is well understood by both civilians and military alike. Over the years, historians and researchers have studied the engagement between the British and Zulus at Rorke's Drift, yet, in terms of military action and the half-dozen major battles during the Anglo-Zulu War, few have acknowledged Rorke's Drift for what it was: a short, sharp engagement lasting just a few hours with barely 100 soldiers engaged. The military in South Africa initially took the event in their stride until the home press and politicians caused underlying resentment among the survivors' fellow officers and soldiers by elevating the survivors' status to that of popular heroes.

Yet curiously, and except in passing, Rorke's Drift was not unduly acknowledged in any contemporary works dealing with the Anglo-Zulu war, even though Queen Victoria appreciated that the role of public opinion had become ever more important in sustaining support for such adventures. The official ratcheting-up of publicity that accompanied the generous distribution of decorations and medals that followed Rorke's Drift only temporarily kept public opinion on board.

Even in Victorian times the British invasion of Zululand must have ranked among the worst military disasters that any nation had the misfortune to suffer. In modern times it is no longer fashionable to take pride in the pointless invasion and destruction of a comparatively unsophisticated and harmless country, especially when the invasion was so brutally conducted. Yet today, the defence of Rorke's Drift is widely considered as one of the greatest epics of British military history, although it was all but forgotten until 1964, when the film *Zulu* and Donald Morris's remarkable book, *The Washing of the Spears* simultaneously elevated Rorke's Drift to excited fame across the land. The book and film respectively portrayed a scenario beloved by the British, of red-coated soldiers in sun-baked Africa, a scenario that became the epic and the legend, myths and all.

Numerous books about Rorke's Drift followed the film *Zulu* but, in my humble opinion, most were hurriedly researched, some lacked references or were regurgitations of previous accounts. Before 1964 the public were in the dark about the Zulu War, and *Zulu* was able to promote many myths, including that of heroic Welsh soldiers and incorrectly identifying the regiment involved. On balance, *The Washing of the Spears* was a remarkably well researched book written in the 1960s by an American intelligence officer from his desk in Berlin without visiting South Africa until years following publication. Likewise, *Zulu* remains a wonderful film which very successfully achieved its aim, to entertain cinema audiences rather than educate them with reality and facts. Sadly, many now treat the film as an educational resource.

Old beliefs and legends can be very enduring when they have lodged themselves into the national psyche, especially when they have remained unchallenged for so long. The phenomenon of widespread acceptance of the mythology surrounding the events of 22 January 1879 would change after 2000 when the author began his meticulous research and intense investigation, mostly on location.

Until 1964 the author was an army officer with the 1st Battalion 41st Welch Regiment and during his service he heard no mention of the Zulu War or Rorke's Drift, yet, today, his regiment's modern equivalent, the Royal Welsh Regiment, annually celebrates 'Rorke's Drift Day' to generously commemorate the South African achievements of the real participants at Rorke's Drift and Isandlwana, the Warwickshire Regiment. On leaving the army the author joined Kent Police. Later, as an experienced detective he became familiar with the process of sifting sound evidence from the dubious or unsubstantiated.

Before commencing his research in 1990 he systematically contacted Rorke's Drift descendants in his quest for fresh material. The response was gratifying and elicited numerous documents, letters, diaries, photographs and reports which had lain unseen since the event, usually in boxes in dark dusty lofts. In one notable instance, following a chance meeting with a descendant of Lieutenant Harford he was given four suitcases of Harford's original Zulu War material to research, most of which was unknown to researchers and included the officer's eye-witness account of the pre-defence of Rorke's Drift. During the following years more significant unknown material was discovered, such as scrapbooks, photographs, handwritten letters and personal journals, including material that was collected and preserved by a young English nurse completing her Zulu War service at Rorke's Drift, Nurse Janet Wells of the Stafford House Committee. His diligent research also uncovered three bundles of Lieutenant Curling's original letters, as well as unearthing the original Isandlwana orders from Lord Chelmsford to Colonel Durnford.

Following an 'after dinner' lecture by the author to a medical conference, a descendant of August Hammar, the real 'Otto Witt' of Rorke's Drift, unexpectedly introduced himself and generously made available the Hammar family's records and letters. Such fresh primary source material explained and corrected many dubious aspects of the defence of Rorke's Drift, previously challenged by respected Zulu War researchers such as Donald Morris and David Rattray.

Over many years the author was privileged to interview and accompany highly accredited historians around and across the battlefield, including David Rattray, Professor Richard Holmes, George Chadwick, Ron Lock, Dr David Payne, Professor John Laband, Peter Quantrill, Lita Webley and David Charles. With the generous translating assistance of Rorke's Drift Resident Reverend Mbatha, many local Zulu officials and guides contributed their understanding of the event. Minister Prince Buthelezi assisted his research and generously supported the *Anglo Zulu War Historical Society*, as well as sponsoring the Society's prestigious annual *Prince Buthelezi Medal* for research and service to the Zulu people. The Society has organised many successful exhibitions and supported Military events celebrating Rorke's Drift, not least at both Brecon and for the 5th Armoured Brigade, the descendants of Lieutenant Chard's regiment.

Adrian Greaves' books are celebrated for their detailed research, narrative clarity and the ability to bring to life the events and personalities of the time. Through his writing and lecturing the author has made a significant contribution to both academic and popular understanding of Rorke's Drift. His research is valued by historians, military enthusiasts and general readers for their insights and depth of analysis.

An engaging and popular after-dinner speaker, he has given 700 Zulu War presentations over a twenty-five-year period, mostly featuring Rorke's Drift, to audiences in the UK, Europe, the USA and to the International Guild of Battlefield Guides. He is a consultant for the BBC *Antiques Roadshow.*

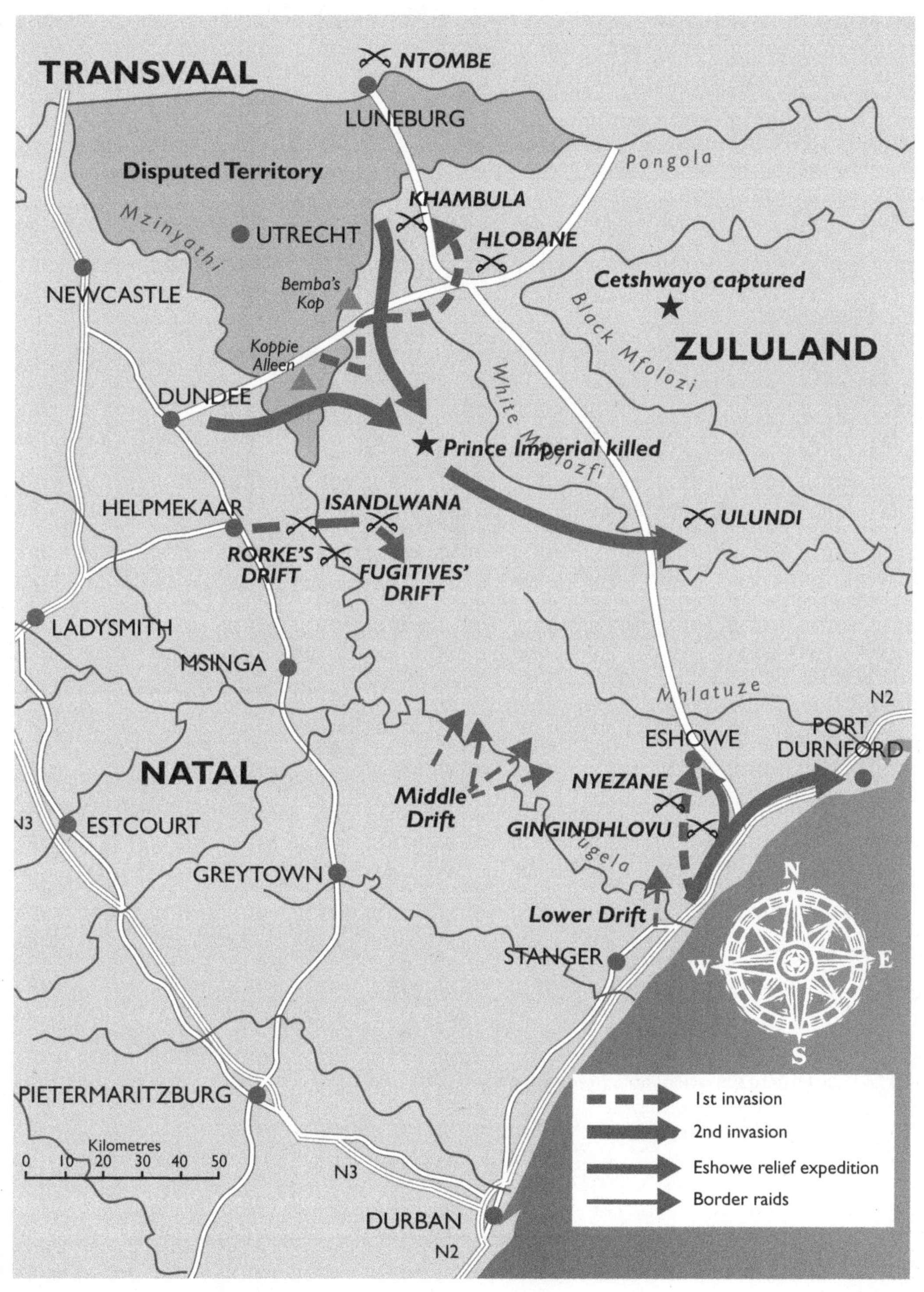

British Invasion Routes into Zululand.

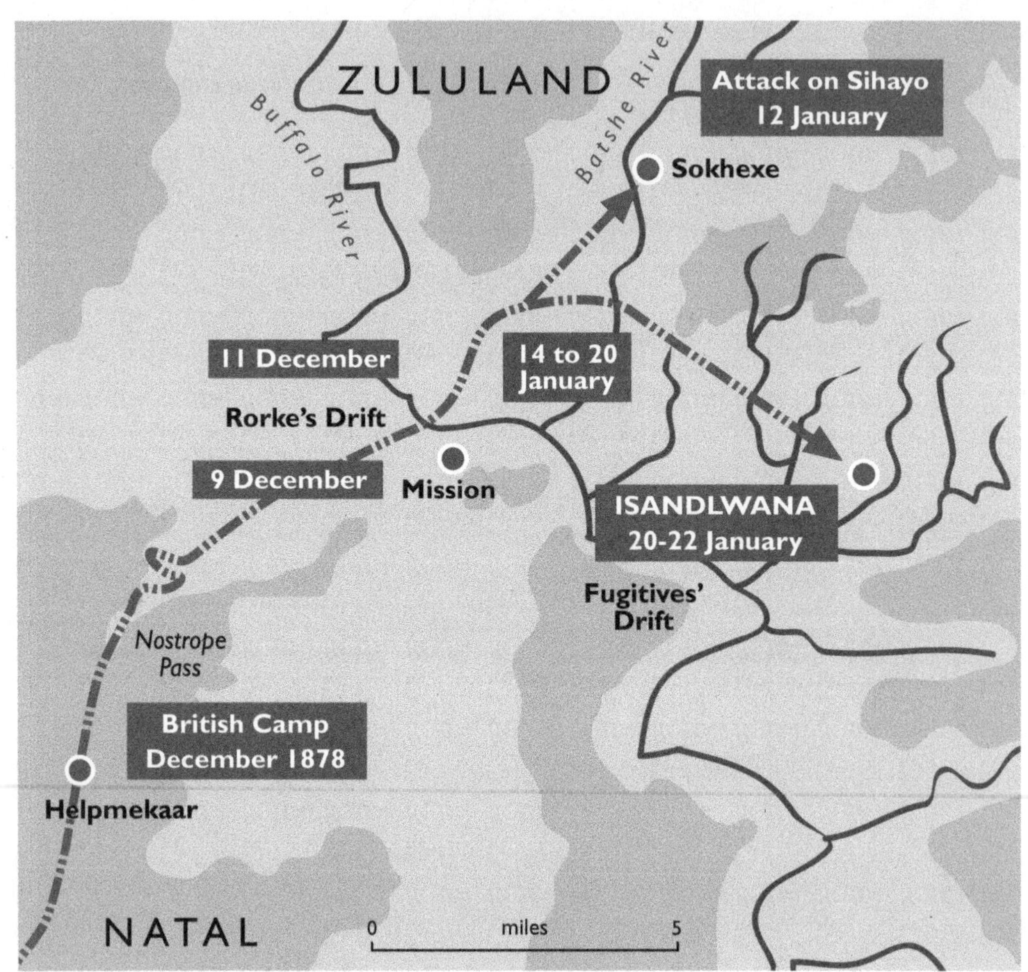

Lord Chelmsford's invasion route from Helpmekaar.

Timescale of Main Events Leading to the Anglo-Zulu War

History may not repeat itself but it rhymes:

1869	Britain, France and Italy take joint control of the finances of bankrupt Tunisia British explorer Samuel Baker annexes the southern Sudan, or Equatoria, on behalf of the Khedive of Egypt
1871	18-year-old British entrepreneur, Cecil Rhodes, on a temporary visit to South Africa, arrives in the new diamond town of Kimberley
1874	The southern region of present-day Ghana becomes a British colony, to be known as the Gold Coast
1875	The beginning of the Balkan crisis, which showed the vulnerability of the Suez Canal to Russian influence. British colonies in India, Australia and South Africa were especially vulnerable
1876	The chaotic government finances of Egypt are placed under joint French and British control, and India becomes the '*Jewel in the Crown*' of Queen Victoria when Benjamin Disraeli secures for her the title 'Empress of India'
1877	Britain annexes the Boer Republic in the Transvaal
1878	Three British armies invade Afghanistan, beginning the second Anglo-Afghan War
1878	Britain invades independent Sekhukhuneland and prepares for the invasion of Zululand
1879	Britain invades Zululand

Causes of Britain's Defeat at Isandlwana by the Zulus on 22 January

The British were defeated by the Zulus at Isandlwana by:

Deliberately ignoring intelligence
Disregarding tactical defensive rules in occupied territory
Relying on tactics from Waterloo
Misunderstanding the drawbacks and efficacy of artillery and Martini-Henry firearms when facing overwhelming odds

And its consequences:

Isandlwana and subsequent defeats by Zulus highlighted Britain's previously perceived world-wide reputation of military prowess and dominance
Following the Anglo-Zulu War, the Transvaal Pedi people won a second victory over the British, mainly due to the causes above
Having witnessed British humiliating failures and losses in 1879, the Transvaal Boers were confident enough to initiate the First Boer War of 1880, a war of attrition won only by the British outnumbering the Boers
With Britain's military reputation compromised, Britain was thereafter compelled to defend her Empire in the following wars.

1878–1880	Second Anglo-Afghan War
1879	Second Sekhukhune War
1879–1882	Urabi Revolt
1880–1881	Basuto Gun War
1880–1881	First Boer War
1881–1899	Mahdist War
1885	Third Anglo-Burmese War
1888	Sikkim Expedition
1891	Anglo-Manipur War
1893–1894	First Matabele War
1896	Anglo-Zanzibar War

1896–1897	Second Matabele War
1898–1899	Second Samoan Civil War
1899–1901	Boxer Rebellion
1899–1902	Second Boer War
1903–1904	British expedition to Tibet
1914–1918	First World War
1919	Third Afghan War
1939–1945	Second World War

Personae

Colonel Stanley, the Secretary of State for War in London
Benjamin Disraeli, Prime Minister
Sir Stafford Northcote, Chancellor of the Exchequer
Sir Frederic Thesiger (shortly to become Lord Chelmsford)
Lord Chelmsford, General Commanding British Forces in South Africa
Lord Carnarvon, then Colonial Secretary
Sir Bartle Frere, the High Commissioner
Theophilus Shepstone, the Natal Secretary for Native Affairs
Sir Henry Bulwer, Governor of Natal, a long-time friend of the Zulu people
Michael Gallwey, a barrister who had become the Attorney General of Natal in 1857 at the age of thirty-one
Lieutenant Colonel Anthony Durnford RE, who had served in South Africa for many years and thoroughly knew the area and the Zulus. Killed at Isandlwana
John Shepstone, brother and deputy of the Secretary for Native Affairs.
Sir Michael Hicks Beach, Secretary of State for the Colonies
Colonial Foreign Secretary Lord Edward Henry Stanley,

Chapter 1

Rorke's Drift

Today, Rorke's Drift ranks as one of the most popular British battlefields in the world.

Brian Best Chairman *Victoria Cross Society*

There have been occasions in the past when Britain exercised power in a way, to put it mildly, that was not appreciated by the rest of the world. A classic example during the country's golden age of domination was Britain's 1879 unwarranted invasion of Zululand in Southern Africa. Military victories have long been defining moments in the nation's supremacy and since 1879 historians and researchers have discussed the Anglo-Zulu war in general terms, a war which commenced with Britain's unexpected invasion of previously friendly Zululand. Just days later, on 22 January 1879, the Zulus retaliated by attacking and destroying the main camp of the British invasion force at Isandlwana, a prominent isolated rocky outcrop in Zululand, and inflicting an unbelievable total defeat of the invaders. Within an hour the garrison of some 1,500 troops were slaughtered (only a handful of escapees – an estimated 76) managed to evade the encircling massed ranks of some 30,000 Zulus and lived to tell the tale.

On the British invasion route from Natal, just 10 miles from the disaster at Isandlwana, was the insignificant and desolate mission station and border river crossing at Rorke's Drift. Just days before, Lord Chelmsford's passing invading army had converted its two small thatched buildings into a temporary staging post and makeshift hospital covering an area no larger than two tennis courts. That afternoon the mission was manned by 100 men of B Company, 2nd Battalion, 24th Regiment, all completely unaware of their invading column's fate. Then, three mounted escapees from Isandlwana, including Lieutenants Vaine and Adendorff, breathlessly arrived at the drift with the unbelievable news of the British defeat and, worse, a large force of Zulus was well on its way to attack their mission base. Less than an hour later the unbloodied 4,000 strong reserve from the main victorious Zulu army arrived. Not having been required to participate in the Zulu success at Isandlwana they were keen to see action and as darkness fell commenced their assault with probing attacks against the defenders. After a five-hour series of such attacks, many fought hand-to-hand, the Zulus departed and the small garrison of young soldiers miraculously survived, albeit with the loss of 13 killed and many wounded. Rorke's Drift was the last part of the Zulu attack that fateful day and the successful defence of the mission would create the newsflash to mitigate the appalling news of Britain's defeat at Isandlwana. These events on 22 January set in motion the start of the six-month Anglo-Zulu War that would witness two separate British invasions of Zululand.

But it is Rorke's Drift that has fascinated the public. In isolation from Isandlwana and the other skirmishes and battles of the Zulu War, this distant short battle has influenced the work of filmmakers and authors and given the event an enduring cultural afterlife. Yet in terms of military action and the half-dozen other major battles fought during the short six-month Anglo-Zulu War, few have acknowledged Rorke's Drift for what it truly was: a short sharp minor engagement lasting just a few hours with barely 100 soldiers engaged, most of whom survived. For those involved and for the military in South Africa, all stoically took the event in their stride for being a typical engagement of its time. However, when news of the defeat at Isandlwana and survival of Rorke's Drift reached London, the press and politicians successfully softened the dramatic impact of Isandlwana by creating a national mood of pride focusing on the Rorke's Drift survivors. For those in power it was an effective distraction from defeat at Isandlwana, but it was a ruse that caused resentment and incredulity amongst the military in South Africa. Such praise elevated the defenders' status to that of popular heroes, and the swift issuing of a glut of medals and decorations was not appreciated by all. And yet, by the end of 1879, events in South Africa were a distant memory for the public at home who, having enjoyed an uneventful summer, were settling down to follow the course of yet another routine war, this time to wrest Afghanistan from the Russians who were showing increasing interest in India.

Even with the benefit of hindsight it is almost inexplicable how the events that day came about, fought largely by British foot soldiers across an African boulder-strewn wasteland. covering over 150 square miles. By shaking the Zulu War tree this fresh research gives a detailed account of events, both before and after the four well-equipped British columns, each of some 3,000 trained and experienced soldiers, supported by a similar number of locally recruited volunteers, unsuccessfully invaded previously friendly Zululand.

It was during the late morning of 22 January 1879 when the temporary overnight Isandlwana camp of the confident British invasion force began to be dismantled before moving further into Zululand. The camp was manned by:

> N Battery 5th Brigade Royal Artillery; 5th Field Company Royal Engineers, 5 companies of the 1st Battalion 2/24th (2nd Warwickshire) Regiment, G company of the 2nd Battalion 2/24th (Warwickshire) Regiment; plus detachments from other companies of the 2nd Battalion 2/24th (Warwickshire) Regiment, the 90th Foot, the Army Service Corps, Army Hospital and Army Pay Corps. Detachments of the Mounted Infantry, Natal Volunteer Corps from the Natal Carbineers, Newcastle Mounted Rifles and the Buffalo Border Guard. They were supported by an estimated 600 black Natal Pioneer Corps troops of the Colonial 3rd Regiment Natal Native Contingency (NNC).
>
> The total force consisted of 67 Officers and 1,707 men commanded by Brevet Lieutenant Colonel H. Pulleine 1/24th (2nd Warwickshire) Regiment.[1]

During the morning two reports of distant Zulu groups in large numbers reached the camp, but the observations largely went unheeded – in the baking hazy heat of the day they appeared to be bypassing the camp without posing any threat. Then, at midday, the Zulus suddenly changed direction and 30,000 warriors swiftly surrounded the camp. The massed Zulu army was about to fight to the death to keep the British from their lands.

Two linked battles then took place, firstly beneath a hill known as Isandlwana, situated just 10 miles into Zululand from the Tugela River boundary between British-controlled Natal and King Cetshwayo's autonomous Zululand. The second battle, really an overflow of Isandlwana, was at Rorke's Drift, the nearby but previously unknown and desolate border river crossing point used by occasional traders bartering gin and cooking utensils for ivory and skins. The desolate location, set on the Natal river border with Zululand, was discreetly overlooked by two small thatched stone buildings, the home of its resident Swedish missionary, Otto Witt, his wife and 3-year-old daughter Ida Wilhelmina.

The fighting that day saw both armies display heroism and bravery, but both suffered appalling losses. The Battle of Isandlwana took place in open country and lasted only one hour, with only seventy-six men managing to escape. As the sun went down more than 5,000 bodies lay before the cliffs of Isandlwana, to be left to the vicissitudes of the elements and wild animals. The estimated 4,000 Zulus slain by volleys of Martini-Henry rifle fire lay mixed among the estimated 1,500 slaughtered British garrison of 52 officers and 806 white troops, plus over 500 NNC, all killed by Zulu stabbing spears. At Rorke's Drift, built amidst scattered boulders from the adjacent Oskarsberg hill, and manned by just 140 defenders, the fighting lasted five hours with a British loss of 13 soldiers and an estimated 550 Zulus killed.

Then, for the British people initially stunned by the loss at Isandlwana, the subsequent and politically orchestrated publicity glorifying Rorke's Drift provided temporary respite and hope. Since then, and due to the public's lasting fascination for tales of heroism, volumes have been written about Rorke's Drift. This now famous and dramatic battle naturally attracted the attention of historians and filmmakers, too many of whom relied upon replicating time-worn and sometimes inaccurate accounts blended with generally accepted facts. By perpetuating the many myths surrounding Rorke's Drift, and omitting the true causes of actual events that fateful day, subsequent implications for world history have generally been overlooked. Post Rorke's Drift and Isandlwana, the broadening consequences steadily unfurled, resulting in long-lasting international developments, ominously not to Britain's advantage. Most seriously, losing Isandlwana, a battle fought against an ill-equipped and untrained native army, revealed Britain's military weakness to her antagonists. This realisation would unavoidably produce dangerous worldwide repercussions and, in time, would create dramatically unstoppable consequences to drive Britain into a corner, both militarily and politically, firstly, and soon, against the Boers.

But why invade unexplored Zululand? Advised by its resident officials in the Cape, the High Commissioner, Sir Bartle Frere, and his army commander, Lord Chelmsford (formerly Sir Frederic Thesiger of the Grenadier Guards), the British government in London had erroneously been led to believe there was a potentially serious risk that King Cetshwayo's fearsome Zulus could sweep across the long and unprotected border and invade British controlled Natal. Even so, no authority for action against the Zulus was authorised by the home government. In Natal, the growing belief that a Zulu invasion was likely had been steadily promulgated by Frere and Chelmsford, and as a result of their orchestrated rumours, they had caused serious alarm to spread among the growing immigrant white farming community, now amounting to some 25,000 people. Nevertheless, this propaganda and local public disquiet encouraged Frere and Chelmsford to act independently to neutralise their fabricated Zulu threat. In reality, there was no such threat. Unbeknown to the increasingly anxious Natal population, a Zulu invasion was neither possible nor probable. Nevertheless, Frere and Chelmsford chose to resolve the dubitable invasion threat by wilfully serving the Zulus with an impossible ultimatum. The terms were deliberately set by Frere's officials to be far beyond the bounds of anything the Zulu king could agree to, and so Zulu non-fulfilment of the ultimatum terms became the official justification for Frere and Chelmsford to fulfil their collective personal pre-retirement ambition – to invade Zululand with their 18,000 strong army and for Britain to win an easy and painless war.[2]

It was a war initiated solely by Frere and Chelmsford in total disregard for the rights of the Zulus. The pair unleashed a war in the belief that the campaign would be easy, with victory achieved in a matter of weeks – and with minimal loss or cost to Britain. They knew that, assuming the invasion of Zululand went according to plan, their decision to invade would be met with the effusive approval of the home government and the British people, whose experience of colonialism long since led them to expect only quick and easy victories. But Frere and Chelmsford were taking calculated risks; no one outside South Africa was aware of their proposed invasion which would commit all their available resources to the campaign against the unknown capabilities of the Zulus.

Their failure to understand the Zulus was desperately perilous; these two highly placed and experienced British officials completely miscalculated the effect of their actions. Instead of a quick and successful campaign, and glory at home, they committed Britain to a humiliating, expensive and tragic war that accentuated her army's previously unknown deficiencies, some of which had already been highlighted by Frere's failed and secret campaign the previous year to subdue King Sekhukhune's Pedi nation in the neighbouring Transvaal. (See Chapter 2)

At the beginning of 1879 the plans for the invasion of Zululand were known only to a handful of Frere's local politicians. Then, on 12 January, British forces in South Africa invaded Zululand without the knowledge or agreement of the home government. Twelve days later the armies of Britain and Zululand met beneath the rocky hillside at Isandlwana, where the day witnessed two separate battles within sight of each other. As the ancient Greek, Herodotus, once wrote: 'Africa is the land of surprises.' This the British invaders were about to discover. In vastly overwhelming numbers the Zulus swiftly killed them all before laying waste to the massive camp of some 500 tents that had been carefully constructed, street by street, in accordance with strict army regulations.[3]

Without pausing, the unbloodied Zulu reserve of some 4,000 warriors then moved on to attack the column's makeshift hospital, which they could see through the heat haze, just 10 miles away at Rorke's Drift and defended by a mere 100 British soldiers. It would be a brave but unsuccessful Zulu attack on a defiant unsuspecting British rear guard left behind to protect the invading column's temporary camp hospital and river crossing at Rorke's Drift.

The story of Rorke's Drift has long since become immortalised in the psyche of the British people, who traditionally have a proud interest in their history and they have always strongly supported their army. History shows us that the British Army almost always fought for good reason and in a disciplined manner; it has neither murdered its prisoners nor molested the women of the defeated. Americans prefer not to talk about Vietnam; the Germans and French are reluctant to discuss the Second World War. By mentioning these examples, we see the first clues to explain why some wars and battles do indeed become forgotten; the two prime factors appear to involve military defeat and national embarrassment. Conversely, victory and pride play a role in ensuring good memories remain; for example, British film makers have a history of glorifying the subject of British battles and in this respect, *Zulu* and *Zulu Dawn* fit neatly into this category for the benefit of audiences who know no better. Sadly, many now treat the film *Zulu*, designed to entertain, as an educational resource.

Regardless of the high-profile newspaper accounts of the engagement, the war in Zululand never appealed to the public, who widely disapproved of it, especially when it was learned that Britain had unnecessarily invaded Zululand. Yet curiously, and except in passing, Rorke's Drift was hardly acknowledged in any contemporary works dealing with the Anglo-Zulu war, even though Queen Victoria appreciated that the role of public opinion had become ever more important in sustaining support for such ventures. The official ratcheting-up of publicity that accompanied the generous distribution of decorations and medals that followed Rorke's Drift only temporarily kept public opinion on board before it was all but forgotten. Queen Victoria wrote in her diaries that she was well aware of what the press were saying about the issues of the day and perspicaciously commented of Rorke's Drift that 'this was another event that would be eulogised in some quarters'.[4]

Then, at the conclusion of the Zulu campaign, instead of returning home, British forces recovering from fighting the Zulus would have to be re-committed to a fresh and costly campaign against King Sekhukhune's defiant Pedi people. Then, equally enthused by Britain's poor performance in southern Africa, Natal's neighbours, the Transvaal Boers, rose up against British rule, which led to the disastrous Transvaal rebellion followed by, without pause, two disastrous Anglo-Boer wars which fed growing anti-British animosity within Europe. Isandlwana and Rorke's Drift were soon forgotten.

Before the making of the films *Zulu* and *Zulu Dawn*, little was known of Rorke's Drift. So much so that when in March 1914 General Sir Reginald Hart VC unveiled the 24th Regiment's obelisk on the Isandlwana battlefield, he wrote:

> 'The terrible disaster that overwhelmed the old 24th regiment will always be remembered not so much as a disaster, but as an example of heroism like that of Leonidas and the three hundred Spartans who fell at the pass of Thermopylae'.

He omitted any mention of Rorke's Drift.

At first glance it is difficult to comprehend how the modern perception of Rorke's Drift developed into such national pride. After all, the incident was the consequence of a small insignificant and peaceful nation making a brave stand against being invaded by the world's most powerful Empire. Before 1964 the public were in the dark about the Anglo-Zulu War, and *Zulu* was able to promulgate many myths, including that of heroic Welsh soldiers and the incorrect identification of the regiment involved. Conversely, the 1964 book, *The Washing of the Spears,* was a remarkably well-researched book written in the 1960s by a senior American army intelligence officer from his desk in Berlin without him visiting South Africa until years following publication.[5]

On reflection, this classic film has much to answer for. It helped create and maintain our collective awareness of events at Rorke's Drift. Conversely, it made many mistakes which ensured that what is remembered of these events has distorted the reality of Rorke's Drift and created enduring myths by replacing actual history with attractive film fiction. Film producers are employed to make money by entertaining us and so they naturally endeavour to fulfil audience expectations. In the case of *Zulu*, this excellent film skilfully transformed well-known actors into heroic characters and brought awesome scenery with evocative music to stimulate viewers' expectations – but with the historical content trailing behind. *Zulu* is so seriously flawed historically that, for example, it has encouraged many Welsh people to believe the Warwickshire Regiment, the defenders of Rorke's Drift, was a Welsh regiment from Brecon. And on 22 January each year, the British Army's Royal Welsh Regiment still proudly celebrates Rorke's Drift Day with rousing versions of *Men of Harlech* rather than the more appropriate and correct *Warwickshire Lad*.[6]

Apart from *Zulu* honouring the Battle of Rorke's Drift, statistically the most repeated film broadcast on television, other battles fought during this short campaign, significant or otherwise, all share the combined fate of having been ignored, regardless of whether they were victories or punishing defeats. The Anglo-Zulu War remains a popular war for both historians and publishers while their reading public generally considers it a romantic war. *Zulu*'s portrayal of Rorke's Drift is of dignified and painless combat fought in sun-drenched South Africa between red-coated soldiers, avoiding the dirt and unemployment of civilian life at home and following Queen Victoria's orders against brave Zulu warriors defending their king and country. The film's enduring popularity has kept Rorke's Drift to the fore while the remaining battles of this campaign, all fierce and bloody, have been consigned to the occasional mention in books where the outline of events is vague and lacks humanity.[7]

References

1. *Imperial survivors.* Captains Essex and Gardner; Lieutenants Cochrane, Curling and Smith-Dorrien plus a small number of mounted soldiers from the following units; Royal Artillery, 1st Sqd. Mounted Infantry and Column Headquarters staff.
   Colonial survivors. Captains Barton, Nourse, and Stafford; Lieutenants Adendorff, Higginson, Raw, Vause, Henderson, Andrews, Davies, Erskine, Vaine and Quartermaster McPhail. A small number of individually mounted troopers from the following units also survived: Natal Mounted Police, Natal Carbineers, Newcastle Mounted Rifles, Buffalo Border Guard, 3rd Regiment NNC.
   In total, 76 whites. Figures from *David Rattray's Guidebook to the Anglo-Zulu War Battlefields.*
2. See Appendix 1.
3. *Army Field Exercise Guide* 1870 (still current in 1879). Isandlwana camp consisted of some 500 tents neatly erected according to strict military regulations, company by company, street by street, over an area nearly one-mile square. There were troop tents, numerous headquarters and administration tents together with hospital and messing tents. Within hours, the area was transformed into a thriving bustling tent town. The bell tents each provided cramped accommodation for sixteen private soldiers sleeping in a circle with their feet towards their single centre pole. Sergeants and above fared better, mostly enjoying an individual tent. Each tent, including the space around it that accommodated the ropes and pegs, occupied 1,440 square feet or thirty tents to the acre, more or less.
   The regulations for the laying out and erection of tents saw the British Army at its ritualistic best:

   > The NCOs in charge of squads will be extended 16 paces from the left by Officers Commanding Companies in prolongation of their arms and turned to the right. The senior Major will dress the NCOs of the first row of tents, along the front of the column, so that they will stand exactly on the line marked out as the front of the camp and the Captain of each Company will, from them, dress the NCOs of his squads who whilst being so dressed will stand to attention. After being dressed, No. 7 of each squad will drive a peg in-between the heels of his NCO, who will, after turning about, take 18 paces to the front where another peg will be driven in a similar manner.
   >
   > On the order being given to strike tents, all ropes except the corner ones, will be quickly undone and hanked up (*sic*) close to the flies; walls will be unlaced and packed into bags.
   >
   > The corner ropes will then be loosened and the tents dropped on the bugle sound 'G'. Nos 1, 2, 3, 4 and 10 will remove poles, bank corner ropes, fold up flies and lace them carefully up in the hold-alls, while Nos 5, 6, 7 and 8 take out pegs, count them, and pack them in the peg bag.

   As the Zulus attacked Isandlwana, complying with such a time-consuming drill to 'break camp' would have caused confusion, if not panic, among the troops.
4. Queen Victoria had been very moved by the events of the war, particularly the defence of Rorke's Drift. She had followed the news with a deep fascination and in August 1879 it was announced that the Queen had commissioned Elizabeth, Lady Butler (1846–1933) – incidentally, husband of General Sir William Butler GCB, late of 69th Foot – for a fee of £1,000 to paint a representation of the defence of Rorke's Drift. Lady Butler's painting

of Rorke's Drift (1193mm x 2133mm) is in the Royal Collection and hangs at the top of the main staircase in The State Apartments in St James's Palace.

5. It is pure coincidence that, as a British Army officer in Berlin, the author was occasionally debriefed by Colonel Donald Morris USA Intelligence, as part of their respective duties.
6. See Chapter 12.
7. See Chapter 2 for the expedition account. At the conclusion of the Zulu campaign, instead of returning home, British forces recovering from fighting the Zulus would have to be re-committed to a fresh campaign against King Sekhukhune's defiant Pedi people. Enthused by Britain's poor performance in southern Africa, the Transvaal Boers rose up against British domination. They rebelled, which forced Britain into two disastrous Anglo-Boer wars and fed growing anti-British animosity within Europe.

Chapter 2

The Stalking Russian Bear

In order to understand the true historical significance of Rorke's Drift with its consequences for subsequent British and world history, we should briefly consider the innovative British foreign policy operating in South Africa which, indirectly, led to the 1879 Anglo-Zulu war. Earlier, in 1806, Southern Africa's Dutch Cape Colony was surrendered to Britain along with its total 60,000 population, made up mainly of the original Khoikhoi and Hottentot people living in family groups alongside some 20,000 white settlers, mostly from Europe and known as Boers. They considered the colony to be their promised land and kept apart from the increasing number of British settlers arriving at the Cape who viewed the Boers as 'uncouth and backwards'. Both sides remained firmly apart until, frustrated by increasing British domination and taxation, the Boers trekked inland and away from British rule – only to collide with the steady migration of Xhose people coming from the north. The Xhose were part of the larger mass Bantu migration which had originated in west and central Africa and were now only 500 miles from the Cape. The Boer interaction with the Xhosa was invariably violent. By the 1870s other South African Bantu tribes, including the Basotho, Mfengu, Swazi and the Zulus became more disposed to the British, especially when the Boers began encroaching into Zululand. Matters came to a head when Britain became responsible for the Boers following Britain's annexation of the Boer Transvaal in 1878. With the transgressing Boers now British subjects their belligerence towards the Zulus immediately created an unsolvable problem for Britain, who faced either ordering the Boers from Zululand or rendering the Zulus powerless to resist the Boers. One side had to be brought to heel but it would lead Britain to war; firstly in 1879 against King Cetshwayo and then against the Boers in 1899 and 1902.

South Africa had an insignificantly small European population compared with 'Fortress' England's vast empire, now including South Africa. Britain needed to militarily protect and administer her wealthy but sprawling overseas colonies. Both Germany and Russia were progressively developing aggressive foreign interests in Britain's overseas affairs, with Germany openly seeking to establish colonies near to or adjacent to British interests to further increase its status as both a European and a world power. In Germany's fledgling colonies, official colonial policy was directed at social differentiation and segregation in order to maintain their perceived racial purity and German superiority. By then, German cultural ideology, founded on the innate German urge for domination, was firmly anchored to the basic principle that subject natives must be made to work for their new overlords, and without any rights; concomitantly, German colonial military law required harsh measures to maintain or enforce order.

As Africa entered the twentieth century, the German agenda was set for the most unpleasant action, action that paved the way for the worst excesses of atrocities against those hapless tribes who found themselves under German military occupation. For example, the first years of the early 1900s witnessed the European 'scramble for Africa' during which German troops officially and systematically used brutality and mass murder of local populations as an acceptable means of gaining and maintaining control across their new dominions. Records reveal that some 80,000 resisting *Herero* and *Namaqua* people in German South West Africa (Namibia) and over 250,000 people in German East Africa (Tanzania) were killed by over-work/exhaustion, starvation or mass murder.

Britain responded with Confederation, a policy which was designed and developed to protect the Empire. This policy was a result of expensive lessons learned by Britain while maintaining its military presence and administering her valuable but distant colonies and lands. During the 1870s, Confederation was becoming an increasingly important factor in British foreign policy following its successful implementation in lands as distant as India, Australia, the Leeward Islands and most recently and successfully, Canada, mostly under the guidance of Lord Carnarvon, then Colonial Secretary. With such a policy, these areas prospered, became self-sufficient and in due course this resulted in highly profitable trade with Britain. Such a unified area then developed its own military system, albeit trained and supervised by British officers, which neatly solved the problem of Britain supplying and maintaining hugely expensive Imperial troops for distant peacekeeping. Without such policies, responsibilities such as Imperial administration and economic success were previously a heavy financial burden on Britain. Inadvertently, it was a route that would lead to the unintended encounter at Rorke's Drift.

It is in the light of their successes that this policy was considered essential and suitable for British-controlled southern Africa, especially with its then diverse and mutually antagonistic populations. Such mutual support across this vast landmass would directly resolve a number of developing and complex issues already drifting towards conflict with the Zulus and Boers. However, Britain's overseas trade routes were beyond the influence of such support, making the importance of safe sea routes vital to Britain's trade. The sea occupies about 70 per cent of the entire earth's surface and is singly the most important geopolitical factor in trade, global politics and military-strategic affairs. Since the mid-1850s, while the Crimean War progressed, officials in India, led by an Imperial administrator of India and Zanzibar, Sir Bartle Frere, began to ponder the vulnerability of India to the growing attention of Russian warships.

Frere, better remembered for his later mishandling of the South African Zulus and Boers, had enjoyed a glittering career as a successful Indian administrator who had founded Karachi and rebuilt Bombay. He had brought East African slavery to a close and then planned the defence of India from possible Russian incursion. He also studied the vulnerability of Britain's world trade to the presence of lurking foreign raider (privateer) ships. Britain's Royal Navy had already assumed strategic responsibility for the Indian Ocean, and apart from her dominant home naval power, Britain had developed naval bases around the world where its warships could refuel (initially with coal and later with oil), replenish fresh water and provisions, and carry out essential maintenance without having to return to distant Britain. Theoretically, these locations also protected Britain's important overseas interests in South Africa, where its base in Simonstown protected the vital passage around the Cape of Good Hope to the Far East and Australia; while Bahrain controlled the sea lane through the Persian Gulf; Trincomalee in Ceylon controlled the sea lane across the North Indian Ocean; and Singapore protected the southern entrance to the Straits of Malacca. The logical core of British naval strategy was to prevent rival powers from establishing a naval base anywhere in the Indian Ocean. Clearly, without access to fuel and supplies from a friendly base, no hostile warship could operate in this vast oceanic expanse for any length of time.

But since 1860 Russia had been on the move. China provided Russia with a long strip of Pacific coastline to build a substantial naval base at Vladivostok. The systematic Russian conquest of Turkistan alarmed the British authorities in India, especially Frere, who correctly feared growing Russian interference in Afghanistan. British confidence in its military nevertheless remained at a high level; after all, the British Army of 1878 fielded over 100 fully-manned regiments across the Empire, each made up of eight companies. The senior twenty-five regiments of the army, mainly those serving overseas, had two battalions, usually for the home based battalion to train and maintain a steady flow of home recruits. But army tactics had changed little since Waterloo; British troops still wore bright red uniform jackets and were trained to fight in traditional squares using controlled volley fire from elderly Martini-Henry rifles. Meanwhile, their European counterparts began to retrain with smaller attacking groups using the terrain, modern smokeless rifles and camouflage to reduce their visibility. While military over-confidence at home satisfied the public, the country's diminishing naval ability was another matter.

Since 1875 British politicians had become increasingly concerned for their overseas possessions due to the vulnerability of the Suez Canal to increasing Russian presence in the eastern Mediterranean, making British colonies in India, Australia and South Africa especially vulnerable to any malevolent threat. The British government knew only too well that the defences of the Cape were entirely obsolete and undermanned. That year Parliamentary papers recorded the complaint by Vice Admiral Hornby:

> 'We are sadly deficient in ships to furnish reliefs to those on foreign stations and we have no reserve whatsoever. Five out of 20 frigates, 25 out of 32 corvettes, 16 out of 25 sloops and 36 out of 59 gunboats were unseaworthy'.[1]

This caused the British cabinet collectively but slowly to understand South Africa's vulnerability. It was noted by the Colonial Committee with responsibility for the protection of British sea routes that 'if such a misfortune as a war with Russia were to occur, it would be everything to have it in our power to deal a sudden and crushing blow in Asia'.[2]

Russia's growing influence at sea was blatant, while Britain's Royal Navy, with many of its active warships still resembling Nelson's navy, was languishing and mockingly described as being in 'the dark ages'. Lord Cardigan was so concerned the Russians might strike that he resigned, fearing the Empire might be set to the torch. His successor, Sir Michael Hicks Beach, agreed. Frere wrote to the government that:

> 'In the largest and most important of this group of colonies there is absolutely no military element whatsoever. No effectual measures have been organised for making military defence, whether against privateering at sea or against a Kaffir (*sic*) rising by land'.[3]

Another report in 1878 confirmed the Russian threat when it revealed a Russian naval squadron had disappeared and sailed completely undetected from Europe to America. Had it gone to the Cape it could have easily overwhelmed any British vessels, as Cape Town was defenceless. This deteriorating situation coincided with a review of British defence by a Colonial Defence Committee concerning the Cape's vulnerability, which commented that the Cape's coaling station was vital to the Empire but agreed with Frere's warning that its defences were obsolete.

Frere considered Cape Town to be 'utterly defenceless' and had long since expressed his concern over the vulnerability of the Cape to enemy warships since witnessing the construction of the Suez Canal when passing through on his return to England from India where he had served as the British colonial administrator. Frere was constantly worried over the possibility of Russian threats to his beloved India and to British-controlled South and East Africa. He noted:

> 'I have no doubt that a telegraph to the Cape would be very valuable both in an Imperial and a Colonial point of view and ... still more valuable for military reasons ... I am bound to say I think the telegraph is important; for at any moment the Cape may become to us a station of first class value'.[4]

Frere knew the Cape was the key to protecting Britain's trade routes with India and the Far East, but the government had ensured the Admiralty was seriously handicapped financially. Such complacency stemmed from the belief that Britain still possessed the most powerful land army, but Frere knew this would not protect the Cape without telegraphic communication, meaning that Britain could lose one South African colony after another, and worse, her world supremacy. But Frere had an ally in the Chancellor of the Exchequer, Sir Stafford Northcote who commented, 'Every precaution therefore that can properly be adopted will be wise'.[5]

With the writing on the wall, the cautious Colonial Secretary, Lord Carnarvon, had sensibly obtained permission from Prime Minister Disraeli to send Frere to South Africa to activate Confederation and ensure the defence of the two main ports, Cape Town and Durban. Frere's role was to effect the unification of these territories under British rule and bring into line the militantly-chaotic and bankrupt Boer republics to the north of the Cape. Frere's sincere and dominating belief was that war with Russia was inevitably looming and that South African ports were vulnerable to attack by Russian warships and privateers. He was seriously perturbed by knowing the Cape was defenceless while at the same time the unanticipated threat of rebellion by the disgruntled neighbouring Boer Republic was worsening – a huge problem to solve even for an accomplished Colonial expert like Frere.

By the time of Frere's arrival in the Cape the growing reality of a cascade of growing problems was evident to Frere and his officials. The Xhosa tribes across the Eastern Cape were disgruntled with British rule and there was a strong possibility of an 'anti Britain' rebellion by the Boers to the north in the neighbouring Transvaal. Of increasing concern to the white population was the possibility of a Zulu attack against the Transvaal border which could overflow into Natal. To these difficulties, Frere had to consider the likelihood of Russian warships molesting the Cape's shipping and even landing marines. Frere wrote to Carnarvon: 'The Cape had the mere skeleton of a garrison – and the batteries for the defence of Simon's Town could be taken from the rear'.[6]

Frere set to work; he instigated a survey as to how Cape Town could be defended. Nearby Simon's Town was more easily defended but was a week away for marching soldiers or a day's sailing, even if a British ship happened to be in harbour. Frere promptly gave orders for four gun batteries to be constructed with an additional floating battery to be positioned at the mouth of the harbour, despite official foot dragging in London. Frere's plate was now overloaded. Sir Michael Hicks Beach, Secretary of State for the Colonies, downgraded the seriousness of a Russian threat to the Cape, and wrote to Frere:

> 'I hope your harbours and stores at Cape Town are to some extent protected: at least sufficiently so to defeat the only kind of attack likely to be made on them by a stray cruiser or privateer'.[7]

Frere knew only too well that such stray cruisers and privateers were a real threat. The *Shenandoah,* a powerful Confederate privateer, had already wreaked havoc worldwide, when operating in the Southern oceans by capturing six ships, and in the North Pacific where she captured thirty-two Union vessels. She had proved to be fast enough to outpace British ships, being able to maintain a speed of 12 knots, potentially allowing her to attack civilian shipping off Cape Town and disappear before the Royal Navy could intervene. Frere understood the implications for the British Empire; merchant shipping would have to re-route, if possible, or stay in port while Britain's trade would dry up. Shipping insurance rates would become untenable and maintaining the military power of the Empire would become a financial and military crisis. Frere responded by submitting a further warning citing his anxiety for the safety of the Empire's ports:

> 'I wish it were … easy to defend our ports from Privateers, should you be unable to avert a European war. The subject was one of the first things I attended to when I came out … This was only managed by commencing work at my own risk …But Table Bay is still open to any vessel with a single rifled gun, and a Privateer might levy a contribution from our Banks before a man-of-war could come to our help. The Russians know this well, and when their Squadron was here two or three years ago, the officers used to tell their partners at balls that "they did not intend to wait to be taken by the English Channel or Mediterranean fleets, but to pay visits to the Cape and Indian ports where they would levy contributions, on their way to Petrapaulovski!". Meantime the enclosed Memo shows the guns Colonel Hassard asks for, and if you could only get the War Office to send us some of them … I could make a beginning and not run the

> risk of having to report your flag hauled down and a contribution of half a million or more levied by some wretched Alabama cruiser or Privateer'.[8]

Meanwhile, anti-Russian rumours and gossip had long been rife at all levels of the British Government as, on occasions, it appeared that foreign agents somehow had access to British secrets just as war with Russia seemed imminent. The press and parliament were about to experience a major scandal! The news broke that Lady Derby, the wife of the Colonial Foreign Secretary Lord Edward Henry Stanley, was in a relationship with the Russian ambassador to London, Pyotr Shuvalov. As the wife of the Secretary of State for Foreign Affairs, Lady Derby had long been an unofficial advisor to both British diplomats and ministers, but that privilege should not have extended to passing secret British Cabinet naval material to the Russian government. Queen Victoria was informed and, not amused, she instructed her chaplain to write to Lady Derby. Lord Derby resigned. In open parliament Lord Blake observed:

> 'Derby surely must be the only Foreign Secretary in British history to reveal the innermost secrets of the Cabinet to the ambassador of a foreign power in order to frustrate the presumed intentions of his own Prime Minister'.[9]

These perceived dangers to the Cape were not baseless; the Russians were already agitating along the vast Asian border with India, which directly led to the Second Anglo-Afghan War, and Russian diplomats were active in the Balkans. Russian warships began making exploratory long-range deployments to the Indian Ocean and the Persian Gulf as part of their strategy of expanding Russian naval capabilities in the Pacific.

By then, the only telegraph cable to Japan ran overland through Russian territory to Vladivostok and from there to Japan by a line maintained by the Russians. Russian naval presence in the Pacific and Indian Oceans greatly increased Russia's international prestige and helped to strengthen the country's authority in those regions. While coastal defences at British-controlled overseas ports were either negligible or entirely lacking, Russia selected Australia as the prime target because there was less chance of Russian vessels encountering a British fleet during the return voyage to a neutral or friendly port on the west coast of the United States. The object of the Russian plan was to destroy as much unprotected coastal shipping as possible and to raid the ports of Sydney and Melbourne, where it was expected that gold bullion worth at least £6 million could be obtained under threat of bombardment. Remarkably similar plans of attack had been discovered earlier in 1864 but officially denied by the Russians. On Admiralty advice, coastal defences in Australia were strengthened.

To add to his growing list of woes, other simmering problems were beginning to sharply focus Frere's attention. Since the Boers first crossed the Drakensberg Mountains in 1836, their dusty settlements had continued to spread progressively towards the more fertile heartland of Zululand, itself protected by a natural boundary, the Tugela River. This temporarily deterred further encroachment by the Boers, but by the mid-1870s Boer settlers again began surreptitiously moving into Zululand and these incursions were opposed with increasing vigour. One such area of heightened tension was an unofficial extension of the (Boer) Transvaal into Zululand which lay between the Buffalo and Blood rivers immediately north of the isolated Rorke's Drift mission station. It was evident to the British, Boers and Zulus that relationships between the Boers and Zulus were seriously deteriorating and decisive action needed to be taken with increasing urgency.

Frere then received news from Theophilus Shepstone, Natal Secretary for Native Affairs, that due to the recent and unexpected crash of the Boer economy and the threat of an attack against the Boers by either or both of the adjacent Pedi and Zulu nations, the Boer government had reluctantly agreed to British annexation for protection. Not all Boers were prepared to accept annexation, and within days a deputation of senior Boer politicians, led by Paul Kruger, set sail for London to argue against the British move. Then international politics took a turn for the worse. Russia declared war on Turkey, which strengthened Frere's fear of growing Russian influence, especially as he knew South Africa had no telegraphic communication to the outside world and that, even with such communication, there were usually no Royal Navy ships even within weeks of the Cape.

North of the Cape, the Boers were openly taking initial steps to gain independent access to the Indian Ocean, thereby becoming independent of any British control or interference. The situation then deteriorated as the threat of rebellion by the disgruntled neighbouring Boer Republic began to outweigh Frere's fears about Russian interference. Meanwhile the Boers watched on, biding their time. Fortunately for Britain, by 1879 internal turmoil in Russia eliminated that particular naval threat.

Meanwhile, King Cetshwayo had traditionally regarded the encroaching land-stealing Boers as his enemy and treated them with great suspicion, whereas he regarded the British as his true friends. During April 1877, a serious confrontation between the Zulus and Boers began to develop as a result of trekkers moving on to land unanimously recognised to be Zulu territory. The king finally decided to resolve the problem by massing his combined *impis* (regiments), amounting to over 30,000 warriors, at strategic crossing points along the Boers' Transvaal border.

Before Cetshwayo could give the order for a full scale Zulu attack, two events occurred simultaneously, either by coincidence or by astute British diplomatic design. Firstly, the local Secretary for Native Affairs, Sir Theophilus Shepstone, ordered the king to withdraw his army. Cetshwayo reluctantly complied but sent a strong letter warning Shepstone that he had intended driving the Boers 'beyond the Vaal River'. Secondly, on the very same day (12 April 1877), Shepstone was actually attending a secret meeting with the Boers with the sole intention of persuading the Boers to surrender the Transvaal to British authority on the logical grounds that the Transvaal government was bankrupt and the Zulus were about to attack. Shepstone wrote to Lord Carnarvon: 'The sooner the root of the evil, which I consider to be the Zulu power and military organisation, is dealt with, the easier our task will be'.[10]

Agreement was quickly reached, whereupon Shepstone annexed the Transvaal to the Crown. The declaration was read to the assembled Boers by the Secretary to the Mission, Melmoth Osborn. He appeared to suffer from a bout of chronic anxiety mid-proclamation; he commenced trembling and his voice failed. Shepstone's twenty-year-old clerk, H. Rider Haggard, stepped forwards to continue reading the script.

The Zulus believe to this day that Shepstone encouraged Cetshwayo to mass his fighting *impis* on the Transvaal border in order to coerce the Boers into submission.

Shepstone's motive behind this annexation was to initiate Confederation across southern Africa, but, in pursuing this policy, Shepstone had unwittingly inherited responsibility for the developing Boer and Zulu land dispute. Prior to annexation, the British had viewed the Boers as 'foreigners' but, overnight, they had involuntarily become British subjects by virtue of the annexation. The problem of the disputed territory had unwittingly converted itself from being an insignificant Boer-Zulu dispute to a potentially serious military confrontation between Britain and the Zulus. The Zulu king, Cetshwayo, had welcomed the British annexation of the Transvaal, as he believed it would protect Zululand from further Boer incursions. Cetshwayo informed Shepstone, 'I am glad to know the Transvaal is English ground; perhaps now there may be rest'. Mr. Rider Haggard wrote that the financial effects of annexation on the Transvaalers were magical: credit and commerce were at once restored and that:

> 'When the recollection of their difficulties had grown faint, when their debts had been paid and their enemies (Zulus) quietened, they began to think that they would like to get rid of us again, and start fresh on their own account with a clean sheet'.[11]

But, by annexing the Boer Transvaal, Britain unintentionally annexed neighbouring Sekhukhuneland. Its king, Sekhukhune, never accepted this demarcation of boundaries and subsequent British attempts to establish authority over his Pedi people were firmly rejected by the king, now in a state of rebellion against anyone white and who encouraged his warriors to regularly raid British lines of communication between Natal and Pretoria. Britain first had to neutralise the Pedi to pacify and protect the Boers, now inadvertent British subjects and clamouring for British protection from Pedi raids.

In response the British sent a small mounted column under the command of a Captain Clarke to subdue the Pedi, but his force was ignominiously routed with heavy loss of life and Clarke barely escaped with this life while withdrawing. With planning for the British invasion of Zululand well underway, the British commander, Lord Chelmsford, did not want a rebellious Pedi army actively operating behind his northern supply lines into Zululand, and in August despatched Colonel Rowlands VC with a fully equipped force of 1,800 men to defeat Sekhukhune. On 3 October 1878 Rowlands also had to accept defeat. Overcome by constant sniping from the Pedi at night and suffering intense daytime heat, his demoralized and exhausted force withdrew, a British fiasco that was swiftly brought to the Zulu king's attention. It would also create a detrimental consequence on Britain's long-held reputation for invincibility; if Britain could not contain an unknown local chief how could they successfully contain the Zulus? In the longer term, Rowland's defeat seriously fortified the Boers resistance to Britain's recent annexation of the Transvaal: they realised that opposing the British militarily in order to recover their Transvaal might not be that difficult.

This highlighted another smouldering dispute. A number of Boer and displaced native settlers had joined those already illicitly farming in a particularly sensitive Zulu area – the same area which was generally becoming known as the 'Disputed Territory', directly north of and adjacent to Rorke's Drift and, for the first time, putting the location firmly on the map.

At the persistent request of the Governor of Natal, Sir Henry Bulwer, a long-time friend of the Zulu people, and in the British tradition of apparent compromise, Frere agreed to defer the problem by reluctantly constituting an independent Boundary Commission which was to sit at Rorke's Drift. The location was central to the dispute, with easy access for its members. The Commission was to adjudicate on ownership to the disputed territory; simply, did it belong to the Boers or Zulus? Cetshwayo was consulted and he agreed to abide by the Commission's decision on the condition that he could nominate three senior *indunas* to participate.

The Commission's principal members consisted of three highly respected officials led by Michael Gallwey, a barrister who had become the Attorney General of Natal in 1857 at the age of thirty-one. The other two members were Lieutenant Colonel Anthony Durnford RE, who had served in South Africa for many years and knew the area and the Zulu thoroughly, and John Shepstone, brother and deputy of the Secretary for Native Affairs. The Boers sent three noted representatives: Piet Uys, a farmer who had lost relatives to Dingane's *impis*; Adrian Rudolph, the Boer Landdrost of Utrecht: and Henrique Shepstone, who served on his father's staff in Pretoria.

The Commission sat for nearly five weeks, during which time they considered voluminous verbal and written representations. Gallwey utilised all his legal training to impartially evaluate the material, a task made especially difficult because several Boer documents proved to be fraudulent while a number of Zulu reports were manifestly unreliable. Gallwey concentrated the Commission's attention on two main issues, firstly, who owned the land prior to the dispute, and secondly, had any land under dispute been properly purchased or ceded?

It has to be remembered that between the Zulus and Boers no boundary line had ever been agreed, and that for many years the local Zulu chiefs had repeatedly implored the British Governor in Natal for advice and help in dealing with examples of blatant Boer encroachment. It had long been Boer policy – if policy it may be called – to force the Zulus gradually to edge further and further from their lush pasture lands. Hitherto, little notice had been taken of their petitions. The Boundary Commission finally decided, against all expectations, that the disputed land had always belonged to the Zulus and furthermore, the fledgling Boer settlement of Utrecht must also be surrendered. The Boundary Commission eventually delivered their stunning findings and verdict in late 1878 to an astonished Sir Bartle Frere, who simply locked the report away until severely rebuked by the Colonial Secretary for not informing the Zulus of the result.

Frere was obliged to realise that publication of the Commission's findings could unleash powerful forces against Britain, both from other native nations who would believe their campaign against progressive European settlement was vindicated, and from furious Boers who could well retaliate against Britain by resorting to military action against British-controlled Natal. Frere was also aware that alienating the Boers might provoke additional antagonism from a number of the Boers' European allies, especially Holland and Germany. Lord Carnarvon, then Colonial Secretary, further warned that if Britain did not act to support the Boers, 'Germany would be induced to undertake the protection of the Transvaal'.[12] This possible complication would be most inconvenient, as Britain was becoming seriously engaged in waging a major war against

Afghanistan while at the same time diplomatic relationships with Germany and Russia were fragile.

But Frere had not been idle since activating the Boundary Commission. He and his staff, encouraged by Theophilus Shepstone in the Transvaal, had wrongly anticipated that the Commission would find for the Boers, leading Shepstone to believe that the Zulus might retaliate against Britain with a military offensive into Natal. In consequence, plans were already well advanced for a British pre-emptive invasion of Zululand, partly to placate the increasingly militant Boers but also to finally neutralise the Zulus and facilitate Confederation. Invading Zululand meant other significant benefits would accrue to Frere; not least it would placate the Boers by allowing Boer farmers to continue encroaching further into Zululand, and under British protections. It would also dissuade other Bantu nations who might consider making a stand against British expansion. A British invasion would overturn the Zulu king by eradicating his military potential and freeing a valuable source of labour for developing British and Boer commercial activities. Accordingly, Frere ordered his General Commanding British Forces in South Africa, Sir Frederic Thesiger (shortly to become Lord Chelmsford), to proceed to Natal to secretly mobilise his forces for an immediate invasion and a brief war against the Zulus. There were also important personal considerations for both Frere and Chelmsford. Success for Frere would strengthen his already glittering career, and for Chelmsford an early defeat of the Zulu army would be popular and ensure him a heroic return to England. Meanwhile, Frere pondered the Boundary Commission's pro-Zulu findings and decided that inactivity was the best, if temporary, solution.

Frere gained more time by forwarding the report's findings to Hicks Beach, the new Colonial Secretary in London (who had succeeded Lord Carnarvon). He also requested additional Imperial troops, ostensibly to protect Natal and the Boer families still within the area. Frere knew full well that Hicks Beach's official reply would take several months to reach him.

Meanwhile, and fearful of informing the Boers that the Boundary Commission had found against them, Frere played his master stroke of turning a blind eye to the Boers' expansion into Zululand by presenting the Zulus with an impossible ultimatum to disarm or be invaded. Knowing the Zulus were unable to comply with the ultimatum, Frere and Chelmsford prepared for war. Hicks Beach's reply suggesting caution finally reached Frere and it was, as Frere fully anticipated, an indication that Hicks Beach and the government were only interested in the perceived Russian threat. Britain was economically depressed and any unnecessary expenditure on military adventures should be avoided. The reply reads:

> 'Her Majesty's Government are (*sic*) not prepared to comply with a request for reinforcement of troops. All the information that has hitherto reached them with respect to the position of affairs in Zululand appears to justify a confident hope that by the exercise of prudence and by meeting the Zulus in a spirit of forbearance and reasonable compromise it will be possible to avert the very serious evil of a war with Cetshwayo'.[13]

Frere took Hicks Beach's faint-hearted reply as authority to launch his war. He was fully aware that, once started, the British government was powerless to stop him as it took about three months for a message to travel to London and back; his exploitation of the delay, on the grounds of the tension and urgency he had created, was blatant. In total confidence that Cetshwayo could not comply with the ultimatum, Frere slipped the leash and, supported by Chelmsford, the pair went to war.[14]

With Chelmsford's assembled military force fully prepared, the British invasion was soon advancing in four columns of troops and artillery, spaced out over a broad front of 100 miles, towards the river border between Natal and Zululand. Chelmsford accompanied the main thrust of the invasion, the Central Column, intending to use Rorke's Drift as his main assembly area and start line for the invasion.

Cetshwayo's five years of comparative peace were coming to an end. Admittedly there had been some minor border incidents, but they were petty and of no concern to the British except that the Boer-Zulu confrontation was steadily maturing to the point of a full scale war between the pair.[15]

Frere had earlier made representations to the Boers for support, believing that by allying itself to the Boer cause and preparing for war against the Zulus, the Boers would support British action. Following a meeting at Utrecht on 5 December 1878 between Frere's representative and local meetings with the Boers, they agreed their assistance would be forthcoming to the point that pay would be five shillings per day per Boer, provisions, arms and ammunition would be provided and loot must be equally shared. The Boers would serve under their own officers. Wood was promised he would have several thousand Boers under his command. Three days later the Boers discovered the Boundary Commission had found against them. Realising the deception, the Boers accordingly withdrew their support – with the exception of isolated individuals, most notably Piet Uys, whose father and brother had earlier been killed by the Zulus.

With their retirements approaching, and to further enhance their reputations, Chelmsford and Frere were now at war against the Zulus. Apart from losing Boer support, there were three additional serious flaws in their plan:

1. They had duped the British government in London into falsely believing that there was a serious risk of King Cetshwayo's Zulus invading British controlled Natal. Failure of their invasion would be disastrous to both.
2. Believing in their military supremacy, they ignored the embarrassing defeat and implications of their two recently failed and secretive expeditions against King Sekhukhune's Pedi people.
3. Frere and Chelmsford ignored military intelligence reports of Zulu preparations for war, choosing instead to believe the Zulu army was spread across Zululand making mobilisation impractical, whereas the Zulu army was already assembled at Ulundi for the major event of the Zulu calendar, and preparing for war.

These two very senior officials sincerely believed the Zulu campaign would be over before any message to London could be acted upon, but they were taking a huge personal risk; no one outside their immediate circle of advisors and senior officers was aware of their recent rout by the Pedi or of their proposed Zululand invasion, which would commit all British and colonial resources in South Africa to the campaign. Furthermore, they believed their imminent invasion of Zululand would be successful and meet with the fulsome approval of the British government and people, whose experience of colonialism had led them to expect only quick and easy victories. This enthusiasm and belief in success was remarkable, based on inaccurate British intelligence estimates of the Zulus' military strength, which was as desperately inaccurate as the army's maps they were about to rely upon.

Yet Frere was a trusted and experienced official and Chelmsford enjoyed a sound military reputation. Neither had reason to believe that the outcome of the invasion would be anything other than a swift and complete success and no one in southern Africa really anticipated even a single significant battle. The possibility of any military obstacle did not enter their minds: defeat was unthinkable. After all, Britain was a highly industrialised nation with a modern well-equipped and trained army seeking nothing more than to subdue a seemingly chaotic, uneducated, ill-equipped and inexperienced native population – whose only offence was a minor degree of insignificant non-cooperation. There was now nothing to stop Frere and Chelmsford's deceitful masquerade or deter them from their unauthorised invasion.

Chelmsford's confidence had been further strengthened after reading the 1838 *History of the Boer Invasion of Zululand* when 440 Boer men survived against an attacking Zulu force of some 12,000 warriors. Chelmsford wrote to Colonel Wood prior to invasion suggesting British infantry could do even better than the Boers forty years previously:

> 'Pretorious, when he invaded Zululand to avenge the massacre of Retief's people, had 440 men with him and with these he easily beat off the 12,000 warriors who attacked him. The Zulus in those days were warriors flushed with repeated victories. I doubt the present Zulus making a more determined fight'.[16]

But no modern army had ever fought the Zulus.

References

1. *Her Majesty's Fleet* 1875 Carnarvon Papers PRO 30/6/115.
2. Carnarvon to Salisbury 25 Dec 1876. PRO 30/6/7.
3. Memorandum to the government CDS 1/5, 24 February 1877.
4. Carnarvon 17 Nov 1877 PRO CP 30/6/3 No. 55.
5. 25 Dec 1876 PRO No. 110.
6. Frere to Carnarvon PRO 30/6/122.
7. Narrative of facts respecting the *Shenandoah* whilst in the port of Melbourne. PRO FO5 1388.
8. Frere to Lord Cranbourne cited in Martineau, Vol 1.
9. *The Zulu and the Raj. Life and Times of Sir Bartle-Frere*, O'Connor D. 2002.
10. *AZWHS* Journal 1. Letter dated 11 December 1877.
11. *An Illustrated Tour of the 1879 Anglo-Zulu Battlefields*, Greaves A., Pen & Sword 2023.
12. *The Road to Isandlwana*, Gon P. AD Donker (Pty)Ltd 1979.
13. *An Illustrated Tour of the 1879 Anglo-Zulu Battlefields.*
14. For detail of the ultimatum, see Appendix 1.
15. 1. On 28 July 1878, an incident had occurred that Frere used to encourage widespread anti-Zulu sentiments. Some of the sons of a local chief, Sihayo, crossed the river border to restrain two of their father's absconding wives who had been accused of adultery. The women were duly apprehended and marched back across the border, only to be clubbed to death in accordance with established Zulu tradition. In Natal the incident received officially orchestrated publicity, out of all proportion to the event, in order to further inflame public antagonism against King Cetshwayo. Even the pro-Zulu Bulwer was forced to agree that the danger of collision with the Zulu was growing and wrote that the system of government in the Zulu country is: 'so bad that any improvement was hopeless – we should, if necessary, be justified in deposing Cetshwayo'.
    2. Two British surveyors checking the border had temporarily been detained by a curious Zulu patrol but then released unharmed.
16. *Blood on the Painted Mountain*, Lock, R., Greenhill Publishing, 1995.

Chapter 3

The Road to Rorke's Drift

Military victories have long been defining moments in Britain's history and Rorke's Drift is a classic example well understood by both civilians and the military. Over the years, noted historians and researchers have studied the engagement between the British and Zulus at Rorke's Drift, yet, in terms of military action and compared with the half-dozen major battles during the Anglo-Zulu War, few have acknowledged Rorke's Drift for what it was: a short sharp minor engagement lasting just a few hours with barely a hundred soldiers engaged. The military in South Africa initially took the event in their stride as just another skirmish. The press and politicians at home then unwittingly created an air of resentment and incredulity amongst the survivors' fellow officers and soldiers when the Rorke's Drift survivors' status was elevated to that of popular heroes. And yet, by the end of 1879, events in South Africa were a distant memory for the British, whose foreign policy was fast becoming overshadowed by Disraeli's Government wrestling with the problem of Irish Home Rule. The British Army was gearing up for war on India's North West Frontier, where the British felt vulnerable to Russia's steady absorption of the vast territories east of the Caspian Sea. Fighting had also broken out in Afghanistan and the British had occupied the capital, Kabul, and installed a puppet ruler. An uneasy peace lasted but a few months until the British Political Officer, Major Sir Louis Cavagnari and his escort, were slaughtered. It was prophetic that Cavagnari, piqued by the lack of press interest, had previously written:

> 'I am afraid there is no denying the fact that the British public require a blunder and a huge disaster to excite their interest'.[1]

The British public were about to have their blunder. The post-battle consequences of the disaster at Isandlwana, mitigated by the encounter at Rorke's Drift, then steadily unfurled, resulting in long-lasting international developments, ominously not to Britain's advantage. Events that day, 22 January 1879, unavoidably became an irreversible flash point soon to ignite worldwide repercussions and create dramatically unstoppable consequences that would drive Britain into a corner, both militarily and politically. Meanwhile, for the British people, stunned by the loss at Isandlwana, only the subsequent and politically orchestrated mass publicity of Rorke's Drift could provide temporary respite and hope.

But how did the engagement at Rorke's Drift come about? By shaking the Anglo-Zulu War tree, it is now possible to have a more thorough understanding of events both before and after four columns of well-trained British soldiers unnecessarily invaded previously friendly Zululand in South Africa.

Volumes have been written on the subject of the Anglo-Zulu War with its most famous battle, Rorke's Drift, attracting enduring attention from historians and filmmakers, some of whom have relied upon replicating time-worn and sometimes inaccurate accounts blended with commonly-known facts. By perpetuating the many myths surrounding Rorke's Drift and omitting the true causes and consequences of the actual events of that fateful day, the subsequent implications for world history have been overlooked, not least involving Britain in nearly twenty subsequent wars.[2]

Yet the Anglo-Zulu war lasted only six months and witnessed two separate British invasions of previously friendly Zululand. Unlike most wars, the war in Zululand was unexpected beyond South Africa, especially by British politicians in London and their public, who were just settling down to follow the course of another routine war to wrest Afghanistan from the Russians who were showing a growing interest in India. But why invade Zululand?

Unbeknown to most British politicians, the end of 1878 witnessed mounting discontent and uncertainty being deliberately fermented across southern Africa. Advised by its resident officials in the Cape, the High Commissioner Sir Bartle Frere (Frere) and his army commander Lord Chelmsford, the British government in London had erroneously been led to believe there was a potentially serious risk that King Cetshwayo's fearsome Zulus could sweep across the long and unprotected border and invade British controlled Natal. Indeed, local fears of a Zulu invasion were being quietly stoked by Frere and Chelmsford and grew as a result of their orchestrated rumours. Serious alarm had spread among the growing white population, now amounting to some 25,000 people. Such alarm was also endemic through Natal's black population of some 250,000 souls who had, over many years, sought sanctuary by fleeing the autocratic and often violent way of life under a succession of Zulu kings.

In turn, this propaganda and public disquiet gave Frere and Chelmsford authority to neutralise the perceived Zulu threat. In reality, there was no such threat; a Zulu invasion was neither possible nor probable and so perception of the situation by Colonial Office officials in London was as indifferent as, conversely, the increasing fear of terrified Natalian civilians. Nevertheless, Frere and Chelmsford chose to resolve the dubitable threat of a Zulu invasion by wilfully serving the Zulus with an impossible ultimatum with terms deliberately set so that Zulu non-fulfilment became the official justification for the invasion of Zululand.

It was a war initiated solely by Frere and Chelmsford in total disregard of the rights of the Zulus. The pair unleashed a war in the belief that the campaign would be easy and over in weeks, and with minimal loss or cost to Britain. They knew that, assuming the invasion of Zululand went according to plan, their decision would then be met with the effusive approval of both the home government and the British people. But Frere and Chelmsford were taking two calculated risks; no one outside South Africa was aware of their proposed invasion, which would commit all their available resources to the campaign against the unknown capabilities of the Zulus.

Their failure to understand the Zulus was desperately perilous; these two highly placed and experienced British officials completely miscalculated the effect of their actions. Instead of a quick and successful campaign, and glory at home, they committed Britain to a humiliating, expensive and tragic war that accentuated her army's previously unknown deficiencies, some of which had already been highlighted by its recent failed and secret campaign to subdue King Sekhukhune's Pedi nation in the neighbouring Transvaal.

On 12 January 1879, British forces in South Africa invaded Zululand with four well-equipped columns without the knowledge or agreement of the home government. The invasion front was some 300 miles wide extending from the shores of the Indian Ocean to the borders with Swaziland and the Transvaal. The terrain was mostly unmapped and uninhabited, consisting of vast rolling plains strewn with rivers and ranges of unusual flat topped mountain ranges. The route for Chelmsford's No. 3 column was directly into the area known as 'the Disputed Territory', the subject of the earlier Boundary Commission, having long been disputed by the Boers and Zulus. Twelve days later the armies of Britain and Zululand met beneath the rocky hillside at Isandlwana, where the day witnessed two separate battles within sight of each other. The British invaders were about to discover the truth behind the observation of the ancient Greek, Herodotus, who wrote 'Africa is the land of surprises'. The engagement commenced when vastly overwhelming numbers of Zulus, some 30,000 warriors, surprised then crushed the hastily-assembled line of defenders guarding the unprepared British invasion column's camp at Isandlwana, inflicting an unimaginably total and inglorious defeat for the British with a loss of some 1,500 troops killed before the Zulus laid waste to the massive tented camp. Without pausing, the unbloodied Zulu 4,000-strong reserve, which had watched the battle from a nearby hillock, then moved on to attack the column's makeshift hospital at nearby Rorke's Drift, just 10 miles away and defended by just 140 soldiers of B Company of the 24th Regiment.

Not having been required in the battle for Isandlwana, the Zulu reserve moved on to attack the tiny British garrison that they could see in the hazy distance. It was a brave but unsuccessful Zulu attack on an unsuspecting but defiant rear guard left behind to protect the invading column's temporary hospital and river crossing at Rorke's Drift. It is the story of Rorke's Drift that has long since become immortalised in the psyche of the British people who traditionally have a proud interest in their history, even if it is casual and hazy, and they have always strongly supported their army. History shows us that the British Army almost always fought for good reason and in a disciplined manner. Americans prefer not to talk about Vietnam, while the Germans and French are reluctant to discuss the Second World War. And by mentioning these examples, we see the first clues to explain why some wars and battles do indeed become forgotten; the two prime factors appear to involve military defeat and national embarrassment. Conversely, victory and pride play a role in ensuring good memories remain; for example, British filmmakers have a history of glorifying British battles and in this respect, *Zulu* and *Zulu Dawn* fit neatly into this category for the benefit of audiences who knew no better. Sadly, many now treat the film as an educational resource.

When news of the invasion of Zululand first reached London, the event was considered so insignificant that only one of the London newspapers bothered to send a correspondent to cover the event. Instead, all efforts were focused upon Afghanistan where, in the event, the British had a comparatively easy advance. Regardless of the subsequent high-profile newspaper accounts of the engagement, the Zulu War never appealed to the public who widely disapproved of it, especially when it was learned that Britain had invaded the small friendly country of Zululand. Yet curiously, and except in passing, Rorke's Drift was not unduly acknowledged in any contemporary publications dealing with the Anglo-Zulu war, even though Queen Victoria appreciated that the role of public opinion had become ever more important in sustaining support for such adventures. The official ratcheting-up of publicity that accompanied the generous distribution of decorations and medals that followed Rorke's Drift only temporarily kept public opinion on board. Queen Victoria wrote in her diaries that she was well aware of what the press were saying about the issues of the day and commented perspicaciously of Rorke's Drift 'this was another event that would be eulogised in some quarters'.[3]

Thereafter little was known of Rorke's Drift and at first glance it is difficult to see why the modern perception of Rorke's Drift is one of such national pride. After all, the incident was the consequence of a small insignificant and peaceful nation making a brave stand against invasion by the world's most powerful Empire. Indeed, before 1964 when the film *Zulu* was released, the public were in the dark about the Zulu War, enabling the film to promulgate many myths, including that of heroic Welsh soldiers and the incorrect identity of the regiment involved. On balance, the 1960s book, *The Washing of the Spears,* was a remarkably well-researched book written by an American intelligence colonel from his desk in Berlin without him visiting South Africa until years following publication.[4] Likewise, *Zulu* remains a wonderful film which very successfully achieved its aim, to entertain cinema audiences rather than educate them with reality and facts. Sadly, many now treat the film as an educational resource.

This classic film has much to answer for; it helped create and maintain our collective awareness of events at Rorke's Drift, and to a lesser extent of the Battle of Isandlwana. Conversely, this dramatic film has many mistakes which has ensured that what is remembered of these events has distorted the reality of Rorke's Drift and created enduring myths by replacing actual history with attractive fiction. Film producers are employed to make money by entertaining us and so they naturally endeavour to fulfil audience expectations. In the case of, for example, *Zulu* and *Lawrence of Arabia*, these films skilfully transformed well-known actors into heroic characters and brought awesome scenery with evocative music to stimulate viewers' expectations, but with the historical content trailing behind. *Zulu* is so seriously flawed historically with mistakes that, for example, a majority of Welsh people now believe that the Warwickshire Regiment, who fought at Rorke's Drift, was a Welsh regiment from Brecon. And on 22 January each year, the British Army's Royal Welsh Regiment proudly celebrates Rorke's Drift Day with rousing versions of *Men of Harlech* rather than the more appropriate and correct *Warwickshire Lad.*

Apart from *Zulu* honouring the Battle of Rorke's Drift, statistically the most repeated film ever broadcast on television, other battles fought during this short campaign, significant or otherwise, share the combined fate of having become forgotten, regardless of whether they were glorious victories or punishing defeats. The Zulu War remains a popular war for both historians and publishers while their reading public generally considers it a romantic war; *Zulu*'s portrayal of Rorke's Drift is of a dignified combat fought in sun-drenched South Africa between red-coated soldiers following Queen Victoria's orders against brave Zulu warriors defending their king and country.

References

1. *The Zulu and the Raj*, O'Connor, 2002.
2. See the *Introduction* for the list. At the conclusion of the Zulu campaign, instead of returning home, British forces recovering from fighting the Zulus would have to be re-committed to a fresh campaign against King Sekhukhune's defiant Pedi people before going on to tackle the even more disastrous Transvaal rebellion, which swiftly led to the two Anglo-Boer wars and growing European animosity towards Britain.
3. Queen Victoria had been very moved by the events of the war, particularly the defence of Rorke's Drift. She had followed the news with a deep fascination and in August 1879 it was announced that the Queen had commissioned Elizabeth, Lady Butler (1846–1933) (incidentally, husband of General Sir William Butler GCB, late of 69th Foot) for a fee of £1,000 to paint a representation of the defence of Rorke's Drift. Lady Butler's painting of Rorke's Drift (1193mm x 2133mm) is in the Royal Collection and hangs at the top of the main staircase in the State Apartments in St James's Palace.
4. It is pure coincidence that the author, as a junior officer in Berlin, was occasionally debriefed by Colonel Donald Morris as part of their respective duties.

Chapter 4

King Cetshwayo Says 'No'

King Cetshwayo was now fully aware that his attempts to pacify the British had failed. At far off Ulundi, his royal capital on the rolling Mahlabathini plain, he ordered wild animal hunts to be held along the borders of neighbouring British Natal. The Zulu hunters were instructed to ensure that Chelmsford's spies observed the Zulus' advanced state of preparedness as well as strutting the strength of the Zulus opposing them.

Cetshwayo then played his master card by ordering his whole Zulu army to assemble before him at Ulundi, as it did each year, at the gathering known as the 'first fruits' ceremony. By the time the British ultimatum[1] reached Cetshwayo, just a week before the invasion, most of the *amabutho*, a total of 50,000 warriors, was already gathered and the ritual preparations for war had begun. Notwithstanding soothing reassurances from Henrique Shepstone, Cetshwayo was not to be caught off balance. Shrewdly, he decided to wait and watch. He sent a number of *induna* emissaries to implore British restraint but on presentation of their credentials they were arrested and imprisoned.

Updated by his flow of spies' reports, Cetshwayo knew exactly where the British were amassing their forces. He correctly presumed their main objective was the main column approaching Rorke's Drift and singled it out as the most dangerous force. The time for peaceful negotiation had passed; both sides were ready for war.

Although Britain had presented Cetshwayo with an impossible ultimatum, including the disbandment of the Zulu army, and had moved their massed troops along the whole length of the Zululand border, Cetshwayo still withheld the order for his army to attack in the hope that his final request to delay the implementation of the ultimatum would be accepted. Cetshwayo had given up trying to understand why the British, his former friends, were now his enemy. Anticipating rejection, he secretly gave his *indunas* their orders for a specific attack on Chelmsford's main central column, though with certain restrictions; he insisted his army must not attack any fortified or static position and not cross the British Natal border. Presuming his orders would be complied with, he was confident that his army's presence would, by itself, force a British withdrawal back to Natal and gain him additional time to state his case but he nevertheless sent one final plea. It said:

> 'What have I done to the great house of England, which placed my father, Mpande, over the Zulu nation, and after his death, put me in power? What have I done to the great white chief? I hear from all parts that the soldiers are around me, and the Zulu nation asks me, what have I said to the white people.
>
> 'I hear that war is intended, and the reason for it and that the reason for it is that I said I was as great as the Queen of England.
>
> 'I feel the English have stopped the rain, and the land is being destroyed. They have told me that a kraal of blood cannot stand, and I wish to sit quietly according to their orders, and cultivate the land. I do not know anything about war and want the great chiefs to send me the rain'.[2]

Even by this late stage, and notwithstanding the impossible nature of the ultimatum, King Cetshwayo sent a conciliatory message to Sir Henry Bulwer, the Lieutenant Governor of Natal stating:

> 'Cetshwayo hereby swears, in presence of Oham, Mnyamana, Ntshingwayo and all his other chiefs, that he has no intention or wish to quarrel with the English'.[3]

Again, this faithful endeavour for peace was ignored. In conversation with his advisor, John Dunn, Chelmsford expressed his concern that he might not be able to get Cetshwayo to fight and made the chilling observation:

> 'I must [then] drive him into a corner and make him fight'.[4]

In the weeks leading to the British invasion, Cetshwayo had been fully aware that events were rapidly moving beyond his control. In anticipation of trouble, Zulu women and children living along the border with Natal could be seen moving their cattle away from the probable British invasion routes and going into hiding. Notwithstanding soothing reassurances from Henrique Shepstone, Cetshwayo was not to be caught off-guard; shrewdly, he decided to wait, prepare and watch. Aware of the growing consternation of his people at the menacing gathering of British troops along the Natal border, the king sent a number of senior emissaries to implore British restraint but on presentation of their credentials they were arrested and imprisoned. In the meantime, the British invasion force was already gathering at strategic crossing points along the river border of Zululand in total confidence that King Cetshwayo could not comply with the ultimatum.

Viewed overall, Chelmsford's main invasion force was remarkably small when the magnitude of the undertaking is considered. His force of regular troops consisted of the two battalions of the 24th; the 90th; single battalions of the 2nd Regiment, 3rd Brigade, and the 1st Regiment, 13th Brigade; and a battalion of the 80th Regiment held in reserve at Luneburg. This force was initially divided into four columns (the Number 2 column under Colonel Durnford consisted of locally raised troops) and amounted to a total of nearly 6,000 highly professional and well-armed soldiers. In support were a similar number of native troops, known disparagingly as the 'untrained untrainables', who were divided into seven battalions and led by white officers and NCOs, not necessarily with any military training. To this force irregular units were added based on the quasi-military Natal Police, together with frontier guards and local defence groups with grand names such as the Natal Hussars, Natal Carbineers and Durban Rangers.

King Cetshwayo and his chiefs and advisors were now focused on resisting the inevitable British invasion. Knowing he had achieved unity across Zululand, Cetshwayo made one final attempt to prevent the British invasion. He ordered a herd of royal cattle to be taken across the river as a peace offering, along with a request that the ultimatum date be deferred to allow further negotiation – both of which the British refused. Totally unbeknown to Chelmsford, the timing of the ultimatum was unwittingly in favour of Cetshwayo, whose army was, by coincidence, already assembling at Ulundi for the annual *umKhosi*, the first fruits ceremony. This was traditionally held at Ulundi each year before the king to allow him to review his army and herds. Chelmsford's intelligence officers were unaware that the next gathering was due to take place on 8 January at Ulundi – just three days before the expiry of the British ultimatum. Had Chelmsford selected an invasion date a week either side of the *umKhosi* the Zulu army would have been scattered across the country leaving Zululand defenceless. As an additional precaution, instructions were given that warriors were to come to Ulundi prepared for war. Cetshwayo left a token force in place to watch the border river crossing points and called for his spies to report on British movements. Cetshwayo now decided to resist the British, even if it meant outright war.

At each year's *umKhosi*, young men who had attained the age of about sixteen were formed into companies, or *amaviyo*, which after a year's probation was placed in an *ibutho*, or regiment. This first year also symbolized the transition from boyhood to manhood as a warrior. The new company might either belong to another regiment into which the young one was incorporated, or it might be newly formed. As a rule, several regiments of different ages were combined and resided at the same *ikhanda* barracks, so that the young soldiers might have the benefit of the experience of their seniors. In this manner loyal corps were formed, occasionally some thousands strong.

The Zulu army now gathering was soundly structured and consisted of twelve such corps, each with one or more regiments with its own *ikhanda*. These corps necessarily contained men of all ages, some married, others unmarried, some old men scarcely able to walk, and others boys. Five of these corps consisted of a single regiment, while the remaining corps comprised several regiments. Each corps or regiment possessed its own military *ikhanda* and was controlled by one commander, one second-in-command and several junior commanders who controlled the flanks in action. The uniform of the Zulu army was clearly laid down and was different in each corps. The great distinction was between the married and unmarried regiments. The total number of regiments in the Zulu army amounted to thirty-four, of whom eighteen were married and sixteen unmarried. Seven of the former comprised men over sixty years of age, so that for practical purposes there were only twenty-seven Zulu fighting regiments amounting to some 44,000 warriors. British intelligence figures of the day estimated these as 17,000 men between 20- and 30-years-of-age, 14,500 between 30- and 40-years-old, 5,900 between 40- and 50-years-old, and 4,500 aged between 50 and 60. There were twenty-seven *amakhanda*, or royal homesteads, scattered about the kingdom, thirteen of them being located in the region of Mahlabatini Plain, near Cetshwayo's residence at Ulundi. Ulundi itself was a huge complex of some 1,200 huts whose garrison was more or less permanently in residence.

Unlike the unwieldy British invasion force being laboriously assembled, the Zulu army required but little commissariat and no lumbering transport. Three or four days' provisions consisting of maize or millet and a herd of beef cattle were prepared to accompany each regiment. The older boys were briefed to follow their allocated regiment and assist in driving the cattle. They also carried the provisions, cooking utensils and spare spears.

Before marching, a circle was formed by each regiment, each company together and their officers in an inner ring with the first and second in command at the centre. The regiment then proceeded to break into companies, beginning from the left-hand side. Each company formed a circle and then marched off, followed by *uDibi* boys. The company officers marched immediately in rear of their men, the second in command in rear of the left wing, and the commanding officer in rear of the right.

Ignorant of the Zulus' readiness to fight, Frere and Chelmsford's deceitful masquerade initiated the invasion. In the hope that his final request to delay the implementation of the ultimatum would be accepted, Cetshwayo withheld the order for his army to attack, but had secretly given his *izinDuna* their orders for a specific attack on Chelmsford's main Centre Column. Based on reports from the Pedi defeat of the British, Cetshwayo ordered there must be no attacks on the British while they were on the move or attack on any fortified or static position, and the British Natal border was not to be threatened. Presuming his orders would be complied with, he was confident that his army's presence would, by itself, encourage a British withdrawal back to Natal.

By now Chelmsford was receiving reports of massive concentrations of Zulu warriors at Ulundi and clearly preparing to move in Chelmsford's direction; the reports were correct, Cetshwayo had assembled the main *Ulundi* Corp (8,000 warriors), the *Nokenke* (2,000), the *Ngobamakosi* (5,000), the *Umcityu* (4,000), the *Nodwengo* (2,000), the *Mbonambi* (3,000) and the *UDloko* (1,000), making a total of more than 20,000 fit young warriors. But the supremely confident Chelmsford did not want to be bothered with the facts – he treated the reports, most of them accurate, with indifference and ignored them. It was a simple case of 'having made up his mind he did not want to be confused by the facts'. Britain was now committed by Frere and Chelmsford to invade Zululand with the main advance across the Buffalo River at Rorke's Drift. The date was set for the invasion, 12 January. King Cetshwayo and his Zulu nation were about to defiantly stand their ground to protect their country.

The main Zulu tactic was based on the encircling movement, often wider than a mile across, which had developed over hundreds of years when hunting large herds of game. The actual Zulu battle formation resembled a crescent shape with two flanks moving to encircle the enemy. The formation was invariably known by Europeans as the 'horns of the bull' and by the Zulus as the *impondo zankomo*.

The fast-moving encircling horns consisted of the younger fitter warriors, with the body or 'chest' made up of the more seasoned warriors who would bear the brunt of a frontal attack. The tactic was most successful when the two horns completed the encirclement of the enemy and relied, in part, on the main body of warriors remaining out of sight until the horns met. They would then rise up and close in to slaughter the victims. A large body of troops were also kept in hand as a reserve; they were usually held with their backs to the enemy to prevent their over-excitement. This tried and tested tactic would now be put into operation to defend Zululand from the massing British invasion force.

The Zulu king was also a shrewd diplomat. Cetshwayo knew that if the British invasion force could be trapped he could seriously embarrass Britain internationally and even force her invading army commanders to sue for peace. Unfortunately for Cetshwayo, his field commanders would, instead, take autonomous action, either unable or unwilling to follow the king's orders.

By 21 January, most of the British invading force had arrived at Isandlwana. The location was ideal as there was an ample supply of both water and wood for cooking; and the position was elevated, with a sheer rock face to its rear and, therefore, it appeared easy to defend. It dominated the vast open plain towards the Zulu capital at Ulundi so that any approaching Zulu force, advancing from Ulundi would be observed for several miles before it could form up for an attack. The British camp under construction would hold some 500 tents, neatly erected according to strict military regulations, company by company, street by street, over an area nearly 1 square mile, and all under the gaze of Cetshwayo's spies looking down on the camp from the Nqutu Plateau less than one mile distant.[5]

References

1. Appendix 3.
2. *Destruction of the Zulu Kingdom*, Guy 1979.
3. British Parliamentary Papers 2308.
4. Dunn J. 1886.
5. *Army Field Exercise Guide* 1870, still current in 1879. See ref.[2] Chapter 1.

Chapter 5

Rorke's Drift Base and Attack on Sihayo's Homestead

The main focus for the senior British officers invading Zululand was intelligence gathering to learn the Zulus' intentions and predict their tactics. Henry Curling wrote that the advance into Zululand was handicapped by a lack of accurate maps.[1] Chelmsford was invading Zululand blindly and so had to rely on local information for his intelligence, which came from local officials; men such as John Robson and Henry Fynn, both local magistrates who were familiar with the countryside and Zulu ways. As late as 6 January, Robson's string of agents were reporting regular patrols of well-armed Zulus on their side of the Buffalo River who appeared to be eager for a fight. Right up to the point of the British invasion, a flow of reports was reaching Chelmsford that indicated massive concentrations of Zulu warriors between Ulundi and Isandlwana. The reports were correct. Cetshwayo had assembled the *Ulundi* Corp (8,000 warriors), the *Nokenke* (2,000), the *Ngobamakosi* (5,000), the *Umcityu* (4,000), the *Nodwengo* (2,000), the *Mbonambi* (3,000), and the *UDloko* (1,000), making a total of more than 30,000 warriors. The supremely confident Chelmsford did not want to be bothered with the facts – he treated the reports, most of them accurate, with indifference and ignored them.

For his first main move Chelmsford ordered the Centre Column, the largest of the four invading columns under the command of Colonel Glyn, an experienced officer and a Crimea veteran, to assemble at Helpmekaar some 12 miles from the border of Zululand at Rorke's Drift. At the beginning of January and following the arrival of their sister battalion, the 2nd Battalion the 24th Regiment (2/24th), the 1st Battalion the 24th Regiment (1/24th) arrived at Helpmekaar. At an informal mess dinner on 9 January, just a few days short of the thirtieth anniversary of the 24th Regiment's unfortunate experience at the Battle of Chillianwallah, the officers of both battalions, sitting on supply boxes, shared supper at which a toast was proposed: 'That we may not get into such a mess and have better luck next time'.[2] The following day, and with the band playing stirring regimental music, the troops marched the 12 miles from their camp at Helpmekaar on the high Biggarsberg escarpment by descending the steep winding track that led to the river border crossing at Rorke's Drift between British-controlled Natal and Zululand. Chelmsford had already visited both Helpmekaar and Rorke's Drift on 4 January and had then ridden on to the Mangeni waterfall which he identified as suitable for a camp further into Zululand. He was impressed by the readiness and enthusiasm of his gathering invasion force.

In 1879 the Swedish mission station at Rorke's Drift was situated on the Natal side of the border with Zululand immediately adjacent to the Buffalo River crossing. It was located on a level elevated ledge of rock and commanded a magnificent view across the river into Zululand. The two small mission buildings consisted of the missionary's house and a small store which doubled as a church on Sundays; both were solidly made of stone collected from the 500-foot-high Oskarsberg hill overlooking the mission station, with roofs thatched with reeds from the nearby river.

The mission was financed by patrons in Sweden and named 'Oskarsberg' by the Swedish missionary, Otto Witt, in acknowledgement of his Swedish king. Surrounding the homestead were three acres of carefully cultivated land that included an orchard of grape vines, orange, apricot, apple, peach, fig, pomegranate and other fruit trees, all bordered by an assortment of lime trees and quince bushes. Between the well-tended vegetable garden and the Mission was a 120-foot long, 5-foot high, stone wall. Witt's home was the larger of the two buildings and was nearly thirty yards long and spacious. Forty yards away was Witt's small and dignified store-cum-church; it was used by the missionary in his daily work with the local community. Immediately beyond the church was a small stone cattle kraal and then, below the rock terrace on which the buildings nestled, there was a similar but larger cattle kraal that could hold 100 cattle. The sole link between the mission station and the rest of Natal was a little-used dirt track that led westwards towards the high escarpment of the Biggarsberg and thence to the small settlement at Helpmekaar. In the other direction, the track led to the nearby Buffalo River and for the occasional traders plying their wares among the Zulus, this was the only safe route across the river into Zululand.

For those at Rorke's Drift on 9 January the tranquillity and peace of the mission was severely disturbed by the arrival of nearly 6,000 troops from Helpmekaar and all the impedimenta of Chelmsford's invasion force. Row upon row of white canvas Bell tents were erected in neat formations on the half-mile grassy slope between the riverbank and the mission station, while, for reasons of hygiene, the Natal Native Contingent (NNC) were instructed to camp downstream of the Europeans. A few days earlier, *The Natal Witness* reported British confidence at a high level:

> 'No attempt to cross the river will be made if opposed, except under the protection of the battery. These Zulus do not yet know what a shell is like or what effect it will have upon them. May they soon learn, and the larger the quantity that is present the better the effect will be'.[3]

Notwithstanding the protestations of Otto Witt at being allowed to retain only one small room in his house, the commissary staff commandeered his two buildings on behalf of the Crown. In despair at the damage caused by converting his home and church into defensive positions, Witt dispatched his wife and small children to stay with friends at nearby Msinga, some 10 miles south of Helpmekaar. Exasperated by Witt's unrelenting complaining, which was clearly based on the question of compensation, Witt was ordered out of the camp and set off to follow his family, leaving behind his recently arrived young Swedish friend, August Hammar, to protect his interests. By the day of the invasion, Witt's house was converted into a makeshift hospital to cater for the growing number of fever cases and a few soldiers with damaged limbs caused by a number of wagon-related incidents. The church became a supplies store.

Historians and filmmakers have preferred to exaggerate and dramatize the effort taken to defend Rorke's Drift during the hour or so before the Zulu attack by magnifying their focus upon the perceived predicament of a small band of brave British soldiers, far from home, having to defend an unprepared position. *Zulu* shows the whole pre-defence and battle fought in brilliant sunshine, whereas the whole event took place after dark. Such inaccuracies and dramatization only serves to warp the history of the whole story. The film myth that Rorke's Drift was undefended before the Zulus attacked has long been a focal point of Zulu war historians, because few Zulu War researchers or commentators have known of, or given credit for, actual preparations for the pre-battle defence of Rorke's Drift prior to the invasion of Zululand.

While reluctant to spoil a good story with evidence to the contrary, the reality is very different. Based on personal accounts by a number of unbiased well-placed individuals present at Rorke's Drift before the battle, it is clear the mission was correctly prepared for defence as long as ten days before the British invasion of Zululand. These defences were ordered by Chelmsford as a standard military procedure in enemy territory, and he accordingly wrote to Frere on 2 January: 'The more I see of the Buffalo border, the more I am convinced that we must hold both sides of the river, if Natal is to be made more secure in the future from raidings'.[4]

This makes perfect military sense; the British realised a Zulu attack on Rorke's Drift posed little risk to the Zulus but, if successful, it would pose a serious risk to their supply line, hence the need for the mission to be properly protected.

Further, should the advancing column need to fall back on Rorke's Drift, it would have been imperative that the column's stores of food and ammunition remained intact, and to have left such a forward position wide open and vulnerable would have openly encouraged a Zulu attack.

During the intense aftermath of the Zulu War Chelmsford came under pressure to explain certain aspects about the defence of Rorke's Drift and Isandlwana camps. He wrote in his own defence:

> 'The labour of getting troops and supplies across the Buffalo River, and of making the roads passable for wheeled transport, absorbed nearly the entire strength of No. 3 Column from its arrival on the banks of the river, to its advance to Sandhlwana (*sic*). I know, however, that Colonel Glyn had given orders to Lieutenant Chard, Royal Engineers, to construct an entrenched post on the Natal side and that it had been commenced by the detachments left behind before the column moved off. So long as the force was in occupation of the position at Sandhlwana it covered directly the ford on the Buffalo River'.[5]

Earlier, just a week prior to the invasion, the press reporter accompanying Lord Chelmsford en route from Mooi River to Helpmekaar, Charles Norris-Newman, was fully aware of significant intelligence reaching Chelmsford that large numbers of Zulus were assembling to oppose the Centre Column. He wrote the following: (unabridged)

> 'A mounted orderly arrived just after midnight (6 January) with important despatches from Helpmekaar, and the General was roused in consequence. The intelligence was connected with the presence of several thousand Zulus near Rorke's Drift. Similar intelligence reached Chelmsford in the following days'.[6]

Such intelligence would have become widely known by the invasion column's senior officers and, according to Norris-Newman, there was already a 'temporary fortification of mealie-sacks, biscuit-boxes, etc., etc. constructed at Helpmekaar'. This camp was itself some 12 miles inland from the British camp at the Zululand border at Rorke's Drift, so not to have constructed any form of defence at the actual crossing point into Zululand would have been inconceivable. Norris-Newman's statement is supported by the recently discovered paintings of Helpmekaar by Lieutenant Lloyd of the 24th Regiment, which show that Helpmekaar had also been well prepared for defence prior to the British invasion of Zululand.

A week before the disaster at Isandlwana, Chelmsford had ordered subordinates that 'the great thing will be for you to make yourself thoroughly secure wherever you take up your position'.[7] With Chelmsford's advance instructions to fortify camps during the invasion in senior officers' minds, it is unlikely Major Spalding, the commander at Rorke's Drift, would have ignored such an order. Spalding's Commissary officer, Dalton, had already fortified and entrenched the area around the mission's two buildings, with the bulk of the work completed by 11 January. This is independently confirmed by Lieutenant Charles Harford, who accompanied the main invasion force as it passed through Rorke's Drift. He wrote that Rorke's Drift was being used as a fort and was entrenched as early as 11 January. This supports August Hammar's account of Witt's house being prepared for defence at the same time. Harford wrote in his diary:

> 'On the 11 January the 3rd Column crossed the Buffalo into Zululand, the troops making their way over at different points. The Artillery and the 24th Regiment went over by degrees in the pontoon, a little above the main drift, (a shallow crossing point) known as Rorke's Drift after the Dutchman Jim Rorke, whose house and farm buildings were occupied by us as a Fort after being entrenched'.[8]

Harford was an experienced army officer, a noted entomologist and a popular young officer on loan to the NNC from the 99th Regiment. The NNC consisted of some 7,000 locally-recruited Bantu from Natal. Harford would have understood the words 'Fort' and 'entrenched' so they would have only been used in their correct military context and, having been present at Rorke's Drift prior to the Zulu attack, he is unlikely to have made a mistake. He clearly observed some form of defensive measures sufficient to describe the result as a 'fort'. Furthermore, the official *Army Field Exercise Guide* of 1870 specifically defines 'entrench' as follows:

> 'To increase the power of defence of a position by the use of field-works, defensible posts, or even shelter trenches'.[9]

Additionally, the account of Lieutenant Colonel F. Whitton CMG, thought to be the most factual and authoritative of the time, supports Harford's statement. The account was published in 1934 by *Blackwood's Magazine*. It states:

> 'The instructions to strengthen and hold the post at Rorke's Drift had been given before the force at Isandlwana was attacked, and when it was even believed that the Zulus might pass by that place in their eagerness'.[10]

Whitton added that once the news of the approaching Zulus reached the British 'the wall of mealie-bags was raised to a height of four feet', which confirms there was already a wall of mealie bags. The contemporary researcher and author Lee Stevenson wrote:

> 'In a very short space of time all vestiges of his (Reverend Otto Witt) Mission had disappeared beneath a pile of mealie bags and supplies as the British Army arrived to take control. B Company 2/24th under the command of Lieutenant Bromhead took up positions at Rorke's Drift to protect both the crossing and the stores'.[11]

August Hammar, the twenty-two-year-old Swedish family friend of Witt, had temporarily been resident at Rorke's Drift during the two weeks leading up to the British invasion of Zululand. As a young surveyor unable to find work in Sweden, Hammar had set out for South Africa to stay with Witt before searching for suitable work. When Witt departed from Rorke's Drift prior to the Zulu attack, he left Hammar to oversee the Mission. Hammar wrote that he had to sleep outside Witt's house because the British had knocked the walls into defensive positions. This is an impartial eye-witness account recently translated from one of Hammar's original letters, dated 6 January, in Swedish, to his family back in Sweden.[12]

Harford also wrote about Dalton who had supervised the defence of the mission station:

> 'At the moment when warning was received of the nearness of the Zulus, [Dalton] devised all the rapid arrangements for the defence as well as working like a Trojan himself with the men at the barricades …'.[13]

If they were building barricades surely he would have said so instead of 'being at the barricades'? Such a statement chimes with Chelmsford, who also subsequently supported the Harford and Hammar accounts when he confirmed to parliament that he had ordered Glyn to organize the defence of the mission prior to the invasion on 11 January and that he 'understood Glyn had done this'.[14]

Defended or not, Chelmsford had arrived at Rorke's Drift with his entourage of staff officers during the evening of 10 January, a visible sign to the awaiting troops that the invasion was imminent. During the night, the six guns of N Battery Royal Artillery, commanded by Lieutenant Colonel Harness RA, were relocated to an adjacent small rise overlooking the river crossing in order to cover the massed troops assembling for the ponts. Shortly after 2.00 am reveille was sounded and within the hour the column approached the river crossing point.

One minor diversion occurred when it was discovered that a trader's supply wagon had been looted and a cursory search failed to discover the culprits or the stolen stores. By daybreak, the river was covered in a heavy soaking mist. No sound could be heard and as the mist gradually lifted above the river, the far bank and surrounding countryside were bathed in bright sunshine. There were no Zulus; they were 60 miles away at Ulundi undergoing pre-battle rituals in preparation for the defence of their country.

The swollen river they were about to cross was a daunting sight for the 5,000-strong No. 3 Column with all their oxen, supply wagons and guns of the Royal Artillery. First to cross were the Natal Mounted Police followed by the Natal Carbineers, the Buffalo Border Guard and then the Newcastle Mounted Rifles. They were closely followed by the infantry and the 24th Regiment, who were ferried across the river to form up in traditional squares on the Zulu bank. Between the invasion force and the column's first staging post at Isandlwana was a ridge of cliffs and low hills, home of Cetshwayo's friend, Chief Sihayo, and his scattered homesteads. It was obvious to all that these could cause a problem by sitting on the column's main supply route into Zululand.

The British Attack Chief Sihayo's Homestead 12 January 1879

Sirhayo (sic) has about 8,000 men ready to oppose the crossing; I hope it may be true.[15]

Despite the enthusiasm of the Imperial troops, there was one section that was less than happy. Unexpectedly, Chelmsford was faced with the unbelievable threat of mutiny by his previously loyal Colonial troops, who took exception to an inadvertent snub to their commanding officer, Major Dartnell. According to paragraph 144 of the *Regulations for Field Forces in South Africa* any colonial officer, regardless of his rank, was barred from having command over Imperial troops. Chelmsford had previously decreed that all commanders would be Imperial officers and command of the Natal Mounted Police together with all the Natal volunteer units had been given to Brevet Major John Russell of the Mounted Infantry, which insensitively ignored their own experienced Major Dartnell. This ruling infuriated the Colonials who paraded at Helpmekaar to take a vote on the matter; they unanimously decided to refuse orders unless they were given by Dartnell, a highly respected officer, especially in the field of African warfare. Bearing in mind the earlier loss of Boer support, Chelmsford wisely relented; he resolved the issue by promoting Dartnell to the British rank of Lieutenant Colonel and gave him authority over Russell. After a short discussion, the Colonials accepted the decision and followed the main column down to Rorke's Drift, and there the matter ended.

The soldiers marching from Helpmekaar anticipated some comfort at Witt's Rorke's Drift's, whose two buildings were conveniently sited on an elevated small level plateau of rock and commanded a magnificent view over the Buffalo River into Zululand. The two mission buildings consisted of the missionary's house next to a small store which doubled as a church on Sundays; both were solidly made of local stone with thatched roofs. Sheltering the mission was the nearby 500-foot high Oskarsberg hill. Witt's home was the larger of the two buildings and was nearly thirty yards long and spacious. The sole link between the mission station and the rest of Natal was a dirt track that led westwards towards the high escarpment of the Biggarsberg and thence to the small settlement at Helpmekaar.

By the day of the invasion, Witt's twelve-roomed house was converted into a makeshift hospital to cater for the growing number of fever cases and a few soldiers with damaged limbs caused by a number of wagon-related incidents, while the church became an ammunition store. When Witt departed from Rorke's Drift prior to the Zulu attack, he left Hammar to oversee his interests at the Mission. Hammar wrote that he had to sleep outside. During the evening of 10 January, Chelmsford had arrived at Rorke's Drift with his entourage of staff officers, a visible sign to the awaiting troops that the invasion would take place the following morning. The excitement throughout the camp was so infectious that few men slept. During the night, the six guns of N Battery commanded by Lieutenant Colonel Harness RA were relocated to an adjacent small rise overlooking the river in order to cover the troops while crossing. Shortly after midnight reveille was sounded and within the hour the column approached the river crossing point.

The advance guard of mounted troops cautiously rode their horses through the deep swirling waters of the Buffalo River using the submerged flat rocks at the original traders' crossing point. In anticipation of a Zulu attack, they spread out in a wide semi-circle but all they found were three Zulu boys tending their cattle. The infantry were then slowly ferried across the river, followed by the NNC auxiliaries who had to be cajoled by their officers towards the fast-flowing muddy water. They began the crossing in their customary style by linking arms and entering the water in a 'V' formation, those in the front apex being pushed across by those in the rear. Once across, they pulled their colleagues over, losing several men in the crossing, but as their officers didn't know how many men they commanded, little concern was shown.

Within a quarter hour the mounted patrols confirmed the absence of Zulu defenders. A new campsite was prepared on the hillside that looks back at

Rorke's Drift and by noon, the slow process of bringing stores and wagons across from Rorke's Drift was virtually completed. Mid-morning, and with all going well, Chelmsford had ridden off to liaise with Colonel Wood, commander of the Northern Column, with regard to the non-appearance of the Zulus. Wood was already well into Zululand about 30 miles to the north, having 'jumped the gun' by ignoring the ultimatum expiry date and crossing into Zululand on 6 January. Chelmsford ordered him to halt his advance while the Centre and Coastal columns caught up. Lieutenant Harford wrote of the crossing in his diary:

> 'On the 11 January the 3rd Column crossed the Buffalo into Zululand, the troops making their way over at different points. The Artillery and the 24th Regiment went over by degrees in the pontoon, a little above the main drift, (a shallow crossing point) known as Rorke's Drift after the Dutchman Jim Rorke, whose house and farm buildings were occupied by us as a Fort, after being entrenched. I was ordered to find a crossing for the 2nd/3rd Natal Native Contingent, higher up the river. The fog was so dense one could barely see anything a yard in front, but at last, after hugging the bank very closely for about half a mile or more, we came to a spot that looked worth a trial. So I put my pony at it and got across all right, the bed of the river being nice and hard; but the water came up to the saddle flaps, and there was a nasty bank to scramble up on the opposite side. However, that did not matter, it was good enough.
>
> 'Then followed a truly unforgettable scene, firstly of the natives crossing over and then of the impressive ceremony when the regiment had formed up again on the other side and were addressed by old Ingabangi, the witch-doctor. In order to scare away any crocodiles that might be lurking in the vicinity, the leading company formed a double chain right across the river, leaving a pathway between for the remainder to pass through. The men forming the chain clasped hands together, and the moment they entered the water they started to hum a kind of war-chant, which was taken up by every company as they passed over. The sound that this produced was like a gigantic swarm of bees buzzing about us, and sufficient to scare crocodiles or anything else away. Altogether, it was both a curious and grand sight.
>
> 'All being safely over, the men were formed up in quarter-column on the hillside, and one or two officers on their ponies were sent out in different directions to try and find out in the dense fog where any of the other troops were, and what was going on. While this was in progress, an elderly Zulu, Ingabangi, asked permission to address the men. Never shall I forget his extraordinary elocutionary power, and the splendid oration he delivered. The old fellow got to the head of the Column and then started off at a

> trot, going backwards and forwards at this pace for nearly an hour. He would have gone on much longer, had we not received orders to move. Without stopping to take breath, he recounted the history of the Zulu nation, which was frequently applauded by a loud "Gee!" and rattling of assegais on shields from the whole Contingent. It was a wonderfully impressive scene, and one which will always remain fresh in my memory. The drift at which we crossed was subsequently known as Harford's Drift, but I don't suppose it has been used since.
>
> 'Our scouts eventually got in touch with the 24th Regiment, and as we moved up to support them the fog gradually lifted. Then a very pretty sight presented itself as the troops were dotted about over the rolling hills in 'Receive Cavalry' squares formation, their red coats showing up distinctly in the clear atmosphere. No further advance was made that day, owing to the difficulties of getting the Transport across. So we camped where we were'.[16]

In the early hours of the next day, 12 January, the centre column commenced the slow advance towards Ulundi with the intention of constructing a supply depot at a rocky hill inland from Rorke's Drift, then known to the British as *Isandula.* Isandlwana lay about 10 miles from the river crossing and was an ideal site with fresh water and firewood readily available. In between Rorke's Drift and Isandlwana, some 5 miles into Zululand, was a high row of steep red cliffs that formed the backdrop to the homestead of the Zulu Chief Sihayo ka Xongo, an anglophile who wore European clothes, owned two fine English shotguns, and who was a good friend of James 'Jem' Rorke. It was Sihayo's sons who had murdered two of their father's adulterous wives within sight of the mission station a month earlier, an act that was used by the British as one of the grounds for the invasion. More to the point, Sihayo's homestead lay directly in the path of the invading column's main supply route; Chelmsford had already ordered that the stronghold be neutralized and during the day, Major Dartnell with a few Mounted Police was sent on a reconnaissance, and took Harford with him as Staff Officer. On their way to the Bashee Valley, which led towards Chief Sihayo's homestead, they heard a war-song being sung, evidently by a large body of natives; but where they were, or what became of them, the reconnaissance party were unable to discover. However, as this was the ground over which they were going to attack the next day, it looked as if they would meet with some opposition. Other scouting parties from the column had also been out in various directions, and had captured a considerable number of Zulu cattle.

On 12 January, Chelmsford and most of his Centre Column formed up to watch as the NNC, the Natal-recruited auxiliaries of Commandant Rupert La

Trobe Lonsdale, formerly of the 74th Regiment (Black Watch), spearheaded the first attack of the invasion against Sihayo's nearby homestead and village of Sokexe. Chelmsford commented:

> 'I am inclined to think that the first experience of the power of the Martini-Henrys will be such a surprise to the Zulus that they will not be formidable after the first effort'.[17]

Colonel Glyn was in overall command, with responsibility for leading the attack passed to Major Black's Staff Officer, Lieutenant Charles Harford. This was to be the first engagement of the Centre Column which sensed some fun to be had from watching Harford and his 'untrained untrainables' under their equally-untrained hotchpotch of Colonial NCOs, going into action against the Zulus. Led by Harford in his first ever action, the attacking NNC warily advanced towards the steep cliffs and soon came under desultory fire from a handful of Zulus who had been left to protect the homestead; they were armed with ancient muskets and a mixture of old rifles. Under wild and inaccurate fire from the Zulus, who had taken shelter in caves set deeply into the rock face, the NNC adopted the attack formation rehearsed only the day before and then bravely stormed the stronghold supported by the 2/24th, who ponderously clambered over the rocky terrain several hundred yards to the rear. Bearing the brunt of the mostly inaccurate Zulu fire, the NNC steadily advanced but such was the rate of Zulu firing that the NNC soon lost half a dozen men killed to random shots, with a similar number badly wounded, while the 24th, who remained well to the rear, sustained no casualties. The Zulus, on the other hand, lost over 30 old men and boys killed in hand-to-hand fighting, including one of Sihayo's sons. Sihayo's base at nearby Sokexe was burnt to the ground and his cattle seized. The column then moved on to the proposed campsite at Isandlwana.

Following the skirmish, several captured Zulus, including a number badly wounded, had been taken prisoner and forcefully interrogated, an unpleasant process but normal British Army procedure of that time. It was a procedure that was to seriously rebound on the British a few days later. The tortured Zulus nevertheless kept the secret that a great force of 25,000 warriors, accompanied by another 10,000 reserves and camp followers, was steadily approaching the invading British column from Ulundi and was already approaching Isipezi Mountain, just 20 miles distant. Released the following day, the captured Zulus took refuge at the neighbouring village 5 miles downstream which spanned both sides of the river border at Sotondose's Drift, soon to be known as Fugitives' Drift. Angered by the destruction of their village and the death of one of Chief Sihayo's sons, and with their own brutal treatment, not to mention the theft of their 400 head of cattle, they would not be well disposed to the British fugitives who were to flee from Isandlwana through Sotondose's Drift a few days later. News of the British attack on Sihayo's defenceless *umuzi* soon reached Ulundi, and further angered the gathered Zulus.

Later that day Harford wrote a detailed account of the skirmish; it is so vivid that it is reproduced here unabridged:

> 'Reveille sounded very early, about 3.00 am the next morning, and we marched to attack Sirayo's kraal, up the Bashee valley, through thick bush. It was most unpleasant going, for above us, on our right, were hills with the usual cavernous rocks encircling them a little below their crests. It was evident that the warriors we had heard singing their war-chant the day before were ensconced in these caves, for the instant the troops got within range a continuous popping went on from these places. The crack, crack, crack of their guns and rifles echoed and re-echoed among the hills in the still morning air and made it impossible to detect exactly where the shots were coming from. Now and again a Zulu was seen in the open, and on one such occasion I saw the man taking deliberate aim at Colonel Glyn who was standing in an open patch above me. Shouting as loud as I could, I told him to get out of the way before the shot was fired.
>
> 'Colonel Glyn was in command of the troops, and Lord Chelmsford took up a position with his staff on the opposite side of the valley, to watch operations. Colonel Degacher commanded the 2nd Battalion, 24th Regiment, and Major Black our Contingent, as Lonsdale was still in hospital. We started skirmishing through the bush, Major Black leading the 1st Battalion NNC under Commandant Hamilton-Browne, and I following in support with the 2nd Battalion under Commandant Cooper. Before many minutes, bullets were whizzing about in all directions, and one of our Natives, who was close by my side, got a bullet in the thigh, breaking the bone. A short distance further on, seeing two NCOs sheltering behind a rock instead of leading their men, I went to drive them on; and had just got them away when 'ping' came a bullet and cut away a bough just at the spot where my head was a second before. This was luck!
>
> 'As we got further into the bush all sorts of obstacles, such as rocky ground, ravines, and especially thick masses of creepers, prevented any sort of formation being properly kept, in consequence of which the firing line and supports soon got mingled together. Nevertheless, the men were kept well in hand. Before very long I could hear Major Black's shrill voice in broad Scotch urging his men on, and, making my way up to him with supports, I found that he and Commandant Hamilton-Browne were in

a hot corner close to some caves, with hand-to-hand fighting going on. When I was within about twenty or thirty yards of the place, one of their men fell almost at my feet with a terrible assegai wound, which had nearly cut him in half, right down the back. The poor fellow was not dead, and although I could see it was only a matter of minutes my feelings almost led me to try to put him out of his misery with my revolver. But I abstained. I went on to the ridge of the spur of the hill in front of me as fast as I could, with some men, to see what was on the other side and to assist on Major Black's flank.

'Eventually, on reaching the foot of a ledge of rocks, where they curved in a horse-shoe bend overhanging a deep valley, a somewhat grim sight presented itself. Confronting me across the bend was a large, open-mouthed cave, apparently capable of holding a good number of men, and hanging below it were several dead Zulus, caught in the monkey-rope creepers and bits of bush. They had evidently been shot and had either fallen out, or been thrown out, by their comrades when killed. Later on, I learned that a Company of the 24th Regiment had been firing at this particular cave for some time, and had been ordered to cease firing on it when our men came up. It was an uncommonly awkward place to get at, as it meant climbing over nothing but huge rocks and in many places having to work one's way like a crab, besides which a loss of foothold might have landed one in the valley below. However, there was not much time to think, and I determined to make an attempt, so, sending some men to work round below, I took a European NCO who was close at hand, and told him to follow me. Clambering at once over a big piece of rock, I got rather a rude shock on finding a Zulu sitting in a squatting position behind another rock, almost at my elbow. His head showed above the rock, and his wide-open eyes glared at me; but I soon discovered that he was dead.

'Scarcely had I left this apparition behind than a live Zulu suddenly jumped up from his hiding place and, putting the muzzle of his rifle within a couple of feet of my face, pulled the trigger. But the cap snapped, whereupon he dropped his rifle and made off over the rocks for the cave, as hard as he could go. Providence had again come to my aid, and away I went after him, emptying my revolver at him as we scrambled up. Out of my six shots only one hit him, but not mortally. I stopped for a second to reload, but finding the wretched thing stuck I threw it down into the valley below, at the same time turning round and shouting to the NCO, who I thought was following me, to let me have his revolver. But he remained behind, where I had left him at the start, and all he did was to call out, as loud as he could, *"Captain Harford is killed!"* However, I soon put this right by shouting down, *"No, he is not, he is very much alive!"*

'All this was a matter of seconds, and after pronouncing my blessings pretty freely on the Corporal, followed up my quarry, who by this time was standing in the mouth of the cave. Speaking to him in Kaffir, I called upon him to surrender, explaining that I had no intention to harm him in any way and would see to it that he was not ill-treated by anyone. He then squatted down in submission. Before getting up into the cave myself, not caring to run my head into a noose thoughtlessly, I demanded to know if there was anyone else inside and was assured that there was no-one, and as all was quiet, although I must say I had some slight misgivings, I clambered in.

'Close to the entrance lay a wounded man with his feet towards me. Although unable to rise, he clutched hold of an assegai that was by his side, but I told him at once to drop it, that I was going to do him no harm, and questioned him as to who was with him in the cave. He stoutly denied that there were any others there. By this time I was getting accustomed to the darkness, and saw several likely-looking boltholes and kept on repeating that I knew there were others somewhere in hiding and that they were telling me lies. At the same time adding, in a tone loud enough to be heard by anyone near the place, that if they would come out I would promise on oath that no harm should be done to them and that I would accompany them myself to the General, who would see that they were well treated.

'In a short time this had the desired effect, and presently a head appeared from a hole, and as the object crept out I kept careful watch for any sort of weapon that might emerge with it; another and then another crawled out from the same spot. All were unarmed, and squatted down close to me. I then wanted to know where the others were, but they swore that there was no-one else. As this seemed to be the case, I moved off with my four prisoners, leaving the badly-wounded man in the cave. We soon made our way down the valley to where the General and his staff were, and I was met by Major Clery, the Adjutant-General, who greeted me with, 'Well, Harford, I congratulate you on your capture, the General and I have been watching your gallantry for some time'.[18]

Harford was then taken before Chelmsford to discuss the day's action. Chelmsford was sufficiently impressed by Harford's bravery to raise the question of a decoration. Embarrassed by the suggestion and by the presence of watching senior officers, Harford declined saying he was just doing his duty, which Chelmsford accepted. It was a comment Harford bitterly regretted making for the remainder of his service having unintentionally talked his way out of the first Victoria Cross of the campaign.

After a short rest and a meal the whole force returned to camp, drenched to the skin in a thunderstorm. After a day's rest to clean arms and dry clothing, camp was moved forward to the Bashee Valley, not far from the scene of operations two days before, and here they remained for the next four or five days, the 24th working hard at making and repairing roads for the advance to Isandlwana on the 20th. *The Natal Times* on 16 January enthusiastically reported the engagement at Sihayo's homestead:

> 'Up to 9 o'clock last night no intimation had been received from the front of shots being fired in any quarter; but at that hour we received the following important telegram, notifying the repulse and flight of the Zulus, with great loss on their side, at the first encounter. It will be seen that the initiative in attack came from the enemy, and, as has been expected it was from Uirajo's (Sihayo's) people. We regret to see that one of Lonsdale's officers has been killed, and, we fear, two of the Natal Mounted Police; but the telegram leaves room for a probability that the latter have only been wounded. They were probably chasing the flying enemy. The prediction of those best acquainted with the Zulus, that they would never stand the fire of regular forces, has been abundantly verified'.[19]

Following the skirmish at Sihayo's homestead, the subject of Sihayo's Zulu cattle captured during the skirmish caused much discontent among participating column troops who were all entitled to a fair but small share of the plunder, based on the current market price. Evidently, the 400 head of cattle captured at Sihayo's homestead and the surrounding area had been sold cheaply to contractors; the cattle for the sum of £2 a head, the goats for 2s 6d and the sheep for 6s. The troops who captured the cattle would be due a monetary reward based on the contractors' price and word of the price spread quickly through the column.[20]

The Natal Witness reporter with the Carbineers submitted the following perceptive despatch to his newspaper on 18 January:

> 'We have already had three different patrols into the enemy's quarters. Rumour had it that there were thousands near to us: but, though we hunted up hill and down dale, *saw we never none*. It is impossible to know what to believe. The Zulus must assuredly be somewhere, but wherever we go, we only come across deserted huts'.[21]

Britain's invasion into Zululand obliged Cetshwayo to finally confront the problems being forced upon him by the formidable British. Following the invasion, the British received the sixth appeal from Cetshwayo to negotiate. Bulwer simply replied that he should communicate with the British commander, General Lord Chelmsford. The Zulu nation had been at peace for twenty-three years and no British settler or traveller had ever been harmed. The scene was now set for a dramatic confrontation between the British and Zulus. A hush of anxious suspense descended across Natal and Zululand, both sides fearing invasion by the other, and all without the knowledge of anyone in Britain. Over the next two days several local Zulus reported to Chelmsford that King Cetshwayo intended to decoy the British and then make for Natal. Chelmsford dismissed their warning and resolved to push on deeper into Zululand without delay. Isandlwana was now just 3 miles away.

It was now that Lieutenant Harford wrote home to his mother. His recently discovered letter (unabridged) reads:

Zululand 1879
Jan 14th 1879 Just across Rorke's Drift

My dearest mother and everyone. I've never sent a line to a soul since I left Maritzburg. I wrote to you from there though I was awfully busy the whole time and told you I was placed as staff officer to Lonsdale. I can tell you it has been a most awful time with these people, but I will say one thing the European officer and NCO are a thousand per cent worse than the natives, no one hardly speaks a word of Kafir and the Zulu interpreter can't always be present so it is a lucky thing I have not forgotten mine and am picking up a good deal more so that I really am 'Comd off Adj Qm and Zulu' everyone comes to me white and black and my life is an incessant force, but in the midst of all I can't help laughing all round no matter who it is. I'm glad however, things are beginning to get a little ship shape. We have crept along here by degrees staying for about a week just across the river to show the Zulus we were prepared. There are besides ourselves here (of the 3rd Column) 2 Co 1/24, 4 Co 2/24, Dartnell's Police, troop mounted infantry, Battery of Artillery and the troop of Natal Carbineers under officer Henrique Shepstone. The Ultimatum having gone and no answer received except a message from Cetewayo (*sic*) to say that he was tired of talking with us, so on the 11th we crossed the border encamped the night and next morning at day break (the day before yesterday we started off for Sirayo's (*sic*) kraal about 6 or 7 miles off to see what could be found. We got up to the kloof a most abominable place to get at a lot of men fired upon us from a cave. And we had a nasty bit of fighting to get them out, fearful climbing and boulders and not much footing. The Native Force wanted a deal of urging on I had to threaten several men's lives before getting them to budge, they were in such a fright hearing the bullets go past. Taking such a small affair we came off rather badly we had 2 men killed and 13 wounded (2 more dead). I was very nearly killed twice. I had a bough cut off close to my cheek once and the other time - there had been a great many shots fired from a certain cave and the occupant doing a lot of damage - no nigger would go up and it was a long time before I could get a soul to come up. So as we could drive certain parties who were hidden out before we got to it, at last a fellow volunteered and up we went of course, then a lot followed but I got almost on the edge of the cave which happened to be round the corner slightly when a fellow took a deliberate pot at me but the cap snapped I gave him four barrels of a revolver which wounded him slightly and put him in such a fright that he gave in and caught him. I then pulled 4 more out, so I got the whole five, two were badly wounded and 2 died just outside the mouth of the cave. I took a couple of guns and heaps of assegais and which I should like to keep of course but can't get no one to carry the things. I know you would like to know all so I tell you. The Colonel and the Chief of his Staff who saw the whole proceeding complimented me very much on my success and the manner in which I got up to the cave so I hope it may do me good. My commandant specially mentioned me in his report to the General so I dare say I may have been mentioned in despatches. I expect we shall have a rough time of it and the young boys of Cetewayo intend giving battles. They are determined to fight, it will be the best thing that possibly can happen for the Colony. All 3 columns, Col Wood, VC CB 90th, Col Pearson CB 3rd Buffs, Col Glynn CB 24th, all meet somewhere by Cetewayo's kraal and we shall give him a tremendous thrashing he won't ever forget and we have taken heaps of cattle already so I hope to get some prize money as well…

Happy return of the years…

H. Harford[22]

Over the next two days several local Zulus reported to Chelmsford that Cetshwayo intended to decoy the British and then make for Natal. Chelmsford dismissed their warning and resolved to push on deeper into Zululand without delay. Isandlwana was now just 3 miles away. Chelmsford could now relax; his fear of a sizeable Zulu force sitting across his supply line was proved empty; Sihayo's warriors had long since departed for Ulundi.

The engagement at Sihayo's homestead was, in reality, a token demonstration of British invincibility to the handful of Zulus guarding Chief Sihayo's homestead. Although of no real military significance, it was reported to the invasion force as a success, even though the Zulu opposition had largely consisted of a few old men and boys left to guard the homestead. As an exercise, it gave the inexperienced and nervous NNC their first taste of fighting, even though they heavily outnumbered the Zulus. However, the engagement was highly significant as it gave Chelmsford and his staff officers' false courage, as they wrongly presumed the Zulus were not seeking to engage them in combat. It also convinced the troops that, as they had been told by their officers, the Zulus would run away rather than stand and fight. From the Zulus' perspective, news of the attack against Sihayo's homestead reached Ulundi and sufficiently provoked King Cetshwayo and his chiefs to finally order the main Zulu army to attack Chelmsford's centre column. Chelmsford's presence during the attack also convinced the king that the centre column was the most dangerous of the three and therefore must be the first invading column to be attacked using the full might of the Zulu army.

Earlier, on 17 January while the British were settling in at Rorke's Drift, the Zulu army, totally inexperienced in warfare apart from a handful of older chiefs, formed up to undergo the final ritual purification against evil influences during the coming conflict. This purification was performed by two war-doctors, one with special 'powers' to reduce the effect of British bullets. Later that same day the Zulu army began leaving its base on the Mahlabatini Plain to face the invaders, and the trail they left in the grass was to remain visible for many months. Their orders were to march slowly so as to conserve their energy. Their destination was a gorge, 50 miles distant, near the border with Natal, and just 3 miles from an unknown rock outcrop known locally as Isandlwana. Faced with the inevitable British invasion of Zululand, Cetshwayo's overall strategy was to either trap, or inflict a decisive preliminary defeat on the British invaders. Knowing the British possessed overwhelming firepower, Cetshwayo decided against the traditional Zulu mass frontal attack, preferring the use of siege tactics. He remembered the reports from his spies during the recent Pedi expedition – that the British were weak and relatively defenceless when in the open or on the move. He reasoned that, once trapped or starved into submission, the invaders would be forced to withdraw to Natal rather than face a humiliating defeat on the battlefield. He accordingly instructed his generals to harass the invading columns and isolate them from their supply lines.

As already noted, Cetshwayo was an astute diplomat and knew that once the British invasion force was trapped he could seriously embarrass Britain internationally and even force her invading army commanders to sue for peace. Unfortunately for Cetshwayo, his field commanders would, instead, take autonomous action, being either unable or unwilling to follow the king's orders not to attack defended positions.

By 21 January, most of the British invading force had passed through Rorke's Drift and arrived at Isandlwana. The location was ideal as there was an ample supply of both water and wood for cooking; and the position in front of the mountain was elevated with a sheer rock face to its rear and, therefore, the large spread out camp appeared easy to defend. It dominated the vast open plain towards the Zulu capital at Ulundi so that any approaching Zulu force, advancing from Ulundi, would be observed for several miles before it could form up for an attack. The camp under construction would hold some 750 tents, neatly erected according to strict military regulations, company by company, street by street, over an area nearly one square mile and all under the gaze of Cetshwayo's spies, watching from the adjacent plateau unseen from the camp.

Having settled the British invasion column into the camp site at Isandlwana, considerable misgivings on the part of certain experienced officers soon arose, including Major Dartnell. All were alarmed with regard to the selection of the site, owing principally to the broken and wooded country to its immediate rear which would offer ample cover for a large force of Zulus to concentrate unseen and to attack suddenly. To an officer of the Natal Mounted Police who had suggested to one of Chelmsford's staff officers that the British camp might be attacked from the rear, Chelmsford retorted, 'tell the police officer my troops will do all the attacking'. Major Dunbar and Lieutenant Melvill also registered their concern with the comment, 'Do the staff think we are going to meet an army of schoolgirls? Why in the name of all that is holy do we not laager?'[23]

That morning, several locals from the Natal side of the nearby river came into the camp with a warning for Chelmsford that Cetshwayo intended to decoy the British and, when lured into the bush, the Zulu army would make for Natal. The same report arrived from Chelmsford's own local advisor, Mr. Fannin; Chelmsford dismissed their multiple warnings. He believed the river crossing points were adequately covered and resolved to push on deeper into Zululand without delay and commented:

> 'We have already had three different patrols into the enemy's quarters. Rumour had it that there were thousands near to us: but, though we hunted up hill and down dale, "saw we never none." It is impossible to know what to believe. The Zulus must assuredly be somewhere, but wherever we go, we only come across deserted huts. It is evident that a large number of the people have taken to flight, but whether they have done so through fear of us, or of their own 'noble savage' defenders, I cannot undertake to say. As a change, however, on the last occasion we came across a Zulu, whom we took prisoner. On questioning him as to why there were so

> few men about, he said that they were quite scared away at the manner in which we had taken their mountain fortress (Sihayo's) from them – as they had not ever dreamt that we should venture up it. This amount of fear does not look very much like the wonderful prowess of the Zulus, of which we heard so much in Natal. I imagine they are much like other natives – very great at bragging, but easily depressed and panic-stricken by any sudden reverse'.[24]

As the day progressed, Chelmsford experienced frustration heaped upon frustration. The initial stage of the Zulu action was effective and resulted in a perplexing tangle of information and disinformation reaching the British headquarters. Chelmsford's situation was made worse by a local Zulu chief, Gamdana, arriving at the camp. Gamdana had considered defecting to the British but was still wavering. As a sop to Chelmsford, Gamdana correctly reported that the Zulu army was approaching Isipezi Hill, but he and his information were dismissed. Rebuffed by Chelmsford, Gamdana was able to assess the strength and layout of the British camp, a point of accusation that would later be levelled against Chelmsford by some of his own staff officers. That afternoon, Chelmsford received incorrect reports from Dartnell's reconnaissance party that they had found the approaching Zulu army. Dartnell was sent orders to attack the Zulus the following day and supplies of food were sent out from the camp to sustain Dartnell's force of mainly NNC, some 12 miles from Isandlwana.

Later that afternoon Chelmsford decided to accompany a reconnaissance to the top of the Nqutu Plateau. One of the officers leading the patrol, Lieutenant Milne RN, later wrote:

> 'On reaching the summit of the highest hill I counted fourteen Zulu horsemen watching us at a distance of about 4 miles; they ultimately disappeared over a slight rise. There were two vedettes at the spot from where I saw these horsemen; they said they had seen these men several times during the day, and had reported the fact. From this point the ground was nearly level; there were slight rises, however, every now and again, which would prevent our seeing any men who did not wish it'.[25]

From their vantage point high on the plateau, these Zulu chiefs were reconnoitring the British position around Isandlwana. Neither Chelmsford nor his accompanying officers realised the significance of so many mounted Zulus; only senior Zulu chiefs rode horses and no one expressed any curiosity as to why the riders were there. Throughout that night the Zulu army silently consolidated its position in the valleys on the plateau and their scouts were sent forward to observe the unsuspecting British sleeping on the plain below. On one occasion, less than 2 miles from the main camp, some Zulu scouts came so close to an NNC piquet on Magaga hill that they conversed with them.[26]

References

1. Curling letters of the Anglo-Zulu War.
2. *SWB*, Atkinson C.T., Cambridge University Press, 1937.
3. *The Natal Witness*, 6 January 1879.
4. *Chelmsford.*
5. PRO WO 33/34 56333.
6. Letter dated 28 Jan 1879 to Chelmsford. See *South Africa's Uprising from 1851.*
7. a. David Rattray collection. *Harford*, Payne, D. Nb. Following a chance meeting in 2012 with Lieutenant Harford's descendants, the author was loaned four suitcases of Harford's Zulu War material to research, most of which was unknown to researchers and included the officer's eye-witness account of the pre-defence of Rorke's Drift.
   b. See *Natal Archives*, Sir Evelyn Wood Papers, 16 Jan. 1879.
8. Harford.
9. Note; still current in 1879.
10. *Blackwood's Magazine*, 1934.
11. *The Rorke's Drift Doctor*, 2001.
12. *A Handful of Heroes*, Stossel K. Pen & Sword. Hammar's letters reproduced in Chapter 10.
13. a. *Harford*, Payne, D.
   b. Also, *Invasion of Zululand 1879*, (Clarke, Sonia, The Brenthurst Press 1979). is confirmation of the defences being reduced in size as the Zulus approached Rorke's Drift, indicating a pre-defence.
14. Quoted in Hansard, 1880.
15. *Chelmsford.*
16. Harford Payne, D. Also, on 11 January 1879, while No. 3 Column was crossing the Buffalo River into Zululand, a private of the mounted infantry became de-horsed in the river and would have drowned had it not been for the swift action of Captain David J. Hayes of the Natal Native Contingent, who saved him. This act, although not under fire, was probably the first occasion of the war that resulted in a mention in despatches.
17. Dispatch from Lord Chelmsford at Pietermaritzburg to Col. Wood 23 November 1878
18. Harford Payne, D.
19. *The Natal Times*, 16 January, published on 23 January.
20. *A Lost Legionary in South Africa.*
21. *Natal Witness*, published on 23 January.
22. Harford Payne, D.
23. *A Lost Legionary in South Africa*, Hamilton-Browne, quoted by Captain Duncombe to Commandant Hamilton-Browne.
24. Natal Witness reporter with the Carbineers submitted the despatch to his newspaper on 18 January. PRO WO 33/34 S 6333.
25. Milne to his father, 10 February 1879.
26. Confirmed by The Hon. Lieutenant Vereker. See Higginson WO 33/34 S6333.

Chapter 6

Defeat at Isandlwana

Helpmekaar, the name translates as 'help-one-another' in Afrikaans (named 'Helpmakaar' by the British), was a flat area on the twenty-mile-long Biggarsberg plateau some 5 miles inland from the Buffalo River overlooking the border with Zululand. Before the invasion there was little at Helpmekaar other than two small rough farmers' cottages and the remains of a tiny church built by Berlin missionary Jacob Dohne. Helpmekaar provided access off the plateau via the steep Nostrope Pass to the vast level grasslands below, with a convenient traders' track leading to the rarely used river crossing at Rorke's Drift.[1] The advance of Lord Chelmsford's Centre Column from across Natal to Helpmekaar progressed through December 1878 and was uneventful; it was to be the last main supply camp before the invasion of Zululand. Several hundred tents were erected for the 4,700 men and pens constructed for the 1,500 oxen needed to pull the column's 300 wagons and carts. The surrounding area was given over to an extensive storage complex encompassing pens to hold large numbers of horses. As it was flat and level, it was an ideal location for the British to accumulate their vast quantity of supplies prior to the invasion of Zululand, but to the weary soldiers, the location was flat, featureless, remote and bleak. Accompanying the invasion force was Lieutenant Colonel Arthur Harness RA who described the whole plateau area as devoid of vegetation 'Like the bottom of the sea with grass on it.' Within days it was a confusing mass of tents, stores and supply wagons and, due to the summer deluges, there were unavoidable obnoxious quagmires of mud mixed with sewage. Dysentery soon followed. Nevertheless, with the return of hot weather Chelmsford's force prepared to move to the Zulu border. From the top of the winding Nostrope Pass, the advancing column had a spectacular view of the Buffalo River which formed the natural border between British Natal and Zululand. The Oskarsberg hill overlooking Rorke's Drift could clearly be seen standing alone, with the dominating peak of Isandlwana in the further hazy distance of Zululand.

During the first week of January Glyn's massive bustling Central Column descended off the plateau to reassemble at Rorke's Drift, previously reconnoitred and approved by Lord Chelmsford. There they waited for 11 January and the expiry of the British ultimatum before advancing towards the hill at Isandlwana.

The column's troops considered themselves invincible. The backbone of this force were the two battalions, the 1st and 2nd, of the 24th (2nd Warwickshire) Regiment. The Royal Artillery had four 7-pounder horse-drawn rifled muzzle loading guns. The proven tactic of the British was well-aimed volley fire by calm experienced troops, supported by artillery. The soldier's standard issue weapon was the Martini-Henry rifle, a real man-stopper accurate to well over 200 yards. The one-ounce soft lead slug flattened on impact, causing massive tissue damage. Even if it did not kill, the victim would soon die of shock or appalling trauma. British soldiers had been informed that King Cetshwayo's army was inexperienced in actual warfare other than local domestic skirmishing with hide shields, long throwing spears, clubs and the *assegai* – a short stabbing spear traditionally designed for hand-to-hand fighting.

Meanwhile, with all-out war inevitable, King Cetshwayo planned for his main attack on the British column now advancing towards Isandlwana, not least because it was accompanied by Chelmsford, and posed the nearest threat to his capital at Ulundi. He meanwhile dispatched token forces to deter the subsidiary four columns of British troops facing Zululand from molesting his supply lines. Colonel Rowlands VC was in the Transvaal to keep watch on the Boers, Colonel Pearson was at the coast, Colonel Wood to the north and Colonel Durnford facing the Middle Drift crossing point at the Tugela River. Zulu spies had reassuringly reported that these British columns were unlikely to pose an immediate threat to Ulundi due to their smaller size and the difficult terrain facing them. With the doctoring rituals of the assembled Zulu army completed, especially with potions to 'neutralise' British bullets, Cetshwayo's regiments departed Ulundi on 17 January full of confidence that they would easily rout the invaders. They left a small reserve to protect Ulundi consisting of the iNdabakawombe *amabutho*, most nearing sixty years of age.

The main mighty Zulu column of 25,000 warriors together with 10,000 *uDibi* boys and camp followers carrying food and spare weapons was led by the veteran chief, the 70-year-old Ntshingwayo and his deputy, the younger Ntuli chief, Mavumengwana ka Ndlela. Accompanying the Zulu commanders was Mehlokazulu, one of Sihayo's sons who had returned from his enforced exile after having riled the British authorities for murdering his mother. By the second day the army reached the Isipezi *ikhanda*, just 15 miles from Isandlwana, before dividing into two more manageable columns. The following day the huge army continued its advance, with the two columns marching side by side. Some of Sihayo's men had horses and, knowing the area, they rode ahead of the columns to deal with any British scouts. In accordance with the king's orders, the army marched slowly so as to conserve its energy, taking three days instead of the usual two to cover the 50 miles to their destination. On 21 January, the

Zulu army passed the lower reaches of the Isipezi Mountain and under cover of darkness moved to the nearby Ngwebeni River depression, 6 miles to the north and out of sight of the British at Isandlwana.

With the British column arriving at Isandlwana, Glyn initiated Chelmsford's instructions for the layout and defence of the camp, but within the hour he was over-ruled by Chelmsford who was reluctant to fortify the extensive position. Another standard precaution against a surprise attack was the spreading of broken glass around a temporary camp perimeter but this precaution was not taken. Chelmsford's intention was to overnight at Isandlwana before moving further into Zululand next morning at daybreak. Chelmsford reasoned that the ground was too hard and the ox drawn supply wagons had to be kept moving day and night to bring in necessary supplies. Once in Zululand each battalion needed a ton each of food and fuel per day, overall Chelmsford's column needed some 2,500 tons of supplies for every week of the campaign.

Ntshingwayo learned from his scouts that the British had erected their tents over a wide area on the gentle downward slope on the south side of Isandlwana, and the extensive camp appeared to be undefended. Ntshingwayo shared his scouts' collective opinion that the British camp's officers appeared oblivious of the Zulus' presence. The main Zulu army's actual advance had been so well hidden from Chelmsford's camp that Chelmsford continued to ignore the trend of his scouts' intelligence reports warning of the possible approach of the Zulu army. He preferred to believe his own plan, to discover then defeat the main Zulu army he believed would be advancing from Ulundi. During the previous two days, Chelmsford and his escort had indeed fleetingly observed Zulu movements to the distant east, the direction of Ulundi. This was confirmed by his scouts mistakenly reporting seeing the same Zulus advancing from the east. They were wrong; what they had seen were groups of Chief Matyana's warriors on their way back from Ulundi to their own tribal lands following a leadership dispute between Matyana and Chief Tshingwayo as to who would be in overall command of the advancing Zulu army. Matyana had stormed off, taking his warriors with him. It was this force returning from Ulundi that Chelmsford's scouts had seen, albeit some 10 miles distant from Isandlwana. Faced with this incorrect report of a growing Zulu presence Chelmsford accepted their reports which supported his incorrect belief that the Zulu army was approaching his position from Ulundi to the east.

That late afternoon of 21 January Chelmsford despatched Major Dartnell to the Isipezi hills with a large detachment of four companies to investigate and locate this imaginary Zulu force. In spite of exhausting and fruitless patrols no Zulu force could be found. During the latter part of the evening Ntshingwayo gave orders for the preparation of an elaborate decoy. He instructed that, after dark, camp fires should be lit across the first range of hills some 12 miles from Isandlwana. The decoy was intended to suggest the Zulus were closing on Isandlwana from the east, whereas Ntshingwayo's army was already in a valley to the north of the British camp, and undetected. As a result, as darkness fell, Dartnell saw hundreds of Zulu cooking fires suggesting a massive Zulu army was indeed approaching from the direction of Ulundi. Convinced he had found the main Zulu army, Dartnell sent an urgent report to Chelmsford requesting immediate assistance. Events were about to get messy and uncomfortable for the British; the final stage of the Zulu decoy was underway.

It was around midnight when Chelmsford received Dartnell's confirmation that, on the basis of the fire decoys, he had found the Zulu army. Within the hour Chelmsford committed the cardinal sin for a general in occupied territory: unaware of the true location of his enemy he divided his force. Anticipating the battle he so urgently sought, he ordered one infantry battalion, the 2/24th Battalion Warwickshire Regiment, and a battalion of the NNC to march out at midnight to support Dartnell, all under the command of Colonel Glyn. Those left in camp under the command of Colonel Pulleine included the 1st Battalion of the 24th Warwickshire Regiment.

As dawn broke on 22 January, the remaining Zulu forces arrived from Isipezi Hill to join the final massive advance on Isandlwana camp. News from Zulu scouts began reaching Ntshingwayo that Dartnell's column had remained 10 miles out from Isandlwana. Even better, the scouts reported they were actively engaged in searching the empty hills between Isipezi and Mangeni looking for the Zulu army. Fresh information from his scouts then began coming to Ntshingwayo that another column, accompanied by both Chelmsford and Glyn, had unexpectedly departed the British Isandlwana camp and was at that very moment busy joining Dartnell's men searching for the imagined Zulu army.

For breaking his own orders to defend Isandlwana camp Chelmsford would suffer an unimaginable defeat and seriously alarm Parliament – so much so that when later discussing the question of the policy of the war, which proceeded with criticism of the military operations, reference was focused on the defeat at Isandlwana, especially upon the conduct of Lord Chelmsford:

> 'By dividing his force, leaving one part in an unintrenched (*sic*) camp, while he proceeded in two columns into the interior of the enemy's country, without establishing a communication with the force left in the camp, the result being the capture of the camp with all its stores, and the destruction of the force left in charge; arguing, (as was understood) that a general who had so mismanaged a single expedition was not fit to be left in the supreme management of a company'.[2]

The Zulu decoy had succeeded beyond Ntshingwayo's expectations. He later said:

> 'You gave us the battle that day, for you dispersed your army in small parties all over the country'.[3]

In the early hours before dawn, those left at Isandlwana camp, some 1,600 men in all, had heard Chelmsford's relief column march out of camp. Pulleine dispatched his remaining infantry to form an extended 1-mile line facing Ulundi, approximately 1,000 yards to the left front of the camp with several yards between each soldier. At dawn, further positions to the north of the camp along the base of the Nqutu Plateau were taken up by several companies of the NNC, while a mounted patrol was sent to observe the top of the Nqutu Plateau less than one mile distant. Pulleine and his officers were totally unaware of their looming predicament. Their camp was now highly vulnerable to the unseen massed Zulu army hidden on their flank, only 5 miles away. The British were unwittingly spreading over a vast area, from Rorke's Drift to Isipezi Hill, and from the Ngwebeni Valley to Mangeni; they were all in the wrong place covering an unmanageable 150 square miles. Worse, the wagon route back to Rorke's Drift and the rear of Isandlwana camp was unprotected. Colonel Pulleine believed any Zulu attack would come from a frontal attack on his fallacious assumption that the Zulus would not use their standard tactic – to envelop an enemy.

The emerging plight for Chelmsford's column unimaginably worsened. Ten miles to the east of the Isandlwana camp, other Zulu decoys deliberately confused Dartnell's and Chelmsford's forces by appearing on hilltops, then disappearing, encouraging the searching troops to be lured even further away from Isandlwana towards Ulundi, leaving the main Zulu army preparing to advance undetected on both the unprotected flank and rear of the British camp. Having sent his chiefs forward to the edge of the Nqutu heights overlooking the British camp to make their final reconnaissance, Ntshingwayo ordered his army into action. The Zulu main army then began to move in force towards the rim of the Nqutu Plateau, still unseen by the unsuspecting British camp a half-mile below them.

At the same time, the bugle call for breakfast sounded across the British camp followed by normal camp activities. Then things began to go wrong. Spreading out over a four mile front and in places, a half-mile deep, Ntshingwayo's advancing army began approaching Isandlwana camp, unseen by the main British force, until they reached a long slope off the plateau less than a mile from the camp. Under orders, the Zulus approached at a fast walking pace as, completely unexpected by Pulleine and his officers taking breakfast, the leading edge of the main advancing Zulu army was clearly seen moving off the plateau. Overlooking the camp from their vantage point the senior Zulu chiefs became busy directing the various *impis* to assembly areas before attacking the unsuspecting camp. The Zulu commander, Ntshingwayo, now fully appreciated that the British were unprepared for his imminent attack.

An alarming report then reached Pulleine from a patrol on a nearby hill that a large Zulu force was indeed advancing from the north-east of the Nqutu Plateau towards the camp. The bugler sounded 'Stand To'. Breakfast was abandoned. The men quickly gathered their weapons and assembled to prepare for action. They were then rushed to the east of their camp and formed up in a thin line over a half-mile in length to face any attack. In the still African morning, nothing appeared to happen and the soldiers soon relaxed believing it was another false alarm. Then, from the east and the direction of Ulundi, larger groups of Zulus appeared to be steadily approaching the camp. Again, Pulleine's front line was made ready for action. Confusingly, another mass of Zulu warriors was reported advancing towards the unprotected rear of Isandlwana, but behind the hill, they were unseen from the camp; the British ignored the report.

Further positions were then taken up by several companies of the NNC. These faced the base and shoulder of the Nqutu Plateau to the northeast of the camp, while a mounted patrol was sent to observe the unseen top of the plateau itself. Pulleine and his officers were totally unaware of their looming predicament. Chelmsford's main invasion column's camp was now highly vulnerable not only to the massing Zulu army on their flank, only 5 miles distant, but to the Zulus approaching behind the hill to their unprotected rear.

British scouts' reports to Pulleine confirmed a sizeable force of Zulus was steadily advancing on the camp from both the north, the direction of the Nqutu Plateau, and from the east. This caused Pulleine and his officers some confusion; they anticipated the Zulus would be to their east-facing front, not on their northern left flank. Nevertheless, Pulleine strengthened his front line of infantry with the two guns of the Royal Artillery. One engineer officer, Lieutenant Chard, who had earlier witnessed the first group of Zulus watching the camp, had been sufficiently concerned by events that he was already returning to Rorke's Drift, rightly anticipating that his detachment at the garrison could be in danger.

For the next hour, the soldiers were alternately stood to, or stood down, during which time the still unsuspecting Pulleine inexplicably busied himself with Chelmsford's order to dismantle the camp in anticipation of their next move. Half his force had been allocated to the task and were thus employed when Captain Gardner and Captain Henrique Shepstone breathlessly arrived at Pulleine's tent pointing at the Zulu regiments now pouring off the plateau towards the camp. Shepstone noted that Pulleine was still focused on Chelmsford's last order – to strike camp and move to re-join Chelmsford's advance.

By late morning it was already a baking hot day when the central body of the main Zulu force, consisting of some 15,000 warriors, formed up ready to attack the camp. The bugle call to prepare for action sounded for the final time. To the horror of the soldiers, now spread out before the camp in a thin line, six feet between each man, the central body of the main Zulu force steadily advanced at the run, en masse towards them. It must have been an awesome sight for the soldiers, for most of them this would be their first experience of both seeing and hearing the vastly overwhelming numbers of charging Zulus. Within minutes the Zulus crashed into the camp. What the front line soldiers could not see was the other Zulu force from behind Isandlwana now charging through the unprotected rear of the camp.

Directed by Major Stuart Smith and Lieutenant Curling, the guns of the Royal Artillery had opened fire using close range shrapnel. The charging Zulus observed the gun crews' firing procedure, throwing themselves to the ground as each gun was fired making Lieutenant Higginson later report that the artillery 'swept them away'. This may have been wishful thinking; Zulu accounts state that the artillery did little damage. These accounts were probably correct due to the convex nature of the terrain; half of the British front line was unable to see most of the advancing Zulus massing in the dead ground east of the camp. From the relative safety of this unseen dead ground the massed Zulus charged the British infantry line either side of the guns. Using this depression was an important aspect of the Zulu attack and they had used it to their full advantage to form up, mostly unseen, for the final attack.

Because the line of British infantry and artillery gunners facing east could not see the massing Zulus in the dead ground to their front, they sought to rectify their disadvantage by advancing their line another 100 yards in the hope of getting a better view of the approaching Zulus. In so doing, they advanced far enough that Pulleine and his headquarters officers could no longer see their own front line. Pulleine would have been further dispirited had he known a third force of Zulus was already attacking his unprotected camp from behind. Unable to see the Zulu columns, the most senior British officer in the camp was now fighting 'battle blind'.

The British opened with volley fire. To the right of the guns, the three *amabutho* making up the main Zulu army, the iNgobamakhosi, uKhandempemvu and uMbonambi, had moved to the south and then charged, but soon began to suffer heavily from British rifle fire as they charged on the British front line across the last 100 yards of open terrain. The officers and NCOs calmly controlled their men's volley fire and the main Zulu attack faltered then stopped. The soldiers reportedly laughed and joked about the drubbing they were giving the Zulus even though, due to the black smoke of their own volley fire, they might not have seen that the advancing Zulu warriors were a half-mile deep. The long line of redcoats still fully anticipated victory; after all, victory was always expected. To make matters worse for Pulleine, he and his camp officers could now see yet another massive force of Zulus pouring off the Nqutu Plateau and heading for the small conical hill one mile in front of the camp. They would shortly drive a wedge between the distant Chelmsford and the camp by massing beyond the dead ground at the east of the camp. The tactic succeeded brilliantly; the Zulus had manoeuvred and advanced the main body of their army into full view of the British while the right horn slipped unnoticed behind Isandlwana, encircling the British position. The British were only aware of the right horn when it emerged in force from behind the mountain, driving the column's bellowing and terrified cattle from the undefended wagon park straight into the unprotected rear of the British camp.

But British volley fire was too slow to have the necessary impact on thousands of fast running Zulus. As the charging stabbing Zulu masses emerged from the protection of the dead ground, now only 50 yards in front of the British firing line, each volley of Martini-Henry rifles, firing black powder cartridges, created a dense wall of black smoke just ten feet in front of the line through which the soldiers could only fire blindly. Conversely, the same smoke created a protective smokescreen that enabled the Zulus to charge into the British line like ghosts through the thick smoke, largely unseen until the last moment. The day was baking hot and there was not even a breath of wind to clear the smoke. It was evident to the Zulus that even sustained British volley fire was no longer going to stop them. Orders could not be heard even though the volleys had given way to single shots.

This smoke hypothesis is supported by an item in a contemporary army instruction manual: 'In firing volleys by sections it is well to commence from the section on the leeward flank, in order that the smoke may not inconvenience the remainder'. After several volleys in still air, the British line at Isandlwana may well have fought blindly in a dense fog of their own gun smoke before withdrawing back to the camp – only to encounter the massive Zulu right horn as its 4,000 warriors charged through the unprotected camp into the rear of the retreating British troops.[4] Lieutenant Smith-Dorrien survived the downfall of the camp and chillingly wrote:

> 'Before we knew where we were they came right into the camp, assegaing everybody left and right. Everybody who then had a horse turned to fly. The enemy were going at a kind of fast half-walk half-run. On looking round we saw that we were completely surrounded and the road to Rorke's Drift was cut off'.[5]

Lieutenant Wilkinson, a veteran of several Zulu War battles, subsequently made a relevant and revealing observation:

> 'and we followed suit, firing volleys by sections in order to prevent the smoke obscuring the enemy, and we had repeatedly to cease fire to allow the smoke to clear off, as some young aspirants out of hand paid little attention to section firing. One lesson we learnt in our fight was, that with the Martini-Henry, men must fire by word of command either by individuals, or at most, by sections: independent firing means firing in twenty seconds, firing at nothing; and only helped our daring opponents to get close up under cover of our smoke. Officers had to be everywhere, and to expose themselves to regulate the fire within bounds, and I feel sure that for the future, only volleys by sections will be fired'.[6]

In camp, the scene was beyond nightmarish – gunfire, screaming, noise, terror, confusion and wholesale slaughter. The thick black smoke from the rifle fire just added to the pandemonium. For the dying and wounded British soldiers across the camp, no wounded man could be cared for. Obeying the law of survival, anyone still alive had to flee or be killed. The road to Rorke's Drift earlier taken by those who had fled was now a mass of stabbing Zulu warriors killing fleeing fugitives. With no other way being open, the remaining fugitives attempted to escape across the rocky terrain towards a nearby ravine. In moments the fleet-of-foot Zulus were among them, stabbing men as they ran.

The Zulus still had to deal with clusters of soldiers who obeyed their orders, trying to remain in extended line right up to the final bugle call to retreat. Too late, the desperately-awaited call sounded. Overwhelming numbers of Zulus smashed through the last clusters of soldiers fighting back-to-back or retreating, stabbing and slashing as they ran. Curling wrote of the Zulu attack 'once amongst their enemy, the short stabbing spear or assegai proved most effective, killing men as fast as they came out of their tents'. This statement suggests that not all available troops were on the front line – some were still engaged in packing the tents for the move to join Chelmsford's column when the Zulus so dramatically swept through the camp. The fighting and merciless slaughter raged for no more than a half hour; by then the overwhelming force of Zulus had killed the last surviving soldiers. Apart from the loss of the camp, the British lost 52 officers, 730 white troops and some 700 plus NNC and native troops. Zulu losses are estimated between 2,000 and 3,000.

Towards the end of the battle, and without giving any further orders, Pulleine retired into his tent. Various Zulu accounts claim Pulleine was killed at the height of the battle while still writing at his desk. Wherever he was, he had lost everything. Yet, at the height of the main attack, the few survivors and Zulu accounts all agreed the British soldiers obeyed their orders to stand firm, and died bravely, even as the Zulus overwhelmed them. Whilst no front line foot soldier lived to tell the tale, several accounts survive from Zulu warriors interviewed after the battle:

> 'Ah, those red soldiers at Isandlwana, how few they were, and how they fought! They fell like stones – each man in his place'.[7]

> 'They threw down their guns, when the ammunition was done, and then commenced with their pistols, which they fired as long as their ammunition lasted; and then they formed a line, shoulder to shoulder, and back to back, and fought with their knives'.[8]

> 'Some covered their faces with their hands, not wishing to see death. Some ran around. Some entered into their tents. Others were indignant; although badly wounded they died where they stood, at their post'.[9]

Due to the rough terrain, the artillery's gun carriages were swiftly overtaken and their crews killed. On seeing his guns were lost, Curling rode off, his horse picking its way across the rocky ground. He was hotly pursued for about 5 miles until he came to a cliff overhanging the river. As he began to lead his horse down the boulder strewn slope to the river he saw a number of the survivors fall, seriously injuring themselves, including his senior officer, Major Smith. Curling got down safely and jumped his horse into the turbulent flowing river, 100-yards wide, very deep and dangerously fast flowing. Once in the water he collected up three floundering soldiers, who desperately clung to his swimming horse. The bedraggled group eventually reached the safety of the Natal bank. Many of the exhausted survivors who attempted to cross the river were swept away and drowned as they tried to reach the safety of Natal, and a number of swimmers caught in a whirlpool were shot by the chasing Zulus. Private Westwood reached the river but was trapped in the surging whirlpool. His plight was spotted by Private Wassal of the 80th (South Staffordshire Regiment) who tied his horse to a branch then successfully swam to rescue Westwood. They untied Wassall's horse and, hanging on to the saddle, they plunged back into the river. Due to the horse managing the strong current the pair crossed the river and escaped. For his actions Wassal received the first VC of the day.[10] Those without a horse who reached the safety of the Natal bank were cut down by the local natives who, a few days before, had suffered the first British attack at nearby Sihayo's homestead.

Back at Isandlwana, the scene in camp had been one of nightmare proportions. The gunfire, the noise of shouting and screaming and terrified panic and confusion at the sight of the slaughter being unleashed was now subsiding. Once they were in the ascendancy, the Zulus busied themselves with killing anything still alive, soldiers trying to hide or feigning death, the soldiers' horses, cattle and camp dogs; such was their fury, before laying waste to the massive tented camp. By early afternoon, only one British soldier remained alive. He had climbed up the steep side of Isandlwana and took refuge in a small cave beneath a sheer cliff. For another two hours, according to Zulu reports, this soldier husbanded his ammunition and killed any Zulu who approached the cave. Eventually, the Zulus lost patience with this lone sniper and gathered a force armed with captured Martini-Henry rifles. They poured volley after volley into the cave until the soldier was killed. His body was discovered some ten months later by Captain Mainwaring's burial party, with a rope around his neck. Zulu folklore records their sorrow at having had to kill such a brave man. His name and regiment remain unknown.

Mehlokazulu kaSihayo, son of Sihayo and an attendant of King Cetshwayo, was present at Isandlwana with the iNgobamakhosi regiment. In his account of the war, which was recorded in September 1879, he made various references to the subject of stripping and disembowelling the Isandlwana dead:

> 'As a rule we took off the upper garments, but left the trousers, but if we saw blood upon the garments we did not bother. All the dead bodies were cut open, because if that had not been done the Zulus would have become swollen like the dead bodies. I heard that some bodies were otherwise mutilated'.[11]

At Isandlwana, some bodies were disembowelled immediately. Trooper Richard Stevens of the Natal Mounted Police survived the battle, and recorded his shock of the practice:

> 'I stopped in the camp as long as possible, and saw one of the most horrid sights I ever wish to see. The Zulus were in the camp, ripping our men up, and also the tents and everything they came across, with their assegais. They were not content with killing, but were ripping the men up afterwards'.[12]

One aspect of Zulu ritual that did result in mutilation of the dead was the removal of body parts from a fallen enemy that could be added to the ritual medicines used to prepare the Zulu army before a campaign. These medicines were known as *intelezi*, and were sprinkled on the warriors by *izinyanga*, war-doctors, before the army set off on campaign. Parts from a dead enemy, especially one who had fought bravely, would be an enormous boost to Zulu morale, thus ensuring supremacy in battle. Since a number of *izinyanga* accompanied the army that triumphed at Isandlwana, they would certainly have taken the opportunity to collect the raw materials for such medicine from dead soldiers. Archibald Forbes' graphic account of the state of the bodies at the time of the first burial expedition to Isandlwana in May 1879 is highly suggestive; 'Every man had been disembowelled, some were scalped, and others subject to yet ghastlier mutilations'.[13]

These mutilations included the disarticulation by the Zulus of dead soldiers' jawbones for trophies, complete with beards. Facial hair was relatively unknown to the warriors and the luxurious beards worn by the soldiers fascinated them. Despite the soldiers' deep-seated fears that these mutilations were carried out before death, and therefore amounted to torture, there is no evidence that this was in fact the case.

Following the battle, the victorious Zulus gathered up their walking wounded and in accordance with Zulu custom, dispatched those too injured to walk. They then plundered the camp, and there was much to be plundered, including rifles, nearly a half million rounds remaining in abundance on the wagons, neatly parked nearly a mile from the left of the British line. Also lost was Paymaster White's box of gold sovereigns intended to bribe any local Zulu chiefs from aggression. The victorious Zulus were in no hurry to depart Isandlwana as there was no sign of movement from Chelmsford's column, which was still more than 10 miles off and oblivious of the camp's fate.

There was much that was new to the victorious Zulus, and even more to plunder. The concept of tinned food was still unknown to them so tins were stabbed and medicine bottles smashed or drunk, making a number seriously ill or incapable. As dusk began to fall, Chelmsford's distant column could be seen cautiously approaching. Now alert to the fate of the camp and their colleagues, it was still several miles distant, giving the Zulus a good two hours to depart. The Zulus calmly gathered themselves and set off carrying what they could. They all headed back to their previous night's campsite on the Nqutu Plateau, where they remained for several days tending their wounded and burying those that died of their wounds. The Zulus had lost a significant number of men. The first few British volleys, especially those at close range, would certainly have accounted for between 1,000 and 2,000 warriors, and perhaps another 1,000 or even 2,000 were seriously wounded. The Zulus had not previously witnessed the effects of Martini-Henry or artillery fire and many had appalling wounds and died in agony.

The post-battle tradition of a victorious Zulu army was to return to Ulundi where the chiefs could report their success to the king. Although it is acknowledged that Isandlwana was a great Zulu victory, the Zulus had lost so many men killed and wounded that any euphoria was short lived. Uncharacteristically, instead of making for Ulundi, the majority of the warriors returned to their homesteads. Undoubtedly, many would have been too badly wounded, in shock or just too exhausted to walk the 50 miles to Ulundi. After the Zulu success at Isandlwana, Natal was utterly helpless to defend itself. The British invasion force was in part defeated and Pearson's coastal column was surrounded at Eshowe, yet Cetshwayo was unwilling to capitalize on his victory. Had he ordered his army into Natal, the consequences for the Natal population and the subsequent history of southern Africa would have been difficult to imagine.[14]

Meanwhile, the Zulu reserve that had not participated at Isandlwana, nor been fed for two days, headed off towards Natal in search of food and chasing stray fugitives – against the king's orders. They split into small raiding parties to focus on looting along the border with Natal – but Rorke's Drift was in their way. It was now for Rorke's Drift to make amends for Isandlwana.

This unexpected defeat by the Zulu army at Isandlwana would shake Victorian Britain and its proud army.[15]

Chelmsford was clearly a shattered man by the time he returned to the devastation of Isandlwana. He managed to make a sorry bewildered statement: 'I can't understand it, I left a thousand men here'.[16]

But who was to blame? Chelmsford's false account claiming the disaster fell squarely in Durnford's lap has long since confused historians. A modern investigation by the *AZWHS* discovered the final orders from Chelmsford's staff officer, Colonel Crealock received by Durnford at Rorke's Drift on 22 January. Because they are so ambiguous, they are reproduced exactly:

> 'You are to march to this camp at once with all the force you have with you of No.2 Column.
>
> 'Major Bengough's battalion is to move to Rorke's Drift as ordered yesterday. 2/24th, Artillery and mounted men with the General and Colonel Glyn move off at once to attack a Zulu force about 10 miles distant'.

Armed with this instruction, together with the orders from the General dated 19 January, Colonel Durnford's orders were clear. He was not instructed to take command of the camp – and indeed had freedom of action to use his independent No. 2 Column. On his arrival at Isandlwana and seeing the Zulus approach in force, he consulted Colonel Pulleine before embarking on a logical course of action to hinder their progress towards the camp.[17]

Although Durnford was senior in service to Pulleine, the presumption could be that command of the camp naturally devolved upon Durnford thus relieving Pulleine of overall responsibility, for which Pulleine would undoubtedly have been grateful. The facts are different; he was the Commander of the second column and no orders were given to merge the two columns. Durnford nevertheless met with Pulleine in his headquarters tent to discuss the sightings of the Zulus, and a brief discussion followed after which Durnford detailed patrols of his men to ride to the plateau and ascertain what was happening.

One patrol was led by Captain Shepstone of the Natal Native Horse. Lieutenant Cochrane, who arrived at Isandlwana with Durnford, wrote that a number of Zulus had been seen since an early hour on the top of the adjacent hills and that an attack was expected. A note from another patrol confirmed the Zulus were moving east. Indeed, according to Lieutenant Curling's evidence to the subsequent Court of Inquiry, they could be seen from the camp. Durnford correctly concluded that a large enemy force was deploying along the plateau, possibly to drive a wedge between Chelmsford's force and Isandlwana camp. Pulleine no doubt accepted Durnford's calm analysis with some relief and gave the order for his men to 'Stand Down' but keep on their accoutrements. Astonishingly, preparations went ahead for the camp move, which is confirmed by Chelmsford's order to Commandant Hamilton-Brown after Chelmsford realised he had been duped by the Zulus. The order reads:

> 'Commandant Brown, I want you to return at once to camp (with your men) and assist Colonel Pulleine to strike camp and come on here'.[18]

Durnford took his force to intercept this Zulu threat, departing the camp, according to Curling, shortly before midday. Out on the firing line, Lieutenant Charlie Pope, 2/24th, somehow managed to scribble a diary line. This direct personal observation provided confirmatory evidence that a large Zulu force was sighted. Furthermore, the deployment was taking place prior to Durnford's arrival. This is a valuable, and completely uncorrupted, collateral source report. It reads:

> 'Alarm 3 Columns Zulus and mounted men on hill E. Turn Out 7,000 (!!!) more E.N.E., 4,000 of whom went around Lion's Kop. (Isandlwana Hill) Durnford's Basutos arrive and pursue'.[19]

Safely back in Natal, Chelmsford lost no time in convening a Court of Enquiry to investigate the loss at Isandlwana. Its terms and purpose were, at best, curious. Certainly Crealock deliberately lied when he told the Court that he had issued orders to Durnford to 'take command of it', referring to the camp, when in fact this was not the case. Chelmsford then drove in the final nail to damn Durnford; he informed the House of Lords on 19 August 1880 that 'In the final analysis, it was Durnford's disregard of orders that had brought about its (Isandlwana) destruction'.[20]

This statement was compounded by Major the Hon. Gerald French DSO who commented:

> 'As to Lord Chelmsford's orders to Colonels Pulleine and Durnford before leaving the camp on the morning of 22 January the evidence adduced before the court of Inquiry conclusively proved that the former was directed to defend the camp whilst the latter was to move up from Rorke's Drift and take command of it on his arrival. Colonel Durnford would consequently, on assuming command, take over and "be subject to the orders given to Colonel Pulleine by Lord Chelmsford"'.[21]

It was therefore presumed that Durnford had failed to assume command of the camp from the subordinate Pulleine and then disobeyed orders by taking his men off to chase the Zulus. The Court's findings enabled Chelmsford to escape the blame, and his account to the House of Lords relied on these findings to blame Durnford. Sadly, Chelmsford joined his staff in their attempt to blame both Durnford and Glyn but this tactic backfired when Glyn accepted partial blame. Durnford and most of his troop died in sight of the camp when overwhelmed by the advancing Zulus. The original orders issued to Durnford were later discovered on his body and are proof Crealock lied, whereas Durnford obeyed his orders.[22]

There is now conclusive evidence to prove that Durnford behaved correctly and bravely according to his orders. His reputation should be seen in the same light as his military record; exemplary. Attempts to trace Durnford's descendants have not succeeded, although folklore claims his daughter lived in South Africa. She subsequently married a local (unknown) farmer.

With the unbelievable Zulu victory at Isandlwana, the first cracks in the reputation of the British Empire would quickly be noted by Britain's enemies.

References

1. Since 1879 little has changed at Helpmekaar; it now consists of an isolated two-man police station and a cluster of mostly deserted and dilapidated buildings alongside the overgrown British cemetery.
2. a. The Hon. Member Mr E. Jenkins Volume 2/255 Thursday 19 August 1889.
   b. Pulleine's orders were to defend the camp but these were overruled by Chelmsford as the camp would shortly move out.

3. *The Annuls of History*, Hattersley 1938.
4. *Appendix to Field Exercises – Rifle and Carbine Exercises and Musketry Instructions*, p 252–253.
5. Smith-Dorrien to his father, 25 January 1879.
6. *The Red Soldier*, Emery, F., Hodder & Stoughton, 1977, also;
   a. Such smoke was a vital component of the battle, usually overlooked by most authors and historians, and
   b. an examination of some of the contemporary paintings of the time, often painted from descriptions given by actual combatants, clearly reveal palls of smoke on various Zulu War battlefields. This effect can be seen in, amongst others, C.E. Fripp's painting of *Isandlwana*, De Neuville's *Rorke's Drift*, Lieutenant Evelyn's two sketches of *Nyezane*, Crealock's *Final Repulse* of Gingindlovu, Orlando Norie's watercolour of *Kambula* and the equally famous *Illustrated London News 'Square at Ulundi'*.
7. *Zulu War Then and Now*, Knight, I., 1993.
8. *Curling Letters of the Zulu War*, Greaves & Best, 2001 (Clery letter 16 May 1879).
9. *Rope of Sand*, Laband, 1995.
10. Wassel VC. See Chapter 9 for citation.
11. *Natal Mercury*, 27 September 1879.
12. *Natal Colonist*, 17 April 1879.
13. Post Isandlwana, the practice of shaving became widespread throughout the army; soldiers accepted the necessity of dying for their country but were reluctant to be disarticulated after death on the battlefield. The gulf of cultural misunderstanding was so wide that, after Isandlwana, any Zulu who fell into British hands was doomed.
14. As a gesture, he offered the surrounded Eshowe column safe passage back to Natal.
15. *British Battles on Land and Sea*, 1892. Cassel.
16. *David Rattray's Guidebook*, Rattray and Greaves, 2003. It was not until 21 May that Chelmsford instructed the Isandlwana bodies to be buried. The task was conducted by the 17th Lancers, the King's Dragoon Guards and four companies of the 24th, a force of 2,500 men. One reason for the delay was the initial overpowering stench from the thousands of rotting bodies under a hot African sun. By 21 May the bodies had dried out, causing less trauma to the burial party, although the battlefield was still strewn with bones.
17. Chelmsford's orders to Durnford – later recovered from Durnford's body.
18. *A Lost Legionary in South Africa*, Hamilton-Browne, 1890.
19. Extract from Lieutenant Pope's diary, later recovered from the battlefield.
20. *Lord Chelmsford and the Zulu War*, French, Unwin Bros, 1939.
21. Ditto.
22. *Isandlwana*, Greaves. A., Cassel, 2001. This work contains the full examination of Durnford's role, with photographs of Chelmsford's actual orders to Durnford discovered in Durnford's jacket pocket, and the subsequent investigation and Court of Inquiry.

Chapter 7

The Battle for Rorke's Drift, 22 January 1879

Note a: The timings of some events during the engagement are uncertain because the accounts of the various participants do not always tally. They were, after all, preoccupied with fighting for their lives. Few officers had watches; they were both rare and inaccurate. Chronology is therefore no more than approximate. Specific timings are taken from Chard's account, which probably reflects a consensus.

Note b: The engagement at Rorke's Drift must be considered together with that of Isandlwana, as both were part of the same battle fought on the same day across a desert-like boulder-strewn wasteland covering some 150 square miles.

Note c: The Zulus reached Rorke's Drift at sunset; the battle took place at night in unusual darkness, moonless and described by the Zulus as the night of the 'dead moon'. The Zulus withdrew at dawn.

When British forces invaded Zululand on 11 January 1879 they left Lieutenant Gonville Bromhead and nearly 100 soldiers of B Company 2/24th (The 2nd Warwickshire) Regiment to guard the fast-flowing river crossing and the Central Column's supply base and temporary hospital at Natal's Rorke's Drift. Following breakfast on the morning of 22 January, the recently-arrived Lieutenant Chard, a Royal Engineers officer, rode to Isandlwana to join the column and to receive his orders. On arriving at Isandlwana there were no orders for Chard but there was a buzz of excitement running through the camp as clusters of Zulus could clearly be seen watching the camp from the rim of the Nqutu Plateau that overlooked the British position just one mile distant. For most of the soldiers, this was their first view of the Zulu army, but this event caused no concern other than curiosity. On hearing of an outpost report from nearer the plateau that a large party of Zulus was moving north west across the plateau behind Isandlwana, Chard decided to return to Rorke's Drift in case, as he surmised, the Zulus intended 'to have a dash at the drift'.[1] Chard headed back to Rorke's Drift, arriving at noon to report to Major Spalding, the officer commanding Rorke's Drift, that Zulus had been seen in the vicinity of Isandlwana. Spalding, on loan from the 104th Regiment, was aware that two companies of the 2/24th Regiment were two days overdue at the drift from Helpmekaar, some 10 miles distant. Following a brief conversation with Bromhead and Chard, Spalding considered sending a message to Helpmekaar to speed their progress but, unconcerned with Chard's account, took no action.

Meanwhile, Chelmsford's marching force was twelve miles further into Zululand from the unprepared British camp at Isandlwana when, at about midday, the massed Zulu army suddenly appeared from the plateau overlooking Isandlwana camp and attacked the unprotected east flank of the unprepared defenders. The hitherto invincible soldiers began falling back in a mass rout while taking appalling casualties at the hands of an overwhelming but untrained native army armed with spears and clubs. Within the hour, Isandlwana camp was destroyed and some 1,400 troops lay massacred and disembowelled.

Following their swift victory, the Zulus despatched their reserve force to cross into Natal to find food, without realising there was a small British garrison at the Rorke's Drift Swedish mission. Rorke's Drift is in sight of Isandlwana, less than ten miles to the northwest but, unlike Isandlwana, Rorke's Drift camp covered a very small area, no larger than two tennis courts. The terrain around the two buildings was rough vegetation broken with clumps of bush, gulleys, caverns and boulders, all of which would give excellent cover to the advancing Zulus. To the north-west of the hospital stretched thick bush, through which a wagon track and Witt's garden had been constructed. This scrub and a taller clump of trees, along with a garden wall just twenty feet from Witt's house, would provide shelter to the first Zulus who would shortly approach the mission. The steep Oskarsberg rock outcrop, just 50 yards away, overlooked the rear of the two buildings.

Meanwhile, the small Rorke's Drift garrison were blissfully unaware of the disaster at Isandlwana or that the untested reserve of the victorious Zulu army, which had not been required in the battle, was now streaming towards them. The reserve consisted of an estimated 4,500 warriors led by Prince Dabulamanzi, King Cetshwayo's half-brother. By midday Spalding, now more aware of rumours of Zulus in the vicinity, left for Helpmekaar to speed the companies ordered to support the mission. He left instructions with Chard, the senior of the two lieutenants present, to take charge, but no action was taken, probably because Spalding told him that 'nothing would happen'. Leaving Chard in command due to his seniority, he declared, '*and I shall be back again this evening, early*'. With that comment, Spalding rode off and threw away the certainty of receiving the Victoria Cross as the senior officer present – had he stayed. His departure would later stimulate a lively discussion through the army's officer corps as to why Spalding, as the senior officer at Rorke's Drift, would leave his command and set off to Helpmekaar merely to speed-up the two delayed 24th companies due to reinforce B Company already at the drift. It would have been more logical to send Bromhead, of the same regiment, or one of Bromhead's many NCOs, especially as Chard had already warned Spalding of the possibility of approaching Zulus. Oblivious of the battle being fought at Isandlwana, Chard then went to his tent at the river to have lunch and to supervise the security of the ferry ponts.[2]

Two days before, a small group from the camp, including Colour Sergeant Bourne, Sergeants Smith, Gallagher, Windridge and Wilson, had visited the crest of the Oskarsberg, but the Isandlwana camp was obscured by low cloud. At midday of 22 January the weather had cleared so, highly curious and with nothing else to do that afternoon, the Swedish missionary's friend, August Hammar, along with the Reverend George Smith with his telescope, the 34-year-old Surgeon Reynolds, and Private Wall of the 24th, set out to ride to the summit of the Oskarsberg in the hope of being able to see the progress of Chelmsford's column into Zululand. From their high vantage point they were instead bemused to hear gunfire from the direction of Isandlwana; this was not heard by Bromhead at the Mission, perhaps due to his partial deafness, nor by Chard whose campsite was in a depression by the river and out of sight of Isandlwana.

Through the afternoon heat haze the summit group were surprised to see three distant columns of natives moving towards the Buffalo River from the direction of Isandlwana. Reverend Smith's first impressions were that these columns were detachments of NNC returning to Rorke's Drift, until Smith noticed that there were two Zulus on white horses leading an obvious *impi* of warriors. Ahead of the *impi*, they saw scouting patrols of Zulus who appeared to be searching in wide sweeps and occasionally firing into the bush. They remained watching the advancing Zulus until Surgeon Reynolds noticed two riders, Lieutenants Vaine and Adendorff of the NNH, approaching the mission from the direction of the drift crossing; thinking that they might need medical attention, he set off down the hillside. Realising the significance of what they were watching the group rushed back to camp and reported what they had seen to Lieutenant Bromhead. There was now no doubt that an unusual event must have occurred to allow such a large Zulu force to bypass Chelmsford's main column and, completely unhindered by British troops, they were now heading for Rorke's Drift.

The approaching Zulus, led by Prince Dabulamanzi, a half-brother of the king, formed the reserve of the main attacking Zulu army at Isandlwana, that had not taken part in the battle. They included the UThulwana, iNdlondlo and uDloko *ibutho*. It is this force of Zulus who harried the Isandlwana fugitives cross-country from Isandlwana down to the river border with Natal. At the river crossing point the king's younger brother, Prince Ndabuko kaMpande, had urged his uMbonambi warriors to join Dabulamanzi's force crossing into Natal. Because of their orders not to cross into Natal they declined and returned to plunder Isandlwana, leaving Dabulamanzi's force to cross the river between Rorke's and Sotondose's Drifts. Not having eaten for two days, they divided into raiding *impis* and set out to find food from any local homesteads they could raid. Equally important, not having participated in the victory at Isandlwana, they needed action of some kind to maintain their honour. Since the time of Shaka, warriors returning from battle without having 'washed their spears' were viewed as cowards.

The Zulu reserve then crossed the Buffalo River by jumping across the narrow rocky and boulder strewn gorge some three miles below Rorke's Drift. Having crossed the border into Natal, Dabulamanzi's force was intent on some serious plunder and 'spear washing'. They could still gain prestige and glory by killing any Natal natives they came across between Helpmekaar and the river by burning their farms and plundering their cattle. Rorke's Drift just happened to be in their way. After taking snuff and quenching their thirst, the Zulus divided into several groups; some headed off towards the low hills towards Helpmekaar where they would shortly meet Major Spalding and his relief column and force them back to Helpmekaar. Another group continued along the river towards Rorke's Drift, unaware it was manned by B Company. En route they came across a farm belonging to local farmer, Edward Woodroffe, which they burned to the ground.

From the river crossing point, the Zulu scouts from the main iNdluyengwe force advanced along the Natal river bank and began assembling on the low plateau behind the Mission, a mere 500 yards from the two buildings. According to local folklore, they came across the weakly defended British position by accident and, even if they had known of the two buildings, there is no evidence they knew they were occupied by troops. Professor Laband believes the Zulu attack against Rorke's Drift was unintended, as the Zulus had crossed into Natal for 'short term plunder'. Furthermore, his extensive research contends that the defence of Rorke's Drift merely diverted a large Zulu raiding party from 'going about its short-term business of ravaging the Buffalo River valley'. Had the mission been their primary target, it is unlikely the Zulus would have divided into foraging *impis*.[3]

Meanwhile, a native horseman of the Edendale Contingent had just delivered a note to Bromhead written by Captain Essex, an Isandlwana escapee. Essex unequivocally reported the loss of the British camp. Oblivious of events at the Mission, Chard was enjoying his afternoon rest on the riverbank when he noticed two horsemen galloping towards the drift from the direction of Isandlwana. The pair plunged their horses into the river shouting to Chard that the Zulus were approaching; the two riders were Lieutenants Vaine and Adendorff of the Natal Native Horse, both escapees from the battle at Isandlwana. Vaine was exhausted and Adendorff, a Boer, was incoherent, made worse by English not being his main language. The two rode off with Adendorff seemingly calling out that he would remain to fight.

This unbelievable news was the first intimation Chard had of the disaster at Isandlwana; before he had time to react, a messenger arrived from Bromhead suggesting that Chard should strike his tents, load his tools into his wagon and return immediately to the Mission. Chard then despatched a message to Bromhead stating that he would return once he had gathered his working party.

At the mission, Bromhead pondered his situation. Commissary Dalton, a former British Army sergeant trained in constructing defensive positions, was ordered by Bromhead to collapse the company's tents to widen their field of fire and to strengthen the perimeter walls with bags of Indian corn (mealies) and boxes of biscuits. Believing the Zulus were fast approaching the Mission, Bromhead urgently despatched a rider with a note to the garrison at Helpmekaar. Bromhead's note reads;

> 'Sir,
>
> 'Intelligence has just reached camp that the camp at Isandula (*sic*) Hill is taken by the enemy.
>
> 'Bromhead'[4]

It is likely that the rider was given Reverend Smith's horse as when Smith decided that, not being a fighting man, it was time for him to leave Rorke's Drift, his horse could not be found – obliging him to become another defender.

Now late afternoon, Chard and his men retired to the mission with the water cart and tools. It was this water cart that Chard left outside the final defensive position at the mission that would later lead to his bayonet charge to recover it. Lieutenant Henderson, with a large party of Durnford's Horse, then galloped in and was ordered to guard the ferry crossing. Chard returned to the mission and after discussing their predicament, Bromhead ordered the reserve ammunition to be issued and bayonets fixed. A lookout was posted on the ridge of the store.

It was realized by Chard and Bromhead that, with some thirty-five injured or sick soldiers in the hospital, they should urgently consider making their escape to Helpmekaar ten miles away. Their two ox-drawn wagons were brought to the hospital but both officers quickly realised their small cumbersome convoy was no match for the fleet-of-foot Zulus. They decided instead to defend the mission, which, in compliance with Chelmsford's orders for the Mission, had already been prepared for defence with trenches and a low embankment around the two buildings.

Supervised by Commissary Dalton, the existing barricade was strengthened by additionally stacking heavy sacks of mealie corn and biscuit boxes around the mission perimeter and building the two wagons into the south wall. Available to help were 300 NNC auxiliaries under the command of their colonial officer, Captain Stephenson.

Chard ordered Stephenson to help strengthen the barricades and the NNC reacted in traditional manner, with gusto and singing war-songs. All went well until a party of mounted auxiliaries rode up from the Drift. These were some of Colonel Durnford's command who had survived Isandlwana; they were mostly followers of the BaSotho chief, Hlubi, and they were under the command of a Lieutenant Henderson. These mounted NNC had escaped before the Zulu cordon around Isandlwana was completed and crossed the Mzinyathi (Buffalo River) downstream at Sotondosa's Drift, later known as Fugitives' Drift. Henderson reported to Chard, who asked him to deploy his men beyond the Oskarsberg in the direction of the Zulu advance, the intention being to deter or delay the Zulu attack as long as possible.

As the Native Horse prepared to ride off it seems one of their number shouted to the garrison that the Zulus were nearly upon them and, unhelpfully, that they would all die; they ignored Henderson's order to remain and galloped off towards Helpmekaar. This was too much for Stephenson's NNC; these terrified black auxiliaries simply deserted en masse, jumping over the barricades to follow Henderson's Native Horse as fast as they could. They were hotly followed by Stephenson and his white NCOs and in doing so, their departure reduced the effective strength of the garrison from 450 to 104, including the Reverend Smith and thirty-six sick in Surgeon Reynolds' care.[5] No action was ever taken against Henderson.

While the garrison had clearly not expected much from the NNC rank and file, they were infuriated by the sight of their white NCOs in flight. Several soldiers fired at the fleeing deserters and one fell dead. It is generally accepted that he was Corporal Anderson, the only man of the NNC who was killed in the battle whose death is not accounted for by other evidence. Curiously, even though he was shot whilst deserting he was buried alongside those killed during the action whereas Mr. Byrne, because he was a civilian, was buried elsewhere; his resting place remains unknown.

Colour Sergeant Bourne later declared that:

> 'The strength of our small garrison at the Drift was two combatant and six departmental officers, and one hundred and thirty-three non-commissioned officers and men, thirty-six of whom were sick, leaving about one hundred fighting men. Remember that twelve hundred men had just been massacred at Isandlwana.
>
> '... the desertion of these detachments of 200 men appeared at first sight to be a great loss, with only a hundred of us left, but the feeling afterwards was that we could not have trusted them, and also our defences were too small to accommodate them anyhow'.[6]

The garrison then heard distant firing. With the exception of a few Boer NCOs not from Stephenson's company, who were patients in the makeshift hospital and who distinguished themselves in the fight, there was no further NNC involvement during the action. Meanwhile, now that the area of the garrison had been severely depleted, men were taken from the outer line to rapidly construct an additional low wall within the perimeter to the corner of the store. This became the famous wall of biscuit boxes that would provide the second and last line of defence. Outside this final line was the hospital, already barricaded and loop-holed. Bromhead directed six soldiers to defend the building from behind the doors and windows now being sealed with sacks and boxes while Bourne volunteered to take a skirmishing party to delay the approaching Zulus. The Zulus were then seen spreading out into their classic attacking 'horns' formation just 200 yards from the mission. In the last minutes of daylight they progressively forced Bourne's outnumbered skirmishers back to the post.

Having detected the mission, Zulu scouts reported back to their main force following behind before testing the defences of the defending soldiers. The first group of warriors moved forward and advanced at a slow run darting behind their shields to confuse the soldiers' aim. At the Commissariat Store, Private Hitch had been detailed to act as lookout from the top of the thatched roof of the building. As dusk fell, he urgently shouted a warning that other groups of Zulus were approaching. These first thirty or so Zulus were the iNdluyengwe scouts who had probed ahead of Dabulamanzi's marauding force. As Hitch watched, another *impi* of several hundred warriors arrived and silently joined the scouts in the classic 'horns' attack formation. Once in position, they began to advance at a run towards the outpost's south wall between the hospital and storeroom. The defenders immediately opened fire with volleys controlled by Chard and Bromhead; the distance was between 2–300 yards and a scattering of warriors fell. As the defenders warmed to their task, they became more accurate with their fire, which was fortuitous because, as the warriors ran forwards to point blank range, they darted from whatever cover they could find while wildly firing their own guns, albeit ineffectively. The Zulus were rehearsed at using their shields to distract an enemy or prey, and to confuse the soldiers' aim they now advanced with their shields held away from their bodies in the anticipation that the soldiers would fire at the steadily held shields and not the darting bodies holding them. In this way, many Zulus got to within fifty yards of the outpost with their very first charge before the British volleys forced them to take cover behind the numerous boulders that littered the area. The battle for Rorke's Drift had begun.

Under the cover of darkness, the warriors then retreated and regrouped some sixty yards away while others gathered behind the five-foot high garden wall facing the ledge in front of the mission. They soon came under a heavy crossfire from the two buildings and those warriors unprotected by the wall sought whatever cover they could find in the orchard and stream beds whilst those Zulus behind the buildings, who bore the brunt of the initial volleys, took cover in the area of the cookhouse ovens in front of the Oskarsberg.

The initial attack on the south of the defences was contained and the leading Zulu ranks were successfully pinned down by rifle fire. When the Zulus were in sufficient strength, their main attack diverted to the west of the hospital and along the thinly held north-west wall. Persistent wild Zulu sniping from the Oskarsberg then began. Initially, the Zulu attacks were uncoordinated and lacked any real determination or aggression. The Zulus were skilled at hunting but had received no training for warfare against an enemy armed with accurate rifles. Instead they were indoctrinated with a lifetime of parade-ground rituals, which included imitating their *giya* tactic, based upon a mock-battle display, and they approached the British position using this method, the only tactic known to them. As the author discovered during his research of local Zulu folklore relating to their tactics:

> 'They made a number of prancing attacks at a slow run, showing they cared little for the slaughter awaiting them, and each time they would advance, then halt for a moment, and then advance again quietly, but running quickly, taking advantage of every bit of cover'.[7]

This tactic suggests the front line of the Zulu attack was a deliberate ploy enabling the chiefs to identify where the defenders' fire was coming from. Modern local belief supports this theory and suggests the Zulus deliberately attacked in a very deliberate manner, more akin to their traditional *giya* dancing, by prancing and high kicking as they attacked. They also maintain that the Zulu chiefs present had expected to surprise the camp and that by their melodramatic approach to Rorke's Drift they would scare the defenders into fleeing deeper into Natal.

By using this tactic, many Zulus got to within 50 yards of the first barrier until the soldiers' sustained volley fire forced the surviving warriors to take refuge among the many boulders littering the lower slope of the Oskarsberg. One of the first Zulus to fall was a chief shot by Private Dunbar, an excellent shot and a marksman later identified for praise having calmly accounted for eight Zulus with as many shots. It took the inexperienced Zulus a few moments to realise what was happening, but having witnessed the unexpected carnage, the remainder hesitated, broke ranks, and scattered to their left and occupied the garden and orchard, where there was plenty of cover. As more Zulus arrived, many took refuge behind the long five-foot-high garden wall directly in front of Witt's house. It is presumed that the soldiers had left the wall to use as a defensive position, without realising it would provide the Zulus with cover, which now enabled them to creep to within 20 yards of the British defending the inner low wall of mealie bags.

There were twenty bed-bound patients in the hospital, formally Witt's house, so six soldiers of B Company were directed to take up defensive positions in the building; they were Privates Joseph Williams, John Williams (real name Fielding), Robert Jones and William Jones, Henry Hook and Thomas Cole. Those patients who were 'walking sick' were issued with rifles; they were Gunner Howard and Privates Adams, Horrigan and Waters. Under the supervision of Commissary Dalton, each defender was given a haversack full of ammunition and allocated a room to defend; then all the doors and windows were blocked off and sealed with sacks and boxes and final improvements were made to the loopholes. Due to the intensive activity, no one questioned the fact that access from the rooms was only to the outside and that, once barricaded into their rooms, there was no access to the other rooms within the hospital; the defenders and patients were now effectively trapped inside their allotted rooms.

Dalton was industriously opening ammunition boxes and supervising distribution of rounds to the soldiers manning its defensive wall. In his blue jacket and slouch hat Dalton, a big man and well over six feet tall, must have stood out among the red-coated soldiers whose average height was less than five feet six. Chard suddenly remembered that there were several casks of medicinal rum in the store building and knowing only too well the British soldiers' insatiable desire for alcohol, gave orders to Sergeant Windridge that the spirit was not to be touched. Windridge was in temporary charge of the storeroom and he detailed the nearest soldier to guard the rum with orders that, after giving the standard military warning of 'Stop or I fire', he was to shoot anyone who attempted to touch the spirit. Having given the order, Windridge continued supervising the defence of the Commissariat store, cutting loopholes through the walls and strengthening barricades around the building.

According to Colour Sergeant Bourne, Zulu marksmen with Martini-Henry rifles, looted when they overran a dozen soldiers of the Royal Engineers working on the track leading to Isandlwana, were soon sniping into the backs of Bromhead's soldiers from the Oskarsberg caves, merely 200 yards away; fortunately, they were unfamiliar with the rifle sights and being poor shots, casualties were few. Conversely, the defenders' well aimed close-range volleys blasted each Zulu attack and those who survived could then only run onto the defenders' waiting blooded bayonets. Chard and Bromhead controlled the outpost from a central position and when a gap appeared, one or other would step forward to assist the fight to ensure each wave of Zulus was forced to retreat. When Dalton was shot at close range he handed his rifle to Chard before collapsing. Surgeon Reynolds dressed the wound and, within minutes, Dalton was back on his feet encouraging the defenders. Unable to reach his patients in the hospital, Reynolds bravely used his time issuing ammunition and offering words of encouragement to the soldiers around the perimeter.

Numerous dead and dying Zulus now slumped against the inner wall and the following waves of warriors tried in vain to climb or jump over their bodies but were unable to reach the barricade, now awash with slippery blood. With no time to reload their rifles, the soldiers fought with their fixed bayonets and, although the Zulus ordinarily relished close combat, British bayonets from behind the high mealie bag wall forced their retreat. Such tactics were new to the soldiers who were now fighting for their lives. Dead and wounded Zulus soon lay several deep around the position.

With the noise of the battle raging, Chard could no longer communicate with those still in the hospital, just forty yards away and now surrounded on three sides by packed ranks of Zulus. A soldier then shouted that he saw marching redcoats approaching from the direction of Helpmekaar. This set the men cheering, which confused the Zulus; they momentarily withdrew but no relieving troops came. After a pause of about ten minutes, the Zulus re-grouped for the next assault. Chard wrote of this incident:

> 'Some of the men said they saw the redcoats coming on the Helpmekaar road. The rumour passed quickly round – I could see nothing of the sort myself, but some men said they could. A cheer was raised, and the enemy seemed to pause, to know what it meant, but there was no answer to it, and darkness came. It is very strange that this report should have arisen amongst us, for the two companies 24th Regiment from Helpmekaar did come down to the foot of the hill, but not, I believe, in sight of us.
>
> 'They marched back to Helpmekaar on the report of Rorke's Drift having fallen'.[8]

It will be remembered that Major Spalding, the officer commanding Rorke's Drift, had earlier ridden to Helpmekaar to speed up the overdue reinforcements. By late afternoon he was within sight of the steep pass that led to Helpmekaar when he saw the two delayed companies of the 24th approaching him having descended the pass. Spalding rode to join them and discussed the situation with their officers and, in view of the uncertainty of events and the note which had just arrived from Bromhead that Isandlwana had fallen (see [8] above), Spalding took with him Mr. Dickson of the local Buffalo Border Guard and the pair retraced the track back towards Rorke's Drift to try and make sense of the situation. As they began crossing the open plain they saw the first native fugitives approaching them from the direction of the drift. Puzzled, they rode on until they met with the first fugitives from the Mounted Infantry escaping from Isandlwana. All told the same story: Isandlwana had fallen to the Zulus and Rorke's Drift was about to suffer the same fate. Dickson wrote:

> 'Every single white fugitive asserted that the mission house was captured'.[9]

Stunned by the news and assuming it was true, Spalding was uncertain of the best course of action. The pair rode on against the increasing trickle of fugitives until they gained a low crest; from this distant vantage point they could indeed see Zulus surrounding the mission. Spalding and Dickson then saw, from a dried river bed a half-mile distant, a large group of Zulu skirmishers approaching them. The Zulus steadily came on to within 200 yards and then began to form into their traditional encircling attack formation, whereupon Spalding and Dickson retreated at a gallop back to the marching column, now only two miles distant. Spalding found himself in a dilemma: should he proceed to relieve Rorke's Drift or return to the base at Helpmekaar. On reaching the column, Spalding was informed that other Zulu raiding parties could be seen approaching the pass they had earlier descended. In the light of this alarming information, and with darkness soon upon them, Spalding and the column commander, Major Upcher, decided to retreat back up the pass rather than get caught in the open. They ordered the column to 'about turn' and the two companies, along with all their wagons, laboriously turned round and began to urgently trudge back to the pass. There can be little doubt that the defenders at Rorke's Drift, even in the failing light, had somehow seen the far-off approaching column – indeed, Spalding reached a position less than two miles from Rorke's Drift before he retreated; this would have placed the marching column about four miles from Rorke's Drift. Due to its size and associated dust cloud from the marching men, wagons and oxen, the relieving column would have been comparatively easy to see at that distance. With nightfall upon them it was undoubtedly a nerve-wracking experience for the retreating column. As they began the laborious task of ascending the steep pass, Zulus could be heard calling each other on the nearby cliffs around the retreating soldiers. The oxen with Upcher's party were already exhausted and bellowing their unwillingness to return back up the steep track. Excruciatingly slowly the column climbed back up the hill; the soldiers could now see the red glow behind them hanging over Rorke's Drift. On their eventual arrival at Helpmekaar, there was no rest; it was now well after midnight and the defences had to be manned in case the Zulus arrived. The remaining garrison was 'stood to' awaiting the Zulu attack.

Meanwhile, at Rorke's Drift the defence of the hospital was about to become a battle within a battle. The defenders were mostly isolated from each other by walls and partitions so the initial fighting was by individual soldiers fighting for their lives and unsupported by their colleagues. Initially, and for a brief moment, their firing through the loopholes was effective but the Zulus soon managed to gather either side of the looped holes and could tug at the rifle barrels making firing by the defenders impossible. In the din of the battle, the thatch began to smoulder and then part caught fire, probably from an oil lamp that had somehow overturned in the chaos. The choking smoke from the smouldering thatch soon forced some of the defenders to smash through the thin inner wall and retreat to safer rooms.

Private Joseph Williams had kept up sustained fire from a window in the hospital before running out of ammunition. The Zulus then forced the door protecting the unfortunate soldier and dragged him outside where they stabbed him to death. Privates John Williams and Hook then found themselves in a room occupied with patients just as the Zulus began breaking down the very door they intended to use for their escape. Now trapped, and with minutes left before the Zulus would have broken through, Williams took a pickaxe and knocked a hole in the far wall while Hook stabbed with his bayonet at the Zulus trying to push through the gap. As the last patient was pushed through the escape hole, Hook jumped through and joined them in the next room. With Hook now defending this hole, Williams smashed a fresh hole in the far wall which gave them access into a small room occupied by Privates William and Robert Jones. They had been defending this room for some time taking turns in preventing the Zulus entering and defended the post to the last, until six out of the seven patients had been removed. The seventh, Sergeant Maxfield, 2/24th, was delirious with fever. When Private Jones returned to endeavour to carry him away, he found him being speared to death by the Zulus as he lay on his bed.

The Zulus began clawing at the barricaded doors which soon began to give way under the relentless attack. Private Cole, who suffered from claustrophobia, and Privates Howard, Beckett and Waters fled the hospital. Cole and Beckett were killed as they fled and Private Adams was killed inside. Howard and Waters escaped when part of the hospital roof collapsed; they dashed outside and survived the night by hiding amongst dead Zulus. Being trapped, John Williams smashed a hole through an inner wall whilst Joseph Williams and Horrigan held the Zulus at bay with their bayonets. John Williams pulled three patients through the hole before the Zulus burst in; they killed the remaining patients in the room.

In desperate hand-to-hand fighting the remaining soldiers occupying the hospital were forced to retreat, room-by-room, through the building until they reached the high window. The two Privates Jones helped four patients to escape through the smoke of the smouldering hospital to the window overlooking the courtyard, but still with thirty yards of exposed yard to cross under wild musket fire and the more serious threat of being speared by the Zulus. Through the haze and glow of the roof fire Chard saw the defenders lowering the hospital patients one by one, to the ground into the yard between the two buildings.

Seeing the plight of the hospital defenders, their colleagues put down several volleys into the Zulus enabling their miraculous escape. Even so, Trooper Hunter of the Natal Mounted Police hesitated in the confusion and fell to a lethal spear thrust from a Zulu who vaulted the barrier to reach him. Private Hook was the last to leave the hospital, he later wrote that they 'were like rats in a trap'. The hospital was now abandoned to the Zulus, with six of the seven patients saved; Sergeant Maxwell had to be left behind. The burning thatch would illuminate the area for the next hour or so, enabling the defenders better able to see the attacking Zulus and help keep them at bay.

Throughout the action Corporal Attwood of the Army Service Corps had defended an upper window in the store and now performed the vital task of shooting at warriors trying to climb across the barricades. Until the end of the battle, he held his position and kept the Zulus at bay. Nevertheless, the pressure of sporadic hand-to-hand fighting continued and eventually the British holding the outer wall of the cattle kraal were forced to retire behind the inner mealie bag wall, an area about half the size of a tennis court. This was to be the final British position, there could be no further retreat.

Although wounded, both Hook and Robert Jones joined the rest of the Company in continuing their desperate defence. Hook later descriptively wrote:

> 'The Zulus were swarming around us, and there was an extraordinary rattle as the bullets struck the biscuit boxes, and queer thuds as they plumped into the bags of mealies. And then there was the wiz and rip of the assegais, of which I had experienced during the campaign of 1877–78'.[10]

Chard and Dunn, assisted by four soldiers, then began the task of converting the two large piles of bagged maize into a small redoubt to become the final position for the wounded and, if the final wall was eventually taken by the Zulus, the few survivors could occupy the redoubt. Access to the core of the pile was by a narrow entrance that could be sealed from the inside. The wounded were then placed inside the new position and Chard detailed marksmen to occupy the upper rampart. This gave them an elevated field of fire, which, with the dying glow of the hospital building, enabled them to accurately fire into the Zulu ranks still crouching behind the earlier abandoned wall of boxes and mealie bags.

Around this inner perimeter, Allen and Hitch, regardless of their wounds, continued to supply ammunition to those manning the final barricade. They were supported by Reverend Smith, who had a haversack full of ammunition from which he issued rounds to the soldiers running low. He would then replenish his supply from the centrally located ammunition boxes in front of the storehouse. A number of the defenders later reported that Reverend Smith constantly exhorted them not to swear by quoting Biblical phrases at them. The irregular Zulu attacks continued until late evening and then the attacks became noticeably less sustained. Eventually the glow from the hospital fire began to dwindle and, as it did, the Zulus' enthusiasm for close combat showed the first signs of waning. By midnight the battle had transformed from coordinated Zulu attacks into a series of isolated probes; this change in Zulu tactics enabled the British to better prepare for each attack, each repulsed with the same deadly vigour that had characterized the whole British defence.

The final attempt by the Zulu to rush the barricades was then made, by which time the opposing sides were physically and emotionally spent. The soldiers had been firing and fighting almost continually for at least five hours. Their hearing was severely dulled from the deafening firing within confined spaces; their heads were pounding, their shoulders badly bruised from the notoriously heavy recoil of their Martini-Henry rifles, and their hands were blistered by the overheated barrels. But still they could not relax their guard one moment during the long night.

The final half-hearted Zulu probe was quickly repulsed as, fortuitously, the British had virtually exhausted their Martini-Henry rounds; only one box remained.

The Zulus were more exhausted than the British, having run from Isandlwana and been without food for two days. At some time around midnight the Zulus fired their final flurry of shots which the defenders later discovered was the time the Zulus began to withdraw and, by dawn, they had departed the scene. Prince Dabulamanzi's men had suffered enormous casualties with nothing to show for their bravery and determination.

Chard took the risk of sending a note by runner to the officer commanding Helpmekaar confirming Rorke's Drift had been held but requesting urgent assistance. As dawn broke at the mission the surviving soldiers took stock of their injuries; all were suffering from bruising and burns caused to their hands by constantly firing their Martini-Henry rifles. In and around the immediate site of the fighting lay pools of congealed blood. Bodies were everywhere, as were discarded spears, empty ammunition boxes and clusters of spent ammunition cases. With the Zulus gone, the weary soldiers left the barricades to find water and contemplate the Zulu dead, sometimes five deep. The dying and wounded warriors and any taken prisoner were given the *coup-de-grace* by bayonet; both sides expected, and received, the same treatment. It was never the policy of either side to take prisoners.

During the night at Helpmekaar, the sentries had peered into the enshrouding mist and for several hours nothing could be seen. Then, after dawn broke, figures could be seen approaching with Bromhead's message and the news was called out that the mission had held. Still uncertain of the veracity of the reports, Spalding took Dickson with a small escort to probe the return route to Rorke's Drift. They shortly met with the local magistrate, Henry Fynn, who confirmed that Chard and the small garrison had survived against all odds. Dickson decided to return to his base at Fort Pine to report the good news to Captain Robson, the officer in command of Fort Pine whose garrison was guarding the Buffalo River from Rorke's Drift to Helpmekaar. Obviously, no one at Rorke's Drift had any definite knowledge of Chelmsford's column or its fate or even if the General had survived. Neither did they know whether Helpmekaar had been attacked.

As dawn lit the summit of the Oskarsberg, the Zulus reappeared on the hill's western slope; the defenders waited, but the Zulus had lost the will to fight, they rested for several minutes, took snuff and then Dabulamanzi led them at a safe distance back towards the drift and Zululand. Chard later wrote that he was glad to seize an opportunity to wash his face in a muddy puddle, in company with Private Bush, a hospital defender whose face was covered with blood from a nose wound caused by the bullet that had passed through and killed Private Cole as he fled.

Then, albeit one mile distant, approaching the drift through the mist hanging low along the river bank, the defenders saw Chelmsford's surviving column approaching. To the Zulus, the column was appearing as if by magic, which shocked the Zulus who believed that the whole of Chelmsford's force had been annihilated. Local folklore suggests that many of the exhausted Zulus believed the whole of Chelmsford's column had been destroyed and that the approaching relief column consisted of 'resurrected ghosts,' making further fighting pointless. They collected themselves together and, leaving several hundred of their warriors dead, along with a similar number of seriously wounded, they retreated towards the river and crossed back into Zululand. On the far side of the river the two opposing columns passed each other less than 200 yards apart. Chelmsford's men had little ammunition and the Zulus were exhausted – neither was in any position to fight the other. Only one warrior ran towards the column and he was shot dead.

Early morning, Lord Chelmsford and the remnants of his column crossed back over the river and rode up to the mission where they were greeted with three cheers from the survivors. Chelmsford, his staff and accompanying troops were shocked by the carnage that greeted them. Hundreds of bodies lay around the Mission and within the smouldering hospital building, and the air still held the nauseous taint of burnt human flesh. Commandant Hamilton-Browne, commander of the NNC wrote: 'The dead Zulus lay in piles, in some places as high as the top of the parapet.'[11]

Chelmsford was devastated to learn that there were no Isandlwana survivors at the Mission and then, over mugs of hot tea, he heard at first hand the accounts of a number of survivors, especially from those defenders who had displayed exceptional bravery. They were interviewed mainly by the staff officers and a few by Chelmsford himself. Private Hook was still engaged with his tea-making when a sergeant called out to him that he was wanted by Lieutenant Bromhead, to which he replied 'Wait till I get a coat on'. The order was repeated with the words 'come as you are' and in Hook's own words: 'I went into the midst of the officers and Lord Chelmsford asked me all about the defence of the hospital as I was the last to leave the building. An officer took down all our names and wrote down what we had done'.[12]

Chelmsford then made a short speech to the assembled defenders in which he thanked them for their endeavours. Gunner Howard repeated some of Chelmsford's words when he wrote home:

> 'The general said we were a brave little garrison, and this showed what a few men could do if they only had pluck'.[13]

Chelmsford remained at Rorke's Drift for a matter of hours before departing at midday with his staff officers for Helpmekaar. He now faced the unenviable task of reporting the defeat of his invasion force and annihilation of a famous British regiment. Colonel Glyn, who was in a complete state of shock at the loss of his regiment, was left in charge of Rorke's Drift with orders to prepare for another Zulu attack. The next day, Chelmsford moved on to Pietermaritzburg to discover panicking colonists had flocked to temporary defensive laagers, about forty in total. Although they were never needed, they remained occupied until early April.

Meanwhile, at Rorke's Drift the mission garrison had increased dramatically from the original defenders, consisting of 'B' Company 2/24th commanded by Lieutenant Bromhead and detachments from the 90th Regiment, the Commissariat, the Army Hospital Corps, the Chaplain's Department and colonial soldiers, amounting to 8 officers. 131 men, of whom 13 men were killed and 1 officer and 8 men were wounded. Now over 700 men, the remnants of Chelmsford's once-proud Central Column, added to the original defenders. The arrivals included the surviving companies of the 2/24th and sixteen companies of the NNC. The mounted troops and the Royal Artillery horses under the command of Colonel Harness were ordered to move on to the high plateau at Helpmekaar, where the air was deemed to be healthier for the horses; the Royal Artillery guns and men remained at Rorke's Drift.

The clearing up then began. The position was repaired and defences strengthened as it was believed the Zulus would return to attack the survivors. The wounded were attended to and orders given for the collection and cremation of the hundreds of Zulu bodies found in and around the Mission. The following day a large number of less-wounded and exhausted Zulus were discovered hiding beyond the Mission among the surrounding rocks and scrub bush. As these were still considered a threat, Hamilton-Browne ordered his men, assisted by numbers of the 24th Regiment, to search the surrounding area and kill any wounded they found along with any Zulus foolish enough to surrender. Due to the lack of ammunition, the soldiers were ordered to use the bayonet or the Zulus' own clubs and spears. According to Hamilton-Browne, 'It was beastly, but there was nothing else to do'. Ruthless as this action was, it was accepted by Glyn and his officers present and it was made easier for the soldiers given the task, knowing that their slain and disembowelled colleagues received no mercy at Isandlwana. Hamilton-Browne took an active part in this patrolling, and personally set the pattern of killing the wounded.

Glyn had a strong perimeter built around the camp and ordered that the survivors slept inside each night. The lack of shelter from the incessant rain soon made the post unsanitary and it was plagued at night by false alarms. Glyn himself withdrew still further into his shell of despondency and took little interest in the misery around him. Without doubt he was displaying all the symptoms of a mental breakdown, grieving for his lost regiment and feeling guilty that he had survived the retreat from Isandlwana.

Column orders for Rorke's Drift garrison dated 2 February indicate that three patrols would reconnoitre the surrounding area at dawn each day to keep the surrounding area free of Zulus. Based on their reports, further action, as necessary, would be detailed. Post war, news of Hamilton-Browne's savagery reached the highest echelons, and despite his seniority and rank, he was refused the South Africa campaign medal having openly ordered the slaughter of injured and captive Zulus at Rorke's Drift.[14] Such routine patrolling continued until the second invasion of Zululand in order to prevent the local Zulus regaining their military balance. Towards the beginning of April reports were received at Rorke's Drift that Zulus were beginning to filter back to their local homesteads. To discourage them, on 9 April Major Dartnell led a force of over 2,000 men in a sweeping raid from Rorke's Drift and into the border area of Zululand and of the Batshe Valley and back to Rorke's Drift via Fugitives' Drift. Seeing the approaching force, the Zulus had time to drive their stock out of harm's way and evacuated the area of fighting warriors. Dartnell experienced no opposition, which enabled his force to destroy Zulu crops and burn down their huts. Dartnell viewed the raid as a total success as it destroyed a total of twelve previously undamaged homesteads within ten miles of Rorke's Drift.

Reports regarding the non-treatment of captured and wounded Zulus soon filtered back to England, and reports of bloodthirsty vengeance for the defeat at Isandlwana even extended to accounts of retribution against wounded and vulnerable Zulus. It is true that, in the aftermath at Rorke's Drift, British troops spared no stragglers or wounded Zulus, particularly in view of the massacre at Isandlwana and the brutal slaying of several defenders in and around the hospital. Records regarding the medical treatment administered to the large number of wounded Zulu warriors after the battle are therefore non-existent. Given the fact that this event has been thoroughly examined by historians and researchers, it is evident that medical care was not administered to wounded Zulus by the British at Rorke's Drift and so the pattern was set for the following military engagements of the war shortly to take place. Later in the war Captain Cardew, acting as staff officer to Major-General John Crealock and the 1st Division, remarked on the bravery of the Zulu warriors and the undeserved brutal treatment of the wounded. He recounted an incident where:

> 'After one of the battles, he himself heard the order given by one general "Let Loose the Murderers," which meant, to order out the native allies to kill the prisoners and all the wounded, and the killing was not confined to the Native allies, but the European soldiers, and even the officers took part in it'.[15]

To add to their woes, the weather then broke and deluged the soldiers with torrential rain from which there was no shelter. Stunned as the Rorke's Drift survivors were, they also feared yet another Zulu attack, especially as their remaining ammunition amounted to just 30 rounds available per man. Without exception, to protect their hands from their red-hot rifle barrels, the defending soldiers had used their red jackets, torn into strips, as a heat-proof protective binding. A quick check of the damaged stores revealed that there were no spare uniforms or tents. Being inventive, they scavenged the heavy and abundant empty mealie sacks littering the ground and cut holes for their heads and arms. They looked odd but the sacks did the job and would do so for several weeks. With no facility for the stores at Pietermaritzburg to issue replacements for battle losses, it took a question in parliament before one flannel shirt and a pair of trousers, but bizarrely no jackets, could be issued to the defenders 'cost free' as compensation for uniforms damaged during the fighting. The news of government 'meanness' leaked out and a question was urgently asked in parliament by *The Referee* newspaper, which then used verse to mock the government into relenting and issuing replacement jackets:

RORKE'S DRIFT

'There was an old soldier named Dan'el
He fought until his clothes were in rags,
So the Government gave him a flannel,
And also a new pair of bags.

'And the news it went over the Channel,
Through Europe it's chaff for the wags,
That we honour our heroes in flannel,
And clothe their achievements in bags.

'Tis a blot on our glorious annals,
Oh, who were the elderly hags,
Who suggested those charity flannels
And ordered those beggarly bags?

'When the public its jury empanels,
'Twill suggest, ere the interest flags,
That the Tories for skirts take the flannels,
And they might put their heads in the bags'.

Historians have long considered the amount of ammunition fired during the fighting. It was historian Donald Morris who stated that 20,000 rounds of Martini-Henry ammunition had been fired in the space of twelve hours by the

104 British combatants. This figure is correct for companies advancing into battle but was it correct for a reserve company guarding stores and a small hospital? This roughly equates to 25 rounds per man per hour, and yet Zulu casualties amounted to not more than (from the battle) 500 at the highest estimate, or roughly 40 rounds to kill one Zulu in the close-range fighting. Archaeological evidence confirms there were few finds of empty ammunition cases, which, if 20,000 brass cases were scattered around this small area, then Chelmsford's surviving column would have soon trampled the frail ammunition cases into the mud, and it was not army policy to collect empty cases after fighting, especially if anticipating another Zulu attack. Commandant Hamilton-Brown clearly believed that the aftermath of the battle suggested the British bayonet had been more effective than the Martin-Henry rifle. He maintained that some were killed by bullets and the wounds, at that short range, were ghastly, but very many were killed by the bayonet. This is echoed by Dr Goldsworthy in his research into ammunition expenditure.

Modern studies suggest that relatively few soldiers, even in the best trained units, actively aim at and seek to kill the enemy in combat, most firing their weapons wildly and some not even firing them at all. Certainly the ratio between the number of rounds fired and the number of casualties inflicted on the enemy in the well-documented combats of the last few centuries has been staggeringly low, usually at several hundred to one.[16]

A logical conclusion to this question is that because so many of the Zulus had died of bayonet wounds, the fighting was more hand-to-hand than previously expected. The saviour of the mission was the bayonet in the hands of trapped and desperate men fighting for their very lives with little chance of survival.

Every officer and soldier remaining at Rorke's Drift was either a defender of the Mission or a surviving member of Chelmsford's column. All were exhausted and most were traumatised by the events of the previous twenty-four hours. The weather broke with torrential rain which would continue for the next week, and without any tents there was no shelter. The survivors of B Company were permitted to use the remains of Witt's roofless house to gain whatever protection they could from the elements. They even found a leaky tarpaulin for cover. Furthermore, a cold and wet Colonel Glyn, left behind by Chelmsford to command the outpost, was deeply traumatised by the loss of his regiment and failed to bring order into the sodden chaos. Glyn had already been advised by a column staff officer that Chelmsford would partly blame him for the loss of Isandlwana, which added to his woes. Captain Walter of the Royal Engineers was unimpressed by Glyn's predicament and opined 'Colonel Glyn does nothing and is *effete*'.[17] Europeans and natives were now crowded together without tents or shelter, and apart from the fear of another Zulu attack keeping everyone alert, such was the depression that no one had any enthusiasm for improving their lot.

With over 1,000 men crammed into a small space, and no respite from the constant alarms, the men were exposed to cold and rain, some sleeping on wet mealie bags, others on the cold waterlogged ground saturated with the overflow from the latrines. The poor sanitation together with their meagre diet soon caused bilious, remittent, or enteric disease among the garrison, which soon included Lieutenant Chard. There was little that could be done for the sick and Chard, because of his new-found status, had to be evacuated. The local press at Durban even reported his death, only to correct their account a few days later.

As a result of the stores lost on 22 January, the medical officer in command at Helpmekaar, Senior Surgeon Dugald Blair-Brown, was left with limited available medical supplies, consisting of two field panniers containing pills, powders, bandages and tourniquets plus brandy and port wine. The risk of epidemics at both Helpmekaar and Rorke's Drift was made known to Chelmsford and his staff, who refrained from taking appropriate action in the interest of military necessities.[18] Although improved entrenched camps were hastily constructed at both locations it did not take long for health problems to develop at Helpmekaar. There, anxiety and poor morale was superseded by malaise with loss of appetite, followed by widespread fever, diarrhoea and dysentery among the vulnerable.

The conditions at Rorke's Drift were only marginally better, with their fever outbreak less severe than at Helpmekaar. Surgeon Reynolds remained at the mission following the battle and it was generally acknowledged that he and the three orderlies of the Army Hospital Corps acquitted themselves commendably. He used the storehouse building as a hospital for the most needy, but was forced to leave the remainder of the garrison prey to the elements. The lack of shelter and rotting mealies in the overcrowded conditions, together with fatigue and declining psychological status inevitably resulted in widespread fever. Surgeon Reynolds described the signs and symptoms specifically, as bilious vomiting, hepatic congestion, delirium with heavy secretions in the upper respiratory tract and mucoid character of the stools. Woolfryes seemed to think that these epidemics were really typho-malarial in origin, as they appeared to be almost identical in character to those identified in various outposts during the Ninth Frontier War.[19] The increasing numbers suffering disease at Rorke's Drift soon included Surgeon Reynolds, who reported sick with acute dysentery on 6 February. He too, was evacuated to Helpmekaar and then on to hospital at Ladysmith, where he made a full recovery. By early April he had returned to his post to continue with his work.

There were very few wounded from the Battle of Isandlwana to care for. At Rorke's Drift, in addition to the fifteen wounded combatants, twenty-six patients had survived the attack on the hospital. Twenty of these sick and wounded survivors from the mission were finally transferred to Helpmekaar on 26 January, using two ambulance wagons. The disbandment of No 3 Column's 3,000 strong NNC in late January helped avoid further congestion and sanitary problems at Helpmekaar and Rorke's Drift. At both stations in the weeks that followed, fevers and dysentery claimed the lives of one officer and 25 other ranks from both battalions of the 24th Regiment. A further 18 officers and 68 other ranks were hospitalised with the same medical symptoms. Arriving at Rorke's Drift on 10 March, Charles Norris-Newman noted that of the garrison's 90 sick soldiers, only 50 enjoyed hospital accommodation. Given the appalling conditions, he was surprised that more men had not been stricken with disease and died. Considering that the months of January, February and March were regarded as the season of sickness, which was usually associated with the heavy rains, dampness and poor water quality, these epidemics were not surprising. Lieutenant Charles Harford, who was stationed at Rorke's Drift after the battle, wrote of the confinement and misery at the station by commenting that:

> 'This terrible state of things, living in such slush, caused a lot of sickness from fever and dysentery which carried off a large number of men and one or two officers. Notwithstanding this, and the knowledge that the Fort was overcrowded, Colonel Glyn declined to have any tents pitched outside to relieve matters …that no-one but the officers and NCOs of the Contingent were allowed outside …'.[20]

However, new epidemics occurred where troops congregated, especially within settlements and garrisons. Post-mortem examinations confirmed enteric fever, though the concept of miasma, zymotic disease and the alleged unhygienic habits of the native troops failed to account for the events.[21] Eventually, upon reflection, Surgeon Ash-Vacy later correctly concluded that germ contamination of water supplies at the army's bases across the war zone was the true cause. The 1878 Field Hospital Regulations ensured that during the weekly health inspection, each medical officer must check mouths for the presence of early signs of scurvy. During the Anglo-Zulu war, in the absence of an available supply of fresh vegetables and fresh meat after the first 14 days in the field, each soldier was required to consume 1oz lime juice daily. Officially, there were eight admissions for scurvy resulting in the men being invalided home during the Anglo-Zulu War, with three of these patients admitted from Rorke's Drift.

All able-bodied soldiers were put to work repairing the mission storeroom and strengthening the existing perimeter fortifications. These had been broken down by the Zulu attacks and were strongly rebuilt with rocks and small boulders brought in from the nearby rock terraces. Later, when Lieutenant Porter's 5th Company of Royal Engineers arrived, the work of building a loop-holed barricade round the entire outpost was commenced. As an additional defence for the anxious outpost, Glyn posted a 7-pound gun at each corner. These were the guns that had accompanied Chelmsford to Mangeni and which had shelled Isandlwana camp on their return.

Immediately outside the Mission barricade were the temporary graves of the men killed during the Zulu attack. Initially, rough wooden crosses were placed over the temporary graves, which were then moved to higher ground between Witt's house and the Oskarsberg. A cemetery with a prestigious stone monument and inscription by the 24th Regiment was then constructed. With the reconstruction of the defences around the Mission came the first semblance of good military order returning to the garrison. Until then, no Regimental Orders were issued at Rorke's Drift. The first was issued on 28 January, due to there being no paper left to produce any daily orders and, even by 2 February, orders for the garrison revolved mainly around the possibility of a renewed Zulu attack. There are a number of documented accounts from those left behind at Rorke's Drift of a lack of paper which, coupled with the severe storms and filthy conditions caused by flooding and sewerage from hundreds of men cooped up, suggests writing anything was problematical. Lieutenant George Banister of the 2/24th was appointed as Garrison Adjutant at Rorke's Drift and in a letter to his father dated 27 January he wrote, 'No paper or pens or in fact any single thing. I have managed to get some foolscap in my extra capacity as Garrison Adjutant'.[22]

It was only following an examination of the report from Captain Higginson, a survivor of Isandlwana and the last man to see the two 24th officers, Lieutenants Coghill and Melvill, that a search for their bodies was undertaken. These two officers had somehow managed to escape from Isandlwana to save their regimental Colour and evaded the chasing Zulus. They then managed to cross the swirling torrent of the Buffalo River to reach what they thought would be safety but were caught and killed on the Natal side of the river by Chief Sihayo's warriors recuperating after having been brutalised by the British troops a few days earlier. On 4 February, a patrol from Rorke's Drift led by Major Wilsone Black discovered their bodies on the upper slope of the Buffalo River gorge at Chief Sotondose's Drift, now known as Fugitives' Drift.

According to a regimental ledger at the 24th Regimental Museum at Brecon, the patrol was accompanied by Captain Harford of the 99th Regiment, with Captain Greaves and Lieutenant Hillier of the NNC when they found the bodies of Coghill and Melvill on the steep hillside overlooking the river. There were additionally two soldiers' bodies discovered alongside Coghill and Melvill, the evidence for which is supplied by the contemporary accounts of two of the officers who accompanied the party. Hillier reported finding four bodies in his letter to the *Telegraph and Eastern Province Standard*, published on 2 February 1879, and this is confirmed by a handwritten entry by Captain Harford in his presentation copy of *In Zululand with the British* by Norris-Newman, presented to him in 1880 by Norris-Newman himself. Harford annotated the book throughout with his own recollections and corrections and with regard to the number of bodies found by the search party he added a handwritten note that the bodies totalled '4'. Reverend Smith accompanied the group and read the burial service as the bodies were buried under a large rock overlooking the Buffalo River in the valley below.

At the end of February, conditions had become so bad that a new fort, initially named 'Fort Revenge' but re-named Fort Melvill on Chelmsford's order (he thought the original name too provocative), was built 800 yards away on an adjacent hillock overlooking the pont river crossing. The defences at Rorke's Drift were abandoned and the stonewalls of the outpost were demolished and used in the construction of Fort Melvill, an oblong fort, flanked with towers, a broad ditch surrounding the walls and built partly of masonry and partly of dry wall. *The Illustrated London News* commented:

> 'Fort Melvill, named after the late Lieutenant Melvill, is an oblong fort with flanking towers, built partly in masonry, partly with dry wall, loop-holed throughout, and surrounded by a ditch, with an obstacle formed of aloes planted on the glacis. It is constructed on a height 150 yards from, and overlooking and commanding, the ponts by which the invading army crossed on January 11th last. Lieutenant da Costa Porter, RE, has superintended its erection; and manned with 200 Europeans, it may be considered impregnable against any number of Zulus. A large stone store, roofed with galvanised iron, has been built inside, to hold commissariat supplies'.

References

1. Chard Second Report.
2. Lieutenant Chard, an engineer officer, had unexpectedly arrived at Rorke's Drift the day before but kept away from Bromhead's detachment as engineer officers were still not thought of by their regular army peers as 'proper officers'.
3. The attack on Rorke's Drift was initially unintended – the Zulus had crossed the river into Natal merely for short-term plunder. See *Rope of Sand*, Laband, J., Jonathan Ball, Johannesburg 1995.
4. *A Handful of Heroes*, Stossel K., Pen & Sword, 2015.

5. General Order no. 37 of 19 February 1879 stated that the services of Captain Stephenson of the 2/3rd NNC were no longer required, and he was dismissed from the service. A court martial was not possible as Stephenson was technically a civilian. The correct spelling of his name remains in doubt, either Captain William Stevenson or Stephenson NNC. The *Natal Mercury* of 26 November 1878 lists Stephenson as a Captain in the 2nd Regiment (actually 2nd Battalion), but General Orders No. 213 of 3 December lists him as a Captain in the 2nd Battalion of the 3rd Regiment. He was dismissed the service by General Orders No.37 of 19 February 1879 under the name of Stevenson.
6. Bourne's radio broadcast.
7. Author's research at Rorke's Drift.
8. *Chard Report.*
9. *A Handful of Heroes.*
10. *Guidebook*, Rattray.
11. *A Lost Legionary in South Africa,* Hamilton-Browne, 1910.
12. *A Handful of Heroes.*
13. *The Red Soldier*, Emery F.
14. Hamilton-Browne was refused the South Africa campaign medal on the grounds of his slaughter of captured and injured Zulus at Rorke's Drift. The medal he wore following the campaign had been issued to one of his men and the name altered.
15. *Letters of Jane Elizabeth Waterson*, 1866–1905, National Book Printers SA
16. a. Appendix 7.
    b. *Cannae*, Goldsworthy, Dr A., Cassell. This is evidenced in the current (2024) Russian/Ukraine war where the majority (80–90%) of casualties on both sides are from artillery, including mortars, traditional artillery and longer range systems.
17. *A Lost Legionary in South Africa.*
18. *Woolfryes Report*, Medical research by Dr Traverse (2013), p293.
19. Ditto.
20. *Harford.*
21. The medical research by Dr Traverse (2013) quoting *Woolfryes Report*, p. 293.
22. Letter from Lieutenant George Banister of the 2/24th Garrison Adjutant to his father dated 27 January.

Chapter 8

Who Saved the Colour?

This raises the question of the identity of the two soldiers' bodies found alongside those of Lieutenants Coghill and Melvill on the steep rocky slope above Fugitives' Drift. Lieutenant Higginson of the NNC had been with both Melvill and Coghill as they had clung to the rock in the Buffalo River. On reaching the bank, he had promised to fetch horses for them. Instead, once he had found a mount, seized from Trooper Barker, one of his own fugitive troopers, he had ridden off to safety, abandoning Coghill, Melvill, Barker and whoever, to their fate.[1] Certainly, the army of the day would reverently bury their dead soldiers where they fell but not have recorded the details, only specifically caring for the bodies of their fellow officers. Post-battle, and in line with military tradition of the time, the fact that two soldiers had died in the presence of two officers would not necessarily have been deemed relevant or significant.

In 2009 the area around the graves of Coghill and Melvill was examined by researchers from the *AZWHS* looking for evidence of other cairns and, indeed, two unmarked cairns were found nearby. There are no other cairns or graves between these three at Fugitives' Drift and Rorke's Drift, some five miles apart. It is now believed that one of the soldiers who died alongside Coghill and Melvill was Sergeant Cooper of the 1st/24th Regiment, who had fought that same morning at Isandlwana and appears to have made a fighting escape to the river, possibly having been towed across by Curling's horse. Three soldiers were confirmed in Curling's account as having been helped across the fast-flowing flooded river by hanging on to his strong swimmer of a horse. Cooper is officially recorded as being an Isandlwana casualty, probably because he did not survive. However, his family papers and memorial service documents state he was killed at Rorke's Drift. Fugitives' Drift is much closer to Rorke's Drift than Isandlwana. Cooper is not recorded in any of the accounts as having died during the fighting at Rorke's Drift itself, but the logical suggestion is that he died at nearby Fugitives' Drift alongside Coghill and Melvill.

This hypothesis arose when a letter was discovered that had been sent from the officer-in-command of the Rorke's Drift area at nearby Helpmekaar, Major Upcher, to Cooper's sister, addressed as Miss (Mrs) Clements. It informed her of her brother's death on 22 January. Had Cooper been killed at Isandlwana or Rorke's Drift no such letter would have been written. It is possible that

Cooper made his escape along the Fugitives' Trail and across the Buffalo River before being killed alongside Coghill and Melvill. If he had been able to catch or cling to a fleeing horse, the hypothesis has to be reasonable, especially as it is accepted that Lieutenant Curling wrote that his horse pulled three soldiers across the flooded river.[2] The probability is that the body was Cooper and that he was buried alongside Coghill and Melvill. There the matter rested until Major Upcher wrote the following letter to Miss Clements, Cooper's sister. No similar letter has ever been seen by Zulu War researchers or by the curators, former and present, at the Regimental Museum in Brecon. The letter is unique and reads:

> 'Miss Clements
>
> 'I regret to inform you that your brother was killed in action on 22 January 1879, I am sorry that I cannot give you further and fuller information.
>
> 'Helpmekaar
> '11 April 1879
> 'Upcher Major
> 'Commanding 24th Regt'.

This poses a question. Whatever caused Major Upcher, then the commanding officer of the 1st Battalion at Helpmekaar, to personally write to Cooper's family on 11 April 1879, when the first attempt to tidy the Isandlwana battlefield and bury the hundreds of bodies didn't take place for another six weeks? No other such letters were sent to casualties' families, either from Helpmekaar, Isandlwana or Rorke's Drift. Furthermore, at a subsequent memorial service held for Cooper by his family, the memorial cards state that Cooper's death occurred, not at Isandlwana, but at Rorke's Drift, then the nearest identifiable location to where the fugitives crossed the river.

Had Cooper been killed at Isandlwana or on the Fugitives' Trail, his death would not have been drawn to the attention of anyone, least of all Major Upcher. Conversely, if Cooper had been killed during the defence of Rorke's Drift he would undoubtedly have been buried with the other fatalities from that engagement and memorialised with them, which did not happen. In view of the connecting circumstances, the most likely venue for Cooper's death is Fugitives' Drift alongside Coghill and Melvill. Both Rorke's Drift and Fugitives' Drift then came under the Regimental Headquarters at Helpmekaar. As with many of the uncertainties of that day, the death of Sergeant Cooper remains shrouded in mystery. Was he the soldier, or one of the two soldiers' bodies actually discovered along with Coghill and Melvill and buried under one of the adjacent cairns? Two soldiers' bodies were seen by Lieutenant Hillier and Captain Harford and this information was important enough to be passed back to Glyn, who mentioned the matter in his report to Colonel Crealock, Chelmsford's Military Secretary on 1 Feb 1879:

> 'I sent a party down the river to see if they could discover Melvill's and Coghill's bodies. They found them lying on a path [in a glen about five miles off and about 300 yards from the river on this (Natal) side.] Coghill had been stripped with the exception of his boots and socks, his spurs were lying at his side. Just below him Melvill was lying in his uniform apparently untouched. Below them again was a soldier and a number of the enemy. I think both Melvill and Coghill had been shot as their bodies were not mutilated'.

The party collected various personal items such as rings and spurs from the two officers' bodies to return to their families, a normal procedure with officers' bodies. The sergeant would not have had such items, but a quick search of his body would have revealed any family letter to identify him before burial.

The Times of Natal special war correspondent, Charles Norris-Newman, wrote that corresponding with family and friends back in the British Isles was the soldiers' principal recreation. On campaign, soldiers traditionally carried cherished letters in their pockets as they had no other storage facility – so it is perfectly feasible that, if the body of the soldier was Cooper, the jacket contained such a letter from his sister, a letter which would positively identify both the soldier's body and the letter writer's address. It is reasonable to expect that those who found the body would have passed such a letter 'up the line' to Major Upcher along with the items recovered from Coghill and Melvill for their respective relatives.

Otherwise, what caused Colonel Glyn to mention it and for Major Upcher, by then commanding the 1/24th at Helpmekaar and Rorke's Drift, to write a one-off personal letter to Cooper's sister on 11 April 1879? Coincidentally this was sent about the same time that details of the deaths of Coghill and Melvill were forwarded from Helpmekaar to Horse Guards. Furthermore, the first serious attempt to identify and bury the Isandlwana battlefield bodies did not take place until later, on 21 May of that year and so, until then, no one knew where the Isandlwana bodies were. This author can find no alternative logical explanation for the Upcher letter to Cooper's sister other than a letter from her having been recovered from Cooper's body. No similar letter to a dead soldier's relatives, either from Rorke's Drift or Isandlwana, has ever been seen.

This author's presumption for why the Cooper family held the belief that he had been killed at Rorke's Drift, and then conducting his memorial service accordingly, is based on Upcher's letter to Cooper's sister being signed off at Helpmekaar. Any enquiry by the family would reveal that Helpmekaar was also the headquarters for Rorke's Drift. Cooper had previously served with Coghill and Melvill at Gibraltar. This might also explain why he went to the aid of the officers after Higginson left them; Cooper had served with them since 1874.

The usual manner by which relatives discovered the death of a soldier was from other soldiers' letters, newspaper articles or lists published in major towns. Officers' deaths in action were formally notified by Horse Guards to the *Times* newspaper and in the case of the Isandlwana officer casualties, the *Times* list of those killed was published on 12 February. Major Upcher sent the Clements' letter on 11 April, which roughly coincides with the actual details of the deaths of Coghill and Melvill being sent from Helpmekaar to London. The official notification of the actual circumstances of the deaths of the two officers at Fugitives' Drift was sent on from Horse Guards to their respective families and is dated 21 April 1879, which indicates that the news of the three deaths in question was sent from South Africa at about the same time.

Meanwhile, the Coghill family in Ireland had already been contacted by Captain Higginson, the NNC Adjutant who had abandoned Coghill and Melvill to their fate, with an account of the death of their son. This prompted a letter from Coghill senior to the *Irish Times*, published on 8 April, acknowledging that Higginson 'did everything that an unarmed and dismounted man could do to succour poor Melvill and my son'. The account unsurprisingly put Higginson in a good light and was presumably sent by Higginson in an attempt to ameliorate growing accusations of his cowardice for leaving Coghill and Melvill then taking Trooper Barker's horse and abandoning them all to their fate.

In 2009 the area around the graves of Coghill and Melvill was examined by this author accompanied by David Rattray and David Payne seeking evidence of other cairns and, indeed, an unmarked burial cairn was discovered. The group then searched the route between Fugitives' Drift and Rorke's Drift seeking evidence of any other cairns but found nothing. This ties in neatly with the belief of those who later lived in the area, including George Bunting, who lived most of his life at Umzinyati House at Fugitives' Drift overlooking the graves of Coghill and Melvill. In the 1930s one of Bunting's regular visitors was the historian J. L. Smail who recorded the following in his 1965 book *Historical Monuments and Battlefields in Natal and Zululand.* He quotes Bunting:

> Lieutenant Melvill VC and Lieutenant Coghill VC. The cairns nearby conceal the remains of others. Bodies found on 1/2/1879 and buried under a common cairn by the Rev. Smith on 3/2/1879. At a later date the bodies of the two officers were reinterred in two separate graves'.[3]

A further search by the same group that discovered the bodies then found the Queen's Colour, lost by Coghill and Melvill, among the boulders in the now calm and shallow river just 200 yards downstream from the drift. Back where the bodies were found a cairn of stones was erected over the bodies and the waterlogged Colour was taken back to Rorke's Drift. Glyn was moved to tears when he received the flag and learned of the fate of his favourite young officers.

As already noted, according to a regimental ledger at 24th Regimental Museum at Brecon, the patrol was accompanied by Captain Harford of the 99th Regiment, with Captain Greaves and Lieutenant Hillier of the NNC, when they found the bodies of Coghill and Melvill on the steep hillside overlooking the river. Two soldiers' bodies were discovered alongside Coghill and Melvill, the evidence for which is supplied by the contemporary accounts of two of the officers who accompanied the party. Hillier reported finding four bodies in his letter to the *Telegraph and Eastern Province Standard*, published on 28 February 1879, and this is confirmed by a handwritten entry by Captain Harford in his presentation copy of *In Zululand with the British* by Norris-Newman, presented to him in 1880 by Norris-Newman himself. Harford annotated the book throughout with his own recollections and corrections and with regard to the number of bodies found by the search party he added a handwritten note that the bodies totalled four.

The accounts of officer witnesses confirm the finding of four bodies. Together with the two letters, one from Cooper's sister to her brother and the death notice from Major Upcher to her, logic supports the hypothesis that Sergeant Cooper died alongside Coghill and Melvill. And there the matter rests.

See Appendix 2 for more detail. Regimental Records state that Cooper's personal effects and South Africa Campaign Medal were claimed by his father.

References

1. Lieutenant Higginson of the NNC had been with both Melvill and Coghill as they had clung to the rock in the Buffalo River. On reaching the bank, he had promised to fetch horses for the other two. Instead, once he had found a mount, he had ridden off to safety: his action was reported by another survivor, Trooper Barker of the Natal Carbineers. The adjutant of the NNC, Captain Harford, was meanwhile instructed to arrange the arrest of two NNC officers for desertion; Captain Stephenson for abandoning Rorke's Drift and Captain Higginson for abandoning his men by taking one of their horses to escape and then going absent.
2. *The Curling Letters of the Zulu War*, Greaves and Best, Pen & Sword, 2001.
3. In 1972 the grave of Coghill and Melvill was 'improved' by the South Africa War Graves Board using rounded stones from a pile found nearby. The stones were from a previously unknown Zulu memorial, and, believing their site had been deliberately damaged, the consequence was the desecration of the Coghill and Melvill grave. The matter was eventually resolved with both sites being restored, although the original Coghill and Melvill cross, originally donated by Sir Bartle Frere, had to be replaced. The work was completed in 1973.

Chapter 9

Aftermath and Rewards

One of those things that no fellow can understand
Lieutenant Colonel Pickard of the Royal Household

Following the Battle of Isandlwana, most of the column's survivors who escaped were sent back to Helpmekaar, including numerous Isandlwana and Rorke's Drift casualties. Due to the heavy rains, unhygienic conditions, and lack of medical supplies that followed this battle, many of the Helpmekaar station soon suffered appalling illness and disease. Those who died of their injuries or disease subsequent to the actions on 22 January 1879 are buried in the now-neglected and dilapidated cemetery behind the local police office. Although anticipated, there was no Zulu attack on Helpmekaar. Even with the British victory at Rorke's Drift, conditions for the survivors at the shattered Mission continued to be a severe anti-climax. In the weeks that followed, pollution caused disease and depression, and resulted in the mission having to be abandoned in April in favour of a nearby hillock overlooking the Buffalo River.

Research by Dr Andre Travers[1] into the availability of medical stores at Rorke's Drift revealed that not only had the hospital cot bearers deserted at the same time as the NNC on 22 January, but almost the entire supply of medicines, surgical equipment and six ambulance wagons belonging to Colonel Glyn's column had been lost. The medical officers were left with few supplies, including the pair of field medical panniers at Helpmekaar together with limited quantities that Surgeon Reynolds had been able to save at Rorke's Drift. The urgent need for replenishment medical supplies was technically alleviated by the immediate despatch of substantial bulky stocks from Pietermaritzburg. However, these took almost six weeks to arrive due to the slow pace of the ox wagons and the boggy condition of the tracks. Also, upon receipt of the news of the disaster at Isandlwana, a field hospital of 75 beds was immediately dispatched from Pietermaritzburg for use at Rorke's Drift and Helpmekaar. This also took a similar time to reach its destination as the hospital accompanied the medical supplies convoy. Desperate for medicines such as quinine and pulvis ipecac, the depleted column was supplied by any means, which included postal services and native runners from Pietermaritzburg. In the meantime, a small quantity of medicine was obtained by purchase from the mission station at Umsinga. Glyn's misery was aggravated by the loss at Isandlwana of his regimental medical team, including Surgeon-Major Shepherd, Acting Surgeon Bouee and eleven men of the AHC including Lieutenant of Orderlies, A. Hall.

After the tragedy of Isandlwana, Chelmsford described the survival of Rorke's Drift's as a 'gleam of sunshine'. His report to Colonel Stanley, the Secretary of State for War in London, sent on 8 February, sets out his store. His aim was to justify the invasion of Zululand, but it would be a lengthy one-man quest to make the invasion appear lawful and justified. He wrote:

> 'The defeat of the Zulus at this post and the very heavy loss suffered by them has to a great extent neutralized the effects of the disaster at Isandlwana and it no doubt saved Natal from a serious invasion.
>
> 'The cool determined courage displayed by the gallant garrison is beyond all praise, and will, I feel sure receive ample recognition.
>
> 'As at the present moment the lesson taught by this defence is most valuable I have thought it advisable to publish for general information the report in question (the Chard Report) which I trust will meet with your approval'.[2]

At home massive publicity of the victory at Rorke's Drift initially neutralised Chelmsford's defeat at Isandlwana, although the army, especially in South Africa, more accurately viewed the event as a minor skirmish. News of decorations and medals for those involved inevitably provoked considerable annoyance through the ranks and later earned contempt from General Wolseley, from which many decorated survivors would suffer. It was well understood by the government that the distribution of bravery awards following Rorke's Drift would deter searching questions being asked by the press or public. Likewise, the Queen's intervention on Chelmsford's side discouraged any open resistance from her politicians and senior military officers minded to question her stance. Both Chard and Bromhead were promoted, but their careers thereafter floundered. Encouraged by the popular press, Chelmsford and the politicians successfully used the survival of most of the garrison at Rorke's Drift and turned it into a victory to counter criticism of the defeat at Isandlwana, a defeat produced by his own classic error of dividing his forces in the presence of the enemy and of carelessly dismissing his own military intelligence reports of the growing Zulu presence. General Wolseley wrote on the matter:

> 'It is monstrous making heroes of those who saved or attempted to save their lives by bolting or of those who, shut up in buildings at Rorke's

> Drift, could not bolt, and fought like rats for their lives which they could not otherwise save'.[3]

The engagement at Rorke's Drift was initially viewed by the British military in South Africa as nothing more than a skirmish, and, in military terms, they were correct; it was obvious to those present that a single concerted attack by the Zulus would easily have overwhelmed the small garrison. The praise and fame immediately heaped on the defenders increasingly rankled with many who saw the unexpected status of those involved elevated to that of popular heroes. General Wolseley further expressed his view that he thought the glut of awards was 'monstrous', while Major Clery, one of Chelmsford's staff officers, commented: 'Reputations are being made and lost here in almost comical fashion.'[4]

While the isolated Glyn was suffering both mentally and physically at Rorke's Drift, Chelmsford and his staff attempted to play down their role in the disaster in the face of growing criticism from parliament. Chelmsford indiscreetly suggested that Glyn 'was solely responsible' for the position of the Isandlwana camp, while admitting subtly 'that [while] Colonel Glyn fully and explicitly accepted this responsibility it cannot, however, affect the ultimate responsibility of the General-in-Command'. This attempt to implicate Glyn in the blame game cut little ice with those who knew how limited the Colonel's authority had actually been at both Isandlwana and Rorke's Drift. Anne Glyn, recovering herself from the terrible news of Isandlwana, was incensed at the attempts to blame her husband and was uncharacteristically outspoken in her criticism of Chelmsford, an unusual course of action for an army wife. Glyn himself seemed too numb to do more than briefly give the facts without comment to the Board of Enquiry. In 1882 Glyn was promoted to Major General and appointed a Knight Commander of the Bath. He retired as a Lieutenant General and lived at Mortimer in Berkshire.

British Forces Engaged in the Defence of the Mission at Rorke's Drift:

Unit	Officers	ORs	Sick	Killed	Wounded	Remarks
In Command						
Staff		1				
Royal Artillery		4	3			
Royal Engineers		1				
2/3rd Regiment (Buffs)		1				
1/24th Regiment		11	5	3	2	1 died later
2/24th Regiment	Lt Bromhead	98	17	8	5	1 died later
Commissariat Department	Messrs, Dalton, Byrne & Dunn	1		Mr. Byrne*	Mr Dalton	
Army Medical Department	Surg. Reynolds	3				
Chaplains Department	Rev. George Smith					Civilian
90th Regiment		1	1			
Natal Mounted Police		3	3	1		
Ferryman		1				Civilian. Daniels
	8	131	35	15	9	

* Acting Storekeeper Byrne's grave location is unknown – he was buried as a civilian.

Participants:

Imperial: Lieutenant Chard RE Officer in command. 'B' Company 2/24th (2nd Warwickshire) Regiment commanded by Lieutenant Bromhead together with detachments from the 90th Regiment, the Commissariat, the Army Hospital Corps and the Chaplain's Department.

Colonial: Natal Mounted Police the NNC and a civilian ferryman who was paid £15 per month and provided with free rations as of February 1879, a large sum of money for the job. (See Order no. 85 dated 14 April 1879 published in the *Times of Natal* 21 April 1879.)

Total force: 8 Officers. 131 men.

Casualties, Killed: 17 men, wounded, 1 officer and 8 men.

A full and current nominal roll of Rorke's Drift defenders, along with their personal details, can be obtained from the Regimental Museum at Brecon.

Zulu: Chief Dabulamanzi, a half-brother of King Cetshwayo, in command. The total Zulu force is estimated at 4,000 and consisted of four *amabutho*, or regiments, the UDloko, UThulwana, INdlondlo and INdluyengwe regiments.

Casualties: unknown in total, but some 600 bodies were left around the position perimeter, other bodies found later were cremated or buried in three mass graves.

The homecoming for the Rorke's Drift Zulus was no matter for rejoicing. As a result of their failed action at Rorke's Drift, Dabulamanzi's returning warriors were chided and mocked. Zulu folklore holds that it was said that 'you marched off, you went to dig little bits with your assegais out of the house of Jim that had never done you any harm' and that the surviving warriors who had attacked Rorke's Drift were seriously dejected by their failure and worse was to come. The retreating warriors were jeered and mocked by the villagers through whose homesteads they passed. The gist of the baiting calls included 'shocking cowards' and 'you're just women – running away for no reason at all, just like the wind.'[5]

The day after Isandlwana, most of the NNC crept back to Rorke's Drift, where their future was urgently considered by Chelmsford's staff as to whether or not the demoralised 3rd Regiment could even be kept together. They were certainly no longer a viable fighting force. A number were used to help make good the two damaged buildings and strengthen the perimeter defences. While their future was being urgently reviewed, they were marched off to guard the valley behind the Oskarsberg which the Zulus had originally used to approach the mission. Already without food for three days they became sullen and, in the absence of orders, set about hunting for food and killing any wounded Zulus found hiding in the vicinity.

Within hours Chelmsford finally ordered the disbandment of the NNC and, after being fed and their weapons collected, they were dismissed. They were each issued with an army blanket and, in case there were still marauding Zulus in the area, they were instructed to stay together until they reached Umsinga before making off to their individual homes. Their commandant, Commandant Lonsdale, was despatched to Cape Town to raise a fresh mounted corps. The NNC officers were instructed to remain at Rorke's Drift pending their detachment to other units in the invasion force. The NNC adjutant, Captain Harford, was meanwhile instructed to arrange the arrest of two NNC officers for desertion; Captain Stephenson for abandoning Rorke's Drift and Captain Higginson for abandoning Coghill and Melvill at Fugitives' Drift while fleeing Isandlwana, and then commandeering a trooper's horse to escape and going absent. A letter from Harford clearly shows he was perplexed by having to arrest the two officers:

'NNC
'Rorke's Drift
'From the Officer Comd. 3rd Regt.,
'To the Officer Comd. Troops,

'Jan 31 1879
'Sir,

'I have the honour to state that the two officers *viz* Captain Stephenson and Lieutenant Higginson lately reported as missing after the fight at Isandlwana, and having supposed to have escaped to PM Berg (Pietermaritzburg) have rejoined their Corps, and having been place under arrest in accordance with orders from Commandant Lonsdale, for absenting themselves since the 22nd inst from their Corps without cause and permission.

'I have the honour to request in the absence of Commandant Lonsdale, that I may be informed what steps to take in the matter.

'H.C.H'.[6]

The Rorke's Drift Victoria Cross citations

With regard to the first awards of Zulu War Victoria Crosses, the 2 May 1879 London Gazette citations read:

'The Queen has been graciously pleased to signify her intention to confer the decoration of the Victoria Cross on the under mentioned Officers and Soldiers of Her Majesty's Army, whose claims have been submitted for Her Majesty's approval, for their gallant conduct in the defence of Rorke's Drift, on the occasion of the attack by the Zulus, as recorded against their names'.

LIEUTENANT JOHN ROUSE MARRIOTT CHARD, 5th COMPANY R.E.

LIEUTENANT GONVILLE BROMHEAD, 24th (2nd WARWICKSHIRE) REGIMENT

These two officers' names are forever linked together in one of the greatest feats of the British Army, the defence of Rorke's Drift.

The Mission Station by the west bank of the Buffalo River was taken over by the military as a Commissariat Stores and hospital and it was from there that Chelmsford's invasion force crossed into Zululand. On the morning of 22 January 1879, having been left behind at Rorke's Drift and without clear orders, Lieutenant Chard and his four sappers rode to the camp at Isandlwana to obtain clarification of their duties. Chard's personal orders were to return to Rorke's Drift and keep the ferry ponts in working order and to mount guard over them. As he left Isandlwana, he noticed a large force of Zulus gathering in the distant hills. Chard was probably the last man to leave Isandlwana before the Zulus overwhelmed the camp.

On his return to Rorke's Drift, Chard reported to Major Spalding, the commander and related what he had seen at Isandlwana; furthermore, he expressed his concern that in the event of an attack he would be unable to defend the ponts until the replacement troops arrived. The Company that had been detailed for this defence were several days overdue, so Spalding decided to ride to Helpmekaar to hurry things along. Before he rode off, he gave command of the camp to Chard.

Less than two hours later the Zulus attacked the Mission Station with a force of 4,500 warriors. By comparison, Chard and Bromhead had just 100 fit and thirty-five sick soldiers with which to defend the position. The Zulus commenced their attack at about 4.00 pm on 22 January and sustained their attack until the following morning when Lord Chelmsford relieved the post. For saving the post from the Zulus the two officers were subsequently recommended for the award of the Victoria Cross. Curiously, their well-earned awards were highly irregular; the original recommendation for the Rorke's Drift awards of the Victoria Crosses was in respect of Corporal Allen and Privates Hook, Hitch, Williams and the two Jones, and was submitted by Lieutenant Bromhead in his capacity as commander of B Company, through the correct military channels via Colonel Glyn, his commanding officer. Glyn forwarded these recommendations to Chelmsford on 15 February without further comment by Glyn. It was only when this report reached Chelmsford that he personally added the names of Chard and Bromhead, without the necessary recommendations or referring the matter back to Glyn.[7]

Both officers received their Victoria Crosses from General Wolseley while still serving in Zululand; Bromhead at Utrecht on 11 September 1879, Chard at St. Pauls on 16 July 1879. Their joint citation, prepared in London and not by Chelmsford, reads:

> 'For their gallant conduct at the defence of Rorke's Drift, on the occasion of the attack by the Zulus on the 22 and 23 January, 1879.
>
> 'The Lieutenant General commanding the troops reports that, had it not been for the fine example and behaviour of these two officers under the most trying circumstances, the defence of Rorke's Drift post would not have been conducted with that intelligence and tenacity which so essentially characterised it. The Lieutenant General adds, that its success must, to a great degree, be attributable to the two young Officers who exercised the chief Command on the occasion in question'.

Acting-Assistant Commissary James Dalton, Commissariat And Transport Corps

The two men who managed to escape via Fugitive's Drift had brought a written message from Isandlwana warning the Rorke's Drift garrison of the Zulus' approach. Consulting together, Chard and Bromhead were persuaded by Dalton that it was too dangerous to attempt a retreat to Helpmekaar and risk being attacked in the open. They would not be able to move quickly as the sick from the hospital had to be evacuated and the considerable amount of ammunition and stores would have to be abandoned to the Zulus. The best option was to stay and fight from a good defensive position; something Commissary James Dalton had already set about constructing with piled sacks of corn, biscuit boxes and wagons.

When the Ninth Frontier War broke out in 1877, Dalton came out of retirement and was appointed to the rather cumbersome rank of Acting Assistant Commissary, which gave him officer status.

At this time, Rorke's Drift was home to approximately 84 men of B Company 2/24th, 36 sick or injured men in the hospital, 3 Royal Engineers, 3 Commissariat, 4 medics and 1 detached man of the Buffs. In all, a total of about 140 men. In addition, there were 200–300 African recruits of the Natal Native Contingent. With so many hands, the barricades were all but completed by the time the Zulus appeared. Meanwhile, there was a succession of exhausted and demoralised fugitives passing by who tried to persuade the defenders to run and save their lives. When a large body of Native Horse were seen to head up the road to Helpmekaar, it was too much for the NNC, who with their colonial officer and NCOs, deserted en-masse. This defection meant that the perimeter was too large to defend, so a second defensive line was hurriedly constructed, leaving the hospital out on a limb. Both Chard and Bromhead assisted Dalton to organise the men around the perimeter, making sure there would be a constant supply of ammunition. As the Zulus attacked, Dalton occupied himself around the barricades, encouraging the men and taking shots where necessary. Then, as he leaned over the parapet to take aim, he was hit by a bullet that passed through his right shoulder. Surgeon Reynolds rendered him first aid and after a short rest, Dalton was back passing ammunition and offering advice to the hard-pressed defenders. After the war, James Dalton was promoted to commissariat officer, but he was put on half-pay and returned to England. South Africa was too much of a magnet for him and he returned a few years later and took an interest in a mining company. He was suddenly taken ill and died on 7 January 1887, aged only fifty-four. The citation for Dalton's Victoria Cross was dated the 17 November 1879 and reads:

> 'For his conspicuous gallantry during the attack on Rorke's Drift by the Zulus on the night of the 22 January 1879, when he actively superintended the work of defence, and was amongst the foremost of those who received the first attack at the corner of the hospital, when the deadliness of his fire did great execution, and the mad rush of the Zulus met its first check, and where by his cool courage he saved the life of a man of the Army Hospital Corps by shooting the Zulu, who, having seized the muzzle of the man's rifle, was in the act of assegaing him.
>
> 'This officer, to whose energy much of the defence of the place was due, was severely wounded during the contest, but still continued to give the same example of cool courage'.

PRIVATE JOHN WILLIAMS, 2/24th
PRIVATE HENRY HOOK, 2/24th
PRIVATE WILLIAM JONES, 2/24th
PRIVATE ROBERT JONES, 2/24th
CORPORAL WILLIAM WILSON ALLAN, 2/24th
PRIVATE FREDERICK HITCH, 2/24th

The defence of the hospital was a battle within a battle. The defenders were mostly isolated from each other by walls and partitions so individual soldiers fought without so much as an NCO in command. At first their fire from the loopholes was effective, but once the Zulus had managed to reach the outside walls, the defenders felt their isolation. The Zulus set fire to the roof thatch

Natal to Helpmekaar roadway.

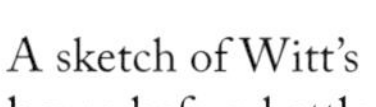

A sketch of Witt's house before battle.

Rorke's house after battle.

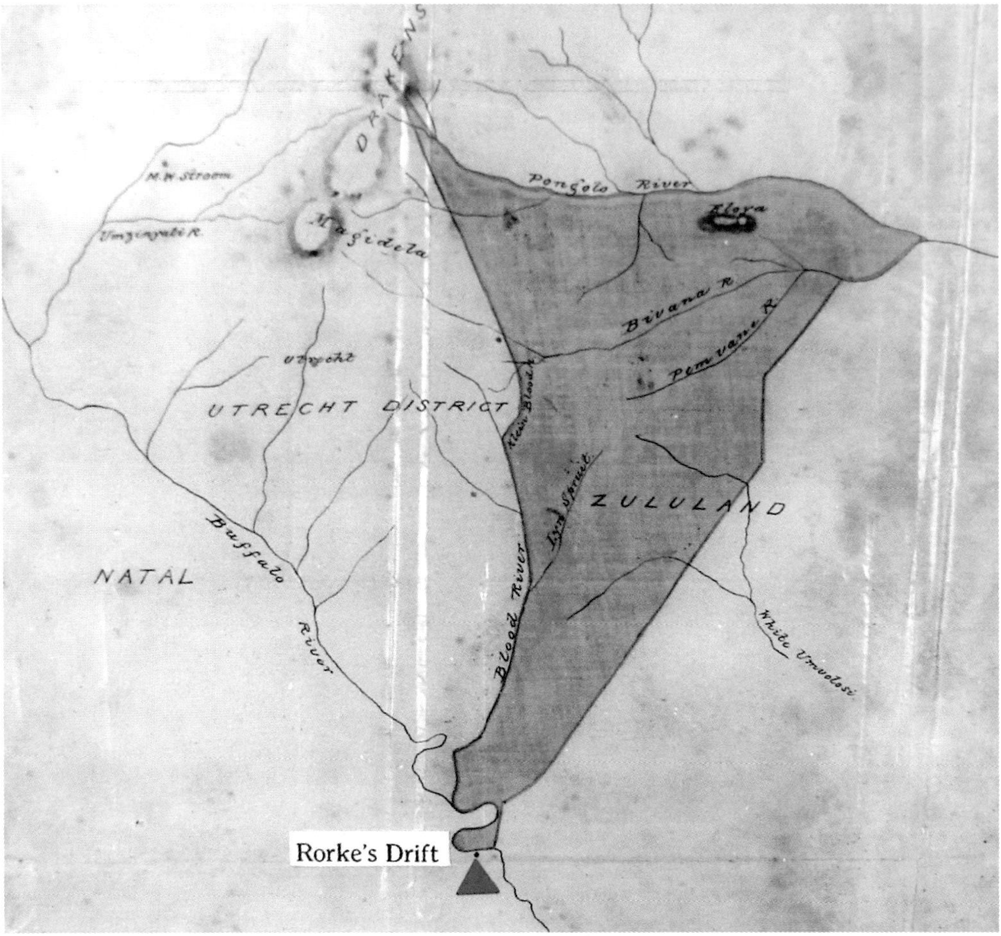

1879 sketch of 'Disputed Territory'.

Reading of the ultimatum to Zulu chiefs.

Rorke's Drift church repaired.

Buffalo River and Oskarsberg.

Rorke's Drift beneath Oskarsberg.

Lord Chelmsford.

Otto Witt.

Buffalo River and Rorke's Drift.

Zulu view of Rorke's Drift from Oskarsberg.

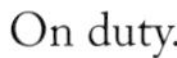

On duty.

Sihayo's homestead near Rorke's Drift.

Zulu view attacking Rorke's Drift.

Zulus attack Rorke's Drift.

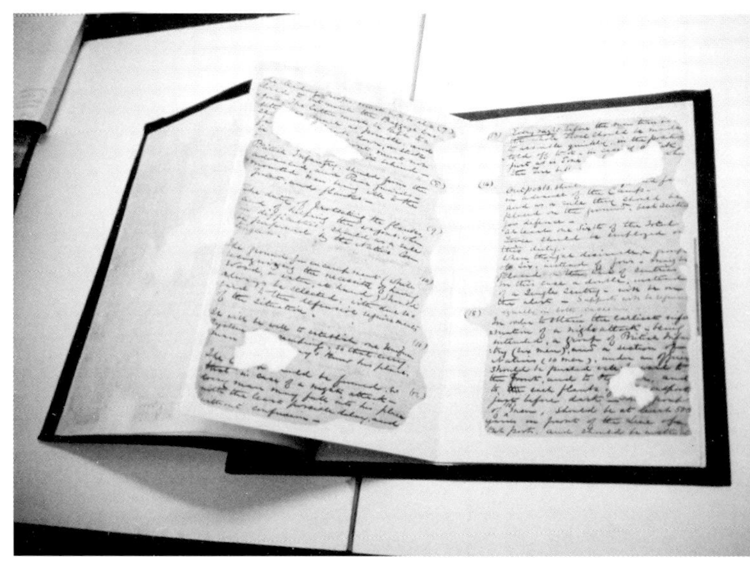

Chelmsford's orders to Durnford.

Initial British graves, post-battle.

Fugitives' Drift memorial overlooking Buffalo River.

Sergeant Cooper's grave at Fugitives' Drift.

Sergeant Cooper's medal.

Lieutenant Adendorff at Rorke's Drift, post-battle.

Fever graves at Rorke's Drift.

Sister Janet's hut at Rorke's Drift.

James Rorke's grave overlooking Rorke's Drift.

Dr Lita Webley supervising excavations at Rorke's Drift.

Tourists visit Oskarsberg post-war.

Rorke's Drift cemetery today.

Approach to Isandlwana.

Rorke's Drift river crossing into Zululand.

The hidden Ngwebeni Valley from where the Zulu army surprised the British.

Chelmsford's next proposed camp at Mangeni.

Final position of the artillery guns on the Isandlwana front line.

Isandlwana battlefield

Wyld's 1879 map of Isandlwana battlefield.

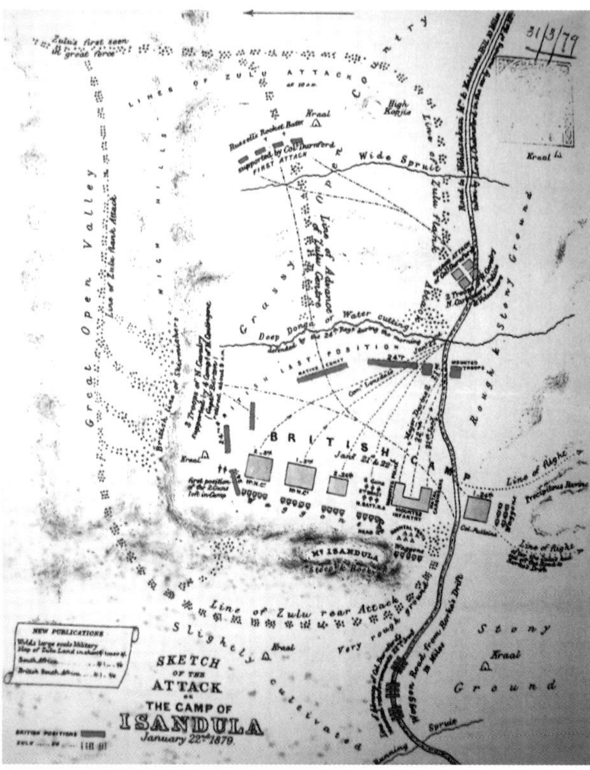

Isandlwana cairns.

Author (right) and David Rattray at Isandlwana.

Archaeologists explore Isandlwana.

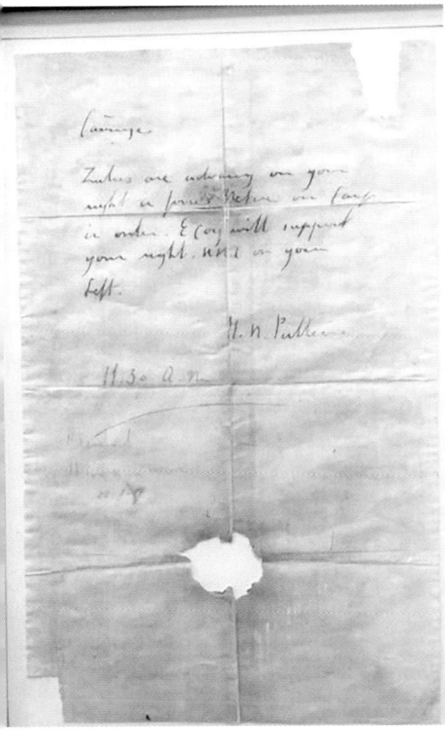

Cavaye

Zulus are advancing on your right & front. Retire on Camp in order. E Coy will support your right. NNC on your left.

H. N. Pulleine

11.30 A.M.

Battlefield orders – fake or genuine?

August Hammar in later life.

King Sekhukhune of the Pedi.

Burying the dead at Isandlwana, May 1879.

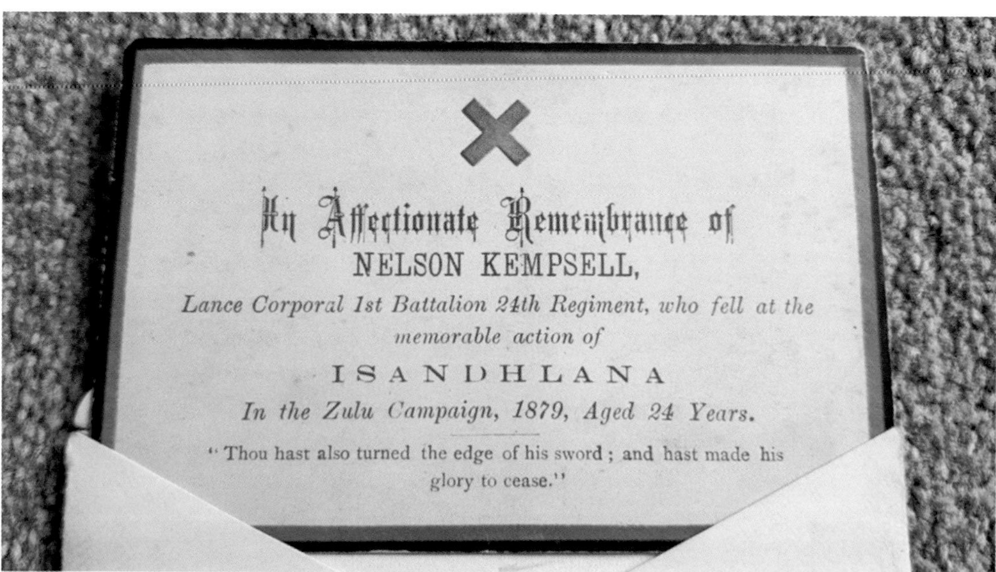

An Affectionate Remembrance of

NELSON KEMPSELL,

Lance Corporal 1st Battalion 24th Regiment, who fell at the memorable action of

ISANDHLANA

In the Zulu Campaign, 1879, Aged 24 Years.

"Thou hast also turned the edge of his sword; and hast made his glory to cease."

Typical Isandlwana memorial card.

and forced some of the defenders to retreat to other rooms. Privates Williams and Hook found themselves in the same room with the Zulus breaking down the door. Using a pickaxe, Williams knocked a hole in the far wall, while Hook, using his bayonet, kept the Zulus from entering. As the last patient was dragged through the escape hole, Hook jumped through and joined them in the next room. With Hook defending this hole, Williams again picked a hole in the far wall and knocked through into a small room occupied by Privates William and Robert Jones. They had been defending this room for some time and had managed to get most of the patients out through the window, while taking turns in preventing the Zulus from entering.

Well defended though they were, the soldiers around the perimeter were taking casualties, mostly from gunfire from the Oskarsberg. Corporal Allan was one of the sharpshooters who tried to dislodge the snipers from their rocky cover. In doing so, he exposed himself to fire over a considerable period of time, even though he was hit in the right arm by a Zulu bullet.

By this time the rest of the defenders had retreated to the new perimeter, leaving defenders and patients with thirty yards of open yard to cross under heavy fire and the threat of being stabbed by the pressing Zulus. Their colleagues laid down covering fire while both Corporal Allen and Private Hitch crossed the yard to assist in bringing back the wounded and sick. It was a miracle that so many did escape thanks in the main to the bravery and coolness of four humble privates.

Although wounded, both Hook and Robert Jones joined the rest of the Company in continuing their desperate defence. With nightfall, the fire from the hospital illuminated the dark and helped the defenders to see any approaching Zulus. Hitch was very prominent during the battle. He was stationed on the thatched roof of the hospital as a lookout and was the first to see the approaching Zulus. He was then sent to help man the weakest part of the defences, the veranda of the hospital. Although the ground sloped away quite steeply in front of the hospital, there had not been enough time to build up the barrier to more than waist height. Also, the warriors could creep up closely through the undergrowth before hurling themselves up the slope. The fixed bayonet soon proved just how effective a weapon it was in a tight defensive role. Most of the fighting here was hand-to-hand as the defenders had little time to reload as wave upon wave of Zulus charged them. Hitch recalled that one large warrior grabbed his rifle and struggled to disarm him. Managing to slip a cartridge into the breech, Hitch fired point-blank and dislodged his assailant.

The fighting had been going on for about an hour and a half and the mounting toll of casualties persuaded Chard to withdraw to the second line of defence, thus abandoning the area between the hospital and the storehouse. The Zulus could not occupy this open ground but could get to the barricades and put down deadly fire. At the most exposed part of the wall, Hitch and Bromhead fought alongside each other, while comrades fell dead or wounded. Finally Hitch, too, was hit in the shoulder, which shattered the bone. Despite this terrible wound, Hitch managed to remove his tunic and strapped his wounded arm under his waist-belt. He borrowed Bromhead's revolver and, with Bromhead's assistance in loading it, carried on firing. He was also later seen delivering ammunition to his comrades.

By being forced to withdraw to the inner defence line, Chard had effectively left the occupants of the hospital to fend for themselves. It should be remembered, however, that the events within the hospital were taking place at the same time as those related above.

The attacks became more sporadic and the last serious attempt by the Zulu to rush the barricades was about 11.00 pm by which time the opposing sides were both physically and emotionally spent.

The soldiers had been firing almost continually for at least six hours. Their hearing was dulled; their heads were pounding, their shoulders badly bruised from the notoriously heavy recoil of their Martini-Henry rifles and hands were blistered by the overheated barrels. But still they could not relax their guard one moment during the long night. A flurry of shots was fired at them around 2.00 am, which they later discovered was the time the Zulus began to withdraw and, by dawn, they had gone. The citations of the above read:

PRIVATE JOHN WILLIAMS

> 'Private John Williams was posted with private Joseph Williams and Private Horrigan, 1st Battalion 24th Regiment, in a distant room of the hospital, which they held for more than one hour, so long as they had a round of ammunition left: as communication was for the time cut off, the Zulus were enabled to advance and burst open the door; they dragged out Private Joseph Williams and two of the patients, and assagaied them. Whilst the Zulus were occupied with the slaughter of these men, a lull took place, during which Private John Williams, who, with two patients, were the only men left alive in this ward, succeeded in knocking a hole in the partition, and taking the two patients into the next ward he found Private Hook'.

John Williams lived to be the last surviving Rorke's Drift VC. He served in India during the period 1880–83 and then various Volunteer battalions until discharged. Because of the events of 22 January, his hair turned prematurely white. This appears to have been the only effect the battle had on him. When the First World War broke out, Williams volunteered for duty at the age of 57 and was taken on as Recruiting Sergeant, Brecon Barracks. Within a few weeks he had lost a son killed in action during the retreat from Mons. After the War, he was still associated with the Regiment when he was kept on the civilian staff at Brecon. When he died on 25 November 1932, he was given a lavish military funeral in keeping with such an extraordinary record of service. He was buried in St. Michael's Churchyard, Llantarnam, Wales.

PRIVATE HENRY HOOK

> 'These two men together, one man working whilst the other man fought and held the enemy at bay with his bayonet, broke through three more petitions, and were thus enabled to bring eight patients through a small window into the inner line of defence'.

Henry Hook uniquely received his Victoria Cross at the site of Rorke's Drift from Sir Garnet Wolseley. He is said to have flinched when his medal was pinned to his tunic as the medal clasp also pierced his breast. The medal fastening at that time was a rather vicious looking double prong designed so that the Queen could dispense the award with one hand while on horseback. It was not till later that a safer brooch fastening was fitted. Along with most of the surviving defenders, Hook had to endure weeks of privation and hardship as they slept rough at Helpmekaar in cold and wet conditions. This, as much as the actual battle, probably prompted him to purchase his discharge and return to London. He joined the British Museum staff and was employed as a cloakroom attendant; in 1893 he again met Wolseley when he visited the museum. Hook remained at the museum until ill health forced his retirement in 1904. He returned to his native Churcham in Gloucestershire, where he died the following year.

PRIVATE WILLIAM JONES AND PRIVATE ROBERT JONES

> 'In another ward, facing the hill, Private William Jones and Private Robert Jones defended the post to the last, until six out of the seven patients had been removed. The seventh, Sergeant Maxfield, 2nd Battalion 24th Regiment, was delirious with fever. Although they had previously dressed him, they were unable to induce him to move. When Private Robert Jones returned to endeavour to carry him away, he found him being stabbed by the Zulus as he lay on his bed'.

William Jones was invalided home suffering from chronic rheumatism, a condition that led to his discharge in 1880. He received his Victoria Cross from the Queen. Unable to find regular work, he performed in theatres, re-enacting the defence of Rorke's Drift. He even appeared with Buffalo Bill's Wild West Show when it toured Britain in the 1880's. Labouring jobs, when he could find work, followed. Poverty, however, forced him to pawn his Cross, which he was never able to redeem. By 1910, recurring nightmares of his ordeal were making him act irrationally. One night he took his small granddaughter from her bed in the belief that the Zulus were attacking and he was later found wandering the back streets of Manchester. He died confused and in great poverty. He was buried in Bradford Cemetery, Manchester, on 21 April 1913.

Robert Jones, William's comrade in the hospital, also had a tragic end. Despite receiving four wounds, he soon recovered and went back on active duty. He received his Victoria Cross at the same time as Major Bromhead. He returned to the regiment and served in India between 1880–81. After years in the Reserve, he was discharged and went to work as a labourer for Major de la Hay in Peterchurch, Herefordshire. Bouts of depression and headaches made Jones increasingly turn to drink for solace. During the summer of 1898 he suffered a fit, which was followed by a blinding headache. Borrowing his employer's gun, Jones said he going to shoot crows. A shot was heard from the garden and a maid found his body. He had apparently committed suicide to end his terrible anguish, but suicides were generally excluded from burial on consecrated ground. The authorities partially relented, and Robert Jones VC was buried in the churchyard of Peterchurch in Herefordshire, but to this day his headstone still faces away from the other graves to signify the nature of his death.

CORPORAL WILLIAM ALLEN AND PRIVATE FREDERICK HITCH

> 'It was chiefly due to the courageous conduct of these men that communication with the hospital was kept up at all. Holding together at all costs a most dangerous post, raked in reverse by the enemy's fire from the hill, they were both severely wounded, but their determined conduct enabled the patients to be withdrawn from the hospital, and when incapacitated by their wounds from fighting, they continued, as soon as their wounds had been dressed, to serve out ammunition to their comrades during the night'.

William Allen was invalided home because of his wound, which never really healed. As a consequence, he received his Victoria Cross from the Queen at Windsor Castle. He served on as a sergeant-instructor of musketry in the 4th

Volunteer Battalion of the South Wales Borderers. He died at Monnow Street, Monmouth on the 12 March 1890, aged only 46 years, from influenza.

Frederick Hitch was also sent home with Allen. His wound was severe and some thirty-nine pieces of bone had to be removed. He, too, received his Victoria Cross from the Sovereign at a ceremony held in the hospital. He was medically discharged and joined the Corps of Commissioners. In 1901, his VC was snatched off his coat and a replacement was presented to him seven years later. He later became a London cab driver and died at home during a taxi strike in 1913. At his funeral, as well as family and military representatives, an estimated 1,500 cabbies paid their respects. His medals were purchased in June 1906 by Philip Wilkins, and they are now deposited at the regimental Museum at Brecon.

SURGEON HENRY JAMES REYNOLDS, ARMY MEDICAL DEPARTMENT

This 35-year-old Irishman had served in the tropics for many years. He had come to South Africa with the 1/24th in 1877 and was experienced enough to treat some battle wounds, but not on the scale or under the conditions he was about to experience. It was about 4.30 pm that the first Zulus were seen approaching from the shoulder of the Oskarsberg Hill that loomed over the mission station to the south. As the Zulus extended to surround the defenders, the soldiers opened fire at about 500 yards and battle commenced.

The Zulus had no plan and attacked in a headlong rush, probing for a weak point. The soldiers were heartened to see how many warriors they were killing, but such was the Zulus' bravery and ferociousness, they kept coming on until they reached the barricades. It then became a primitive struggle of assegai and bayonet, knobkerrie and rifle butt. Slashing, stabbing, clubbing and firing at point blank range. The casualties were not carried to the hospital as portrayed on film, but were treated in a makeshift redoubt in front of the Storehouse by Surgeon Reynolds and his staff. When he was not tending the wounded, Reynolds delivered ammunition through the window of the hospital, which left him very exposed. In fact a bullet passed through his helmet. Dangerous and bloody though the fighting was on the perimeter, the events that unfolded in the hospital were even more dramatic.

For his conspicuous gallantry, he was gazetted on 17 June 1879 to receive the Victoria Cross. He was also mentioned in Despatches and promoted to the rank of Surgeon Major with effect from 23 January 1879. After the battle, he remained at Rorke's Drift and then joined the second invasion of Zululand. He took part in the Battle of Ulundi and on 16 July 1879 at St. Pauls in Zululand, Lord Wolseley presented him and the recently-promoted Major Chard with their Victoria Crosses. Reynolds lived a long and prosperous life until his death in 1932, a month after his eighty-eighth birthday. He was buried at Haslemere in Surrey. His Victoria Cross is held by the Royal Army Medical Corps Museum near Guildford.

PRIVATE SAMUEL WASSALL, 80th (SOUTH STAFFORDSHIRE REGIMENT)

When Lord Chelmsford left his base camp at Isandlwana to reinforce the mounted patrols he had sent out the previous day, he left behind a large widely spread camp at the base of the mountain. Private Wassall, an excellent horseman, was one of the Imperial Mounted Infantry (Carrington's Horse), who had been left in the main camp by Chelmsford. Having no particular duty, he and his fellow Mounted Infantrymen were stood down and in camp when the Zulus struck. As the right flank gave way, it became 'every man for himself'. Wassall, in shirtsleeves and without a weapon, caught a small Basuto pony and joined the ranks of those desperately trying to escape over the narrow pass to the safety of Helpmekaar via Rorke's Drift. Only a few were able to reach safety by this route before the Zulu right horn had reached this escape route and had advanced around the mountain to cut off all retreat. There was no alternative but to head off across rough country and face swimming the Buffalo River.

With the Zulus in close pursuit and due to the steep hills on either side, the escapees had little option but to follow a hazardous six-mile route that led them to a spot known today as Fugitives' Drift. All along the route, men died when the Zulus overtook and killed them, but a number of mounted men did reach the river, including Private Wassall. What he found was a river in full spate and, in normal circumstances, unthinkable to attempt to cross. With Zulus opening fire and closing fast, Wassall urged his pony into the torrent. About halfway across he heard a cry and saw Private Westwood of his regiment being swept round in a raging whirlpool. Despite the approaching Zulus, Wassall turned his mount and returned to the bank, he coolly tied his horse to a bush and waded in after Westwood. Reaching him, Wassall dragged the half-drowned man to the bank and hauled him onto his pony. Then, pursued by a hail of bullets and spears, pony and men plunged back into the river and managed to reach theNatal shore, where they scrambled up the steep sides of the gorge and staggered on to Helpmekaar. The next day, Wassall was back in the saddle and was re-posted to the Northern Column where he saw further action at Hlobane and Khambula.

Although not strictly a Rorke's Drift award, Wassall won his medal at exactly the same time and within sight of Rorke's Drift. His award was the only other Victoria Cross awarded at the time for 22 January 1879.

Wassal's action was observed by two officers and as a result of their report Wassal received his Victoria Cross at Pietermaritzburg a few weeks later; he was, at the age of 23, then the youngest recipient of the award. After he left the Army, he married, raised a family and lived out his life in Barrow-in-Furness until his death in 1927. He was the only survivor of Isandlwana to be awarded a VC.

LIEUTENANT TEIGNMOUTH MELVILL, 1/24th

LIEUTENANT NEVILLE JOSIAH COGHILL, 1/24th

There were several double acts during the Zulu War that resulted in the Victoria Cross award (as with Chard and Bromhead). Although not strictly Rorke's Drift medals, the awards to Coghill and Melvill are probably the most celebrated and were the result of actions at exactly the same time and within sight of Rorke's Drift.

As the Zulus broke through on the British right flank at Isandlwana, Melvill took the Queen's Colour and carried it out of the camp to safety. The Colour was in a black leather case at the end of the long staff, a clumsy object for a rider to handle at the best of times, especially when harried by a determined and fast-closing enemy.

Melvill left the camp on horseback in the company of Lieutenant Walter Higginson, 3rd Battalion Natal Native Contingent, and they followed the cross-country trail of the other fugitives. Contrary to popular belief, Coghill did not accompany Melvill and they descended into the Buffalo River gorge by a different route; the first time they met that day was in the swirling river.

It was unfortunate for Coghill that he was left behind at Isandlwana. He was Colonel Glyn's Orderly Officer and would have accompanied Lord Chelmsford's Column but for the effects of a previous accident. The question has subsequently been raised about Coghill's actions; as a serving officer of the 24th, should his first duty have been to remain with his regiment? Instead, he joined the disorganised every-man-for-himself rabble that headed off across country and away from the battle. Nevertheless, his bravery in returning to save his drowning brother officer is unquestioned.

The fugitives had to run a gauntlet of Zulus, who were not only chasing from behind, but also attacking from the flanks. The fugitives on foot were quickly overwhelmed, and even those on horseback who could not manage more than a cautious trot over the rocky ground were run down and killed. Somehow the three officers variously and independently managed to reach the Buffalo River, closely pressed by the Zulus. Coghill plunged into the torrent ahead of Melvill and attained the Natal bank. While pausing for breath, he looked back and saw the other two in trouble. Higginson was unhorsed and clinging to a rock in midstream. Melvill, still holding on to the Colour that had unbalanced him, was floundering in the river and being swept towards the rock sheltering Higginson. Higginson tried to help Melvill but the current was too strong. Both officers lost their grip on the rock and the Colour was lost.

Seeing their predicament and ignoring the Zulus who were firing from the far bank, Coghill turned to ride back into the river. Almost immediately, his horse was shot and killed. Despite this setback, he swam out to Melvill and Higginson and under heavy fire, all three managed to swim to the Natal bank. With Melvill exhausted and Coghill lame, Higginson set off to find some horses. Exhaustion, heavy wet clothing and Coghill's crippled leg meant they could only climb a short distance before they were caught by previously-friendly local natives and forced to make their last stand, their backs against a large rock.

Some days later, a patrol found their bodies together with a number of dead natives, evidence that Melvill and Coghill had sold their lives dearly. Their attempts to save the Colour and the manner of their deaths made them national heroes, but there was no provision in the warrant to posthumously award them the Victoria Cross. On the contrary, there was some ill feeling that resulted in a sarcastic statement by General Wolseley when he visited their graves. He merely commented that it was 'unfortunate that they had not died on the battlefield'.

On 2 May 1879 two official memoranda appeared in the London Gazette that read:

> 'On account of the gallant efforts made by Lt Melvill to save the Queen's Colour of his regiment, he would have been recommended to her Majesty for the Victoria Cross had he survived'.

Concerning Lieutenant Coghill, the item read:

> 'On account of his heroic conduct in endeavouring to save his brother Officer's life, he would have been recommended to Her Majesty for the Victoria Cross had he survived'.

It was not until the Boer War and the posthumous VC awarded to Lieutenant Frederick Roberts, the son of Field Marshal Lord Roberts, that the relatives of Melvill and Coghill lobbied for the retrospective award. It still took a direct petition by Melvill's widow to Edward VII before the awards were finally made on 15 January 1907, nearly twenty-eight years to the day of the anniversary of their sacrifice.

They were not the only Victoria Cross winners to perish at Isandlwana. Private William Griffiths 2/24th, who won his VC in the Andaman Islands in 1867, also died.

There were two nominations for Rorke's Drift Victoria Crosses which failed:

LIEUTENANT HARFORD, NNC.

He led the first attack of the war at Sihayo's Homestead. Following the success of the engagement, Harford was brought before Lord Chelmsford who had watched this junior officer's action. A decoration was mentioned by Chelmsford but, out of politeness, Harford inferred that he was 'just doing his duty', effectively talking himself out of the war's first VC. Chelmsford, in turn, respected Harford's statement. Harford regretted his comment for the remainder of his long service.

TROOPER BARKER, NNC.

Having escaped Isandlwana and negotiated crossing the river, Barker, along with two other escapees, somehow evaded the local Zulus at the river crossing. Near the top of the steep gorge Barker looked back and saw a distant figure scrambling on foot towards them. Barker left his companions and rode back down the hill to discover the struggling figure was Lieutenant W.C.R. Higginson, the Adjutant of 2/3rd NNC. Higginson intimated to Barker that he had left the horseless Lieutenants Melvill and Coghill near the bottom of the gorge with a promise that he would return with horses. With the hostile natives closing in on Melvill and Coghill, Barker insisted his officer took his horse as it was incapable of carrying them both up the steep slope. Higginson promised that he would wait for Barker at the top of the hill. Higginson dug in his spurs and rode off to safety abandoning Barker to struggle up the slope, now pursued by the same natives who had just killed Melvill and Coghill.

Meanwhile, Higginson had reached Charlie Raw and his group, who recognised Barker's horse. Certain that Barker was now dead, Higginson told them that he had found the horse down by the river. The horse was relinquished in exchange for a spare Basuto pony and Higginson rode off to the safety of Helpmekaar, where he made his report.

Suspicious of Higginson's story, Raw and his companions rode back towards the gorge crest to check for any survivors and came upon Trooper Barker running for his life. He had been pursued for about three miles, managing to fire the occasional pistol round to keep his attackers at a distance.

Within a few days the truth of Higginson's escape and his supposedly humane gesture in searching for horses for Melvill and Coghill became well known. To avoid the shame and ignominy of his action, Higginson left Helpmekaar, complete with a black eye, and quietly disappeared into obscurity.

And there it would have ended but for a visit paid on 17 December 1881 to the Natal Carbineers by the outgoing Military Commander, Sir Evelyn Wood. During his speech to the officers he mentioned:

> 'I have only now heard of a gallant act performed by a straggler, whose late arrival is well explained by his having, during the retreat, given up his horse to an officer, who was exhausted. Into this matter, it will be my pleasure to enquire more'.

Thus Trooper, now Sergeant William Barker, was recommended by Wood for the Victoria Cross. There had already been a reaction in Whitehall over the seemingly lavish dispensing of the Cross and it could not have been such a surprise for Wood to receive the following reply:

> 'Major General Sir Evelyn Wood VC
> 'Sir
> 'I am directed by the Field Marshal Commanding in Chief to acknowledge your letter of the 6th instant, and to acquaint you in reply, that statements re: Trooper Barker, Natal Carbineers, at the Battle of Isandlwana, on 22 January 1879, having carefully been considered, His Royal Highness desires me to state that, while Trooper Barker's conduct on the occasion referred to is deserving of every commendation, there does not appear to be sufficient ground, according to the terms of the statute, for recommending him for the distinction of the Victoria Cross'.

The aftermath and politics of the Anglo-Zulu war had since side-lined official sympathy for the subject, which was demonstrated by questions in parliament relating to possible pensions for next of kin for the Rorke's Drift fallen. The following is of interest:

> (*From Hansard Debate 03 April 1879 Vol 245 cc264–5*)
> 'To the Secretary of State for War from Mr R.W. Duff MP
>
> 'Whether it is true, as stated by a military correspondent of *The Times* of the 28th March, that widows of soldiers who are killed in action are not entitled to any pension from the State; and, if so, whether it is the intention of the War Department to make any provision for the widows and families of the men who lost their lives at Isandlana (*sic*) and Rorke's Drift?'

Secretary of State for War Colonel Stanley replied:

> 'Sir, in answer to the hon. Member, I have to say that the widows and children of the soldiers in question are not entitled to any provision from the State, and that I am unable to propose any regulation to the Government on their behalf. But provision has before now been made from the Patriotic Fund, and communications have been going on with the manager of that Fund, in order to see whether its provisions can be extended to those cases. I am sorry that there are some technical difficulties in the way, and that I cannot give a more positive answer at the present time'.

In December 1879 William Gladstone MP made his feelings known:

> 'In Africa we had the record of 10,000 Zulus slain for no other offence than their attempt to defend their hearths and homes, their wives and their children'.

References

1. Like Chelmsford, and many other commanders including Colonel Hassard, and. Colonel Pearson, Glyn undoubtedly suffered a breakdown following the traumatic events at the war's commencement. Glyn recovered sufficiently to take a minor role in the advance on Ulundi.
2. BPP C.2260.
3. a. *Sir Garnet Wolseley's South African Journal 1880*, Wolseley, entry for 19 March 1880. See in Professor Adrian Preston (ed.), Cape Town, 1973.
   b. *The Zulu War,* Lloyd, A., 1973: *'perhaps no action of such trifling scale and strategic insignificance was ever exulted by so many high awards'.*
4. *The Curling Letters of the Zulu War*, Clery letter 16 May 1879.
5. *A Zulu Boy's Recollections*, Webb, C., University of Natal Press, Durban 1987 for confirmation of the derision of the Zulus who failed to take Rorke's Drift.
6. *Harford.*
7. Military protocol required any recommendation to have been witnessed by the recommending officer.

All Barker's quotations are from *The Natal Carbineers 1855–1911*, Rev. J. Stalker, 1912.

Chapter 10

Rorke's Drift; Was He Really There?

You see, son, there's a lot of people who say they were at Rorke's Drift during the Zulu War. They probably were, months after the battle.[1]

Colour Sergeant George Mabin

This question produces two answers for consideration: one is based on claims made following the Anglo-Zulu War, the second is based on beliefs that important roles and events of the 1964 film *Zulu* are accurate; many are not.

In general terms, the first answer reveals problems which beset those trying to compile a definitive list of Rorke's Drift defenders. There are cases of soldiers who erroneously claimed to have been at Rorke's Drift, or stated they had been present at the Mission during the engagement. Throughout the 1930s and 1940s the pages of the *Regimental Journal* of the South Wales Borderers contain many references to such men, usually in connection with their attendance at the funeral of a former comrade. It must be remembered that the Central Column invaded Zululand from Rorke's Drift, therefore the several thousand men who comprised the column had indeed passed through that place. Furthermore, the force, mainly the 2nd Battalion the 24th Regiment that had accompanied Lord Chelmsford on his sortie from Isandlwana, then returned to Rorke's Drift to increase the garrison there on the day following the battle, 23 January 1879. After Isandlwana, most of the reinforcements to the 2/24th were also posted to Rorke's Drift on arrival in South Africa; consequently, many of the claims to have 'been at Rorke's Drift' are quite justifiable. Problems arise when the timescale of the claim is not made clear. The inference is usually that the claimant was a member of the garrison on 22/23 January 1879 and therefore took part in the defence of Rorke's Drift. Norman Holme ruefully observed:

> 'Undoubtedly a number of veterans encouraged that belief, possibly to increase their standing within the community, or with members of their family. In spite of the absence of any documentary evidence to justify their belief, such spurious claims are now firmly embedded in some families' histories'.[2]

In his seminal work on the rolls of the 24th Regiment at Isandlwana and Rorke's Drift, Holme noted that:

> 'The defenders of Rorke's Drift were comparatively few in number; furthermore the garrison mainly consisted of soldiers belonging to one Company of a particular Regiment. On the basis of these facts the accurate identification of the individual men present during the action on 22/23 January 1879 would appear to be a relatively simple task; however, such is not the case'.[3]

Despite the continuing interest in the subject and for the twenty-five years since Holme made that remark, the task has not become any easier. This chapter will consider such claimants as Reverend Otto Witt; Lieutenant Gert Adendorff NNC; Private G. Langridge 24th and Private David Jenkins 24th.

The fundamental problem that besets researchers is the incompleteness of contemporary records. The only valid sources are the rolls compiled by those who were in a position of authority at the time, and, whilst these agree the identity of the majority of those present, there are contradictions, inaccuracies and omissions and the situation is further complicated because it is impossible to arrive at a definitive conclusion on the question of who *ought* to have been there.

The earliest roll of defenders seems to have been compiled by the senior officer at the action, Lieutenant John Chard of the Royal Engineers. As early as 25 January 1879 – two days after the battle – Chard produced a report of the battle. This was published in the Natal press as early as 8 February. Chard took great pains to identify and acknowledge the role played by numerous individuals during the defence, and the report included a return listing the numbers of men from the various units present who took part. Clearly, this information could not have been arrived at without someone first drawing up a list of the individuals concerned, although no full roll was included with these first publications. Keen to trace that roll, Holme made a diligent search of various official and private archives, but the only surviving document purporting to be a full roll, and signed by Chard, could not be traced back before the 1930s. Moreover, Holme came to the conclusion that this document was most likely a copy, and was perhaps influenced by a veteran of the battle, Bombardier John Cantwell RA, whose widow presented it to the then South Wales Borderers in 1935. Holme offered the opinion that no full roll of the battle had been submitted by Chard to accompany his official report to any higher authority in the immediate aftermath of the battle.

In fact, it seems that whether the 1935 Chard roll was or was not an original document, such a roll did exist, and was compiled, at least on Chard's authority, shortly after the battle. On 1 April 1879 the *Natal Mercury* published an account of the battle by '*An Eyewitness*' (in fact the vicar of Escourt, the Reverend George Smith) which included as an addendum to Chard's report a full roll of the defenders. With very few minor amendments, this contains the same information as the Chard roll associated with Cantwell, suggesting that at the very least they had drawn on the same original document. Quite why the roll was not officially published as part of Chard's report remains unclear although, perhaps in the hurry to send the good news of the defence back to London, an abbreviated return was all that was considered necessary.

As Holme also noted, proof that a roll had been compiled at the time of the battle was further afforded by the publication in the *Natal Colonist* of 15 January 1880 of a roll of the members of the 2/24th present at the battle and signed by Lieutenant Colonel Dunbar, who was a veteran of the campaign and then commanding the 2/24th Regiment. This roll had been compiled in connection with a presentation to the defenders by the Mayor of Durban; it did, however, only list men of the 2nd Battalion and no mention was made of members of other units who were present. Even so, Holme noted that, where relevant, the information it contained was identical to that in the Chard roll. These two mentions in the Natal press confirm that a roll was in existence and was available to the senior military at the time, regardless of whether or not the surviving Chard roll is a copy.

It is unlikely Chard could have been able to complete such a roll without assistance, although, as the temporary senior officer at the Mission, it would have been his duty to approve, sign and submit the document. It was not until 19 January that Chard arrived at the Rorke's Drift river crossing, a mile from the Mission. He was in command of a small detachment of No 5 Field Company, Royal Engineers, and would have undoubtedly met with Bromhead over the next two days. Indeed, since Chard and his men had camped down by the river crossing to make repairs on the over-worked pont, it is highly probable that Chard had nothing to do with the ordinary soldiers of the garrison in the few hours prior to the battle. Any roll signed by him must, therefore, have depended heavily on those who did. It's probable that the other officers present, Lieutenant Bromhead, who commanded B Company of the 2/24th, Acting Assistant Commissary James Dalton and Surgeon James Henry Reynolds were able to provide some details of the men under their command, but the thoroughness of the roll hints at the participation of a good NCO.

The most obvious candidate in this regard is Colour Sergeant Frank Bourne, the senior NCO of B Company who knew his men well. But Holme was of the opinion that Bourne was an unlikely contributor to the Chard roll because in later years he produced a roll of his own – which is, indeed, the second of the only two contemporary rolls in existence. Holme felt that this would have been a pointless duplication of effort on his behalf, and given that in some cases he arrived at different conclusions to Chard, it might even have amounted to a contradiction of earlier work. Yet this is not necessarily the case; being asked to provide help as a young sergeant in the immediate aftermath of an engagement is not the same as attempting to provide a considered document under more mature circumstances years later. Nor was the storage and distribution of information the simple matter then that it is now; Bourne apparently did not have access to any surviving copy of the Chard roll in later life and may simply have decided to draw up a new one from scratch. In addition, the Bourne roll, which is dated 4 July 1910, was apparently compiled 'By Special Request'. By whom? Holme was unable to determine who, but that request might in itself have been sufficient to prompt Bourne to revisit the task. Among the sources used by Bourne were the Regimental pay rolls. Intriguingly, Holme noted that Bourne's original roll, while particularly credible, as might be expected with regard to the men of the 2/24th, whom he knew personally, was less comprehensive than the Chard roll.

In 1937, C.T. Atkinson published his history of *The South Wales Borderers, 24th Foot, 1689–1937*. This included a facsimile copy of the Chard roll, then in the Regimental collection. The publication of this roll seems to have prompted Bourne to return to his personal copy of his own roll, marking each of the names where he was in agreement, and adding most – but not all – of the names he had previously omitted. Thus the two authoritative rolls support one another since, as Holme put it: 'the Chard roll had finally been examined by a known and extremely well qualified authority'.

It is upon these two rolls that all attempts to decide the identities of the men present at Rorke's Drift depend. The problem is that neither is flawless, and there remain differences between them. For example, the Chard roll lists Private Charles Bromwich as being present, but Bourne replaces him with Private 1524 Joseph Bromwich whom, in the light of the pay rolls, Holme agreed was the more likely candidate. Bourne's original roll included three men (Privates W. Buck, P. Caine and T. Williams) who had served with B Company, but in fact these men had been sent to the Depot in Pietermaritzburg at the end of October 1878 and had not rejoined the company, and do not appear on the Chard roll. Private 1374 J. Williams was included on Bourne's original roll but had been imprisoned from 13 October 1878 and not released until 1 February 1879 after the battle was over. As Holme noted, individual soldier's papers were sometimes helpful in resolving these discrepancies and sometimes not. While some papers mentioned the subject's participation in Rorke's Drift, many more did not, and the absence of specific mention of the battle does not by any means suggest that the subject did not take part.

It's worth noting that both rolls have an inevitable bias towards the fixed garrison at the post. Chard's limited knowledge of the members of the garrison has already been noted, although by drawing on others he was presumably able to rectify this to some extent. Bourne would have been intimately acquainted with men of his own Regiment and quite probably acquired a basic working knowledge of the men from other units left or posted there. The garrison was by no means static, and there is at least a hypothetical chance that any men who were passing through Rorke's Drift on 22 January, and who found themselves caught up in the battle, were missed off the roll because they were not personally known to anyone in authority present, and their presence for those few hours, in darkness, was largely missed in the excitement.

Nonetheless, Rorke's Drift was merely a point on the lines of communication, and under normal circumstances any number of men might be expected to be moving forward to join the column, or returning back down the road to Helpmekaar. Lieutenant Smith-Dorrien, the column's junior transport officer, had arrived from Isandlwana shortly after dawn with orders for Durnford's column, then camped on the Zulu bank of the river, to move to Isandlwana. He had visited the Mission to chat with Bromhead before riding back to the column, arriving just before the battle began. Earlier that morning Chard had gone forward to Isandlwana with the Sappers under his command, only to return again, leaving them there, having reassured himself that his personal duties related to the pont. On hearing of the Zulu movements at Isandlwana, Major Spalding, who was in command of the line of communication, decided to ride to Helpmekaar to hurry up two companies of the 24th who had been delayed in their move forward to the drift, but left behind his clerk, Colour Sergeant Mabin. The civilian vicar of Escourt in Natal, the Reverend George Smith, was on his way forward to join the column but had got no further than Rorke's Drift. There was, in short, a steady routine flow of supply wagon traffic up and down the road that day and, for those moving along it, chance alone largely dictated whether they were present at the post when the battle unfolded.

In fairness, it appears that some of those who claimed to have been there, probably just a small minority, can now be proved conclusively not to have been there and were simply liars. In an age when news travelled infinitely more slowly than it does today, and when people travelled slower still, there was very little chance of anyone making false claims being either publicly denounced or being confronted by someone who knew better, and there must have been many old soldiers who succumbed now and then to the comparatively innocent temptation to cadge a few free drinks on the basis that '*I was at Rorke's Drift, you know*'.

While some mischievously claimed to have 'been there', others were to criminally impersonate those who were present. There were at least three cases of the impersonation of John Williams VC. The most famous was a man convicted at Tredegar Court for burglary who sought the compassion of the court claiming he was John Williams VC and received fourteen days' hard labour when his deceit was discovered. On a further occasion a man found guilty at court at Cardiff for theft also claimed to be John Williams VC and that, on conviction, he would forfeit his army pension. He was released with a caution and promptly vanished. Urged by his work colleagues to clear his name, John Williams had a statement printed in the local newspaper denying any involvement. For those who claimed to have been at Rorke's Drift, the situation was more complex.[4]

It was but mere hours after the battle that the remnants of Lord Chelmsford's command returned to the post. While Chelmsford rode on almost immediately to deal with the political and military consequences of the defeat at Isandlwana, his surviving troops were left at Rorke's Drift to provide reinforcements against the probability of further Zulu attacks. Most of these soldiers were still there several miserable weeks later, and many indeed remained there for months. They had arrived in the immediate aftermath of the battle when the ruins of the hospital building were still smoking, and when wounded Zulus still lay scattered around the post. They took part in the grim task of dispatching those wounded, burying the dead and clearing away the debris of battle, and they were condemned to sleep out night after night in the confines of what had been the defended perimeter. They would have formed intense and lasting impressions of their own experiences, and they would have become familiar with the detailed first-hand impressions from the survivors of the garrison. This was probably particularly true of the men of the 2/24th who formed the bulk of Chelmsford's command, and who were, of course, part of the same battalion as B Company. Many of them would have known the men of B Company well, and it is impossible to think that they did not hear first-hand stories of the fight. Chelmsford's men may not have been at the defence but they were indeed at Rorke's Drift immediately afterwards, and these men provided a crucial part of the story of the post's relief. Perhaps a few of them were tempted over the years to embellish their role, but more likely such stories had produced an inevitable confusion in the minds of those who heard them, and had led to the impression that the old soldiers who told them had been present at the battle itself. Today, generations later, this still leads to confusion when the descendants of those who were with Chelmsford's force still cling to the inherited impression that their ancestor had been involved in the battle itself. Yet, even if some dubious claimant had not been in the battle, his experiences were still worthy of recognition in themselves, and should not be dismissed lightly.

August Hammar (1856–1931)

Zulu portrayed the Reverend Otto Witt, (Jack Hawkins), as being present throughout the engagement accompanied by his voluptuous daughter (Ulla Jacobssan) when his real daughter, Ida aged 7 years, was far away with her mother *en route* to Durban. All was revealed when, in 2008, letters from Witt's 23-year-old young Swedish friend, August Hammar, were discovered. He had been staying with Witt at Rorke's Drift when the Zulus attacked.

Historically there is a vague reference that Otto Witt had a visitor staying with him at Rorke's Drift at the time of the Anglo-Zulu War, but no actual account or evidence of any such visitor, even by Otto Witt, was known to exist.

The story of August Hammar came to light in 1985 when Mr C. J. Fourie of the *Natal Library and Museum Service* organised an exhibition of oil paintings depicting scenes of South Africa's landscapes. The artist, August Hammar (1856–1932), was better known as an early explorer of the Victoria Falls and then as Natal's former Surveyor General. In the glossy Exhibition prospectus he described Hammar thus:

> 'He landed at Durban and made his way to the Mission at Rorke's Drift. On his way he witnessed various incidents in the progress of the Zulu war. Engravings based on two sketches he made – British forces crossing the Buffalo River and Chelmsford's forces burning Sirayo's Kraal – appeared in *The Graphic* in London. He had observed the activity of the Battle of Isandlwana at a distance of five to six miles. Returning to the mission he was cut off by a Zulu *impi* and spent the night in the hills watching the epic resistance at Rorke's Drift. Thus, Hammar on arrival in Natal was unexpectedly connected with major events in history'.

The prospectus, clearly based on Hammar's letters, was filed away by the family and there it lay, unrecognised for its historical interest. In 2008, following an after-dinner Rorke's Drift lecture given in London by the author, he was unexpectedly approached by a descendent of Hammar coincidently attending the event. As a result of this meeting, letters from Hammar at Rorke's Drift were subsequently produced, written in Swedish, by Hammar to his family in Sweden. Hammar's role at Rorke's Drift is a remarkable story.

August Hammar was born in 1856 in the small Swedish town of Lund. His father, also August Hammar, was the local parson and rector of the university town of nearby Hälsingborg, a noted seaport. Brought up in a family with a strong academic background, the young August grew up with a love of art, music and history. He studied mathematics and engineering and graduated from university in 1877 as a civil engineer. Whilst a student, he had also spent many hours viewing and noting the work of artists such as Rembrandt, Tintoretto, Van Dyke, Canaletto and Rubens – all represented in the art museum at Göteborg. Like many young graduates fresh from his studies, he knew only too well there was little suitable work in his native Sweden, and August was encouraged to seek employment abroad. He focused his attention on South Africa where Otto Witt, a family friend and the resident pastor at Rorke's Drift, lived. After discussing the matter with his father, August senior wrote a letter to the Witts stating his son was setting out for Africa.

There are numerous letters written by Hammar to his family, but the two in question relating to Otto Witt being present at Rorke's Drift are reproduced below unabridged:

[First letter] … Oskarsburg 26 December 1878. (Two weeks prior to the invasion of Zululand):

'I am staying at Oskarsburg with Otto Witt.

'… Arriving in Natal, conditions were not as described by Ohlsson, concerning the Zulus, their invasion was just a fright, a few hundred Zulus had crossed the Buffalo River in order to chase some escapees who had hidden in a kaffir Kraal, the Zulus behaved somewhat violently.

'… Otto Witt had told a story of 30,000 murderous Zulus, however, the attitudes of the Zulus and the whites are very war-like. Southern Transvaal is disputed; the part which was Transvaal, Natal and UZulu all join. The Zulus have plundered southern Transvaal.

'When I came to Durban I found the situation was very bad. The cost of sea freight had increased 14 times. Because of the long drought and therefore no grass, it would cost between 15 to 20 pounds to go to Potefstroom by post cart, carrying just a night bag. Even by an ox wagon would be beyond my means because of the presence of troops and the drought.

'… I couldn't stay in Port Natal as I had not a penny, fortunately I met the Swiss missionary Flygera with whom I conferred. After much discussion I decided to go first to Oskarsburg and then exchange letters with Mr Persson and await a suitable occasion to go to Potchefstroom.

'… By chance an ox wagon belonging to a friend of Mr Witt leaves any day now, 14 oxen hitched to a wagon. Mr Flygera presented me to the family driving on the wagon, Mr Dohne, his wife, two grown up daughters and a younger son and I got permission to follow the wagon, i.e. I would walk, but leave my luggage on the wagon. The rest of my luggage I left with a merchant known to Mr Witt.

'... Thus began my first journey in Africa, splendid and wild views, the local flora and fauna ... what troubled me most was cutting my leg under the knee while preparing the wood for the fire. I walked 270 kilometres with my stiff knee, through rain, and sleeping rough. We started at 3am to 4am, a pause at 6am, coffee was cooked which was delicious, mid-day and afternoon another pause, and after dark a cup of tea and an interesting talk, the good night. I slept under the wagon.

'... After 11 days we arrived at Dohne's farm. I met Otto Witt and he said 'greetings August'. He had received notification of my arrival. We mounted horses and immediately galloped to Oskarsberg. We made 20 kilometres in 1½ hours. As soon as we arrived Otto's youngest daughter was baptised 'Ida Wilhelmina'. I carried her to the baptism.

'P.S. New Year's Day. The situation is getting critical, all the white people have left, tonight if shots are heard Elin and the children and other women will leave by ox wagon for safety. Otto follows so then I will be alone for a few days on the station until Otto returns'.

[2nd Letter] ... Oskarsberg 6 January 1879:

'I am with the Witts.

'... British officers call today ... they want the house and store and tell Rev Witt to leave. We are very worried about events ... we have put rocks round the outside of the house. Mr Witt and I are the only people left, and he prepares to follow his family tomorrow to safety. I will care after the property.

'... many troops arrive over three days and Otto has left very angry at the damage to his house. There is no more space for tents between the house and the river, it is full of troops, artillery and horses ... and much noise. There are troop tents next to the Witt's store and the troops cook next to the house ... I get nothing from them ... Otto left me some food.

'... I sleep outside under an oilcloth as troops have smashed the Witt house doors for firewood and prepared the house and store if the Zulu attack ... British troops believe the Zulu will attack the river crossing soon ... the house is now a British hospital and will be busy if things go bad ... no sign of the Zulu army but everybody is ready.

'... Otto Witt will return when his family are safe.

'... I am well and I will write again soon'.

This second letter, especially the comment about the house and store prepared for attack, is particularly relevant and it ties in with Captain Charles Harford's diary note of 11 January, a few days later, that the Mission was already fortified.

Due to the activity on the afternoon of 22 January, Hammar would have known full well that a Zulu attack against the Mission was inevitable. As a non-combatant his presence would have been unwelcome and he wrote that he went and hid on the nearby hillside near the Oskarsberg to watch the response of the small garrison to the approaching Zulus. At some point he then moved on to the safety of a high spur of the Biggarsberg hills which gave him a clear view back to Rorke's Drift. In 2015 Dr David Payne walked the same route taken by Hammar and realised that Hammar would have had a clear view of both locations of the Zulu advance from Isandlwana and their attack against the Mission. That night Hammar began walking back to Durban looking for the Witts, but never saw them again. On arrival at Durban and being out of work, hungry and with no immediate prospect of employment, Hammar joined Baker's Horse as a trooper. His unit duly joined Colonel Redvers Buller's scouting forays and on one occasion they were accompanied by the Prince Imperial. At the war's end he took part in the Battle of Ulundi. Senior Surveyor O.G. Reitz wrote about Hammar saying that:

> 'Hammar made a painting of the spot where the prince met his death and that in due course the work was sent to the Empress Eugenie'.[5]

The present location of this valuable painting is unknown to the Hammar family. After the war Hammar was articled to a land surveyor at Verulam and was finally admitted into practice in Natal in 1881. He purchased a small farm near Rorke's Drift and combined surveying with farming.

In January 1884 Hammar completed plans for a visit to the Victoria Falls and Okavango swamps with his friend, Dr Aurel Schulz, a Natal doctor of German descent who lived near Dundee. This was to be an adventure and Hammar took basic surveying equipment while the doctor took appropriate medical supplies. The pair left Natal on foot in January 1884 and travelled north through Pretoria and Rustenburg. They reached the falls on 27 May 1884, some twenty-five years after David Livingstone, and so became among the first recorded visitors to the area. They explored the countryside along the route and Hammar made the first accurate survey of the Victoria Falls, covering nearly 3,000 miles on foot in just one year. On returning to Natal the pair wrote a detailed book of their experiences, *The New Africa* (the family copy now resides with the *AZWHS*). Illustrative engravings in the book are by Hammar, who also made numerous sketches of special views which he later painted in oils, (all in the family or museum possession).

In 1886 Hammar married the daughter of a Yorkshireman who had settled in Natal and in 1887 their first child was born followed by a second in 1889 just as the family moved to Pietermaritzburg; the family were to have two further children.

After the Anglo-Zulu War tribal strife and the formation of the new republic at Vryheid, it was deemed necessary by the government to have a systematic survey of Natal. Geodetic triangulations were undertaken by Hammar between the years 1883 and 1905. During this period, in 1890, Hammar was appointed Government Surveyor to the Colony of Natal and he continued to work in this capacity for the next twenty-five years. In 1893 he was commissioned to survey the Zululand-Transvaal border, and in 1910 he was tasked with surveying the whole length of the Natal and Zululand coast starting at Durban and moving north to St. Lucia and south to the Bashee River. It is the countryside of these locations that form the subject of his paintings. It was a time of war and great upheaval, but his work, of necessity sporadic, was of such a high standard that after 1922 all Hammar's statistics were included in the national trigonometrical survey.

In the course of his surveying in the Camperdown area of Natal, an area was named after Hammar and is today known as Hammarsdale. In 1911 he was owed money by the Natal government who had insufficient funds to pay him and, in lieu of his salary, Hammar was given a vacant farm, Lot 182. He later became an internationally recognized painter of South African landscape scenes and featured in the Durban art gallery prospectus which highlighted his presence at Rorke's Drift.

The account went unnoticed outside of the local Durban art community and remained in obscurity until the author's meeting in London in 2008. Researchers from the *AZWHS* then tracked down Hammar's descendants in Sweden. They were generously offered access to the Hammar family's folder of correspondence from Hammar which included their relatives' own translations of his letters from the original Swedish relating to his time at Rorke's Drift. In due course the *AZWHS* was invited by the family to view a selection of Hammar's famous oil paintings and were loaned copies of the original 1930 translations of Hammar's letters from Rorke's Drift to his family in Sweden. The papers included previously-unknown details of his subsequent military service with Baker's Horse and, to crown the occasion, Hammar's South Africa Campaign medal for his service during the Anglo-Zulu War was produced. Time was then spent verifying the papers and medal; all passed muster. Hammar died in Empangeni Hospital on 16 October 1931. Today his works of art are much sought after and any 'Hammar' coming under the auctioneer's hammer will cost dearly.

Pastor Peter Otto Holgar Witt (1840–1923)

Since the end of the Anglo-Zulu War of 1879, much has been written about the role of the Swedish Missionary, Otto Witt, the incumbent at Rorke's Drift Mission sponsored by Swedish religious charities. At the time of the Zulu attack on 22 January 1879 this previously unknown Swedish missionary, who was represented in *Zulu* by Jack Hawkins, was thereafter thought to have been present throughout the battle. Research has left Witt's credibility rudely exposed. Contemporary accounts unanimously support the belief that Witt was a scoundrel who typically had made up a fanciful account of Rorke's Drift while *en route* to London, having neither seen what he claimed nor been present when the Zulus attacked his Mission. It is probable that Witt's motive behind his illusory account was to gain fame for a series of profitable lectures during his stay in England, and to extract excessive compensation (£600) from the British government for damage to his two buildings.

Until the discovery of the Hammar documents, Witt's personal history was sketchy except for the vital period surrounding 22 January 1879; less well known is how his contemporaries and historians viewed him. The 1936 translations of August Hammar's illuminating letters from Rorke's Drift counter the curious chronology of Witt's account of the battle given to *The Illustrated London News.* Other unabridged accounts strongly challenge Witt's truthfulness and integrity.

For example, *The Times* (Natal). Their reporter wrote '*A short visit to Rorke's Drift*' for the 23 April 1879 edition:

> 'I took with me the description given by that first class impostor and romancer Mr. De Witt to the home papers. He states that the distance between the two places is three miles, and that he could see the place where the camp was pitched, and that he saw the battle and heard the firing from the rifles. The fact that from the highest point of the Ascarberg to Isandhlwana is in a bee line not less than seven miles, that no part of the camping ground is visible, and that he could not have seen the firing, all for the reasons that the hill and ridge hide the camp and battle field. As for his having heard musketry fire at that distance; well, all I can say is, it speaks for the length of his ears. I fancy he will get a very hearty reception should he ever return to the colony'.

Canon Lummis M.C. who wrote the most insightful biography of Padre George Smith, *Padre George Smith of Rorke's Drift*, referred to Witt as follow:

> 'We may consider the picture of him (in the film *Zulu*) as a dipsomaniac unrealistic; but he was certainly no hero. In fact he reached Durban

> eventually and gave a very untruthful and garbled account to English newspapers. He was most unpopular in Zululand. Cetewayo had forbidden him entrance into his territory. With the colonists in Natal he was even more unpopular'.

Donald Morris wrote of Witt in *The Washing of the Spears*:

> 'His wife and three children had left several days earlier in a wagon with a single native retainer to make their way to friends in Durban, and they were, he knew, at the Umsinga Mission. In his excited imagination, nothing stood between them and a bloodthirsty Zulu impi but the Buffalo River and a few miles of open country. Abandoning the last claim to his homestead on the spot, he turned and fled up the track to Helpmekaar to find his family'.

He also added that Witt was never popular in Natal. To be fair to Morris, when writing this he knew nothing of the Hammar letters and naturally relied on a cross-selection of accounts, including Witt's, when putting his synopsis together.

Dr Frank Emery, the Oxford University lecturer and author of *The Red Soldier* wrote of Witt:

> 'The Victorians ...were exploited by Otto Witt, the missionary whose home at Rorke's Drift was the scene of the battle there on 22 January, and who brazenly lectured through England with a false tale of his own experiences'.

The noted South African historian Sonia Clarke confirmed Witt's earlier departure from Rorke's Drift in her *Zululand at War 1879*, adding that Witt enjoyed a short spell of popularity in England claiming to have been present at Isandlwana and Rorke's Drift, but his fraudulent tales were soon dismissed.

In order to try and evaluate what Witt claimed, here is Witt's *The Illustrated London News* and UK press account verbatim, courtesy of the *AZWHS,* together with this author's interpretation of Witt's account. Where there is ambiguity the account refers to these in numerals (1*-18* in brackets) so that the reader can consider material that challenges or counters Witt. Thus, readers can draw their own conclusions as to the veracity of Witt's account, and even ponder how he could have observed the battle at Isandlwana and/or his public claim to have been present at Rorke's Drift when the Zulus attacked.

Witt's *The Illustrated London News* 8 March 1879 (as widely reported in the British press and unabridged):

'It was on January 22 1879. Bright and warm rose the sun over my station, Oskarsburg (1*) situated at the Buffalo River, on the Natal side. At the farm is a drift into the Zulu country, known by the name of Rorke's Drift. Ten minutes' walk from the drift where my houses, two large buildings, situate at the border of the Zulus' country, and at the very place where the greatest resistance from the Zulus was expected. Those buildings were found very fit indeed for military purposes, and at the request of the general commanding the forces I left them at his disposal. A large outhouse, eighty foot by twenty foot, which I used as a church, was turned into a commissariat store, and my dwelling house, sixty foot by eighteen foot was made an hospital, in consequence of which I had to send away my wife and three children. I myself stayed and acted as interpreter between the doctor in charge and the black people. Before the above mentioned day all was quiet, waggons arriving constantly augmenting the store of provisions, and the only variation in this monotony was the reports of skirmishes taking place on this side of the river (2*) – but heavy storm is often preceded by sudden calm.

'The 22 came and witnessed the battle, in which the warriors on both sides showed, or perhaps were compelled to show, a courage that can be denied neither by contemporaries nor by posterity. Behold on the one side one thousand soldiers reinforced by equal their number by black ones, leaving their camp to attack an army more than ten times their number! Behold, on the other side this mass of Zulus, who, close together, walk straight against the mouth of the cannon!(3*) Look how thousands after thousands are killed, and nevertheless the mass prevails, without fear, over the dead bodies of their comrades against the destroying weapon! Behold on the other side a few dozen white troops, the only remainder of the thousand: look how they, after having shot away all their ammunition, keep close together, trying yet awhile, to fight for their lives with the bayonet. Behold, on the other side – the black ones – how they are fighting against the intruder and oppressor, fighting for liberty and independence, coming close to the bayonets and making them harmless by taking the corpses of their brethren and throwing them on them! Who wins your warmest sympathy – the captain, who, knowing that he is lost, stops a moment to spike the cannon and die (4*); or the Zulu, who, in his excitement, leaves his fellow soldiers behind, and alone makes the attack on the hospital at Rorke's Drift, resting his gun on the very barricade, and firing on those inside? (5*) Is your admiration greater for those ninety five who entered the commissariat store at Oskarsburg and defended it against five thousand Zulus than for those five thousand who fought outside the whole night, trying to overpower the whites, and who withdrew at daybreak, leaving one thousand dead, hundreds of whom were lying even on the very veranda of the house? (6*) Indeed, your admiration ought to be as great for the one as for the other. Where did you find greater courage or contempt of death than theirs?

'Dr Reynolds and myself had in the morning made up our minds to pay a visit to a missionary in the neighbourhood. (7*) When about to start at noon we were told that a great fight was taking place over the river. In company with the chaplain of the forces (8*) we ascended a hill 500 feet high, between the station and the river, from which we had an excellent view of what was going on. At a distance of three miles (9*) as the crow flies, we saw the place where the camp was made. The whole spot was filled with black figures swarming about. Down below us, though very hilly and broken, there was a large flat between us and the camp, and on this line we saw three lines drawn, the one end reaching the camp and the other the river. The whole of it was a shocking sight. The heavy firing from the rifles mixed with the rolling sound of the big guns and the movements of the lines, all this caused a nervous feeling that something terrifying was going on.

'My position was on a hill on the other side of the river from where the fight was raging. I watched the Zulus descend and draw themselves in long lines between the camp and the river. From where I stood I could also see the English forces advancing to the attack; (10*) but I could not see any hand-to-hand fighting. I observed that the Zulus were fighting heavily, and presently I saw that the English were surrounded in a Kraal some little distance from the camp. (11*) What I was wroth to learn was the reason why the British troops left their camp to attack, instead of remaining on the defensive. In my opinion, they should never have thus advanced. As the fight progressed, and I saw that the English were being beaten, I prepared to fly, and had my horse saddled with that object in view. At length I noticed that the Zulus were crossing the river. It was not very deep. The water only reached up to their waists as they forded the stream. I saw that there was no time to be lost, and I dashed away on horseback as hard as I could go, chased by the Zulus, who did their best to catch me, but failed. (12*) So far as I have been able I have described the fighting which took place correctly. I could just discern that the Zulus were hurling the bodies of their comrades upon the bayonets of the English as they fought and endeavoured to defend themselves in the kraal, but that was all. The distance I stood from the fight prevented my observing events more closely.

'What struck us in the beginning was that a good many of the officers of the native contingent had one by one crossed the river some miles below the Mission, and came galloping towards it as fast as the horses could carry them; and, on the left hand side, we noticed some of the mounted natives crossing at the drift, and driving some cattle before them. (13*) Although we could not clearly comprehend this movement, we did not pay much attention to it, our minds being far from dreaming of the real facts. In the meantime the three lines had drawn themselves more close together to one spot. Here was a large kaffir kraal, which was gradually surrounded and fired at. How many men had entered it I do not know, and shall probably never learn, because what was inside there was certainly killed by Zulu bullets. After twenty minutes heavy firing the resistance ceased, and the attacking ones divided themselves again. Half of them returned towards the camp, the other half, from 5000 to 6000, approaching the river, and the place where I was. Firing every now and then, they reached at last the river. There another skirmish took place. The spot where they crossed was half a mile below the drift, and defended by a few Natal kaffirs. A tolerably good force could easily have prevented their crossing. Having killed these few Natal kaffirs, they crossed one by one. (14*) This done, they sat down for half an hour in order to get some rest, and to strengthen themselves from the snuff box. Then they separated again, divided into two parties, the one following the course of the river, the other taking its way towards us. We now perceived that the house of a neighbouring farm on the Natal side was on fire; but we were so far from fancying that the Zulus would cross the river that we never had the slightest idea of the real state of things, but were still thinking that the approaching black people were our own troops. They now were so close to us that their bullets could easily have reached us, and we saw that they were all naked. Reality, then, also stood naked for us. The thick mass that swarmed in the camp was the Zulus who had taken possession of it. The light lines firing at the kraal were Zulus, and, finally, those who had crossed the river and were approaching were Zulus. The few whites whom we had seen galloping now and then to the Natal side, perhaps, were the only surviving of all those who a week before had entered the Zulu country. Our eyes were opened, but why had they not been before? How had the idea of the possibility of a disaster on our side been so far from us that the clearest facts had been unable to make it enter our minds? The officers' flight, the burning farm, the immense masses (say 20,000) moving to and fro in light lines, why had not this long ago told us that the Lord's thoughts are not our thoughts nor our ways his? These ideas were crossing my mind while we speedily descended the hill, followed by the Zulus.

'Arrived at the houses, we saw at once a new proof of the sad truth to which our eyes had just been opened. The tents which surrounded the house, (15*) and were used by a company left there under Major Spalding for the protection of the hospital and the commissariat stores, had been pulled down and a temporary barricade of meal sacks was made between the houses, which were a distance of twenty yards from one another. Here we were met by anxious questions from many lips, "do the Zulus come here?" – and compelled to answer "in five minutes they will be here".

'In the same moment the fighting began in the neighbourhood. Though wishing to take part in the defence of my own house, and at the same time in the defence of an important place for the whole colony, yet my thoughts went to my wife and to my children, who were at a short distance from there, and did not know anything of what was going on. Having seen one part of the Zulus going in that direction I followed the desire of my heart, saddled my horse, and started to warn my family. But my poor family had much to suffer before, in five days' journey to Maritzburg, chased by the Zulus, (16*) and frightened by all sorts of reports. I will pass over this as of no interest to other people. The attack on Oskarsburg had been awful.

'Before I started I saw a Zulu alone at the barricade, kneeling and firing. (17*) The whole force drew nearer, and the battle drew on heavier. Soon the hospital was on fire. Our people found it impossible to defend themselves inside the barricade. They must retire within the walls, thus entering the commissariat store. The six people were brought here, except five who could not be removed, and who were stabbed by the Zulus and burnt.[18] That the hospital was set on fire was certainly a great personal loss for me, as all my property was burnt; but it was of great importance for the whole colony, and especially for the people in the commissariat stores, as the flames of the burning house enabled them to aim properly on the Zulus and thus keep them at a fair distance. If the Zulus had known what they ought they should never have put fire to the house, and the heavy darkness of that dreadful night would have made our troops unable to defend themselves as they did'.

The following are inconsistencies;

1*. Witt mis-spells Oskarsberg.
2*. This is not mentioned elsewhere.
3*. Not visible from the Oskarsberg.

4*. The guns were not spiked.
5*. By Witt's own admission he had departed Rorke's Drift before the Zulus arrived.
6*. Ditto.
7*. Witt is not mentioned by Doctor Reynolds.
8*. Witt is not mentioned by Reverend Smith.
9*. Isandlwana from the summit of the Oskarsberg is just over eight miles according to the 1:500,000 S. Africa survey.
10*. Not visible from the Oskarsberg.
11*. Not mentioned elsewhere and no known action took place in an unidentified kraal.
12*. At best, a figment of his imagination, and the river was in full flood.
13*. Unlikely that fleeing riders would drive cattle before them. While still at Rorke's Drift, Witt would have regularly seen riders from routine patrols bringing back captured Zulu cattle which were then sold to the military quartermasters.

This unknown action appears to be Witt's previously mentioned, and unidentified, Zulu kraal. See[11] above.

14*. Raw's men collected themselves on the Natal bank at Fugitives' Drift and gave other fleeing survivors covering fire as they tried to cross the river – but none was killed by the Zulus. Witt could have subsequently heard of this from one of these survivors who, like Witt, made their way back into Natal.
15*. It is well documented that B Company's tents were all together some sixty yards to the east of Witt's house.
16*. They were not chased by any Zulus.
17*. Not mentioned by anyone else.
18*. This was only clarified the following morning.

As most historians and authors have readily identified, Witt's account is false and unreliable, as confirmed by the two Hammar letters. Curiously Witt did not mention Hammar in this or any of his accounts.

By the time the British physically took over the Mission, Witt had already left Rorke's Drift leaving Hammar behind to protect his interests. Hammar tells us that Witt had been ordered to leave by the British, so why would Witt have remained, especially if he was worried about his family? The in-coming British troops knew the Mission was Swedish and found it being looked after by a Swede who spoke no English, and the English spoke no Swedish. The hypothesis has to be that the British naturally presumed Hammar was Witt and, if so, it was certainly Hammar, not Witt, who went to the summit of the Oskarsberg. After all, Hammar's estimate of seeing the battle five to six miles away is reasonably accurate. Hammar's account rings true as he had no motive for giving a false account and, indeed, never promoted his connection with Rorke's Drift. Furthermore, the Oskarsberg was the most likely spot for him to have witnessed fighting at both Isandlwana and Rorke's Drift as mentioned in his letters home.

Finally, if Witt had seen what he claimed, why did he not tell the truth? After all, the facts were far more exciting and punchy than the garbled version he promulgated, all of which Witt could have gleaned from genuine accounts while on his journey back to Durban.

So, until it can be proved otherwise, I believe that the recently arrived British at Rorke's Drift believed Hammar was Witt; this is understandable as neither Hammar nor the British had previously met each other and neither spoke the other's language, and Witt was long gone before the Zulus reached the Mission.

Otto Witt might have had the last laugh. Following hostilities, he returned to rebuild the Rorke's Drift Mission before he retired home to Sweden in 1891. Meanwhile, on 4 February 1884, Witt received notification from the Acting Assistant Colonial Secretary that his application for damages from the British Government had finally been settled in his favour. Witt replied as follows:

> 'Sir,
>
> 'I beg to inform you that I am in receipt of your letter of 4 Feb. stating that the Lord Commissioners of Her Majesty's Treasury have been pleased to sanction the payment of the sum of £450 on account of the damage done during the Zulu War to the Swedish Mission House at Rorke's Drift, and the sum of £200 to me personally.
>
> 'Further I beg to state that I will accept the above named amount viz £450 and £200 in full satisfaction of all demands in connection with these claims, as well from the side of the Mission Society as from my own side.
>
> 'Please be good enough to inform me what I have to do in order to get possession of the money.
>
> 'Otto Witt'.

The letter is to be found in the *KwaZulu Natal Archives*. Whether the money was ever paid has never been ascertained.

There is no mention in the Hammar family documents that Witt and Hammar ever met again or that Hammar ever returned to Rorke's Drift, although he later owned a small farm just twenty miles away. Hammar's travelling companion to the Victoria Falls, Dr Schulz, joined a local Durban defence force during the Anglo-Zulu war. He volunteered as a doctor to accompany Chelmsford's re-invasion force and took part in the Battle for Ulundi for which he received the South Africa Campaign medal. This medal is in the collection of the *AZWHS*.

Lieutenant Adendorff – Natal Native Contingent

Adendorff was unknown to history before the release of *Zulu*, which portrayed him in a role which posed researchers with the problem of matching reality with fiction. Of all the participants at Rorke's Drift, it is Lieutenant Adendorff and his activities that have proved the most difficult to unravel. Adendorff brought news to the garrison of the defeat earlier that day, but whether he stayed on and participated in the defence of Rorke's Drift is still open to debate. If he did remain, why has he gone unrecognised? After all, he would have had the distinction of being the only combatant on the British side to be present at both Isandlwana and Rorke's Drift. Yet the evidence that he did stay is elusive, and as such an air of uncertainty continues to hang round his name as if he 'let the side down', in a way that other survivors of Isandlwana somehow did not. It is significant to this author that Adendorff never claimed to have 'been there'. Rorke's Drift is further complicated because it was fought by men, many of whom did not know each other, it was conducted at night, in darkness and under traumatic conditions. With deaths, injuries, gunfire and violent Zulu attacks unfurling by the minute, the syndrome of false memory would have found many survivors' minds desperate and receptive for any explanation, making it understandable that memories of that night got exaggerated.

Any attempt to rehabilitate Adendorff is further hampered by the fact that very little is known about him. Even his name is in some doubt – he appears variously as Adendorf - one 'f' - and Adendorff - two 'f's – and his initial is variously given as 'J' and 'T', though the former somehow seems more likely ('T' could in any case be a misprint for 'J' – though the reverse could equally be true.). There is nothing unusual about Adendorff's minor role in the war; most of the volunteers and irregulars who served with the Imperial forces in Zululand were shadowy figures from varied nationalities. They rarely merited any mention in official records and then they returned to obscurity.[6] This is particularly true of the officers and NCOs of the NMP and NNC, with whom Adendorff served, and whose records are notoriously incomplete or lost.

There are two basic charges against Adendorff, which, however dressed up, amount to an accusation of cowardice. Since Chard was adamant that Adendorff appeared on the Zulu bank of Rorke's Drift while he, Chard, was still at his tent by the ponts, it is firstly argued that Adendorff must have left the camp at

Isandlwana rather earlier than he should because the Zulu right horn, sweeping down the Manzimyama valley behind Isandlwana, had cut the road to Rorke's Drift long before the majority of the survivors got away. That being the case, those who did manage to escape did so by means of a hair-raising ride across country, swimming the Mzinyathi (Buffalo) several miles downstream from Rorke's Drift at a rocky crossing known as Sothondose's Drift, subsequently known as Fugitives' Drift. Secondly, it is argued that, since there are no references to Adendorff staying at Rorke's Drift, other than his name appearing on the dubious 'Chard Roll', and since all the other fugitives from Isandlwana fled, Adendorff must have done the same.

Quite why Adendorff should be singled out for such disapproval is not explained. No one suggests that there was anything shameful in the conduct of, say, Captains Gardner and Essex, or Lieutenants Curling, Cochrane and Smith-Dorrien, all of whom thought it wiser to head straight for Helpmekaar rather than Rorke's Drift. This despite the fact that these officers were all professional soldiers, while Adendorff, as a Lieutenant in the NNC, was a civilian volunteer. Indeed, given that the survivors from Isandlwana were all exhausted, shocked – even traumatised – and in some cases almost hysterical, it seems absurd that anyone would have thought badly of them for avoiding another fight (which under the circumstances must have seemed pretty hopeless).

Chard was initially sceptical of Adendorff's movements, but was clearly convinced by his explanations. This is only likely to have been the case if Adendorff were able to supply sufficient details of the fighting at Isandlwana to make his story credible. Moreover, Chard fixed the time of Adendorff's arrival at the Drift mid-afternoon, which is consistent with him having left Isandlwana at midday, when the British front line collapsed. In his official report, Chard said simply but emphatically 'I was informed ...[by] Lieutenant Adendorff of Lonsdale's regiment (who later remained to assist in the defence), of the disaster at Isandlwana camp.' In his later, longer account, written at Queen Victoria's request, he expanded on this point:

> 'My attention was called to two horsemen galloping towards us from the direction of Isandlwana. From their gesticulations and their shouts, when they were near enough to be heard, we saw that something was the matter, and on taking them over the river, one of them, Lieutenant Adendorff of Lonsdale's Regiment, Natal Native Contingent, asking if I was an officer, jumped off his horse, took me on one side, and told me the camp was in the hands of the Zulus and the army destroyed; that scarcely a man had got away to tell the tell, and that probably Lord Chelmsford and the rest of the column had shared the same fate. His companion, a Carbineer,

confirmed his story – He was naturally very excited and I am afraid I did not, at first, quite believe him, and intimated that he probably had not remained to see what did occur. I had the saddle put on my horse, and while I was talking to Lieutenant Adendorff, a messenger arrived from Lieutenant Bromhead, who was with his Company at his little camp near the Commissariat Stores, to ask me to come up at once'.

This last comment is significant because, of course, Bromhead had already received a written warning note delivered by a native horseman of the Edendale Contingent, from Captain Essex, who had witnessed Isandlwana. Chard was less confident about Adendorff's role when he presented his second report:

'As far as I know, but one of the fugitives remained with us – Lieutenant Adendorff, whom I have before mentioned. He remained to assist in the defence, and from a loophole in the store building, flanking the wall and Hospital, his rifle did good service'.

The mystery of Chard's misidentification is solved in the 'Chard report' of the Rorke's Drift survivors – presented to Queen Victoria. Corporal Francis Attwood of the Army Service Corp was one of five soldiers who received the Distinguished Service Medal for bravery at Rorke's Drift. In Chard's report of the defenders, Attwood's name is missing whereas Adendorff is named. In his report, Chard describes certain actions of Adendorff but these were well known by those present to have been performed by Attwood. It was an understandable mistake by Chard; the fighting was in darkness and he was among people he didn't know. For the actions believed by Chard to have been performed by Adendorff, Corporal Attwood was awarded the DCM at Pietermaritzburg on 15 November 1879. By then, Adendorff had disappeared into obscurity, although weeks later news reached the garrison at Rorke's Drift that Adendorff had been arrested at Pietermaritzburg for desertion. He was due to face a court-martial but there is no evidence this ever took place. Chard's report that Adendorff had 'stayed to fight' had already been submitted to higher authority and had the trial taken place, Chard would certainly have been called to give evidence, against his own report – and so the matter of Adendorff's court-martial appears to have been quietly dropped.

The Adendorff mystery has evoked much attention amongst writers, with most accepting the Chard report's comment that Adendorff was present without recourse to evidence. Moreover, it is curious that such a controversy even exists to revolve around an unassuming volunteer junior colonial officer of the NNC who for the most part did not influence events nor contribute significantly to any extent and certainly played a very minor role during the Zulu War. Somehow, he has been picked out by historians for special consideration from among the fugitives fleeing the battlefield at Isandlwana, notwithstanding the fact that a number of regular army officers fled too and contributed very little else after crossing into Natal. His treatment has been unfair, especially in light of the fact that the conduct of those other officers has not been shown much attention except for the disdain shown by Chelmsford and Wolseley who felt that they should have stayed with their men since it was their duty to do so. Adendorff did make his way to Rorke's Drift and with others, raised the alarm. For this he must be given some credit. A few days later Adendorff gave up military service when the 3rd NNC was disbanded on account of their poor performance on 22 January when they collectively deserted both at Isandlwana and Rorke's Drift. Due to the lingering debate on the officer's conduct on the subject, the question still remains: did Adendorff stay or leave?

Donald Morris wrote in his classic *The Washing of the Spears* that, after reporting the Zulu approach to Rorke's Drift, both (Vaine and Adendorff) rode on to Helpmekaar and in doing so deserted and had not been part of the action at Rorke's Drift. Morris comments:

> My suspicion that Adendorff did not stay to aid the defence is based on analysis of all the sources listed for both battles. Space precludes a review of the evidence, which I hope to publish separately.

Morris never published that evidence, but what might he have published? He personally knew the Zulu war historian George Chadwick (1923–2000), who spent many years working for the *Natal National Monuments Council* and was on the Board of Trustees of the *Voortrekker Museum,* but his main interest was Rorke's Drift and Isandlwana. Without doubt, Chadwick was the undisputed leader in this field and nobody could rival his breadth of knowledge gained over many years 'on the ground'. Chadwick's '*Visitors' Guide to Rorke's Drift*' makes an intriguing comment about Adendorff's short visit at Rorke's Drift during the afternoon of 22 January:

> 'Although firing could be heard and a black mass moved across the Col (*sic*) at Isandlwana no definite news was received until Lieutenants Vaine and Adendorff arrived at 1400 hrs. They gave the news to Chard, rode off to inform Bromhead and left for Helpmekaar. Chard rode up to the station to find that Bromhead had received the news in a note from Captain Essex. He had already struck the tents and moved two wagons near to the hospital with the intention of moving the sick to Helpmekaar'.

Adendorff could have done what many of the NNC did, briefly report to Helpmekaar but on hearing it was saved, rush back to Rorke's Drift.

Roy Dutton produced in his '*Forgotten Heroes*' an in-depth Anglo-Zulu War medal research publication, first published in 2010, which details the register of Isandlwana fugitives who arrived at Helpmekaar on the night of 22/23 January. On page 449 under the sub heading 'NNC' is the name 'Lieutenant Adendorff', which indicates Adendorff did not remain at Rorke's Drift. The NNC at Rorke's Drift, along with the few surviving NNC from Isandlwana, fled to Helpmekaar on hearing of the defeat at Isandlwana. This register records that Adendorff reported to Helpmekaar. On hearing that Rorke's Drift had held, and possibly to undo his desertion, he then rode back to Rorke's Drift where he was later sketched by Lieutenant Harford presiding over the disbandment of the NNC due to their unreliability.

Lee Stevenson in his '*By Those Who Were There*' (see p. 210) confirms the gist of this account. He states that many of the fleeing NNC from Isandlwana and Rorke's Drift then hid up overnight, only to slip back to Rorke's Drift at dawn and to pretend their bravery. It is totally probable that, having initially made his presence known to Chard, Adendorff then rode off and reported at Helpmekaar, where his arrival was logged. It would then have been easy for him to re-join the NNC hiding in the surrounding hills to slip back under the cover of darkness amidst the post-battle confusion and storytelling to report to his senior, Lieutenant Harford.

Professor Paul Thompson's '*The NNC in the Anglo Zulu War*' is the only published history of the NNC. Thompson conclusively states in the chapter covering Rorke's Drift:

> 'Besides the Company commander, Captain Stephenson, only three corporals appear to have been with the company. No lieutenants and sergeants are mentioned in reports …[and]
>
> 'There was only one man of the Contingent involved in the battle at Rorke's Drift mission station. He was of the iziGqoza. He had been shot in the thigh in the Batshe fight'.

'*The Red Soldier*' by Professor Frank Emery of Oxford University makes no mention of Adendorff being part of the defence at Rorke's Drift; further, Adendorff is not recorded in the book's comprehensive index.

In '*Rorke's Drift – By Those Who Were There*' Lee Stevenson quotes from a letter which refers to Adendorff:

> 'On his arrival at PMB, he (Higginson) and two others of the 3rd NNC who got out of the fight, Lieutenants Vaine and Adendorff, were placed under arrest and ordered back to RD'.

Vaine might have been arrested because his name was not among the forty-eight known survivors from Isandlwana whose arrival was recorded at Helpmekaar. If Adendorff had stayed at Rorke's Drift, then it is time he was rehabilitated and his courageous ride from Isandlwana to Rorke's Drift should be more widely accepted. To have endured the horror of Isandlwana and voluntarily stayed to risk a repetition again at Rorke's Drift, when he might in all conscience have ridden off with the other survivors, shows remarkable strength of character.

Until evidence can be found that he stayed to fight, then Adendorff cannot be remembered as one of the heroes of Rorke's Drift. Chard's comment '*as far as I know Adendorff remained at Rorke's Drift for the defence*' is still the only known reference to him being at Rorke's Drift during the engagement. He was a non-English speaking Boer and this could have precluded him from ever being interviewed by the press, neither is there any record that he spoke of or claimed any 'involvement' at Rorke's Drift.

Private George Thomas Langridge, 2/24th

Private D. Jenkins, 1/24th

The false Rorke's Drift claimant Pte George Thomas Langridge of 24th Regiment is a different matter. Following the war he returned to Sevenoaks in Kent and claimed to have been 'a Rorke's Drift defendant'. He deceived his family and friends for the rest of his life and on his death, according to his local newspaper *The Sevenoaks Chronical* dated 14 March 1924, the South Wales Borderers headquarters also accepted his story and provided a 21-gun salute at his funeral. His case is typical; there were numerous claims by the man himself, but no supporting primary evidence. Today he is officially regarded as yet another Rorke's Drift faker.

'Faking it' went right through the ranks. Whilst his time in Zululand is well documented, Commandant Hamilton-Browne's personal account of his entire career in New Zealand seems to have been appropriated from other men's experiences. Ever the 'rough diamond', he was refused the South Africa Campaign medal for his mass murder of surviving Zulus at Rorke's Drift and, undaunted, had one of his soldier's medals re-engraved with his own name. This medal is part of the Hamilton-Browne medal group owned by a private collector.

In the same vein, an interesting scenario arose during 2012 concerning Private D. Jenkins, G Company, 1/24th following a re-dedication of his grave by family relatives as a 'Rorke's Drift defender'. There is a Private David Jenkins of G Company who wrote a letter home in which he specifically states he survived the Battle of Isandlwana. He wrote of '*being only one of the ten that escaped out of the five companies*'. Yet there is no report of this Jenkins listed as an Isandlwana survivor and, equally oddly, if he was a Rorke's Drift man, Jenkins didn't mention Rorke's Drift in his letter.

The numerous histories, accounts and documents on the subject likewise don't mention this Jenkins being at Rorke's Drift – neither is his name on any of the rolls of participants at Rorke's Drift. Jenkins' own service records make no mention of his presence at either Rorke's Drift or Isandlwana. Army records reveal no clues to evidence this particular Jenkins' whereabouts on 22/23 January 1879. The Chard Report merely states that Chard was given a warning by Private Jenkins of the 24th, but he was probably referring to Private James Jenkins of the 24th, who is correctly recorded on the various nominal rolls as a defender at Rorke's Drift. It is accepted that James Jenkins participated in the battle because he was killed towards the end of the fighting and is buried in the military cemetery at Rorke's Drift.

The art expert, Oliver Millar, wrote at length about Lady Butler's *Rorke's Drift* painting, as Private David Jenkins was a model for the painting, and of one sketch he wrote, '*One of these is inscribed 'Jenkins' by the artist but no soldier of this name is recorded as having been at the action*'. (Other than the Jenkins who was killed).

The '*Rorke's Drift Bible*' inscribed to David Jenkins and donated to the Regimental Museum was a mystery until it was discovered that the distribution of the Bibles was more widespread throughout the regiment than just to those present at Rorke's Drift; the distribution was made on the quayside as the regiment embarked for their return to England.

There is a *Depot Diary* at the Regimental Museum that consolidates various records held in the Depot and which contains names of participants at Rorke's Drift; it tantalisingly includes Private David Jenkins. Curiously, and rather astonishingly, this ledger is not mentioned at all by Welsh military historian and researcher Norman Holme, author of *The Noble 24th*, who, over many years, collated all known records of the 24th in Zululand. His research was conducted with the full support of consecutive 24th Regimental Museum curators, who made available the latest contents of the regimental archives and assisted Holme, in his words, 'on virtually a daily basis'. Holme makes no mention of Private David Jenkins, other than recording that he was present in Zululand at the time; there is not even a claim from David Jenkins himself explaining his movements or stating he was there. The lack of any evidence suggests Jenkins was not a Rorke's Drift defender. Apart from the 2nd Battalion medal roll showing he was in South Africa, no evidence of him being at Isandlwana or Rorke's Drift has ever been found. Holme logged all the 1879 records over many years and in 1998 wrote:

> 'Undoubtedly a number of veterans encouraged the belief [that they were at Rorke's Drift] possibly to increase their standing within the community, or with members of their family. Unfortunately, such spurious claims are now firmly embedded in family folklore'.[7]

In discussion with Brecon Museum's staff, their hypothesis was that the diary entry in question was written as a Depot diary. They believe the diary was overlooked by researchers due to its title being divided into two. They suggest that these researchers collectively saw it as a record of the 2/24th in the Napoleonic period, without noticing the second line and the later dates of the 1/24th records. Furthermore, anyone researching the Anglo-Zulu War could easily be forgiven for missing the second title and not being aware of its existence. In my view, even if all these researchers made the same mistake of misunderstanding the title, I have difficulty accepting they also missed the content of the diary relating to the Anglo-Zulu war. I therefore find this hypothesis hard to accept. The title of the ledger/diary is:

> Records of the 2/24th 1804–1813
> Records of the 1/24th 1689–1905

In Brecon Museum staff's opinion, it is difficult to say who wrote the entry in the diary without a full investigation of the handwriting of various 'potentials'. It is their opinion that the diary consolidated 'various records' held in the Depot. Someone clearly used a book that had space after the 2/24th entries (some 35 pages), to write (initially) a 'catch up' on the records of the 1/24th and subsequent officers have added to it, possibly a Depot Commandant or Depot Adjutant. There are about a hundred pages of considerable detail, written in different handwriting (which you would expect allowing for the length of the period). The important question is, who wrote the 1878/79/80 entries? It is the opinion of Brecon Museum's staff that it looks like the work of Lieutenant George K Moore, an Adjutant of the 1st Battalion South Wales Borderers (SWB) and a participant in the 1879 conflict, not at Isandlwana or Rorke's Drift, but who took part in the march against Ulundi. The fact that he uses the SWB title points to the diary entry having been compiled following the formation of the South Wales Borderers in July 1881. The diary was donated to the Museum in 1950 by the family of an ex-24th officer.

Norman Holme wrote relating to the problem of identity of such claimants in his *The Noble 24th*:

> 'Many soldiers claimed to have been at Rorke's Drift, or stated that they had been one of the garrison at that place. Throughout the 1930s and 1940s the pages of the Regimental journal of the South Wales Borderers contain many references to such men, usually in conjunction with their attendance at the funeral of a former comrade'.

1. Rorke's Drift Roll of Defenders

The so-called original Chard roll, dated 3 February 1879, and apparently authenticated by Chard's signature and correctly addressed to Colonel Glyn, has long been regarded by many to be an official and genuine document. Conversely, Welsh historian Norman Holme had always been sceptical that this report was genuine and undertook his own research between 1964–1971 to establish its authenticity and perhaps the whereabouts of Chard's original roll, if it existed. The number and significance of the various anomalies associated with the 'Chard Roll' aroused Holme's suspicions, not only regarding the authenticity, but also the accuracy of the information on the roll. Although in possession of copies of the official correspondence relating to the Anglo-Zulu War, Holme could find no request for the submission of a list of names of those present at the defence of Rorke's Drift; Chelmsford had indeed made written requests but these were not known to Holme at the time of his research.

It became increasingly evident to Holme that the roll and duplicate copy in the possession of the Regimental Museum at Brecon represented the only known examples attributed to Chard. Logic dictated that the Public Record Office was the obvious depository for such a document, but nothing was known there of Chard's roll, therefore Holme sought assistance from the descendants of Lieutenant Chard. Lieutenant Colonel W. W. M. Chard and Mrs D. Phillips, who actually possessed living memories of John Rouse Merriott Chard, very kindly responded to Holme's request and searched through the papers formerly belonging to their forebear. There was neither trace nor mention of any Rorke's Drift roll. It became a matter of necessity to confirm whether or not Chard had approved and signed the Museum roll bearing his name, so Holme sought the advice of Mr Derek Davies, a well-known expert in forensic handwriting, who undertook an analysis of the roll. An authenticated sample of Chard's handwriting, including his signature, together with a photocopy of the Rorke's Drift roll was submitted. Holme considered the possibility that Lieutenant Bromhead may have been responsible for compiling the roll; accordingly, an authenticated sample of his handwriting was also submitted to enable a comparison of the handwriting on these documents and offer opinions as to authorship.

In due course, Mr. Davis produced a comprehensive report in which he stated;

> 'The handwriting in each document was examined and notes made of the personal handwriting habits, tendencies and formation found. Examination of all notes allowed opinions to be formed as to specific authorship of the documents. In my considered opinion, one person wrote the whole of the Roll, including the headings and the signature of Lieutenant Chard. This includes the names that visually appear to be a different writing. The only clue that I can offer as to the production of the roll is that it is possible that a man from the 2/24th Regiment produced it – due to the use of first names in that regiment. The only name that shows as carefully written is that of Private Michael Kiley, although this may be coincidence. The numbers of the men are mentioned in the 1st and 2/24th Regiment, but omitted from others, as quoted in *The Silver Wreath*'.

As a result of the conclusions contained in the report, it is obvious that Chard did not sign the roll, neither did Bromhead contribute to any part of the document. It must also be remembered that the Chard Roll of Defenders was allegedly signed off by Chard on 3 February 1879 during the acute shortage of paper at Rorke's Drift. It was Holme's personal opinion that the degree of authority attributed to this Chard roll is not supported by the evidence. There are four rolls quoted by Norman Holme; full details of his reservations relating to these rolls can be found in *The Noble 24th* by Norman Holme, published by Savannah Publications.

Of the thirty sources looked at, no less than twenty-four, i.e., 80 percent are factually incorrect and this is a significant number. Any historical error need appear in print only once and is then in danger of 'going viral'. Although it is in a different context altogether, Ron Lock gives the very apt quote that '*History repeats itself. Historians repeat each other*'.[8] This would seem to be the case here, whereby many researchers have simply copied earlier, incorrect secondary sources. The added danger is that future researchers might be tempted to go with the 'majority opinion', even if it is incorrect.

The lesson is clear; always seek evidence by way of corroboration, preferably through definitive, primary sources and not to exclusively trust young soldiers, old soldiers, army records or secondary sources! Sadly, truth remains one of the first casualties of war, a view expressed by the Victorian war historian, Claus Von Clausewitz, who wrote:

> 'The difficulty of seeing things correctly, which is one of the greatest fictions in war, makes things appear quite different from what was expected'.[9]

False claims in letters etc., once written down, and doubtless formulated by the faker with deliberate care to avoid corroboration, inevitably take on the stamp of authority in wider circles. Inevitably, the false written or engraved word can easily lead 'honest others' into accepting its incredibility and a corrupt tale becomes 'accepted'. After all, that is what the faker intended.

Frustrating as it may be, many an attempt to validate any individual's participation at Rorke's Drift is likely to get no further than a brutal truth – if he is not on the rolls, and there is no supporting evidence, then he was not there.

References

1. George Mabin, Major Spalding's clerk, present at the battle as the Colour Sergeant.
2. *The Noble 24th*, Holme, N., Savannah Books, 1999. This work remains an important starting point regarding the records of the men of the 24th who fought at Isandlwana and Rorke's Drift. Julian Whybra's *England's Sons* (GIFT Ltd, 2004) offers a carefully considered and updated roll of the defenders of Rorke's Drift and comments regarding the individuals who survived Isandlwana. Likewise, claiming 'to have been there' was ever a common ruse used by impoverished soldiers returning home from the battles in the hope of obtaining favours and assistance; examples include Waterloo and Custer's Last Stand.
3. Ditto.
4. The position of the *AZWHS* consultants is straightforward; in the absence of any actual evidence, we cannot accept the claim. Neither do we follow the dubious logic of those who collectively agree 'he was there'. The opinion of self-appointed claimants is not history. When we can see one piece of evidence we will positively support their claim.
5. *The South African Survey Journal* (December 1968).
6. *A Biographical Record of the Natal Mounted Police in the Anglo-Zulu War of 1879*, Simpson, C., 2023. Records show that in one unit 155 men were born in England, Ireland 18, India 18, South Africa 11, Scotland 8, Germany 5, France 4, Canada 2, at sea 2, Tasmania 1, Holland 1, Malta 1, Switzerland 1, while 26 could not have their birthplace identified. Six had held commissions in the British Army.
7. *The Noble 24th*.
8. *Isandlwana: The Revelation of a Disaster*, Lock, R., Barnsley, 2017.
9. *On War*, Clausewitz, Claus von, Book 1, Chapter 6.

Chapter 11

Corporal Christian Ferdinand Schiess VC

Gazetted to receive the Victoria Cross 27 November 1879
Presented by Sir Garnet Wolseley at Pietermaritzburg 3 February 1880

While Rorke's Drift visitors have always been and remain fascinated by the accounts of the night's fighting, one character in particular stands out for his acknowledged bravery, especially as he fought on crutches. The fact that he was a Swiss national and, post-battle, was incorrectly believed to have existed in illness and poverty, added to the intrigue. So, who was this brave and enigmatic character, what was he doing at Rorke's Drift and what happened to cause his early death?

He sailed from Hamburg for the Cape on 9 June 1877 as part of a Cape Government scheme to sponsor much needed European farmers and artisans. He arrived in August and took part in the Ninth Cape Frontier War. He then transferred as a Corporal to the newly-formed NNC attached to No 3 Centre Column for the invasion of Zululand and, from Rorke's Drift, participated in the attack on Sihayo's nearby homestead where he sustained a disabling foot injury. He was then hospitalised at the Mission hospital.

It is a sad fact that some survivors of the defence of Rorke's Drift had their lives cut tragically short by illness, or the dire circumstances in which they found themselves in later years. No individual epitomises this more than Corporal Schiess of the NNC, who died on board the troopship H.M.S. *Serapis* on 14 December 1884 while being repatriated to England. He was buried at sea off the west coast of Africa: he was only 28 years old. The captain's log reads:

> 'Sunday 14 December 1884
> '10.20am Departed this life Mr. F.C. Schiess, VC
> '5.10pm Stopped. Committed to the Deep the remains of the late Mr. Schiess, VC
> '5.15pm Proceeded
> 'Ship's Noon observed position: Lat S. 13.00 Long W.7.24'.

Born on 7 April 1856 at Burgdorf among the mountains of Switzerland, Schiess seems to have packed a lot into his short life. Ubiquitous accounts state he was raised for some years in an orphanage adding that, at the age of only 14 or 15 years, he joined the French army where he participated in the Franco-Prussian War of 1870–71. This was not so. Recent research by *AZWHS* members in Switzerland revealed a very different and more likely account.

The enrollment registers of the former orphanage were found to still exist in both the Swiss State Archives and the Municipal Archives in Herisau where Schiess was born. According to these registers, young Christian was enrolled together with his brother Gottfried on 24 September 1861. Christian was 5-years-old, his brother 9. Other children of the Schiess family also ended up there. Registration dates of three more sisters and one other brother were also found.[1]

The civil registry shows the father of the children, stone mason Niklaus Schiess, was born in Herisau on 12 March 1820 and died on 21 September 1893. The mother, Anna Ruchti, was born 19 February 1820 and died at Diemerswil near Bern on 3 November 1863.[2] Christian Ferdinand and his siblings were never orphans, they were there because of poverty. At that time the orphanage provided not only for the care of orphans but also for the care of children from destitute families. The registration of one of Christian Ferdinand's sisters included the telling phrase: 'brought with her only the clothes she wore'.[3]

Christian remained in the orphanage until 26 June 1870, when he was apprenticed to Master Locksmith Säger[4], remaining under the care of the orphanage. The next report that could be found of Schiess is a Herisau police search notice dated September 1871. According to this notice, he abandoned his employer and then disappeared without a trace. This search for him originated from the orphanage still responsible for him.[5] The original notice appeared in the *Amtsblatt* news sheet.

Polizeiliche Ausschreibung.

Christian Ferdinand Schieß von Herisau, geb. den 7. April 1856, hat sich von seinem Arbeitsherrn heimlich entfernt, und es werden die Tit. Polizeistellen hiemit höflichst ersucht, im Betretungsfalle ihn der Waisenbehörde von Herisau zuführen zu lassen. Schieß hat dunkelblonde Haare, ovales Gesicht und ein spitziges Kinn; bei seiner Entfernung trug er dunkelgraue Hosen und Weste, einen hellgrauen Paletot, einen braunen Hut und Bottinen.

Herisau, den 27. September 1871.

Die Kantonspolizeidirektion.

> **'Police Alert**
> **Christian Ferdinand Schiess from Herisau, born on the 7th of April 1856, has secretly distanced himself from his employers, and the different police stations are hereby politely asked by the orphan agency from Herisau to bring him back. Schiess has dark blond hair, an oval face and a pointy chin; at his disappearance he was wearing dark grey trousers and vest, a light grey Paletot (three-quarter length, double-breasted men's coat), a brown hat and boots.**
> **Herisau, 27 September 1871.**
> **The Cantonal Police Department.**

If Schiess disappeared in September 1871, his alleged participation in the Franco-Prussian war must be in doubt. That war ran from July 1870 to the Peace Treaty signed on 10 May 1871. At the same time, from mid-February 1871 to mid-March 1871, a total of 1,584 French soldiers of the 'Bourbaki Army',[6] who had fought in this war, were interned in Herisau pending disbanding. In a municipality of about 9,000 inhabitants, their presence would undoubtedly have impacted on the population, including on the young Schiess. It is possible that he joined this French unit and served under a false name or pseudonym so that he could not be found.

Regardless of whether he took part in the Franco-German war or not, the youngster from Herisau then travelled to South Africa, where he eventually joined the NNC with the rank of corporal. His heroics at Rorke's Drift are well documented and were such that the 'British-only' rule for the award of the Victoria Cross was waived for this Swiss national. Schiess was two months short of his 24th birthday when he received his VC from Sir Garnet Wolseley. He carried his medal to his dying day and it was found in his pocket before his sea burial; it is now on display in the National Army Museum.

Research resolves the mystery of Schiess's activities between 1880 and his death in December 1884. The conventional narrative suggests he worked in the Durban Telegraph Office for some time after leaving the NNC – but then struggled to find work and ended up destitute and ill on the streets of Cape Town until late-1884, when public donations bought him an 'indulgence' ticket to England on board the *Serapis*, which had just docked from India. He died a few days into the voyage and there the matter almost rested.

News of the death of a VC hero in such circumstances was not greeted kindly in some quarters. For example, the British periodical *Truth* offered this rebuke in its issue of 15 January, 1885:

'The case of Corporal Schiess, V.C., does not look particularly creditable to his country. To what regiment Schiess belonged I do not know, but he served through the Zulu campaign, and was awarded the Victoria Cross for distinguished gallantry at Rorke's Drift. After the war he lapsed into absolute poverty at Natal and was lately in such a condition that a subscription was got up to pay his rations home as an indulgence passenger on the Serapis. Want and exposure, however, had so told on him that he died on the voyage. I dare say Schiess himself may have been partly to blame, but we ought to be able to turn a man who could win the Victoria Cross at Rorke's Drift to better account than this'.

This uncharitable article is not notable for its accuracy and it does contain the rather cryptic comment about Schiess himself being 'partly to blame', but it does express a sentiment that was shared in some circles. Further examination of contemporary records and publications cast doubt on this simplified account of Schiess's final years, certainly in terms of the timing. A short piece in *The York House* papers of 8 December 1880 provided more detail. The article reads:

'From Natal I hear that large numbers of citizens have been flocking to Commandant Baker's standard, that gentleman having volunteered to raise a corps of mounted men for service against the Basutos. Among the non-commissioned officers is the familiar figure of Sergeant Scheiss (*sic*) VC, who was decorated with the Cross for valour, in recognition of his distinguished gallantry in Zululand'.

From this, we can see that Schiess had not given up on military service after leaving the NNC and he was obviously a known figure. Proof of his continued service with this mounted troop came from the unlikely source of a provincial Lincolnshire newspaper, the *Stamford Mercury*.[7] On 15 April 1881, under the heading 'With Baker's Horse in Basutoland', it published a letter sent to Mr William Barton, the publisher of the Newspaper, from his son, William Barton, who was serving with Baker's Horse 'which was destined for employment against the Basutos'. The young Mr. Barton recounted the following anecdote in his letter home, dated 2 February 1881:

'I have been out the last few days - one of a party repairing the telegraph wires cut by the enemy; not a nice job for five fellows alone and about ten miles from camp. But we had a good man in charge – corporal Schiess, VC, one of the Rorke's Drift heroes. He is a nice fellow and we are the best of friends. He was born in the Alps, and is Swiss. This mountainous country suits him. When we were out the other day we went and looked for some chamois. We were unsuccessful, of course. I think if he had seen some of the enemy it would not have been a sham. He is a dead shot'.

This takes us to a distance of two years from the exploits at Rorke's Drift with no sign of the destitution or 'absolute poverty' that most authors refer to. There is one more significant twist to the story of Corporal Schiess in the unexpected setting of a royal visit to India at the end of 1883 by the Duke and Duchess of Connaught.[8] The royal event on 1 December 1883 was widely reported in the press, as was the account of the Duke inspecting troops at Allahabad. The following article was printed almost word for word in several publications, including *The Times of India*, dated 18 December 1883:

'On arrival of the special train at Allahabad on the 1st December with their Royal Highnesses the Duke and Duchess of Connaught (after being presented to the notabilities of the station), the Duke proceeded to inspect the guard of honour composed of a very strong muster of the E.I.R. Volunteers. Glancing over the men his quick eye detected one little fellow, Volunteer F.C. Schiess, in the ranks, on whose breast hung the Victoria Cross. With that readiness and good feeling so general with the members of the Royal Family, he at once stepped up to him and, kindly with interest, enquired where and how he had earned the distinguished decoration. I leave it to be imagined with what pride the gallant little fellow answered, possibly "Sir, at Rorke's Drift", such being actually the case. Unfortunately, poor Schiess, having his rifle at the 'present arms', was unable to grasp the ready hand extended to him by the Duke.

So Schiess was still in uniform, and seemingly fit and well although no longer an NCO, and had somehow found his way to India. The E.I.R. Volunteers which proved to be an auxiliary unit, was originally formed as the East Indian Railway Volunteer Rifle Corps whose records are kept in the British Library.[9] As late as 1884 Schiess is recorded in an official directory as being an employee of the East Indian Railway Company and was serving in their Volunteer Rifle Corps. We may never know what took him back to South Africa from India, but there was exactly one year between Schiess being presented to the Duke of Connaught in Allahabad and his boarding H.M.S. *Serapis* in Cape Town for his final journey. Whatever happened in this year must have been fairly sudden and dramatic and not the longer, slower decline that has previously been alleged.

As David Gilmour says in his book, *The British in India*[10]:

'There were also illnesses and diseases in India that would seldom or never have killed people in Britain ...The most common disease for the British was malaria (sometimes known as jungle fever) ...Numerous people died of it when they were in India or after being invalided home to Britain'.

Deaths on long sea journeys were not uncommon at the time, but this voyage was particularly tragic; after the *Serapis* docked, the *Portsmouth Evening News* of 3 January 1885 reported:

'There was an unusually high number of deaths on the homeward voyage, viz 11, and it is an illustration of the effect of the Indian climate that in nearly every instance death resulted from abscess on the liver'.

It is possible Schiess succumbed to an illness such as this, but from this distance in time no one knows. However, the author and *AZWHS* member Colonel Dr Alan Spicer of the RAMC conducted an investigation of the medical records of Surgeon Blair-Brown held at the medical wing of the Wellcome Foundation in London. Once Rorke's Drift had been relieved by Chelmsford's surviving column, and with Surgeon Reynold's medical supplies at Rorke's Drift lost or destroyed, the garrison's most seriously wounded were taken by wagon to Helpmekaar where they were examined and treated by Surgeon Blair-Brown – who fortuitously recorded their details and injuries. Amongst this eminent army surgeon's notes was his written diagnosis and treatment of, allegedly, the seriously injured Schiess. Having read the surgeon's medical notes, it was the opinion of battle-experienced Dr Spicer that Schiess's recorded bullet injury to his head and likely nerve damage sustained at Rorke's Drift, especially in a hot and humid climate, was likely to have progressively contributed to Schiess's deteriorating medical condition in the months before his death. Part of Blair-Brown's notes read:

'Corporal Carl Schiess of the Natal Native Contingent was wounded at Rorke's Drift. The bullet hit the back of the head, at the posterior margin of the left sternomastoid at its origin, and took a course towards the middle of the scapular base, where the bullet lodged subcutaneously, from which position it has been removed when I took charge of him on the 26th January. Here also, the whole shoulder was greatly swollen and painful, requiring poultices. This case, after the usual slough came away, got well'.[11]

However in Blair-Brown's later book he re-apportions the same head and shoulder injury to Corporal C.S. of the NNC, the S.C. possibly having been misinterpreted as Schiess, the real S.C. was most likely to have been Corporal Scammel who had sustained head and shoulder injuries.

What we do know for certain is that this particular hero of Rorke's Drift sustained injuries sufficiently serious to require his evacuation from Rorke's Drift. Sadly, Schiess never got the opportunity to start a new life in the country that had awarded him their highest military decoration, embossed 'For Valour'.

There are no known photographs of Schiess, but Lieutenant Harford, who met Schiess at Rorke's Drift, described him as 'wearing earrings' and 'a very small man with the cut of a seafaring man, which I expect was his real calling'.[12]

References

1. Email to author 10 January 2024 from G. Leipold, Municipal Archive Herisau.
2. Email to author 2 November 2023 from U. Butz State, Archive Herisau.
3. Ditto.
4. Ditto.
5. *Amtsblatt 1871, 2.Teil Bekanntmachungen,* Nr 36 S. 157–158.
6. The Armée de l'Est (Army of the East), also Second Loire Army (nicknamed the 'Bourbaki Army' after its first commander, General Charles Denis Sauter Bourbaki). It was a French army unit that had taken part in the Franco-Prussian War of 1870–1871.
7. *Stamford Mercury.*
8. *The Bengal Directory*, published by Thacker & Co Ltd.
9. Maureen Heath of the Asia and African Studies Reference Section who researched my request and sent me this entry in *Thacker's*. On page 544 of the 1884 edition of this publication is a list of the guards staff at Allahabad Station: among the names is F.C. Schiess, but, unfortunately, there are no precise dates for his employment.
10. Penguin Books, 2019.
11. Courtesy of The Wellcome Foundation, London. See also 'Surgical Experiences in the Zulu and Transvaal Wars', Blair-Brown, D., *The Edinburgh Medical Journal*, October 1883.
12. *Harford – The Writings, Photographs and Sketches,* Payne, D., The Ultimatum Tree Ltd. 2008.

Chapter 12

The Welsh Connection

Following the release of the film *Zulu*, doubts quickly arose about the composition and nationality of the two participating battalions of the 24th Regiment at Rorke's Drift and Isandlwana. The film overlooked the fact that, at the time of the Anglo Zulu War in 1879, the 24th Regiment was the 2nd Warwickshire Regiment and it stayed that way until 1881 when it became The South Wales Borderers. Its Regimental March was 'The Warwickshire Lads', composed in 1769 for the Shakespearean Centenary Celebrations at Stratford-on-Avon. However, *Zulu* portrayed the regiment and soldiers as being Welsh, emphasised by them proudly singing 'Men of Harlech', and due to the popularity of the film, this portrayal became one of popular belief. With regard to the 1/24th lost at Isandlwana, there was virtually no connection with Wales, as the battalion had neither served in the UK since 1867 or ever recruited from Wales. The 2/24th certainly had a small proportion of Welshmen serving in its ranks, but there were many more Irishmen while the greater number by far were English, a fact that is reflected by the composition of B Company 2/24th and the four soldiers of the 1/24th when they defended Rorke's Drift. Since *Zulu* this 'Welsh belief' has been widely accepted.[1]

The question of participants' nationality was highlighted at Southwark Cathedral for the memorial service for the noted historian, David Rattray, when, during his address to the congregation, the regimental Brigadier erroneously stated that 'many of the names in the regiment today such as Evans, Jones and Williams reflected those from Wales who fought at Rorke's Drift and Isandlwana'. The facts are very different. The 24th Regimental depot was founded at Brecon in 1883, simply because it was vacant and the 24th Regiment needed a home base; clearly it could have been anywhere. Thereafter, and until the Zulu War, some recruits were recruited from the counties of Brecknock, Cardigan, Monmouth and Radnor as well as the neighbouring English counties, especially Monmouth, with most of the recruits going to the local 2nd Battalion. The 1st Battalion, though, had seen continuous service in various Mediterranean garrisons for the eight years prior to arriving in South Africa on 4 February 1875.

The 24th had no special depots for recruiting. Had it tried recruiting in Wales or specifically Brecon, it would have encountered a logistical problem as Wales was sparsely populated until the expansion of the coal, iron and steel industries in the late-nineteenth century. For example, until 1880, Brecon had a static population of only 5,000 people covering a wide rural area with only 2,551 males of all ages, so the number of fit men of recruiting age was very small.

Private Robert Jones VC, 2/24th was born in Monmouthshire (then an English county), and awarded the Victoria Cross for his part in the defence of Rorke's Drift. To ponder whether he was English or Welsh probably never occurred to him, but when writing about his experiences, he wrote:

> 'On the 22nd January 1879, the Zulus attacked us, we being only a small band of English soldiers. My thought was only to fight as an English soldier ought to for his most gracious Sovereign, Queen Victoria, and for the benefit of old England'.[2]

In view of the subsequent 1881 change in designation of the 24th into the South Wales Borderers, it is worth considering the actual representation of Welshmen then serving in the two battalions at Isandlwana and Rorke's Drift. With regard to the 1/24th lost at Isandlwana, there was virtually no connection with Wales, as the battalion had neither served in the UK since 1867 or ever recruited from Wales. Indeed, when the news of the loss of the 1/24th reached Britain, *The Daily News* sadly ignored the high proportion of Irishmen serving in both battalions when it commented 'Death had prematurely visited hundreds of peaceful and happy homes in England'.

Throughout the Zulu War, mention of Wales as an entity did not feature in any official or regimental documentation or reports. Following Isandlwana, a famous music hall song, 'The Gallant 24' by Lee and Green, included the words:

> 'In Zululand the Twenty-Forth, a gallant little band
> Of British soldiers bold and true, 'gainst legions made a stand.
> Surrounded by their dusky foe, shut in both left and right,
> 'Gainst fearful odds they fought as none but Englishmen can fight.
>
> 'The name they made will never fade
> And all with pride will tell
> How England's gallant 24th
> As heroes fought and fell'.

This emphasis on 'English' is understandable, simply because the language of the time emphasised the term 'Anglo' as meaning all things 'British' and the term 'English' was similarly used in everyday parlance. In reference to the 24th

Regiment, Lord Chelmsford's copious records always used the term 'English' as he did when referring to all matters relevant to the United Kingdom.

The 2/24th certainly had a small proportion of Welshmen serving in its ranks (born, or living in Wales when recruited). When they defended Rorke's Drift, the composition of the defenders of B Company 2/24th and the four soldiers of the 1/24th was as follows:

<u>1st Battalion</u>

England	1	Staffordshire
Scotland	1	Midlothian
Ireland	1	Dublin
Other	1	Peshawar, India (of British parents)
Total	4	

<u>2nd Battalion</u>

England 42

1 each from; Cheshire; Gloucestershire; Leicestershire; Nottinghamshire; Surrey; Sussex; Worcestershire; Yorkshire.

2 each from; Kent and Middlesex.

3 each from; Herefordshire and Warwickshire.

4 from Somerset.

9 from Lancashire.

11 from London.

Ireland 13

1 each from; Antrim and Limerick.

2 each from; Clare, Cork, Kilkenny, Tipperary.

3 from Dublin

Wales 10

1 each from; Breconshire and Pembrokeshire.

3 from Glamorgan.

5 from Monmouthshire (then an English county).

Other 1

France – of British parents.

With regard to the 24th Rorke's Drift VC recipients, Bromhead was born in France (to a Lincolnshire family), Hook was from Gloucestershire, Allen was born in Northumbria (and considered himself a 'Scotchman' by birth), Hitch was a Londoner, William Jones was from Worcestershire, Robert Jones and John Fielding (alias Williams) were from Monmouthshire (an English county) and Fielding was anyway Irish, although hailing from Abergavenny. According to the *Oxford Names Dictionary*, Jones means 'son of John' – a famously English name.

The statement by the regimental Brigadier that 'many of the names in the regiment today such as Evans, Jones and Williams reflected those from Wales who fought at Rorke's Drift and Isandlwana' neatly takes us to the question of Welsh names, or names commonly associated with Wales. A count of soldiers with these names within the two battalions makes interesting reading. Of course, there are numerous problems using such a rough and completely unscientific method; being named with a Welsh sounding name has absolutely nothing to do with one's heritage. For example, Pte Griffiths VC (killed at Isandlwana) has a Welsh name but he was born in Ireland, was attested in Warwick, and joined the Regiment at Tamworth. With regard to the 1st Battalion, and to a lesser extent the 2nd Battalion, after Isandlwana the battalions were reconstructed with (mainly) recruits from a mix of eighteen UK-based regiments, which makes any analysis virtually impossible.

Medal records are equally ambiguous; many of those new 24th recruits trawled after Isandlwana to replace the losses in the 1st Battalion were posted back to their original units after the war. They were, confusingly, entitled to the South Africa Medal for serving with the 24th, although the 24th would not have been their original unit. Many such medals have no clasp, which indicates that they did not cross into Zululand. Rorke's Drift defenders were a curious exception, as they were all given the clasp yet many never crossed into Zululand. It raises another interesting question: as the 2nd Battalion did not arrive in South Africa until 1878, why did they have 1877–8–9 on their medal bar?[3]

Nevertheless, if one considers the Welsh or Welsh-sounding names of casualties at Isandlwana, then I offer the following:

> 'Casualties with Welsh names at Isandlwana [the author accepts there may well be other Welsh names that he is unaware of].
>
> 'Davis 4, Edwards 4, Evans 2, Griffiths 1, Hughes 5, Jenkins 3, Jones 6, Lewis 2, Lloyd 1, Morgan 2, Parry 2, Thomas 2, Watkins 1, Williams 10'.

One might think that ownership of the 24th Regiment's Colours might clarify the matter, but this is equally misleading. In 1936, the Chillianwalla Colours of the 24th Regiment that were carried in the Second Sikh War of 1849, which had been laid up in St. Mary's Church in Warwick since 1868, were removed to the Regimental Chapel in Brecon Cathedral. The Church Council of St. Mary's Church was not inclined to part with the Colours but the Regiment applied for a faculty for their removal. The case was argued before the Chancellor of the Diocese of Coventry on 6 May 1936, and judgement was given in the Regiment's favour. If fate had taken another turn the 24th might have become an established regiment of Warwickshire and the question of Welshness would never have arisen.

On St David's Day, 1 March 2006, The Royal Welch Fusiliers (23rd Foot) amalgamated with The Royal Regiment of Wales to form The Royal Welsh, (lineage 23rd, 24th, 41st, 69th Foot), the former titles being kept in the battalion designations: i.e. the 1st Battalion, The Royal Welsh (Royal Welch Fusiliers); the 2nd Battalion, The Royal Welsh (The Royal Regiment of Wales); with the 3rd Battalion, The Royal Welsh, being part of the Territorial Army.

So we are left with a meaningless if academic question, and the reality of a fine regiment. The spirit of the 24th Regiment is strongly maintained today by The Royal Welsh. Regardless of names or origins, the regiment is one of the outstanding regiments of the British Army and, since becoming The South Wales Borderers in 1881, one with a distinct Welsh flair. Its motto is proudly displayed on the Regimental Colour – '*Gwell Angau na Chywilydd*' – 'Death rather than Dishonour'.

References

1. Following their return in 1873 from the American War of Independence, the 24th Regiment of Foot was based in Warwickshire. On 31 August 1782 a Royal Warrant conferred county titles on all British regiments. The 24th Regiment was accordingly given the title '2nd Warwickshire' to recruit in that county. Over this period, the posting locations of the regiment's two battalions were:

1st Battalion

The 1st Battalion saw continuous service in various Mediterranean garrisons after 1867, then moved to South Africa on 4 February 1875. As soon as tidings of the disaster at Isandlwana reached England, recruits were urgently drafted from eighteen different regiments to re-form the lost 1st Battalion at Aldershot. On 1 March 1879 a draft of 520 non-commissioned officers and men embarked on the *Clyde* at Woolwich for South Africa. Just six months later, on 27 August, this newly-constituted battalion embarked for the return to England on the *Egypt*, arriving at Portsmouth on 2 October, then moved to New Barracks at Gosport. Men drafted into the reconstituted 1st Battalion after Isandlwana were then permitted to return to their original regiments. Over time, 709 men took the option and were replaced with 358 new recruits.

On 26 November 1880 the battalion was moved by train to Colchester, then in 1885 it was posted to Ireland. In 1889 the regiment was posted to Aldershot.

2nd Battalion

The 2nd Battalion had been based at Aldershot before moving to Dover in August 1875, before moving again to Chatham in 1877. On 1 February, the battalion left Chatham by two special trains for Portsmouth, where it embarked in H.M Troopship *Himalaya* for South Africa and, after three months of training, participated in the Sandilli rebellion.

On 12 February 1880, following the Anglo-Zulu war, the 2nd battalion embarked in the SS. *Ontario* to take up its posting to Gibraltar, going into quarters in Casemate Barracks. On 12 August 1880 the battalion embarked for Bombay on the *Orantes* arriving on 2 September. The battalion remained at Secunderabad from 1880 to February 1884, then moved to Burma until 1892.

Meanwhile, on 1 July 1881 the regiment was ordered to be discontinued, its two battalions, then stationed respectively at Colchester and Secunderabad, to become The South Wales Borderers. Until then neither battalion appears to have had any connection with Brecon or Wales. For further details, see *Records of the 24th Regiment*, Paton, Glennie & Symons. 1892.

2. *The Red Soldier*, Emery.
3. The Text of General Order 103 – August 1880.

In the original text the paragraphs all run together with no spacing. It is reproduced here with spacing between paragraphs for clarity.

The Queen has been graciously pleased to command that, in consideration of the arduous duties performed and the successful conclusion of the operations referred to in the next paragraph, a Medal be granted to her Majesty's Imperial forces, and to such of Her Majesty's colonial forces, European or native, as were regularly organised and disciplined as combatants, whether raised by the Colonial Government or by the General Officer commanding.

The Medal will be granted to the forces employed against

(a) The Galekas, Gaikas and other Caffre *(Sic)* tribes from the 26 September, 1877 to 28 June, 1878 inclusive;
(b) against Pokwani, from 21 to 28 January 1878 inclusive;
(c) against the Griquas, from 24 April to the 13 November 1874 inclusive;
(d) against the Zulus, from the 11 January to the 1 September, 1879 inclusive;
(e) against Secocoeni from the 11 November to the 2 December 1879, and including troops that were stationed at Fort Burghers, Fort Albert Edward, Seven Mile Post, Fort Oliphant, Fort Weeber, and in Secocoeni's valley;
(f) against Moirosi's Stronghold.

Her Majesty has also been pleased to approve of a Clasp being attached to the same Medal, on which will be indicated the year or years in which the recipients of the medal were engaged in the late wars, thus – For operations against the Galekas, &c on Clasp 1877–78; for operations against Pokwani and the Griquas, 1878; for operations in the Zulu and Sekhukhune campaigns respectively, or both, 1879; for operations as specified in Paragraph 2 in 1877–8–9, 1877–8–9; for operations as specified in Paragraph 2 in 1878–9, 1878–9 – the principle being that the year or years of the Clasp cover all the operations in which the recipient may have been engaged in such year or years.

Those troops employed in Natal from the 11 January to the 1 September 1879, but who never crossed the border into Zululand, will be granted the Medal without Clasp.

Chapter 13

Archaeological Investigations at Isandlwana and Rorke's Drift

Very few military items were recovered which support the historical accounts.
Dr Lita Webley, Natal Provincial Museum Service

Regarding battlefield archaeology as a whole, battlefields differ from other areas traditionally looked at by archaeologists in that where a house may indicate how, when and why someone lived, a battlefield often indicates how, when and why somebody died. Similarly, through the various approaches to the study of archaeology ranging from, for example, the cultural-historical approach to the post-processual, studies tend to look at congruence and cooperation such as the spread of agriculture or the building of the pyramids. Therefore, the study of battle is a new dimension in the repertoire of archaeological investigation. The principal differences between history and archaeology are also highlighted in an investigation of this nature, as with many battles involving defeat, the defeated often covered their trail – or in victory exaggerate their success, usually to protect their reputations. Therefore, the benefit of archaeology on this project is that it deals with artefacts which hopefully speak for themselves.

Archaeology at Isandlwana

Over the four-year period, 1987 – 1991, numerous cases of blatant grave robbing were reported from the Isandlwana Battlefield. In each case the motive appeared to be an attempt to obtain military memorabilia for resale. After each reported case KwaZulu Monuments Council staff reinterred all exposed human remains and repacked the cairns. At the time of these re-interments the fragile, fragmented and weathered nature of bone residues was noted. The soils in the region are known to be acidic and together with the former, these have accelerated the natural processes of decay.

In 2000, the author was researching at Fugitives' Drift during the first authorised archaeological investigation on the slopes of Isandlwana (14 August to 12 September). The principal investigator was Dr Tony Pollard of Glasgow

University, later a respected TV presenter, who kindly accepted my occasional presence. It was an important event dealing with the famous Battle of Isandlwana on 22 January 1879 which witnessed the final moments of Chelmsford's Isandlwana camp defenders, some 1,500 troops as well as of several thousand Zulu warriors.

The investigation was the first archaeological investigation at Isandlwana for many years. By then, there were few mortal remains of fallen soldiers, them having been repeatedly re-buried due to the heavy storms and natural erosion processes in the area.

Thanks to previous analysis of the location of bullets and cases previously collected, the firing line had earlier been thought to have occupied ground extending in a broad arc from the northerly section of Isandlwana to Durnford's Donga. Instead, the team found the actual firing line actually extended from the northern section of Isandlwana, covering the ground towards the Conical Koppie, and would have only reached Durnford's Donga following the British retreat. This would be logical from a tactical point of view because if the firing line was that far forward, it would be able to cover the dead ground to the east of Isandlwana, which the previously believed position could not have achieved. The false public image of where the firing line was is most likely due to the locations of the many whitewashed cairns, i.e. they are some 500 yards behind the actual front line. This is primarily because it was four months following the battle before the first burial party attended. The remains had been subject to scavenging and weathering and resembled an abattoir. The burial party focused on collecting up scattered human remains and the bones were reburied communally, closer to the camp. This has long given visitors the impression that soldiers were buried where they had stood, which was thereafter incorrectly assumed to be the firing line.

With regard to the belief of the front line ammunition shortage, archaeologists found ample evidence of ammunition box nails, screws and metal straps reaching to the front line, as well as high concentrations immediately behind the line, suggesting that the soldiers had ample access to ammunition at all stages of the battle.

The dearth of artefacts, the adiagnostic nature of the skeletal remains, and the re-interment procedures that have occurred, collectively suggested that the original cairns have limited archaeological value and do not warrant focused attention in the event of a further large scale archaeological investigation of the site.

Archaeology at Rorke's Drift

It is a curious fact that Sir Bartle Frere was principally responsible for the original interest in archaeological research around Rorke's Drift. Although it was Frere who was responsible for the two 1879 British invasions of Zululand, he had a personal passion for archaeology and anthropology. He was formally the president of The Asiatic Society in 1872, and the following year he became president of The Royal Geographical Society. Before moving to South Africa he was already an avid collector of artefacts; he then turned his interest to Natal and Zululand. Many of Frere's Zulu war items are now deposited with the British Museum in the Department of Ethnography.

Frere was not alone as a number of British officers serving in Zululand collected artefacts; many from Rorke's Drift, others from along the Buffalo River, Isandlwana and Pietermaritzburg. One officer of particular note, Colonel Henry Fielden, not only collected artefacts but, post war, also uniquely established that Bushmen collected glass from soldiers' discarded soda water bottles to make arrowheads. Fielden's Zulu War collection came from his line of march from Newcastle to Rorke's Drift; he wrote that he 'took advantage of every opportunity that arose for leaving the line of march and examining the 'dongas' and denuded surfaces that lay contiguous to this route'.[1]

Artefacts collected by Fielden are now held in the Sturge collection in the British Museum and Liverpool Museum. At first sight, it appears strange that officers would take time from their official duties to study and collect artefacts; yet, perusal of many early collections reveals that army officers were initially responsible for many collections, ranging from the Anglo-Zulu War and the Boer Wars through to the Bechuanaland Expedition of 1884; their endeavours were certainly responsible for spurring initial interest in archaeology in this area.

The most significant Rorke's Drift archaeological excavation was undertaken by Dr Lita Webley in September 1998, with the aim of further elucidating the course of events on that fateful night at the mission station. The first stage was to locate the foundations of the British commissariat store, as well as the hospital burnt down by the Zulu. A preliminary survey with a metal detector provided new information on the Zulu side of the war but very few items were recovered that could be linked unequivocally to the battle, despite the scale of military operations at the site both during and after the conflict of 22 January 1879.

Zulu War authors generally follow the line that British soldiers fired some 20,000 rounds of Martini-Henry ammunition during the battle. Their source appears to be the classic *Washing of the Spears* by Morris. If this were so, the majority of these cartridge cases are likely to have been discarded within the barricades. Following the battle, Rorke's Drift suffered torrential rain and it could be presumed that these spent cartridge cases would have been well trodden into the thick mud. During the archaeological excavations of the site during 1993, virtually none were found, even though excavations were conducted to a depth of 100cm. Visitors to the site would certainly have collected mementos lying around, and metal detectors have since been used, yet the amount found by the archaeologists seems very low. Perhaps the spent rounds were collected and deposited elsewhere, but this seems unlikely given the conditions prevailing at the time and that more urgent survival tasks needed to be performed. There is no evidence that British troops ever collected spent rounds during this war. Subsequent visitors found very little evidence of any conflict at Rorke's Drift:

> 'Few or no traces of the old fortifications remain, but a large house was in the course of construction. Outhouses stood around, hard by was the chapel, belonging to the mission, but of the defences, not a trace'.[2]

Conversely, when Bertram Mitford visited Isandlwana in 1882 he found the site littered with battle debris:

> 'Strewn about are tent pegs, cartridge cases, broken glass, bits of rope, meat tins and sardine boxes pierced with assegai stabs, shrivelled pieces of shoe leather and rubbish of every description; bone of horses and oxen gleam white and ghastly and here and there in the grass one stumbles upon a half-buried skeleton'.[3]

Background to the Excavations[4]

In March 1879 troops started with the construction of Fort Melvill overlooking the river in order to both protect the pont and move the troops out of the old fort, which was very unhealthy. The majority of the troops moved out in April, although some stayed on until the end of the war in July. It is not known when the walls of the old fort were finally dismantled, although the defences of the area were finally abandoned in October 1879. After the war Otto Witt returned and constructed a large house and church on the site. There are no records indicating whether the new mission house was built on top of the foundations of the hospital or whether the church was built on the ruins of the store. It would appear however, that the eight-foot-high stone walling of the old fort was demolished and the stone used in the construction of these new buildings.

Witt's rebuilt house and church are still standing, and while the latter structure continues to function in daily use, the former has now been converted into a museum. The land on which the battlefield is located still belongs to the Evangelical Lutheran Church, but has been let to the Natal Provincial

Administration on a 99-year lease. The battlefield area was declared a National Monument in 1969.

In September 1998 and prior to the conversion of the mission house into a museum, an eminent South African archaeologist, Dr Lita Webley, was requested to undertake an archaeological research programme in order to establish the following:

The original position of the hospital;

The position of the commissariat store;

Whether there was any evidence to substantiate the present position of stones which have been placed to demarcate the original lines of the battle of 22–23 January 1879;

The location of the foundations of Fort Bromhead which was constructed on the site immediately after the battle;

Whether any evidence could be found for the position of Zulu snipers who apparently fired at the British troops from caves in the hillside of Shiyane.

Excavations were also considered to be of a rescue nature as significant artefacts or in-situ features had to be recovered before building contractors destroyed them. There were subsequent fieldtrips in May 1989 and March, June and August 1990. Members of the Evangelical Lutheran Community assisted with the excavations during the first three fieldtrips.

The Location of the Hospital Foundations

Rorke's house, subsequently occupied by Witt, became the field hospital during the Anglo-Zulu War. Burnt down by the Zulus, it is believed that Lutheran missionaries returning to the site rebuilt their mission house on the foundations of the hospital. It is this house that has been converted into a museum.

Some 20 metres were excavated around the house, but no trace of previous foundations was observed. Deposits around the house were not particularly abundant, except for in the kitchen area, where fragments of ceramics, glass and bone were recovered.

A number of trenches were then excavated inside the building. A comparison of the original floor plan of the hospital, drawn by Lieutenant John Chard (who was a Royal Engineer) with that of the plan submitted by Otto Witt when he rebuilt the mission house in 1882, indicates that the former was slightly smaller than the latter. Excavations in Room 7 inside the house uncovered several large quartzite stones that form a neat straight edge, as well as a more roughly constructed inner wall running at right angles. These features probably relate to the foundations of the hospital. The deposit around these stones was rich in charcoal and pieces of melted glass that testify to the blaze relating to the battle itself.

The Commissariat Store

To establish the position of the British Commissariat store a trench was excavated at right angles from the present church across the battlefield towards the rocky ledge for a distance of some 12 metres. As the aim of the excavation was to look for a specific feature, the trench was excavated to varying depths with pick and shovels and no sieving was undertaken. Close to the church the trench reached bedrock at about 1.2m, while near the end of the trench it was reached at only 45cm. This is because there is a pronounced slope down from the church to the cattle kraal and the position of the original redoubt. Most of the historic artefactual remains, such as some Martini-Henry cartridge cases and gin bottle fragments, were found close to these stones. It would appear that the store was built of both sandstone and red brick. Large numbers of gin bottle fragments, rusted iron objects and china were found on the inside (i.e. south) of the line of stones. Excavations however, failed to locate any evidence of an interior floor within the structure.

After following the foundations in a westerly direction, further excavations were undertaken to the east. The excavation of 8 square metres revealed what would appear to be the one corner of the store. The corner was well built and more substantial than the foundation stones in the other excavated areas. In addition, a roughly constructed stone wall angles out from this corner in a northerly direction. It is suggested that this roughly built stonewall is the remains of the fortifications of Fort Bromhead, built immediately after the battle linking the ruins of the hospital with the store and well-built kraal. The stones used for Fort Bromhead were probably used in the construction of the church, mission house and school buildings.

It would appear that the clearly defined row of stones relates to the British Commissariat store and Dr Webley believed that the foundation stones were probably those of the outer or front wall.

Excavations Across the Battlefield

After establishing the position of the 'hospital' and 'store', a number of trenches were excavated to bisect the outer lines of the battlefield. Some trenches were sited along the southern margin while others were intended to sample the top of the rocky ledge to the north. Although the barricades were of a temporary nature, it was incorrectly hypothesized that particularly dense numbers of cartridge cases and other military debris might indicate these lines. The absence of a clear stratigraphy on the battlefield itself suggests that both the levelling of the site prior to the construction of the new mission house and church in 1882 and gardening activities over a period of 100 years have destroyed much of the original stratigraphy. The dark loamy soil contained fragments of yellow clay, red brick lenses and the densest concentration of artefacts at depths of 0.3–0.5m.

It was further hypothesized that artefacts relating to the battle and to the subsequent occupation of the site by British soldiers between February and March 1879 would have been dumped beneath the ledge and would thus be concentrated in this area. Three large areas were therefore excavated immediately below the ledge. Very little artefactual material was recovered from these lower excavations. The dark brown soil was very shallow and overlaid sterile yellow clay. The deposit consisted mainly of recent builders' rubble, with virtually no historic material. An official from the N.P.A. work's branch office in Dundee informed Dr Webley that during the centenary celebrations at Rorke's Drift in 1979, a bulldozer had been used by the event organisers to 'neaten' the area below the ledge. The soil from this area was used to construct the ramp onto the battlefield so that visitors to the site could have more convenient access to the battlefield during the celebrations. In addition, he reported that members of the public had dug extensively at Rorke's Drift and at Fort Melvill during 1979 in search of artefacts relating to the battle and this is confirmed by newspaper reports from that time.

A Metal-Detector Survey of the Slope of Shiyane (Oskarsberg)

One of the aims of the archaeological research had been to attempt to gain new insights into the Zulu side of the battle. With the possible exception of the trade beads, no artefacts were recovered that could unequivocally be linked to them. With this in mind, Dr Webley and her team determined to survey the slopes of Shiyane, in particular examining the caves and ledges from which the Zulus are reported to have fired on the British. Most of the mortalities suffered by the British were as a result of Zulu sharpshooters firing from Shiyane. Since tourists have visited this area for over a hundred years, the team decided that a metal-detector survey would be the most economical means of recovering buried spears and spent bullets. At least three slugs of a .577 calibre were recovered from a cave overlooking the battlefield. They were within a metre of each other and were probably dropped by the same sharpshooter. The calibre of these bullets matched those of a wax-moulded bullet recovered from the front ledge of the battlefield. Furthermore, during the construction of a car park in front of the battlefield similar wax-moulded, fired slugs were recovered. These discoveries suggested that the team were recovering bullets that had been used during the battle of 1879. The fact that many of these slugs were recovered from the car park area (to the north of the battlefield) confirms reports that the Zulus were overshooting their targets.

Of the spent bullets from the car park area, three had rifling marks that suggested to a gun expert that they had been fired from an Enfield rifle. This would confirm observations in an article on firearms in the Zulu kingdom by Professor Guy[5] that muzzleloaders were fairly common in the period up to the 1870's. The Zulus could purchase both percussion Enfields and Tower muskets cheaply from suppliers in Mozambique, but these weapons were frequently obsolete and ineffective.

It is tempting to link the percussion caps found on the front of the rocky ledge to muzzle loaders used by the Zulu during the battle. However, Mechanick[6] has claimed that some of the NNC were still armed with muzzle-loading, percussion Enfields. The percussion caps may well have been dropped prior to the battle and before the NNC fled the scene. However, they may perhaps also be linked to James Rorke's occupation of the site. His will of 1876 lists 'a Rifle, a Dble [double-barrelled] gun and a revolver with cartridges'. We may also assume that since Rorke was a trader he probably dealt in arms and ammunition.

The metal-detector survey also recovered a number of Martini-Henry slugs in the vicinity of the caves on Shiyane, suggesting that the British soldiers were shooting back at a distance of 400 yards or more with their rifles.

Artefactual Remains

Metal

Two iron hoes were recovered behind the mission house next to doorways that have since been bricked in. The hoes were planted vertically in the soil and were used as shoe scrapers by the missionaries. Rusted nails were most commonly recovered. Other finds include buttons, buckles, tins, a spoon and a fork handle, a penknife, a trowel, iron bars, the heel of a boot, watch chains, brass razor blades, regimental buttons, small brass containers and coins including an 1862 Queen Victoria half penny. The sphinx badge (of the 24th Regiment) would probably have been worn on the collar, while the crown badge had probably broken off a helmet.

All that bears testimony to the battle were thirty-three Martini-Henry cartridge cases and seven unfired Martini-Henry bullets. Eleven percussion caps were found to the front of the rocky ledge. Unusual calibres include a .38 Smith and Wesson cartridge. One 12-bore shotgun firing pin was recovered from Extension 5 among all the Martini-Henry cartridges, suggesting that other firearms may also have been used during the battle. It is possible that this cartridge dates to the occupation of the site after the battle, as many officers owned their own hunting rifles. The wax-moulded slug of .577 calibre recovered from the rocky ledge matches slugs found in both a cave on Shiyane and in the car park area to the front of the actual fortified area. They present new light on the Zulu side of the battle.

In conclusion, all the aims of the archaeological project at Rorke's Drift were achieved, but with varying degrees of success. Sections of the foundations of the hospital were recovered under the floor of the present mission house-cum-museum. Charcoal pieces and fragments of melted glass confirm that this structure overlies the ruins of the field hospital burnt down by the Zulu.

The foundation stones of the front wall of the British Commissariat store were also located. It appears to have been largely situated underneath the present church, which would mean that the marker stones used to delineate the position of the store are incorrectly placed. They should be moved back (i.e. southward or toward Shiyane) some 8 metres. Excavations have uncovered 20 metres of the front foundations of the store, and it is therefore quite possible that the store could have been 80 foot in length as described by Otto Witt.

It is clear that the very intensive occupation of the battlefield for some three months after the battle probably resulted in a fairly complex stratigraphy. However, the deposit in and around the battlefield appears to have been subject to considerable disturbance right up to 1979 and it now seems unlikely that much could be gained by more extensive excavations of the area.

In addition to finding the position of the store, excavations also appear to have uncovered at least a portion of the walls of Fort Bromhead. A section of roughly constructed stonewall was found adjoining the back corner of the store, while a substantial portion of walling was also uncovered on the edge of the rocky ledge.

One important discovery, which resulted from the metal-detector survey, is that it appears that the Zulus were indeed over-firing the battlefield. It was recommended that another survey be undertaken of the slopes of Shiyane once the grass has been burnt, even though Dr Webley believed that any accessible material had been collected by visitors to the site during the last 100 years.

Modern aerial photographs of the mission area have highlighted some unusual features, such as cross-hatching in the field in front of the mission house and circular features near the turnstile in front of the rocky ledge. These features may be due to the British occupation of the area in 1879 but they could equally be ascribed to the agricultural activities of the missionaries; only archaeological research will solve this issue. Furthermore, Dr Webley felt that research should also be aimed at integrating the site with Fort Melvill, the military road to

Isandlwana, May's Hotel, Sihayo's kraal and Isandlwana itself, as Rorke's Drift should not be viewed in isolation.

The excavations at Rorke's Drift are a salutary reminder of the significant changes that can occur at a particular site over a very short period of time (archaeologically speaking). Despite the scale of the military conflict at Rorke's Drift, very few military items were recovered that support the historical accounts.

References

1. *AZWHS Journal*, Dec 2000, Dr Peter Mitchel.
2. *The Turbulent Frontier*, as quoted in *The Zulu War and The Colony of Natal*, Henderson. Sheila, edited by G. Chadwick and E. Hobson, 1979.
3. ditto.
4. *AZWHS Journal*, Dec. 2000, Dr Lita Webley.
5. *Journal of African History*, Professor Guy, J. quoting *Firearms in the Zulu Kingdom.*
6. Mechanick, F., '*Firepower and Firearms in the Zulu War of 1879*', *Military History Journal* 4 (6), 1979, 218–220.

Chapter 14

Bromhead Reports and Letters

The Bromhead Report

On 15 February, a report about the bravery of men at Rorke's Drift, subsequently called the Bromhead Report (signed by Bromhead although it is not known who actually wrote it), was submitted to his commanding officer, Colonel Glyn. Glyn simply forwarded it to Chelmsford without comment, although Chelmsford added Bromhead and Chard's names to the report for recognition of their actions. This was done without discussing the matter with Glyn. One could be justified in feeling puzzled as to why Glyn did not make recommendations of awards to these two lieutenants, especially as, being the officer in command, it was his prerogative. The report, submitted on rough paper, is produced here unabridged and unaltered, courtesy of the Royal Welsh Museum; Accession D87.72:

'From: Lieutenant Gonville Bromhead 2/24th Regt.
'To: The Officer Commanding 2/24th Regiment
'Rorke's Drift
'15 February 1879

'Sir,

'I beg to bring to your notice the names of the following men belonging to my Company who specially distinguished themselves during the attack by the Zulus on this Post on the 22nd and 23rd January last; and whose conduct on this occasion came under my personal cognisance.

'No. 1395 Private John Williams was posted by me together with private Joseph Williams and Private William Horrigan 1/24th Regt. in a further room of the Hospital. They held it for more than an hour, so long as they had a round of ammunition left, when, as communication was for the time cut off, the Zulus were enabled to advance and burst open the door. They dragged out Private Joseph Williams and two of the patients by the arms, and assagaied them. Whilst the Zulus were occupied with the slaughter of these unfortunate men, a lull took place, during which Private John Williams – who with two patients were then the only men left alive in this ward – succeeded in knocking a hole in the partition, and taking the two patients with him into the next ward, where he found

'No. 1373 Private Henry Hook. These two men together, one man working whilst the other fought and held the enemy at bay with his bayonet, broke through three more partitions, and were thus enabled to bring eight patients through a small window into our inner line of defence. In another ward, facing the hill, I had placed

'No. 593 Private William Jones &

'No. 716 Private Robert Jones: They defended their post to the last, until six out of the seven patients it contained had been removed. The seventh, Sergeant Maxfield, 2/24th Regt. was delirious from fever. Although they had previously dressed him, they were unable to induce him to move. When Private Robert Jones returned to endeavour to carry him away, he found him being stabbed by the Zulus as he lay on his bed –

'No. 1240 Corporal William Allen &

'No. 1362 Private Frederick Hitch, must also be mentioned. It was chiefly due to their courageous conduct that communication with the Hospital was kept up at all. Holding together at all costs a most dangerous post, raked in reverse by the enemy's fire from the hill, they were both severely wounded, but their determined conduct enabled the patients to be withdrawn from the Hospital, & when incapacitated by their wounds from fighting themselves, they continued, as soon as their wounds had been dressed, to serve out ammunition to their comrades during the night.

'I have the honour to be

'Sir

'Your most obedient servant

'G. Bromhead

'Lieutenant 2/24th Regt.

'Commanding B Company 2/24th Regt.'

Note: It was to this report that, contrary to Army Regulations, Lord Chelmsford added the names of Lieutenants Bromhead and Chard.[1]

Bromhead's letters

The following Bromhead letters are unabridged and unaltered:

Bromhead's letter to Lieutenant Goodwin-Austen

'Rorke's Drift
'19th February 1879
'My Dear Austin, (*sic*)

'I can't tell you how grieved I was to hear on the return of the Column on the 23rd of January that your brother had been left in that fateful camp. He had been attached to B Co at Freetown and we got on so jolly together that he told me he should ask the Colonel to let him stay with the Company, but I am sorry to say it was not to be. The night before the Column transport crossed the river it came out in orders that B Company were to remain here and your brother was sent back to G Company and Griffiths who was Company Officer as usual was posted to the Company. Your brother who was knocked up from over work at the ponts, where he had been working day and night, to get troops across the river had to go sick, but still he march (*sic*) with the Column. I have not got over the dreadful news we received yet, in fact can hardly believe it. We had an awful night of it here as you may fancy. We heard the camp had been taken, and were also afraid that the Column had received a heavy blow, and the Zulus came at us in such force and with such fierce pluck. I thought we should never pull through it, but the Company behaved splendidly (word unknown) as our ammunition held out and we held them back till daylight. We were on the Natal side of the Buffalo but can do nothing as far as I can see until we are fitted up again. I hope they are going to send us out some more troops or you won't see many of us again. The Zulus are so strong we stand a poor chance against them, as it is we expect to be attacked any day.

'I hope the wound is better, and that you do not suffer from it.

'Yours sincerely,
'G. Bromhead'

(Royal Welsh Museum Accession D87.72)

Bromhead's letter to his sister

This was written towards the end of February and it received limited publicity in Britain:

> 'I fear you will be very anxious about me as no doubt we are rather in a fix. I am getting over the excitement of the fight and the sickness and fury at our loss. It is not so much the poor fellows being killed as the way the savages treat them. Having been left alone we have built a mud fort, which I think we ought to hold against any amount of Zulus, till we get help from England. I send you a paper with the report of the fight and the remarks of the General on the behaviour of my company which are flattering. If the Government gives all the steps (promotions) of the poor fellows killed I shall most probably get my company into the 1st Battalion who are to go home directly after the war is finished. I have not got over the wonder of there being one of us left. God was very good to us in giving us a little time to get up a defence, or the black fellows would have taken us by surprise, which they will find hard to do now'.
>
> (Royal Welsh Museum Accession D87.721)

Chapter 15

The Enigma of the Chard Report

The official Chard Report by Lieutenant John Chard of the Royal Engineers, the officer-in-charge during the fighting at Rorke's Drift, has long been regarded as an important historical document which still fascinates and beguiles its readers. It is this initial handwritten account that Lord Chelmsford forwarded to the War Office to become the 'official' report of the attack on the Mission, yet there are curious circumstances surrounding the Report's origin, not least because it was completed and dated one day following the engagement and under the most challenging circumstances.

Although the Zulu attack at Rorke's Drift took place after dark, the Report's events that night have seemingly been well chronicled, and in the absence of other evidence, researchers have largely presumed the recorded sequence of the action is correct. The presumption for this consensus is the apparent acceptance of Chard's account and that what he wrote was accurate, thereby making the report a primary source. Recent investigations by modern researchers suggest the event was not quite as Chard recorded. Like all historical sources, the Chard Report has its own perspective and any researcher should resist the temptation of assuming the events described by this officer were correctly recorded, which, for multiple reasons, this author believes needs challenging.

Due to the passage of time, results from any investigation of the Chard Report can only be deduced by further examination and technical analysis. How the report came to be written must be considered and, by so doing, we can hope to unravel this enigma. For most students of the Anglo-Zulu War, Chard's account has become the settled orthodoxy of Rorke's Drift, with its subtle and articulate undercurrent of British heroism while fighting a ferocious and ingenious foe. What is completely accepted is that the engagement at Rorke's Drift took place and subsequently had a profound effect on Britain's immediate and longer-term history

In the 1990s an in-depth examination of the Chard Report by military archivist and curator of Caernarfon Castle, Norman Holme, proved beyond reasonable doubt the report was not written by Chard. Holme obtained forensic evidence which supported his theory.[1] His doubt is shared by this author, an accredited Zulu War battlefield guide, qualified clinical psychologist and former experienced senior police detective, whose research was from an investigative and psychological perspective. How could Chard, an officer not noted for his mental acuity, have witnessed, remembered and then accurately collated and recorded such a vast amount of information during the hours following the event – fought in darkness by soldiers he didn't know. Chard's report of the engagement, eruditely well-crafted and perfectly sequential report was complete in extraordinary detail, with no mistakes or corrections and written on clean undamaged paper – when all available paper had been burnt in the hospital fire or destroyed during the fighting. Coincidentally, when Chelmsford departed Rorke's Drift for Helpmekaar his staff officer, Major Clery, remained at the Mission and if he or anyone else had paper, it would logically have been made available for the garrison's Daily Orders and records of occurrences and incidents. But none was available. Even the original Bromhead-signed message sent to Colonel Glyn with the names of the six praise-worthy soldiers was written on an unofficial piece of paper and there is documented evidence that for weeks the Mission garrison had to seek out scraps of scorched paper to pen brief notes home.

The day after Isandlwana the bedraggled and exhausted survivors of Chelmsford's column returned to the ruined Mission, now home to 1,000 men. Extreme weather conditions set in and without shelter from the torrential wind and rain the fatigued survivors of both Isandlwana and Rorke's Drift fully expected a renewed Zulu attack at any moment. The Mission's two buildings had been razed to the ground, with their stores burned or destroyed. Clery commented on the conditions when he wrote home on 4 February:

> 'We have lost simply everything we had, except what we stood in – tent, clothing, cooking things, everything in fact – so that when we got anything to eat, we had nothing to cook it in, and when we got something to drink we had nothing to drink it out of.
>
> 'My present abode consists of a tarpaulin held up by some sticks and this I share with Colonel Glyn and the other staff officers. We have a little straw to lie on, but as this is the rainy season and as the rain here comes down in torrents, our straw gets very soaky at times. The ground is too hard for lying on, so one wakes in the morning very tender about one's bones.
>
> 'At first it was very hard on the men for they used to get wet through and had no change; indeed, for that matter there is very little in the way of change for any of us yet, but fortunately the Buffalo River lies close by, so by spending some time every day therein, and utilizing the powerful

rays of this tropical sun for the things we hang out to dry, we are holding on till we get some things from Pietermaritzberg'.

By then the survivors of Rorke's Drift and Isandlwana were all crammed together around the two ruined buildings. Amidst the chaos and without shelter, in increasingly unpleasant sanitary conditions surrounded by hundreds of dead Zulus and incessant downpours of rain, the site quickly became an unhygienic bog, making the preparation and drafting of a clean detailed report even more remarkable. How the report could include accurate timings, precise locations and correctly identify named participants in the dark remains a mystery. Chard had arrived at the Mission moments before the Zulus attacked and could not have known any of the participants except Major Spalding and Lieutenant Bromhead, yet there is no known record of anyone assisting Chard with the report. Chard had a reputation for slothfulness; he was known to both Captain Parke Jones and Lieutenant Curling, who both recorded anecdotes concerning Chard's character. Curling wrote:

> 'It is very amusing to read the accounts of Chard and Bromhead. They are about the most common-placed men in the British Army. Chard is a most insignificant man in appearance and is only about 5 feet 2 or 3 inches in height. Bromhead is a stupid old fellow, as deaf as a post'.

Parke Jones wrote:

> 'Chard makes me very angry, with such a start as he got, he stuck to the company doing nothing'.

Disregarding these difficulties, it was clearly in Lord Chelmsford's interest to obtain and promote a suitably dramatic report of the victory at Rorke's Drift which would deflect those critics seeking to humiliate him for the catastrophic defeat at Isandlwana. Although Chelmsford had not lingered at Rorke's Drift for more than a few hours, his personal notes are evidence that he was expecting a swift and comprehensive report concerning the survival of Rorke's Drift. He also issued instructions for a formal enquiry into the Isandlwana defeat to be immediately conducted at Helpmekaar.

Why Chard wrote the first report is unclear unless Chelmsford's staff took the initiative in ensuring that Chard signed a suitably impressive report, prepared by Chelmsford's staff, in order to offset the anticipated serious repercussions about to be unleashed following Isandlwana.

And so this multi-page, beautifully crafted, meticulously detailed account has become the key to most authors' understanding of events at Rorke's Drift. It was somehow prepared and written, without any mistakes or corrections, and within hours of the fighting, by this junior engineer officer who had no fighting or report writing experience. The swiftly produced report was immediately seized upon by the senior British military in South Africa and politicians at home to explain the inexplicable – how, just hours after the defeat and annihilation of the greater part of the British force invading Zululand, (in less than an hour 1,500 men were killed by the Zulu army at Isandlwana) a small detachment under the command of a junior engineer officer could, within both sight and hours of the appalling loss, snatch such an important victory from certain defeat at the hands of the Zulus? The Chard Report was enthusiastically circulated around the country with the glorious victory of Rorke's Drift masking the inglorious defeat at Isandlwana. Overnight its participants became household names and national heroes. The report was presented to Queen Victoria who then invited Chard, by now the holder of the Victoria Cross and promoted two ranks to Major, to a personal meeting with her at Balmoral. Bromhead was also invited but failed to receive the invitation as he was fishing in Ireland; he was not re-invited.

Chard's Report was pored over by the military and press. It was discussed in Parliament and it remains a masterful and significant account of an important military engagement. Over the years the report, dated 25 January 1879, and accompanying the Nominal Roll of Defenders, dated 3 February 1879, both signed by Chard, have been the focus for historians and authors to write their understanding of the event, usually depending on the Chard Report as their source. These two documents have helped form our collective understanding of what happened. As hand-written documents go, they are well crafted and precise, detailing the names and ranks of personalities involved in the action's many incidents as well as detailing the numerous incidents and phases of the battle with precise timings.

As a result of the considerable research by Norman Holme, doubts about the documents' authenticity lingered on. Holme arranged for their handwriting to be scientifically analysed, which ruled Chard out as its author (see ref.1), although it was signed by Chard so he had clearly allowed himself to be associated with the document. We know Chard was relatively uneducated and his military and academic skill had hitherto not been apparent, so it remains a mystery as to who wrote the actual report, and why. Of those present at Rorke's Drift after the event, only Major Francis Clery, one of Chelmsford's senior staff officers, had the necessary literary skills and it was Clery who remained at Rorke's Drift after Chelmsford departed.

But why Major Clery? Along with Chelmsford, Clery had been culpable in the unfortunate decision-making process that led to the defeat at Isandlwana and he, of all people, would have quickly realized that a dramatic report from Rorke's Drift might deflect the criticism that would undoubtedly be unleashed upon Chelmsford and his staff. Clery was a confidant of Chelmsford and an experienced report writer. He was a staff college graduate, a former Professor of Tactics at Sandhurst Military College and a talented man, although vain, ambitious, and prone to making gossipy judgements about his colleagues.

It would clearly have been in Chelmsford's interest to produce a dramatic report of the victory at Rorke's Drift which would pre-empt any critics seeking to humiliate him for the catastrophic defeat at Isandlwana. Although Chelmsford and his staff officers had not lingered at Rorke's Drift for more than a few hours, Chelmsford's notes reveal he had already requested a report concerning the survival of the Mission, in addition to issuing instructions for a formal enquiry to be conducted at nearby Helpmekaar into the circumstance surrounding the Isandlwana defeat. It is possible that Chelmsford's staff took the initiative by ensuring that Chard, as the senior of the two junior officers at Rorke's Drift, prepared and signed a suitably impressive report sufficiently weighted to offset the serious repercussions about to be unleashed following the appalling losses at Isandlwana. The purpose of an early 'top brass' account of the Rorke's Drift 'victory' was two-fold: it would deter searching and embarrassing questions from lower ranks and at the same time it would create a consensus which would make it impossible for an alternative viewpoint or submission of contradictory evidence. Furthermore, the Chard Report created the illusion of unanimity or 'group think' against which anyone dissenting would be classed as a malcontent and denigrated accordingly.[2]

Two further problems need addressing. Firstly, understanding how Chard managed to obtain all the details and individual experiences of the 130 soldiers present during the battle, bearing in mind he arrived at the Mission just an hour before the Zulus attacked as night fell. Secondly, how could he so accurately remember the overlapping sequence of events, mostly occurring in complete darkness, except for the flickering light thrown up from some smouldering thatch on Witt's house. Chard had not previously been noted for any skill at report writing, neither was he noted for it subsequently. Presumably, on this occasion, this quiet and reserved junior officer rose to the occasion and within hours of the trauma of being attacked for several hours by four thousand Zulus, and with numerous casualties, he not only prepared, but wrote this remarkable report.

For a junior officer to prepare and write the definitive account of any military engagement was unprecedented, so why did Chard even consider writing his account in the first instance – unless significant pressure from a senior officer prevailed upon him. Initially, the engagement at Rorke's Drift was not perceived as being particularly significant, either by the participants or by the army in

South Africa. It was the sum total of these events that would be used in the following weeks and months, first by senior officers and then by politicians, to cover their backs – yet the report had already been written on location and submitted. The questions have to be asked as to why and who had such foresight? Without doubt, the military commanders and politicians involved in the disastrous invasion of Zululand all had well-established reputations at stake and quickly saw the significance of the survival of Rorke's Drift to defend the indefensible. But who could have anticipated that a dramatic report of a stunning 'victory' at Rorke's Drift would mask the inexplicable military defeat at nearby Isandlwana. Perhaps Chelmsford was familiar with Machiavelli who wrote, 'A battle that you win cancels all your mistakes' and the same would apply to a battle that people believed you had won.[3]

This 'use of the event' by those at the highest level of the army occurred when it was quickly realised that the defeat at Isandlwana had serious consequences for Lord Chelmsford and many of his senior staff. Using the relatively insignificant success at Rorke's Drift, just hours following Isandlwana, involved someone deliberately deciding which events, from a massive inventory of possibilities occurring at different locations at different times, could be coordinated to be seen as 'significant'.

For those who survived, the process of someone else writing such an all-encompassing report additionally facilitated their own mental understanding of the confusing sequence of numerous incidents that occurred around them during the hectic six-or-so hours fighting. With their knowledge of such a report, their personal confusion of the previous hours would then have 'morphed' into a more easily understood, logically sanitized and smooth-flowing sequence of events. It is improbable Chard would have understood the significance of the process, let alone possessed the skill or the means to undertake its preparation and writing.

So whoever completed the draft that became the official 'First Chard Report' successfully created a logical firm baseline for all involved by neatly converting the confusing plethora of events into a credible and plausible chronological sequence. For Chard it reinforced and ordered his memories of the chaotic events into a logical and meaningful sequence. In reality, it is difficult to deduce any interpretation of what participants' actually perceived at Rorke's Drift, especially when they were disorientated by the dark of night amidst the chaos, noise, fear and death all around them. Such a scenario would have been fertile ground for a confused person fighting for his life to unwittingly try to make sense of events, especially when, so soon after the event, leading questions, praise or clarifying suggestions are presented to shocked participants (especially by respected people in authority). Attempting to identify who did what, when and where, or whether someone else was even present, must have been difficult for anyone to comprehend. Such questioning would certainly have blurred or confirmed participants' memories of what they actually saw, or what the interviewers wanted the witnesses to remember. It is well known that such questioning, especially if kindly and helpfully led, can seriously influence an individual's memory; this is why 'leading questions' are inadmissible in a modern court of law.

Recollections of traumatic events experienced in the heat of battle are likely to be confused, especially with the distinct probability looming of one's own imminent death. Memories of seeing colleagues being killed and maimed naturally creates shock and the only way to correct the subsequent psychological dissonance is the inadvertent and almost sub-conscious change that can occur to one's perception, interpretation and memory of such reality. In the most horrifying situations a person is likely to perceive and interpret events according to their own personal previous experience. In Chard's case, it was the strict military system that had trained him as an officer and his standing in that fixed hierarchy which would have influenced his recollection of events. It is unlikely that Chard's interpretations and decisions during the flow of battle would have been made with reference to the 'bigger picture' of the subsequent political whitewashing of Isandlwana. Chard's and other defenders' actions, observations and conversations in the battle would, most likely, have focused on their immediate survival – the 'here and now', rather than on how the event would later be portrayed to others.[4] For example, in 2004, Johnson Beharry VC wryly commented on the action in Iraq that earned him the Victoria Cross: 'At the time I was just doing my job, I didn't have time for other thoughts'.

Subsequently, Chard's willing participation in allowing his name to be used for the detailed official report can be understood. He would have long been bound by the strict military tradition requiring officers to conform to the establishment. The effect of the generous accolades he received at the time, were subtle rewards for his compliance with Chelmsford's request for a 'suitable' report. Chard was suddenly the hero, awarded the coveted Victoria Cross, promoted by two ranks and subjected to intense fame and, finally, being invited to meet Queen Victoria.

Chard undoubtedly experienced the psychological phenomena of confabulation; a substantial memory adjustment, usually subconscious, that is characterized by the effect of subsequent statements from influential 'others' that, wittingly or unwittingly, inaccurate or otherwise, alters a witness' perception of a recent event. It is unlikely that the process was deliberate on the part of Chard. This pressure on him, together with the on-going praise, rewards and adulation from those around him, contributed to and encouraged his confabulation.[5]

In the author's professional experience of dealing with serious cases of incident trauma, he and other experienced clinical psychologists[6] understood that the brain will endeavour to fill in memory gaps to make sense of a situation, especially when the individual had been under severe stress or suffering from sleep deprivation. The process is a natural 'defence mechanism' to help bring about normality, which is why confabulation is generally considered by psychologists to be 'honest lying' but is distinct from purposeful lying because there is typically no deliberate intent to deceive. Individuals so influenced are unaware that any manipulation or misinterpretation of their recall is likely to mislead others. Confabulation can also be made to make a complicated or lengthy incident become coherent and logical, and because it is a classic human defence mechanism, it makes sense out of nonsense, fills the gaps and ameliorates stress.

Academic research is conclusive that eyewitnesses to a dramatic event, such as a traffic accident, air crash or major public order incident, produce conflicting witness accounts which rarely concur although invariably made in good faith and honesty believed. Such witness statement disparity relating to serious events prove the inadvertent phenomena of honest 'false memory syndrome' caused by the brain trying to make sense of a sudden and serious event. Human memory has always been creative and easily influenced, and a wide variety of memories can be 'corrected' by suggestions and praise from others. Such 'over-awing' can be seen in Chard's case, of an unknown and exhausted junior officer receiving the praise, earnest attention and intense interest in the event he just survived by his very focused and respected General. Chelmsford's questioning of Chard took place in the immediate aftermath of the fighting in the presence of his senior staff officers, with the two buildings still smouldering and hundreds of bodies littered around. Such intensive and suggestive questioning under such extenuating circumstances is especially relevant where an individual, such as Chard, is also then admiringly applauded for his 'actions' by such highly regarded and respected figures. For Chard, actions that may not have quite occurred as Chard might have otherwise remembered, or were not actually witnessed by him, could be modified by the process of confabulation to become his own memories, otherwise known as 'reconstructed memory syndrome'.

The Chard Report also reveals a number of anomalies of 'perception versus known action' at Rorke's Drift. For example, Chard made no reference to the reason the British were defending Rorke's Drift. This has to be a deliberate omission from the report. He may have relied on Chelmsford's well-known guise of invading Zululand to protect Natal, confirming the historical habit of an aggressor nation to claim it is on the defensive. Chard also described seeing the ramparts around the Mission being built immediately prior to the arrival of the Zulus. What he probably saw was some last-minute preparations being made by soldiers at their individual posts because the Mission had already been fortified and entrenched as early as 11 January; such defences were confirmed in contemporary accounts written before the Zulu attack, both by Lieutenant Harford of the 99th Regiment and August Hammar, the Swedish national and family friend of Witt who was caretaking the Mission during Witt's absence. Chelmsford subsequently supported the Harford and Hammar accounts when he subsequently confirmed he had ordered Glyn to organize the defence of the Mission prior to the invasion on 11 January and that he 'understood Glyn had done this'.[7]

With regard to certain individuals' alleged presence and actions at Rorke's Drift, Chard mentions Reverend Otto Witt being one of the Oskarsberg group who initially witnessed the approaching Zulus yet Witt had departed a few days earlier to follow his wife and infant child having left his friend, August Hammar, in his place. In any event, neither the British nor Hammar could speak the others' language which probably gave rise to the misunderstanding that Hammar was Witt.

And was Lieutenant Adendorff actually present throughout as Chard originally wrote? It is odd that only Chard mentions Adendorff being at Rorke's Drift during the fighting, yet at the same time Adendorff was recorded arriving at Helpmekaar along with the many NNC fleeing back to Natal from Isandlwana and Rorke's Drift.[8] Subsequently, Chard was less confident about Adendorff's presence by writing, 'As far as I know, but one of the fugitives remained with us – Lieutenant Adendorff.' We know Adendorff met Chard at the nearby river crossing point just before the Zulus attacked, and we know he was at Rorke's Drift early the following day because Lieutenant Harford's diary confirms this, and Adendorff is included in Harford's pencil sketch of the disbandment of the NNC.[9] Curiously, various actions performed by Corporal Attwood of the Army Service Corps, for which he received the DCM, were wrongly attributed by Chard to Adendorff. This raises another issue; who nominated Corporal Attwood for his DCM? If it was Bromhead, then this suggests scant liaison even between the two officers post-battle.

Another alarming scenario overlooked by Chard was the unprecedented killing of any wounded and captured Zulus found post event near the Mission. This killing took place over the two days while the Report was being written and is omitted in both of Chard's accounts.

It was such common knowledge that Francis Colenso, the daughter of the Bishop of Natal, later wrote:

> 'The general and his staff hurried on to Pietermaritzberg via Helpmekaar while the garrison at Rorke's Drift was left in utter confusion. – as testified by many present at the time. No one appeared responsible for anything that might happen, and the result was one disgraceful to our English

> name, and to all concerned. A few Zulu prisoners had been taken by our troops – some the day before, others previous to the disaster at Isandlwana, and these prisoners were put to death in cold blood at Rorke's Drift. It was intended to set them free, and they were told to run for their lives, but they were shot down and killed, within sight and sound of the whole force. An eye witness, an officer, described the affair to the present writer, saying that the men he saw killed numbered "not more than seven nor less than five". He said he was standing, with others, in the camp, and hearing shots close behind him, he turned, and saw the prisoners in question in the act of falling beneath the shots and stabs of a party of our own men. The latter, were, indeed, men belonging to the Natal Contingent, but they were supposed to be under white control, and should not have been able to obtain possession of the prisoners under any circumstances.

Was this omission a memory lapse or the result of pressure from others? It is a curious fact that, in the history of warfare, the approval of commanders for the killing of prisoners creates a momentum which defies moral sensibility and discernment, and negates the capacity of the individual to distinguish between right and wrong or, as it appears in Chard's case, to ignore such wrong doing.[10] Confabulation would have allowed Chard to 'twilight' between knowing and not caring what happened to wounded or captured Zulus. Such an 'in between' state of mind allowed him either to accept what he saw as being unworthy of comment, or, whoever finalised the report, censored it by ignoring the matter.

Later in 1879, and safely back in England, Chard was required to submit a further and more detailed report at the request of Queen Victoria, this second report was to include greater detail. Nothing is known of the preparation or research that went into this second report other than the fact that apologies for the year-long delay were given to Queen Victoria as Chard claimed to have 'lost his notes'. No such notes have ever surfaced, which raises yet another question; did they ever exist? After a number of delays due to the 'lost notes', this second Chard Report was eventually submitted to Her Majesty at Windsor Castle on 21 February 1880. This poses another question; did Chard ever have the notes he allegedly lost? He probably had a 'copy' of the first report, because the second report mirrored the first but had more detail; even so it took another year to complete. It should be no surprise that, after the initial glory, Chard's career stalled.

Throughout history, victories have usually been reported as clinically succinct successes. Essentially the Chard accounts don't reflect all of what really occurred, hiding the fear, terror, emotion of killing and pain from being wounded; these memories have been largely omitted by this sanitised, even fantasised account.

How many harrowing scenes does Chard's report describe? None. Why not? Probably to cover the reality of the sheer if understandable brutality of what occurred. Interestingly, the first Chard Report, perhaps because of its preparation so soon after the battle, omits the unimaginable terror and gore at Rorke's Drift whereas, conversely, witnesses of the post-battle carnage at Isandlwana graphically gave full vent in their uncensored descriptions.

Though not all individuals exposed to such pressures will develop inaccurate memories, experiments suggest a significant number of people can be affected, and later, actively defend the existence of events as they subsequently understand them, even if later told they were false and deliberately implanted. An individual's personality structure will naturally play a role in their readiness to confabulate, and in Chard's case his apparent willingness to put his name to the report could be seen as a virtue higher than reflecting on whether his own report of the action tallied with reality. And of considerable importance, in the Victorian army, orders were orders, especially for a junior officer.

In the case of Rorke's Drift, the confabulated memories appear to have created the lasting memory, rather than Chard's and others' actual memories creating the story. Today the Chard Report is the preferred historical source which Lord Chelmsford quickly published regardless of the facts. It was essential for Chelmsford to impose a suitably concocted account of Rorke's Drift on public understanding, and the Chard Report was his means of saving his reputation. At the same time as this report was being prepared, rather than accepting any blame for the loss of the camp at Isandlwana, Chelmsford set out to falsely blame Colonel Durnford of the Royal Engineers. Durnford had conveniently been killed at Isandlwana and was unable to defend himself.[11] Following the defeat at Isandlwana, a Board of Enquiry was convened at Helpmekaar to consider what had occurred, but Chelmsford deliberately arranged that no detailed report was required from actual eyewitness survivors such as Lieutenant Curling of the Royal Artillery. Although long after the event, researchers are still at a loss as to the actual causes of the disaster at Isandlwana, citing various reasons such as inexperience, sealed and 'difficult to open' ammunition boxes, insufficient ammunition supplied to the troops, or a disregard of intelligence, to mention a few conjectures. No jury is needed for Rorke's Drift; based on the Chard Report the magnitude of the 'victory' took possession of the nation's imagination as a great victory.

And there matters rested until the end of 2012 when the Chard Report was further scientifically analysed by Dr David Holmes of The College of New Jersey, USA, in an attempt to establish the Report's author. On seeing this chapter in draft, Professor John Laband commented:

'We are all too often content to take in smooth, well written primary sources at face value and to stop short of proper analysis of the circumstances of their composition. I know only too well, which is why I give my more senior students exercises in document and artefact analysis to alert them to the pitfalls'.

He added:

'Of course, when you look at it, Chard's report was most probably well beyond his capabilities, but there on the spot were Chelmsford (an articulate man who couldn't stop writing if he tried) and Crealock (who knew better than anyone how to spin a situation) and sophisticated Clery too. With all these general and staff officers to help him (and they doubtless had good paper with them still) how could Chard fail to pen a clear, straightforward, effective report? My hunch is that this was a team effort which made all paths straight'.[12]

And so, what does the Chard Report actually leave us with. Probably a carefully cobbled-together account, a Bayeux Tapestry version of an historic event, stitched together by persons unknown to protect reputations.[13]

References

1. See Norman Holme's *The Silver Wreath* for the full account. Further, the author was awaiting publication of a Journal article when he received a call from a friend in South Africa informing him that another handwritten 'Chard Report' had been traced to the Oppenheimer Library in South Africa. He telephoned the library and within a half-hour he received a copy of the signature by fax. Having committed himself in his article to the hypothesis that the known 'Chard Report' was not signed by Chard, he was relieved to see the Oppenheimer handwriting and signatures were not Chard's. This Kimberley document appears to be an additional draft which somehow ended up at the Kimberley Public Library in the Transvaal where it remained undisturbed until it featured, seemingly unnoticed by researchers, in the Kimberley edition of the *Natal Mercury* on 22 January 1929, the event's 50th anniversary. Whether or not this 'Kimberley account' was an original draft or a copy of a draft is unknown. There are spelling variations and its comment that 'The original is in the hands of the Trustees of the Kimberley Library' suggests the possibility of yet another draft of the Chard Report.
2. For an academic account of this subject, see *The Victims of Group Think* by Professor Janis of Yale University.
3. Niccolo Machiavelli, 1469–1527, Italian historian and philosopher.
4. Journal of *The Victoria Cross Society*, January 2012.
5. Greaves. *AZWHS Journal 33.*

6. See 2013, *Journal of Experimental Biology*.
7. Quoted in *Hansard*.
8. *Forgotten Heroes*, Dutton, Roy. 2010: 'The register of Isandlwana fugitives who arrived at Helpmekaar on the night of 22/23 January includes Lieutenant Adendorff among the NNC'.
9. See Dr David Payne's *Harford*.
10. Examples are found in the actions of German soldiers in WWII and American soldiers in Vietnam.
11. For the full account of Chelmsford's plot against Durnford, see Greaves, Adrian. *Isandlwana*, Pen & Sword, Barnsley, 2011.
12. From correspondence between Professor Laband and the *AZWHS*.
13. Dr Greaves explains that the Bayeux Tapestry was woven by skilled English embroiderers at Canterbury based on the input of an unknown person, or people, present at the Battle of Hastings. See *1066 The Hidden History of the Bayeux Tapestry*, Andrew Bridgeford, Harper, 2004.

Chapter 16

The Chard Reports' Analysis

The 'First Chard Report' immediately became the official report concerning the Zulu attack on the mission station and was forwarded by Chelmsford to the War Office to lessen the impact and his culpability for the British defeat at Isandlwana; to this end he succeeded. Then, towards the end of 1879, when Chard was safely back in England, he was commanded to submit a further report to Queen Victoria. Chard was requested to include greater detail, although nothing is known of any preparation or research that went into this second report, other than the fact that apologies for a delay were given to Queen Victoria as Chard claimed to have 'lost his notes'. The identity of the author of the two reports remains unknown, although both documents were signed by Chard. (Both reports are unabridged and unaltered).

The First 'Chard Report'

'Rorke's Drift, 25 January 1879.

'I have the honour to report that, on the 22nd instant, I was left in command at Rorke's Drift by Major Spalding, who went to Helpmekaar to hurry in the company 24th regiment ordered to protect the ponts.

'About 3.15 pm on that day I was at the ponts, when two men came riding from Zululand at a gallop, and shouted to be taken across the river. I was informed by one of them, Lieutenant Adendorff, of Lonsdale's regiment (who remained to assist in the defence), of the disaster at Isandhlwana camp, and that the Zulus were advancing on Rorke's Drift. The other, a carbineer, rode off to take the news to Helpmekaar.

'Almost immediately I received a message from Lieutenant Bromhead, commanding two companies of the 24th Regiment at the camp, near the commissariat stores, asking me to come up at once.

'I gave the order to inspan, strike tents, put all stores &c., into the wagons, and at once made to the commissariat stores, and found that a note had been received from the third column, stating that the enemy were advancing in force against our post, which we were to strengthen, and hold at all costs.

'Lieutenant Bromhead was most actively engaged in loop-holing and barricading the store building and hospital; and connecting the defence of the two buildings by walls of mealie bags and the wagons that were on the ground.

'I held a hurried consultation with him, and with Mr Dalton, of the commissariat (who was actively superintending the work of defence, and whom I cannot sufficiently thank for his most valuable services), and entirely approved of the arrangements made. I went round the position, and then went down to the ponts and brought up the guard of one sergeant and six men, wagons &c. I desire here to mention the offer of the pont-man, Daniels and Sergeant Milne, 3rd Buffs, to move the ponts in the middle of the stream and defend them from their decks with a few men. We arrived at the post at about 3.30 pm. Shortly after, an officer of Durnford's Horse arrived, and asked for orders. I requested him to send a detachment to observe the drifts and ponts, and throw out supports in the direction of the enemy and check and advance as much as possible, falling back upon the post when forced to retire, and assist in its defence.

'I requested Lieutenant Bromhead to post his men; and, having seen his and every man at his post, the work once more went on.

'About 4.20 pm the sound of firing was heard behind the hill to our south. The officer of Durnford's returned, reporting the enemy close upon us, and that his men would not obey his orders, but were going off to Helpmekaar; and I saw them, apparently about 100 in number, going off in that direction. About the same time Captain Stephenson's detachment of the Natal Native Contingent left us, as did the officer himself.

'I saw that our line of defence was too extended for the small number of men now left us, and I at once commenced an entrenchment of biscuit boxes.

'We had now completed a wall two boxes high, when, about 4.30 pm, 500 or 600 of the enemy came in sight around the hill to our south, and advanced at a run against the south wall. They were met by a well sustained fire; but, notwithstanding their heavy loss, continued the advance to within fifty yards of the wall, when they were met by such a heavy fire from the wall, and cross-fire from the store, that they were checked; but, taking advantage of the cover afforded by the cook house, ovens, etc., kept up a heavy fire. The greater number, however, without stopping, moved to the left, round the hospital, and made a rush at our north-west wall of mealie bags, and after a short but desperate struggle, were driven back with heavy loss into the bush around the work. The main body of the enemy were close behind, and had lined the ledge of rocks and caves overlooking us, about 400 yards to our south, from where they kept up a constant fire, and, advancing somewhat more to their left than their first attack, occupied the garden, hollow road, and bush in great force. Taking advantage of the bush, which we had not time to cut down, the enemy were able to advance undercover, close to our wall, and in this part soon held one side of the wall, while we held the other. A series of desperate assaults were made, extending from the hospital along the wall as far as the bush reached but each was most splendidly met and repulsed by our men, with the bayonet; Corporal Schiess, Natal Native Contingent, greatly distinguishing himself by his conspicuous gallantry. The fire from the rocks behind us, though badly directed, took us completely in reverse, and was so heavy that we suffered very severely, and about 6 pm, were forced to retire behind the entrenchment of biscuit boxes.

'All this time, the enemy had been attempting to force the hospital, and shortly after set fire to its roof. The garrison of the hospital defended it room by room, bringing out all the sick who could be moved, before they retired. Privates Williams, Hook, R. Jones, and W. Jones, of the 24th regiment, being the last men to leave, holding the doorway with the bayonet, their own ammunition being expended. From the want of interior communication, and the burning of the house, it was impossible to save all. With most heartfelt sorrow, I regret we could not save these poor fellows from their terrible fate. Seeing the hospital burning, and the desperate attempts of the enemy to fire the roof of the stores, we converted two mealie bag heaps into a sort of redoubt which gave a second line of fire all round – Assistant Commissary Dunn working hard at this, though much exposed, and rendering most valuable assistance. As darkness came on, we were completely surrounded, and after several attempts had been gallantly repulsed, were eventually forced to retire to the middle, and then inner wall, of the kraal on our east. The position we then had retained throughout. A desultory fire was kept up all night, and several assaults were attempted and repulsed; the vigour of the attack continuing until after midnight. Our men firing with the greatest coolness, did not waste a single shot, the light afforded by the burning hospital being of great help to us.

'About 4.00 am on the 23rd instant, the firing ceased, and at daybreak the enemy were out of sight, over the hill to the south-west.

'We patrolled the ground, collecting the arms of the dead Zulus, and strengthened our position as much as possible.

'We were removing the thatch from the roof of the stores, when, about 7.00 am a large body of the enemy appeared on the hills to the south-west.

'I sent a friendly kafir, who had come in shortly before with a note to the officer commanding at Helpmekaar, asking for help.

'About 8.00 am the third column appeared in sight, the enemy, who had been gradually advancing, falling back as they approached. I consider the enemy who attacked us to have numbered about 3,000.

'We killed about 350. Of the steadiness and gallant behaviour of the whole garrison, I cannot speak too highly.

'I wish especially to bring to your notice the conduct of Lieutenant Bromhead 2/24th Regt., and the splendid behaviour of his company, B, 2/24th; Surgeon Reynolds, A.M.D., in his constant attention to the wounded under fire where they fell; Acting Commissary Officer Dalton, to whose energy much of our defences were due, and who was severely wounded while gallantly assisting in the defence; Assistance Commissary Dunn; Acting Storekeeper Byrne (killed); Colour Sergeant Browne, 2/24th; Sergeant Williams, 2/24th, (wounded dangerously); Sergeant Windridge, 2/24th; Corporal Schiess, 2/3 NNC (wounded); 1395 Private Williams, 2/24th; 593 Private Jones, 2/24th; Private McMahon A.H.C.; 716 Private R. Jones, 2/24th; Private H. Hook, 2/24th; Private Roy, 1/24th.

'The following return shows the number present at Rorke's Drift, on the 22nd of January, 1879:

	Officers	N.C. & Men	Sick N.C & Men	Total
Staff		1		1
Royal Artillerymen		1	3	4
Royal Engineers	1	1		2
3rd Buffs		1		1
1/24th Regiment		6	5	11
2/24th Regiment, B Company, 17 casuals sick	1	81	17	99
90th Light Infantry			1	1
Commissariat / Transport Department	3	1		4
Army Medical Department	1	3		4
Chaplain	1			1
Natal Mounted Police			3	3
Natal Native Contingent	1		6	7
Ferryman		1		1
	8	96	35	139

'The following is a list of the killed: -

'Sergeant Maxfield, 2/24th; Private Scanlon 2/24th; Private Hayden, 2/24th; Private Adams, 2/24th; Private Cole, 2/24th; Private Fagan, 2/24th; Private Chick, 2/24th; 1398 Private Williams, 2/24th; Private Nicolls, 1/24th; Private Horrigan, 1/24th; Private Jenkins, 1/24th; Mr. Byrne, Com. Department; Trooper Hunter, NNC; Trooper Anderson, N.N.P

'Private (native) NNC

'Total 15

'* 12 wounded of whom two have since died, viz: -

Sergeant Williams, 2/24th; Private Beckett, 1/24th

'* List already forwarded by medical officer.

'Herewith is appended a plan of the building, showing our lines of defence. The points of the compass referred to in this report are as shown in sketch approximately magnetic.

'I have, &c.

'(Signed) John R. M. Chard

'Lieutenant R.E.

'To Colonel Glynn, C.B., commanding 3rd Column'.

Chelmsford added the following comment to Chard's report;

'Sir,

'It is with much satisfaction that I have the honour to forward the report of the successful defence of Rorke's Drift post on the 22nd and 23rd January.

'The defeat of the Zulus at this post, and the very heavy loss suffered by them, has, to a great extent, neutralised the effect of the disaster at Isandhlwana, and no doubt saved Natal from a serious invasion.

'The cool determined courage displayed by the gallant garrison is beyond all praise, and will, I feel sure, receive ample recognition.

'As at the present moment the lesson taught by this defence is most valuable, I have thought it advisable to publish for general information the report in question which I trust will meet with your approval.

'Chelmsford

'Lieutenant-General'

The report was then urgently forwarded to The Secretary of State for War, The Right. Hon. Frederic Stanley, who promptly replied to Chelmsford:

'From; The Secretary of State For War 20–3–79
'To; Lieutenant General Lord Chelmsford, K.C.B.

'My Lord,

'I have received with great satisfaction your despatch of the 8th Feb. last, and its enclosure from Lieutenant Chard, R.E., containing a narrative of the heroic defence of the Post at Rorke's Drift on the night of the 22nd Jan. last.

'Having laid these documents before the Queen, I have received her Majesty's Commands to express to you her admiration of the gallantry of all who took part in that brilliant defence. The fertility of resource displayed in improvising defences and the cool and determined courage by which they were guarded and maintained have been especially remarked by her Majesty and will worthily take a prominent place in the annals of the British Army.

'I have conferred with H.R.H. the F.M. C. in C., as to the recognition which those officers, N.C.O.'s, Privates and others who are specially mentioned should receive, and I shall lose no time in making the necessary recommendations to Her Majesty on the subject.

'Fred Stanley'

The Second 'Chard Report' (Re-printed with kind permission of H.M. The Queen.)

'RORKE'S DRIFT

'The Defence of Rorke's Drift, 22nd 23rd January 1879
'An account of the defence of Rorke's Drift, written by Major J. R. M. Chard, V.C., R.E., at the personal request of Queen Victoria, and submitted to Her Majesty at Windsor Castle on 21st February 1880.

'Early in January 1879, shortly after the arrival of the 5th Company, Royal Engineers, at Durban, an order came from Lord Chelmsford directing that an officer and a few good men of the R.E., with mining implement, etc., should join the 3rd Column as soon as possible. I was consequently sent on in advance of the company, with a light mule wagon containing the necessary tools, etc., and in which the men could also ride on level ground; with a Corporal[1], three Sappers and one[2] Driver, my batman, who rode one, and looked after my horses. The wagon was driven by a Cape black man, with a Natal Kaffir lad as *vorlooper*. The roads were so bad that in spite of all our exertions, our progress was slow, and although we got a fresh team at Pietermaritzburg, we did not reach Rorke's Drift until the morning of the 19th January 1879. The 3rd Column was encamped on the other side (left bank) of the river Buffalo, and the wagons were still crossing in the ponts. I pitched my two tents on the right (natal) bank of the river, near the ponts, and close to the store accommodation there for keeping them in repair. On the 20th January, the 3rd Column broke up its camp on the Buffalo River and marched to Isandhlwana, where it encamped, and the same evening, or following morning, Colonel Durnford's force arrived and took up its camp near where the 3rd Column had been.

'There were two large ponts at the river, one of which only was in working order, and my sappers were during this time working at the other. Late in the evening of the 21st January I received an order from the 3rd Column to say that the men of the R.E., who had lately arrived, were to proceed to the camp at Isandhlwana at once – I had received no orders concerning myself. I reported this to Major Spalding, who was now in command at Rorke's Drift, and also pointed out to him that the sappers leaving there were no means at my disposal for putting the ponts in working order, or keeping them so. Major Spalding had also received no orders respecting me, except that I was to select a suitable position protecting the ponts, for Captain Rainforth's Company 1/24th to entrench itself. I consequently asked, and obtained permission from Major Spalding, to go to the camp at Isandhlwana and see the orders.

'On the morning of the 22nd January, I put the corporal and three sappers in the empty wagon, with their field kits, etc., to take them to the camp of the 3rd Column; and also rode out myself. The road was very heavy in some places, and the wagon went slowly; so I rode on in advance, arrived at the Isandhlwana Camp, went to the Head-Quarters Tent, and got a copy of the orders as affecting me, and also the road between Helpmekaar and Rorke's Drift and the orders also particularly stated that my duties lay on the right bank of the River Buffalo.

'A N.C.O. of the 24th Regiment lent me a field glass, which was a very good one, and I also looked with my own, and could see the enemy moving on the distant hills, and apparently in great force. Large numbers of them moving to my left, until the lion hill of Isandhlwana, on my left as I looked at them, hid them from my view. The idea struck me that they might be moving in the direction between the camp and Rorke's Drift and prevent my getting back, and also that they might be going to make a dash at the ponts.

'Seeing what my duties were, I left the camp, and a quarter of a mile, or less, out of it met with Colonel Durnford, R.E., riding at the head of his mounted men – I told him what I had seen, and took some orders, and a message all along his line, at his request. At the foot of the hill I met my men in the wagon and made them get out and walk up the hill with Durnford's men. I brought the wagon back with me to Rorke's Drift, where on arrival I found the following order had been issued. The copy below was given me, and preserved from the fact of its being in my pocket during the fight.'

'22nd January 1879'.

'Camp Morning Orders.

'The force under Lieutenant Colonel Durnford, R.E., having departed, a Guard of 6 Privates and 1 N.C.O. will be furnished by the detachment 2/24th Regiment on the ponts.

'A Guard of 50 armed natives will likewise be furnished by Captain Stevenson's detachment at the same spot – The ponts will be invariably drawn over to the Natal side at night. This duty will cease on the arrival of Captain Rainforth's Company, 1/24th Regiment.

'In accordance with para. 19 Regulations for Field Forces in South Africa, Captain Rainforth's Company, 1/24th Regiment, will entrench itself on the spot assigned to it by Column Orders para. – dated –

'H. SPALDING, MAJOR,

'Commanding'.

'The Guard as detailed was over the ponts – Captain Rainforth's Company had not arrived. I went at once to Major Spalding on arrival, told him what I had seen, and pointed out to him that in the event of an attack on the ponts it would be impossible with 7 men (not counting the natives) to make an effective defence. (According to the orders, Captain Rainforth's Company should have been already at Rorke's Drift.)

'Major Spalding told me he was going over to Helpmekaar, and would see about getting it down at once. Just as I was about to ride away he said to me 'Which of you is senior, you or Bromhead?' I said 'I don't know' – he went back into his tent, looked at an Army List, and coming back, said – 'I see you are senior, so you will be in charge, although, of course, nothing will happen, and I shall be back again this evening early.'

'I then went down to my tent by the river, had some lunch comfortably, and was writing a letter home when my attention was called to two horsemen galloping towards us from the direction of Isandhlwana. From their gesticulation and their shouts, when they were near enough to be heard, we saw that something was the matter, and on taking them over the river, one of them, Lieutenant Adendorff of Lonsdale's Regiment, Natal Native Contingent, asking if I was an officer, jumped off his horse, took me on one side, and told me that the camp was in the hands of the Zulus and the army destroyed; that scarcely a man had got away to tell the tale, and that probably Lord Chelmsford and the rest of the column had shared the same fate. His companion, a Carbineer, confirmed his story – He was naturally very excited and I am afraid I did not, at first, quite believe him, and intimated that he probably had not remained to see what did occur. I had the saddle put on my horse, and while I was talking to Lieutenant Adendorff, a messenger arrived from Lieutenant Bromhead, who was with his Company at his little camp near the Commissariat Stores, to ask me to come up at once.

'I gave the order to inspan the wagon and put all the stores, tents, etc., they could into it. I posted the sergeant and six men on the high ground over the pont, behind a natural wall of rocks, forming a strong position from which there was a good view over the river and ground in front, with orders to wait until I came or sent for them. The guard of natives had left some time before and had not been relieved. I galloped up at once to the Commissariat Stores and found that a pencil note had been sent from the 3rd Column by Captain Allan Gardner to state that the enemy were advancing in force against our post – Lieutenant Bromhead had, with the assistance of Mr. Dalton, Dr Reynolds, and the other officers present, commenced barricading and loopholing the store building and the Missionary's house, which was used as a Hospital, and connecting the defence of the two buildings by walls of mealie bags, and two wagons that were on the ground. The Native Contingent, under their officer, Captain Stephenson, were working hard at this with our own men, and the walls were rapidly progressing. A letter describing what had happened had been sent by Bromhead by two men of the Mounted Infantry, who had arrived fugitives from Isandhlwana, to the Officer Commanding at Helpmekaar. These two men crossed the river at Fugitives Drift, with some others and as they have since reported to me, came to give notice of what had happened, to us at Rorke's Drift, of their own accord and without orders from anyone.

'I held a consultation with Lieutenant Bromhead, and with Mr. Dalton, whose energy, intelligence and gallantry were of the greatest service to us, and whom, as I said in my report at the time, and I am sure Bromhead would unite with me in saying again now, I cannot sufficiently thank for his services. I went round the position with them and then rode down to the ponts where I found everything ready for a start, ponts in midstream, hawsers and cables sunk, etc. It was at this time that the Pontman Daniells, and Sergeant Milne, 3rd Buffs, who had been employed for some time in getting the ponts in order, and working them under Lieutenant MacDowell, R.E. (killed at Isandhlwana), offered to defend the ponts, moored in the middle of the river, from their decks with a few men. Sergeant Williams 24th and his little guard were quite ready to join them.

'We arrived at the Commissariat Store about 3.30 pm. Shortly afterwards an officer of Durnford's Horse reported his arrival from Isandhlwana, and I requested him to observe the movements, and check the advance, of the enemy as much as possible until forced to fall back. I saw each man at his post, and then the work went on again. Several fugitives from the Camp arrived, and tried to impress upon us the madness of an attempt to defend the place. Who they were I do not know, but it is scarcely necessary for me to say that there were no officers of H.M. Army among them. They stopped the work very much – it being impossible to prevent the men getting around them in little groups to hear their story. They proved the truth on their belief in what they said by leaving us to our fate, and in the state of mind they were in, I think our little garrison was as well without them. As far as I know, but one of the fugitives remained with us – Lieutenant Adendorff, whom I have before mentioned. He remained to assist in the defence, and from a loophole in the store building, flanking the wall and Hospital, his rifle did good service.

'There were several casks of rum in the Store building, and I gave strict orders to Sergeant Windridge, 24th Regiment, who was in charge (acting as issuer of Commissariat stores to the troops) that the spirit was not to be touched, the man posted nearest it was to be considered on guard over it, and after giving fair warning, was to shoot without altercation anyone attempted to force his post, and Sergeant Windridge being there was to see this carried out. Sergeant Windridge showed great intelligence and energy in arranging the stores for the defence of the Commissariat store, forming loopholes, etc.

'The Reverend George Smith, Vicar of Estcourt, Natal, and acting Army Chaplain, went for a walk (before the news of the disaster reached us) to the top of the Oscarberg, the hill behind Rorke's Drift. Mr. Witt, the missionary, went with him, or met him there. They went to see what could be seen in the direction of the Isandhlwana camp. He saw the force of the enemy which attacked us at Rorke's Drift, cross the river in three bodies – and after snuff-taking, and other ceremonies, advance in our direction. He had been watching them for a long time with interest, and thought they were our own Native Contingent. There were two mounted men leading them, and he did not realize that they were the enemy until they were near enough for him to see that these two men also had black faces. He came running down the hill and was agreeably surprised to find that we were getting ready for the enemy. Mr. Witt, whose wife and family were in a lonely house not very far off, rode off, taking with him a sick officer, who was very ill in hospital and only just able to ride. Mr. Smith, however, although he might well have left, elected to remain with us, and during the attack did good service in supplying the men with ammunition.

'About 4.20 pm the sound of firing was heard behind the Oscarberg. The officer of Durnford's returned, reporting the enemy close upon us, and that his men would not obey his orders but were going off to Helpmekaar, and I saw them, about 100 in number, going off in that direction. I have seen these same men behave so well since that I have spoken with several of their conduct – and they all said, as their excuse, that Durnford was killed, and it was no use. About the same time Captain Stephenson's detachment of Natal Native Contingent left us – probably most fortunately for us. I am sorry to say that their officer, who had been doing good service in getting his men to work, also deserted us. We seemed very few, now all these people had gone, and I saw that our line of defence was too extended, and at once commenced a retrenchment of biscuit boxes, so as to get a place we could fall back upon it we could not hold the whole.

'Private Hitch, 24th, was on the top of the thatch roof of the Commissariat Store keeping a look-out. He was severely wounded early in the evening, but notwithstanding, with Corpl. Allen, 24th, who was also wounded, continued to do good service, and they both when incapacitated by their wounds from using their rifles, still continued under fire serving their comrades with ammunition.

'We had not completed a wall two boxes high when, about 4.30 pm, Hitch cried out that the enemy was in sight, and he saw them, apparently 500 or 600 in number, come around the hill to our south (the Oscarberg) and advance at a run against our south wall.

'We opened fire on them, between five and six hundred yards, at first a little wild, but only for a short time, a chief on horseback was dropped by Private Dunbar, 24th. The men were quite steady, and the Zulus began to fall very thick. However, it did not seem to stop them at all, although they took advantage of the cover and ran stooping with their faces near the ground. It seemed as if nothing would stop them, and they rushed on in spite of their heavy loss to within 50 yards of the wall, when they were taken in flank by the fire from the end wall of the store building, and met with such a heavy direct fire from the mealie wall, and the Hospital at the same time, that they were checked as if by magic.

'They occupied the Cook-house ovens, banks and other cover, but the greater number, without stopping, moved to their left around the Hospital, and made a rush at the end of the Hospital, and at our north-west line of mealie bags. There was a short but desperate struggle during which Mr. Dalton shot a Zulu who was in the act of assegaing a corporal of the Army Hospital Corps, the muzzle of whose rifle he had seized, and with Lieutenant Bromhead and many of the men behaved with great gallantry. The Zulus forced us back from that part of the wall immediately in front of the Hospital, but after suffering very severely in the struggle were driven back into the bush around our position.

'The main body of the enemy were close behind the first force which appeared, and had lined the ledge of rocks and caves in the Oskarsberg overlooking us, and about three or four hundred yards to our south, from where they kept up a constant fire. Advancing somewhat more to their left than the first attack, they occupied the garden, hollow road, and bush in great force. The bush grew close to our wall and we had not had time to cut it down to our wall, and in this part soon held one side of the wall, while we held the other.

'A series of desperate assaults was made, on the Hospital, and extending from the Hospital, as far as the bush reached; but each was most splendidly met and repulsed by our men, with the bayonet. Each time as the attack was repulsed by us, the Zulus close to us seemed to vanish in the bush, those some little distance off keeping up a fire all the time. Then, as if moved by a single impulse, they rose up in the bush as thick as possible, rushing madly up to the wall (some of them being already close to it), seizing, where they could, the muzzles of our men's rifles, or their bayonets, and attempting to use their assegais and to get over the wall. A rapid rattle of fire from our rifles, stabs with the bayonet, and in a few moments the Zulus were driven back, disappearing in the bush as before, and keeping up their fire. A brief interval, and the attack would be again made, and repulsed in the same manner. Over and over again this happened, our men behaving with the greatest coolness and gallantry.

'It is impossible for one individual to see all, but I particularly myself noticed the behaviour of Colonel Sergeant Bourne, 24th, Sergeant Williams 24th, Corpl. Schiess N.N.C., Corpl. Lyons 24th, Private McMahon A.H.C., Privates Roy, Deacon, Bush, Cole, Jenkins 24th, and many others.

'Our fire at the time of these rushes of the Zulus was very rapid – Mr. Dalton dropping a man each time he fired his rifle, while Bromhead and myself used our revolvers. The fire from the rocks and caves on the hill behind us was kept up all this time and took us completely in reverse, and although very badly directed, many shots came among us and caused us some loss – and at about 6.00 pm the enemy extending their attack further to their left, I feared seriously would get in over our wall behind the biscuit boxes. I ran back with 2 or 3 men to this part of the wall and was immediately joined by Bromhead with 2 or 3 more. The enemy stuck to this assault most tenaciously, and on their repulse, and retiring into the bush, I called all the men inside our retrenchment – and the enemy immediately occupied the wall we had abandoned and used it as a breastwork to fire over.

'Mr. Byrne, acting Commissariat Officer, and who had behaved with great coolness and gallantry, was killed instantaneously shortly before this by a bullet through the head, just after he had given a drink of water to a wounded man of the N.N.C.

'All this time the enemy had been attempting to fire the Hospital and had at length set fire to its roof and got in at the far end. I had tried to impress upon the men in the Hospital the necessity for making a communication right through the building – unfortunately this was not done. Probably at the time the men could not see the necessity, and doubtless also there was no time to do it. Without in the least detracting from the gallant fellows who defended the Hospital, and I hope I shall not be misunderstood in saying so, I have always regretted, as I did then, the absence of my four poor sappers, who had only left that morning for Isandhlwana and arrived there just to be killed.

'The garrison of the Hospital defended it with the greatest gallantry, room by room, bringing out all the sick that could be moved, and breaking through some of the partitions while the Zulus were in the building with them. Privates Williams, Hook, R. Jones and W. Jones being the last to leave and holding the doorway with the bayonet, their ammunition being expended. Private Williams's bayonet was wrenched off his rifle by a Zulu, but with the other men he still managed with the muzzle of his rifle to keep the enemy at bay. Surgeon Reynolds carried his arms full of ammunition to the Hospital, a bullet striking his helmet as he did so. But we were too busily engaged outside to be able to do much, and with the Hospital on fire, and no free communication, nothing could have saved it. Sergeant Maxfield 24th might have been saved, but he was delirious with fever, refused to move and resisted the attempts to move him. He was assegaied before our men's eyes.

'Seeing the hospital burning, and the attempts of one enemy to fire the roof of the Store (one man was shot, I believe by Lieutenant Adendorff, who had a light almost touching the thatch), we converted two large heaps of mealie bags into a sort of redoubt which gave a second line of fire all around, in case the store building had to be abandoned, or the enemy broke through elsewhere. Assistant Commissary Dunn worked hard at this, and from his height, being a tall man, he was much exposed, in addition to the fact that the heaps were high above our walls, and that most of the Zulus bullets were high.

'Trooper Hunter, Natal Mounted Police, escaping from the Hospital, stood still for a moment, hesitating which way to go, dazed by the glare of the burning Hospital, and the firing that was going on all around. He was assegaied before our eyes, the Zulu who killed him immediately afterwards falling. While firing from behind the biscuit boxes, Dalton, who had been using his rifle with deadly effect, and by his quickness and coolness had been the means of saving many men's lives, was shot through the body. I was standing near him at the time, and he handed me his rifle so coolly that I had no idea until afterwards of how severely he was wounded. He waited quite quietly for me to take the cartridges he had left out of his pockets. We put him inside one mealie sack redoubt, building it up around him. About this time I noticed Private Dunbar 24th make some splendid shooting, seven or eight Zulus falling on the ledge of rocks in the Oscarberg to as many consecutive shots by him. I saw Corporal Lyons hit by a bullet which lodged in his spine, and fall between an opening we had left in the wall of biscuit boxes. I though he was killed, but looking up he said, 'Oh, Sir! You are not going to leave me here like a dog?' We pulled him in and laid him down behind the boxes where he was immediately looked to by Reynolds.

'Corporal Scammle (Scammell) of the Natal Native Contingent, who was badly wounded through the shoulder, staggered out under fire again, from the Store building where he had been put, and gave me all his cartridges, which in his wounded state he could not use. While I was intently watching to get a fair shot at a Zulu who appeared to be firing rather well, Private Jenkins 24th, saying "Look out, Sir," gave my head a duck down just as a bullet whizzed over it. He had noticed a Zulu who was quite near in another direction taking a deliberate aim at me. For all the man could have known, the shot might have been directed at himself. I mention these facts to show how well the men behaved and how loyally worked together.

'Corporal Schiess, Natal Native Contingent, who was a patient in the Hospital with a wound in the foot, which caused him great pain, behaved with the greatest coolness and gallantry throughout the attack, and at this time creeping out a short distance along the wall we had abandoned, and slowly raising himself, to get a shot at some of the enemy who had been particularly annoying, his hat was blown off by a shot from a Zulu the other side of the wall. He immediately jumped up, bayonetted the Zulu and shot a second, and bayonetted a third who came to their assistance, and then returned to his place.

'As darkness came on we were completely surrounded. The Zulus wrecking the camp of the Company 24th and my wagon which had been left outside, in spite of the efforts of my batman, Driver Robson (the only man of the Royal Engineers with us), who had directed his particular attention to keeping the Zulus off his wagon in which were, as he described it, "Our things."

'They also attacked the east end of our position, and after being several times repulsed, eventually got into the Kraal, which was strongly built with high walls, and drove us to the middle, and then to the inner wall of the Kraal – the enemy occupying the middle wall as we abandoned it. This wall was too high for them to use it effectively to fire over, and a Zulu no sooner showed his head over it than he was dropped, being so close that it was almost impossible to miss him. Shortly before this, some of the men said they saw the red-coats coming on the Helpmekaar road. The rumour passed quickly round – I could see nothing of the sort myself, but some men said they could. A cheer was raised, and the enemy seemed to pause, to know what it meant, but there was no answer to it, and darkness came. It is very strange that this report should have arisen amongst us, for the two companies 24th from Helpmekaar did come down to the foot of the hill, but not, I believe, in sight of us. They marched back to Helpmekaar on the report of Rorke's Drift having fallen.

'After the first onslaught, the most formidable of the enemy's attacks was just before we retired behind our line of biscuit boxes, and for a short time after it, when they had gained great confidence by their success on the Hospital. Although they kept their positions behind the walls we had abandoned, and kept up a heavy fire from all sides until about 12 o'clock, they did not actually charge up in a body to get over our wall after about 9 or 10 o'clock. After this time it became very dark, although the Hospital roof was still burning – it was impossible from below to see what was going on, and Bromhead and myself getting up on the mealie sack redoubt, kept an anxious watch on all sides.

'The enemy were now in strong force all around us, and every now and then a confused shout of 'Usutu' from many voices seemed to show that they were going to attack from one side and immediately the same thing would happen on the other, leaving us in doubt as to where they meant to attack. About midnight or a little after the fire slackened, and after that, although they kept us constantly on the alert, by feigning, as before, to come on at different points, the fire was of a desultory character. Our men were careful, and only fired when they could see a fair chance. The flame of the burning Hospital was now getting low, and as pieces of the roof fell, or hitherto unburnt parts of the thatch ignited, the flames would blaze up illuminating our helmets and faces. A few shots from the Zulus, replied to by our men – again silence, broken only by the same thing repeatedly happening. This sort of thing went on until about 4.00 am and we were anxiously waiting for daybreak and the renewal of the attack, which their comparative, and at length complete silence, led us to expect. But at daybreak the enemy were out of sight, over the hill to our south-west. One Zulu remained in the Kraal and fired a shot among us (without doing any damage) as we stood on the walls, and ran off in the direction of the river – although many shots were fired at him as he ran. I am glad to say the plucky fellow got off.

'Taking care not to be surprised by any ruse of the enemy, we patrolled the ground around the place, collecting the arms, and ammunition, of the dead Zulus.

'Some of the bullet wounds were very curious. One man's head was split open, exactly as if done with an axe. Another had been hit just between the eyes, the bullet carrying away the whole of the back of his head, leaving his face perfect, as though it were a mask, only disfigured by the small hole made by the bullet passing through. One of the wretches we found, one hand grasping a bench that had been dragged from the Hospital, and sustained thus in the position we found him in, while in the other hand he still clutched the knife with which he had mutilated one of our poor fellows, over whom he was still leaning.

'We increased the strength of our defences as much as possible, strengthening and raising our walls, putting sacks on the biscuit boxes, etc., and were removing the thatch from the roof of the Commissariat Store, to avoid being burnt out in case of another attack, when at about 7.00 am a large body of the enemy (I believe the same who had attacked us) appeared on the hills to the south-west. I thought at the time that they were going to attack us, but from what I now know from Zulus, and also of the number we put hors de combat, I do not think so. I think that they came up on the high ground to observe Lord Chelmsford's advance; from there they could see the Column long before it came in sight of us.

'A frightened and fugitive Kaffir came in shortly before, and I sent for Daniells the Pontman, who could speak Zulu a little, to interview him. Daniells had armed himself with Spalding's sword, which he flourished in so wild and eccentric manner that the poor wretch thought his last hour had come. He professed to be friendly and to have escaped from Isandhlwana, and I sent him with a note to the Officer Commanding at Helpmekaar, explaining our situation, and asking for help; for now, although the men were in excellent spirits, and each man had a good supply of ammunition in his pouches, we had only about a box and a half left besides, and at this time we had no definite knowledge of what had happened, and I myself did not know that the part of the Column with Lord Chelmsford had taken any part in the action at Isandhlwana, or whether on the Camp being taken he had fallen back on Helpmekaar.

'The enemy remained on the hill, and still more of them appeared, when about 8.00 am the Column came in sight and the enemy disappeared again. There were a great many of our Native Levies with the Column, and the number of red-coats seemed so few that at first we had grave doubts that the force approaching was the enemy. We improvised a flag, and our signals were soon replied to from the Column. The mounted men crossed the Drift and galloped up to us, headed by Major Cecil Russell and Lieutenant Walsh, and were received by us with a hearty cheer. Lord Chelmsford, with his Staff, shortly after rode up and thanked us all with much emotion for the defence we had made. The Column arrived, crossing by the Ponts, and we then had a busy time in making a strong position for the night.

'I was glad to seize an opportunity to wash my face in a muddy puddle, in company with Private Bush 24th, whose face was covered with blood from a wound in the nose caused by the bullet which had passed through and killed Private Cole 24th. With the politeness of a soldier, he lent me his towel, or, rather, a very dirty half of one, before using it himself, and I was very glad to accept it.

'In wrecking the stores in my wagon, the Zulus had brought to light a forgotten bottle of beer, and Bromhead and I drank it with mutual congratulations on having come safely out of so much danger.

'My wagon driver, a Cape (coloured) man, lost his courage on hearing the first firing around the hill. He let loose his mules and retreated, concealing himself in one of the caves of the Oscarberg. He saw the Zulus run by him and, to his horror, some of them entered the cave he was in, and lying down commenced firing at us. The poor wretch was crouching in the darkness, in the far depths of the cave, afraid to speak or move, and our bullets came into the cave, actually killing one of the Zulus. He did not know from whom he was in the most danger, friends or foes, and came down in the morning looking more dead than alive. The mules we recovered; they were quietly grazing by the riverside.

'On my journey homewards, on arriving at the railway station, Durban, I asked a porter to get me some Kaffirs to carry my bags to the hotel. He sent several, and the first to come running up was my vorlooper boy who had taken me to Rorke's Drift. He stopped short and looked very frightened, and I believe at first thought he saw my ghost. I seized him to prevent his running away, and when he saw that I was flesh and blood he became reassured. He said he thought I got away, he said (the solution of the mystery just striking him), 'I know you rode away on the other horse.' As far as I could learn and according to his own story, the boy had taken the horse I rode from the river to the Commissariat Store, and, wild with terror, had ridden it to Pietermaritzburg without stopping, where he gave it over to the Transport people, but having no certificate to say who he was, they took the horse from him but would not give him any employment.

'During the fight there were some very narrow escapes from the burning Hospital. Private Waters, 24th Regiment, told me that he secreted himself in a cupboard in the room he was defending, and from it shot several Zulus inside the Hospital. He was wounded in the arm, and he remained in the cupboard until the heat and smoke were so great that they threatened to suffocate him. Wrapping himself in a cloak, or skirt of a dress he found in the cupboard, he rushed out into the darkness and made his way into the cook-house. The Zulus were occupying this, and firing at us from the wall nearest us. It was too late to retreat, so he crept softly to the fireplace and, standing up in the chimney, blacked his face and hands with soot. He remained there until the Zulus left. He was very nearly shot in coming out, one of our men at the wall raising his rifle to do so at the sight of his black face and strange costume, but Waters cried out just in time to save himself. He produced the bullet that wounded him, with pardonable pride, and was very amusing in his admiring description of Dr Reynolds' skill in extracting it.

'Gunner Howard, R.A., ran out of the burning Hospital, through the enemy, and lay down on the upper side of the wall in front of our N. Parapet. The bodies of several horses that were killed early in the evening were lying here, and concealed by these and by Zulu bodies and the low grass and bushes, he remained unseen with the Zulus all around him until they left in the morning.

'Private Beckett, 24th Regiment, escaped from the Hospital in the same direction, he was badly wounded with assegais in running through the enemy. He managed to get away and conceal himself in the ditch of the Garden, where we found him next morning. The poor fellow was so weak from loss of blood that he could not walk, and he died shortly afterwards.

'Our mealie-bag walls were afterwards replaced by loopholed walls of stone, the work making rapid progress upon the arrival of half the 5th Company R.E. with Lieutenant Porter. As soon as the Sappers arrived we put a fence around, and a rough wood cross over the graves of our poor men who were killed. This was afterwards replaced by a neat stone monument and inscription by the 24th, who remained to garrison the place.

'I have already, in my report, said how gallantly all behaved, from Lieutenant Bromhead downwards, and I also mentioned those whom I had particularly noticed to have distinguished themselves.

'On the day following, we buried 351 bodies of the enemy in graves not far from the Commissariat Buildings – many bodies were since discovered and buried, and when I was sick at Ladysmith one of our Sergeants, who came down there invalided from Rorke's Drift, where he had been employed in the construction of Fort Melvill, told me that many Zulu bodies were found in the caves and among the rocks, a long distance from the Mission house, when getting stone for that fort. As, in my report, I underestimated the number we killed, so I believe I also underestimated the number of the enemy that attacked us, and from what I have since learnt I believe the Zulus must have numbered at least 4,000.

'As the Reverend George Smith said in a short account he wrote to a Natal paper –

'Whatever signs of approval may be conferred upon the defenders of Rorke's Drift, from high quarters, they will never cease to remember the kind and heartfelt expressions of gratitude which have fallen both from the columns of the Colonial Press and from so many of the Natal Colonists themselves.

'And to this may I add that they will ever remember with heartfelt gratitude the signs of approval that have been conferred upon them by their Sovereign and by the People and the Press of England.

'JOHN R. M. CHARD,

'January 1880. Captain and Bt. Major, R.E.'

The Two Chard Reports – A Scientific Analysis

To endeavour to discover who wrote the two Chard reports the *AZWHS* liaised with Dr David I. Holmes, a noted stylometric expert of The College of New Jersey, USA. A full explanation of the charts, observations and diagrams relating to this analysis is to be found in Appendix 6. They are copyright and courtesy of Dr David Holmes.

Stylometry is a body of scientific techniques used for the statistical analysis of literary style. So, could such an analysis help resolve the authorship of the two reports? These techniques date back to 1851, when the English logician Augustus de Morgan suggested in a letter to a friend that questions of authorship might be settled by determining if one text 'does not deal in longer words' than another. Since then stylometrists such as Dr David Holmes and his team have searched for a reliable way of quantifying the style of a text that may be unique to an author. Growing computer power and the ready availability of machine-readable versions of many literary works have created a plethora of new techniques to examine authorship. Most researchers now believe that common words are the most valuable in characterizing an author's stylometric signature. They study the so-called non-contextual function words – prepositions, conjunctions, articles and adverbs – the 'humble servants' of speech, words that every writer employs subconsciously in a pattern as distinctive as a fingerprint. These two reports are significant for history; it would therefore be helpful to use stylometry to help establish the true identity of their author(s).

In the final analysis, stylometric testing of the Chard report has given us no clear and definite authorship of the report. There is the possibility that an original report by Chard was passed through several hands, with corrections, additions, subtractions and stylistic improvements all building and trimming the final report, which was then transcribed by a totally different hand. Neither do the reports appear to be by Frank Bourne. Bourne may well have added details, but the slightly closer similarity here may reflect the fact that Bourne was very familiar with Chard's first report by the time he gave his own account.

Such important reports, which had in their power the potential to exonerate the senior officers from calamitous blame for Isandlwana, would be likely to have been judiciously reviewed and altered before their final submission. By ratcheting-up the victory at Rorke's Drift, the defeat at Isandlwana could be effectively softened, as it indeed was. No senior officer would allow an unchecked report on such an important event to see the light of day until it had been put into the most favourable form. Thus the Chard report should be viewed in that light and should probably be regarded as a compilation of the available facts, which then was signed by Chard.

According to the researchers, they were left then with the following conclusions:

a. Both the first and second Chard Reports appear to be by the same hand.
b. That hand is not that of Chard or Francis Clery, despite Clery being mooted as a strong contender for authorship. Regrettably, apart from a brief 312-word letter written in September 1879 to Sir John Stokes of *The Royal Engineer Journal*, it may surprise readers to learn that no usable authentic written material from Chard is known to exist.

This research project now lies somewhat tantalizingly on hold, awaiting any future discovery by Anglo-Zulu War historians of new textual material from those who were present at Rorke's Drift.

Chapter 17

Helpmekaar and Chelmsford's Enquiry

At its best, Helpmekaar is a high, open, windswept and desolate location on the edge of the extensive Biggarsberg range of hills with both Rorke's Drift and Isandlwana distantly visible on a clear day. Since 1879 little has changed. Its bleakness is appropriately described by Major Harness RA on arriving at Helpmekaar: 'Like the bottom of the sea with grass on it'. It has not changed over the years. It was never a popular place with British soldiers and its reputation was about to get much worse, especially for the sick and wounded.

When the bedraggled and exhausted survivors from Isandlwana reached Helpmekaar, the sight that greeted them offered little comfort. The bustling depot they had left just a fortnight earlier had been reduced to an unfortified wind-swept and storm sodden area consisting of three corrugated store sheds and a few battered tents belonging to a section of infantry that had been left behind as guards. As news of Isandlwana arrived the senior officer present, Captain Essex, took command and organised its defence with the few tools that he had at his disposal. He made a small laager by surrounding the main zinc shed with the three wagons left and infilling the gaps with sacks of mealies. At this time there were forty-eight people, including volunteers, camp followers and three farmers with their families who sought protection. For several anxious hours, there were just twenty-eight rifles to defend Helpmekaar from the attack that was fully expected.

The fatigued volunteers had little enthusiasm for fighting and began to take their horses and drift away. When Essex realized that his force was melting away he threatened to shoot all the horses to stop further desertions, which lowered morale still further. Now aware that a disaster had occurred, and with refugees steadily arriving, a register of refugees and their accounts of Isandlwana and Rorke's Drift was opened to record who had survived, what had occurred and where.[1] Three of these survivors also rode off and were to become figures of controversy. Lieutenant Higginson of the NNC had been with both Melvill and Coghill as they had clung to the rock in the Buffalo River. On reaching the bank, he had promised to fetch horses for the other two. Instead, once he had found a mount, he had ridden off to safety. His action was reported by another survivor, Trooper Barker of the Natal Carbineers. At the same time, Captain

Stephenson of the NNC had deserted from Rorke's Drift as the Zulus were about to attack; at Helpmekaar he registered as a Rorke's Drift survivor before riding off, only to be later arrested, court-martialled and dismissed the service. Lieutenant Adendorff was also recorded as a deserter from Rorke's Drift but because Chard's account of the action at Rorke's Drift included Adendorff his case was quietly dropped.

Lieutenant Curling RA who had, alone, survived the front line at Isandlwana and escaped to Helpmekaar wrote to his mother on 30 January, mentioning that life at Helpmekaar was grim: 'We have 30 sick and wounded men inside and several typhoid patients who however are left in a tent outside where of course they will at once be killed if we are attacked'. In the aftermath of Isandlwana, there was a climate of suspicion and paranoia about any native caught near both Rorke's Drift and Helpmekaar. On a visit to Rorke's Drift Curling had seen a Zulu hanging from a tree and several natives met a similar fate at Helpmekaar, even though they were probably entirely innocent. On 2 February Curling wrote:

> 'What is going to happen to us, no one knows. We have made a strong entrenchment and are pretty safe even should we be attacked. The only thing we are afraid of is sickness. There are 50 sick and wounded already who are jammed up at night in the fort. The smell is terrible, 800 men cooped up in so small a place. Food, fortunately, is plentiful and we have a three months' supply. All spys (*sic*) taken now are shot: we have disposed of three or four already. Formally (*sic*), they were allowed anywhere and our disaster is a great extent due to their accurate information of the General's movements. What excitement this will cause in England and what indignation'.

The suggestion that a Zulu spy network was the cause of Chelmsford's defeat was indicative of the wild theories, rumours and excuses circulating around the British camps. Curling was right, though, about the shock and outrage with which the news of the disaster was received in Britain.

Following the British defeat at Isandlwana, Lord Chelmsford paused at Helpmekaar long enough to convene a Court of Enquiry to investigate Isandlwana. It consisted of senior officers then at Helpmekaar and commenced its deliberations five days later, on 27 January 1879. The court president was Colonel F.C. Hassard with Lieutenant Colonel Law RA and Lieutenant Colonel Harness RA as court members. The nature of the enquiry was extraordinary when compared with standard military procedures; their brief was merely to 'enquire into the loss of the camp' at Isandlwana. Although a number of officers and men had been required to make statements relating to their escape from Isandlwana, the Court recorded only such evidence of Majors Clery and Crealock, Captains Essex, Gardner, and Cochrane, Lieutenants Curling and Smith-Dorrien, and NNC Captain Nourse. It was subsequently argued, within the army and the press, both in the UK and South Africa, that insufficient evidence was heard in order to divert the blame away from Chelmsford. Harness was later to defend himself by stating, 'it seemed to me useless to record statements hardly bearing on the loss of the camp but giving doubtful particulars of small incidents more or less ghastly in their nature'. The final line of his report indicated his defensive attitude:

> 'The duty of the Court was to sift the evidence and record what was of value: if it was simply to take down a mass of statements the court might as well have been composed of three subalterns or three clerks'.

The modern historian is left to ponder by what criteria Harness decided which statements were 'unreliable and worthless.'[2] It was a transparent exercise and, at best, Harness saw the Court as a means of obtaining information about the defeat for Chelmsford. However, it served no real purpose apart from giving Chelmsford time to prepare his explanatory speech before he returned to England to present his case before the awaiting press and Parliament. The initial observations of the Court certainly enabled the blame for the British defeat to be squarely laid upon the NNC and Lieutenant Colonel Durnford. At the Inquiry, Colonel Crealock deliberately gave false evidence stating that he had ordered Durnford, on behalf of Chelmsford, to take command of the camp; this persuasive evidence totally exonerated Chelmsford in the eyes of the Inquiry. Durnford was convenient as a scapegoat; he was dead. Furthermore, he was not from a respected infantry regiment of the line. In addition, and it would become the subject of much subsequent debate, he was the senior officer present. The finding of the court conveniently accepted, on Crealock's false evidence, that Durnford had been in charge, that there had been a defeat, and accordingly highlighted Durnford's various deficiencies to the point that the Deputy Adjutant General, Colonel Bellairs, forwarded the court's findings to Lord Chelmsford with the following observation:

> 'From the statements made to the Court, it may be gathered that the cause of the reverse suffered at Isandwana (*sic*) was that Colonel Durnford, as senior officer, overruled the orders which Lieutenant Colonel Pulleine had received to defend the camp, and directed that the troops should be moved into the open, in support of the Native Contingent which he had brought up and which was engaging the enemy'.

Helpmekaar now became the focal point for further recriminations. Not content with blaming Durnford, Chelmsford's staff then began focusing their attention on Colonel Glyn, Chelmsford's second-in command, now isolated from any news at Rorke's Drift. While the alienated Glyn was suffering both mentally and physically, Chelmsford and his followers began to play down their personal roles in the Isandlwana disaster. In a subtle piece of responsibility shifting, Chelmsford stated that: 'Colonel Glyn was solely responsible' and 'that Colonel Glyn fully and explicitly accepted this responsibility cannot, however, affect the ultimate responsibility of the General-in-Command'. This attempt to share the blame with Glyn rang hollow, as it was generally known that Glyn had little say in matters where Chelmsford gave the orders. Chelmsford's staff contributed to the growing controversy by saying that it was Glyn's failure to entrench Isandlwana camp that caused it to be overrun: whereas it was Chelmsford who had overruled Glyn to defend the camp, as it was temporary. Chelmsford's staff deemed that, as Glyn was commander of the Central Column, the blame should be firmly laid at his door. Glyn was sent a number of official memoranda requiring him to account for his interpretation of orders relating to the camp at Isandlwana. Glyn recognised the possible entrapment and returned the memoranda, unanswered, but with the comment, 'Odd the general asking me to tell him what he knows more than I do'. Glyn finally accepted all responsibility for details, but declined to admit any responsibility for the movement of any portion of troops in or out of camp. The acrimony continued with Chelmsford even suggesting that it was Glyn's duty to protest at any decisions with which he did not agree. Glyn maintained his position by stating that it was his duty to obey his commander's orders. Little was said beyond this point; with considerable dignity, Glyn remained silent and loyal to his general but Mrs. Glyn robustly defended her husband in the coming months.

There was no defence for the NNC and initially there was no defence for Durnford. Chelmsford finally damned Durnford's reputation in his speech to the House of Lords on 19 August 1880. Chelmsford stated that 'in the final analysis, it was Durnford's disregard of orders that had brought about its (the camp's) destruction'.[3] It was thereafter widely believed by the enquiry that Durnford had failed to assume command of the camp from the subordinate Colonel Pulleine and had then irresponsibly taken his men off to chase some Zulus.

With regard to Major Spalding's departure from Rorke's Drift, little was ever said that was sympathetic. Many believed that, if only he had remained at his post as the commanding officer, he would have automatically been awarded the Victoria Cross. After all, there was no valid reason for him personally to ride to Helpmekaar, especially as Chard had already informed him that the Zulus were possibly approaching the position; and there were several under-employed officers who could easily have undertaken the task. It was also generally believed that, on his return, having reached a point less than 3 miles from the beleaguered Mission Station, Spalding and the two companies of the 24th could easily have pressed on to relieve Rorke's Drift. Perhaps it was to save him from embarrassment that no official questions were asked, although Major Clery came straight to the point in one of his letters home. He wrote from Helpmekaar on 13 April: 'Spalding is utterly worthless, so that the general was – as regards an opinion on any subject – practically without an adjutant or quarter-master.'

As well as being the officer commanding Rorke's Drift, Spalding was also the deputy assistant adjutant and quartermaster General. Spalding nevertheless submitted a full report detailing his actions on the day. He wrote:

> 'At 2.00 pm on the 22nd instant I left Rorke's Drift for Helpmekaar, leaving a second horse at Varmaaks. My intention was to bring up Captain Rainforth's company, 1st Battalion 24th Regiment, to protect the ponts. Lieutenant Chard, R.E., on returning from the camp, Isandula (*sic*), had observed Zulus on the neighbouring heights. I thought they might make a dash for the ponts during the night.
>
> 'Between Varmaaks and Helpmekaar, where I arrived 3.45 pm, I met two companies 1st Battalion 24th Regiment under Major Upcher; on returning from Helpmekaar, I met Major Upcher, who informed me of the disaster at Isandula.
>
> 'We advanced as far as Varmaaks with the troops. I then pushed on to the foot of the Berg, accompanied by Mr. Dickson, of the Buffalo Border Guard. The road was covered with fugitives, chiefly Basutos and people in civilians' clothes, but there were one or two mounted infantry. Several of these I ordered to accompany me, but all except two slipped away when my back was turned. My object was to ascertain whether the post at Rorke's Drift still held out. In this case I should have sent word to Major Upcher to advance and endeavour to throw myself into it.
>
> 'But every single white fugitive asserted that the mission house was captured; and at about three miles from the same I came across a body of Zulus in extended order across the road. They were 50 yards off; a deep (ravine) donga was behind them, capable of concealing a large force. They threw out flankers as if to surround the party.
>
> 'On reaching the summit of a hill from which the mission house is visible it was observed to be in flames; this confirmed the statement of the fugitives, that the post had been captured. This being the case it was determined to save, if possible, Helpmekaar and its depot of stores.

'It was growing dusk; the oxen had already had a long trek; the hill had to be re-ascended, and the heights were said to be lined with Zulus. I examined them with my glass, but could not observe the enemy. There may have been a few detached parties, however, as these were observed by competent witnesses. No attack was made by them, and the column reached Helpmekaar by 9.00 pm, when a waggon laager was formed around the commissariat stores. Colonel Hassard, R.E., met us half-way up the Berg, and took over command from me.

'The following morning a dense fog prevailed. About 9.00 am a note arrived from Lieutenant Chard, R.E., stating that Rorke's Drift still held out, and begging for assistance. It was considered imprudent to risk the safety of Helpmekaar by denuding it of its garrison, and probable that Rorke's Drift had already been relieved by the column under the General. It was determined to push down to the drift some mounted men to gather intelligence. I was in command. A short distance from Helpmekaar Mr. Fynn was met, who communicated the fact that the General's Column had relieved Rorke's Drift. At the top of the Berg I met Lieutenant-Colonel Russell, who confirmed the news. At about noon I reached Rorke's Drift and reported myself to the General.

'(Signed) H. S. SPALDING,

'Major, D.A.A.G.'[4]

While Chelmsford pondered the political implications of events, the sick and wounded apparently received scant consideration from their general. On their arrival at Helpmekaar, the more seriously wounded from Rorke's Drift were accommodated at the end of a corrugated zinc shed, one of several filled with commissariat stores, chiefly fermenting bags of maize that had been repeatedly soaked by heavy rains during their transportation from Pietermaritzberg. These many tons of damp bagged maize were then stored, decomposing and giving off the most offensive smell. For the seriously sick and wounded, the only bedding consisted of long square biscuit boxes that were arranged along the inside of the building that then had empty sacks laid over them. This was all the bedding that was obtainable for more than a fortnight, during which time replacement stores were slowly making their way from the base of operations at Pietermaritzburg. The station's medical stores were non-existent, as all such stores had been allocated to the Column's hospital at Rorke's Drift where all equipment and medicines had been destroyed in the fire. Fortunately, the surgeon at Helpmekaar, Surgeon Blair-Brown, had one small personal medical kit that contained a mixture of pills, powders, bandages, and a tourniquet; unfortunately, the labels of the pills and medication had been washed off in a storm and the doctor relied on his intuition and luck when dispensing to the patients. Blair-Brown wisely took control of a crate containing bottles of brandy and port wine; this form of medication proved very popular and efficacious in treating most conditions. With the decline in morale and general health, the doctor was kept very busy, 646 soldiers reported sick or sought treatment during their first week at Helpmekaar. A week later about 600 more men from the 4th Regiment augmented the Helpmekaar force. The treatment list during the first weeks was as follows:

	OFFICERS	MEN
Royal Artillery	4	66
1st 13th Regiment	1	73
1st 24th Regiment	7	110
2nd 24th Regiment	0	45
Medical Department	2	3
Commissariat Department	1	6
Veterinary Department	1	0
Mounted Infantry	4	95
Natal Mounted Police	3	84
Natal Mounted Volunteers	4	49
Royal Engineers	2	2
Mounted Basutos	4	80
TOTALS	33	613

When the shocked survivors from Chelmsford's column re-entered the camp at Helpmekaar, one of the greatest fears was of a Zulu night attack, even though the Zulus rarely, if ever, attacked at night. Consequently, Captain Walter Parke Jones, RE, and his able subordinate Lieutenant Porter commenced the construction of a substantial entrenchment; Porter subsequently wrote a prize-winning dissertation on military fortifications. Jones described the fort's location as 'vile', its position having been determined by Chelmsford who insisted that its construction must defend the existing iron storehouses. Jones thought the position was unsuitable as it was prone to become waterlogged whenever it rained. Indeed, after one particularly heavy downpour, the defensive camp ditch was filled with water to a depth of six feet.

Chelmsford and his staff remained at Helpmekaar just long enough to give instructions for the Inquiry, leaving Colonel F.C. Hassard in charge. Hassard proved to be a weak commander. He occupied himself with strengthening the fort and then resolutely remained within the defences. One week later, command at

Helpmekaar was given to Colonel E.W. Bray, who did what he could to improve the appalling conditions around the fort. Chelmsford's staff officer, Major Clery, once commented that the original store site had been so located 'with regard to nothing but the convenience of the contractor erecting them'. On the positive side, the re-construction of Helpmekaar fort was comparatively easy as the soil was soft but firm; an earthen parapet and deep ditch were soon constructed, and the whole fort was surrounded by strong earthworks. A drawbridge made from bundles of brushwood was constructed to make a bulletproof barrier across the entrance at night. For added protection, the guns of Harness's RA detachment were brought from Rorke's Drift and positioned at three corners.

And then it rained; and when it rained, the fort quickly became waterlogged and a virtual swamp. Immediately following Isandlwana, there were few stores or tents and the men slept packed together within the fort; when supplies arrived from Pietermaritzburg, tents were erected outside the fortifications but due to the close proximity of fit and sick men, the tents were moved on 31 March to a new location five hundred yards away, and a wagon laager was built to house the hospital tents.

Due to the constant fear of Zulu night attacks, the whole garrison was confined within the fort between sunset and sunrise, with uniform and boots worn at all times; the men were then released in groups and always under a police escort. Much discomfort arose from the total loss of personal possessions looted from Isandlwana, and with few stores, no comforts and constant driving rain, life at Helpmekaar was physically and mentally exhausting. Washing facilities were limited to one bathe per week in a nearby stream and men and officers had to let their beards grow. Improvisation and invention flourished and rubbish heaps were scoured for empty tins that could be used to fashion knives, and forks, and numerous items such as combs and brushes were created from pieces of wood. The Natal Mounted Police and Natal Carbineers shared these miserable conditions describing the men therein as:

> 'in a beastly mess and as no arrangements had been made for drainage the natural consequence, after a few days' rain, can better be imagined than described. The inside of the laager was like a pond, the stench overpowering, and the men all huddled inside at night but with one blanket apiece. The hospitals were in such a disgraceful state that dying men preferred to keep out of them'.[5]

At first the whole garrison was shut in every night and marched out an hour before daybreak under a police escort. As clothing and bedding were scarce, the people of Ladysmith sent a wagonload of useful articles for the police, who by the middle of February were more comfortably encamped. Then in early February the Natal press were informed of the plight of the Colonial volunteers.

'TO THE EDITOR OF THE NATAL MERCURY.

'Sir, - The following notice appears on the Government notice board, in an 'extra' published in the *Times*:

> "NOTICE. – The Carbineers having suffered the loss of all their clothing, it is urgently requested that they be supplied with the following articles, each: - 2 shirts, 2 pair socks, 1 pair breeches, 1 blanket, 1 pair boots. Contributions for procuring above, either in money or kind, may be sent to Holliday's Mart. – J D Holliday, Volunteer Agent, Pietermaritzburg."

'Does this mean that the Imperial authorities have taken no measure to supply these men with clothing in place of that burnt at the camp, and that unless contributions come in, the poor fellows are to be without these actual necessaries? What notice has been issued, signed by authority, that parents or wives are required to provide such articles to send to the front? Should it be left to a private individual to suggest and make provision for such necessities?

'The Imperial Government, for Imperial policy, called these young fellows out, and now, through some unexplained blunder, they have been deprived of everything but what they stand in. The Imperial authorities seem so paralysed that they cannot even issue an order that an outfit similar to that lost shall be issued, but leave it to private subscription to send; and if private subscription fail, the poor fellows are to be left in the field destitute.

'Why do not the Government authorities provide the things necessary, without delay, as they would be obliged to do for regulars in the same position? Should subscriptions be raised, there will be difficulty in expending the money for the good of those at the front'.

When news of the appalling conditions reached the people of Pietermaritzburg, they collected and despatched food, clothing and washing equipment for the colonial troops, most of whom came from the town. There was little comfort for the Imperial troops who had to wait until March before they were re-supplied. The only personal equipment to be purchased was that previously belonging to the officers and men killed at Isandlwana, including the possessions of Major Stuart Smith, which fetched high prices.

The garrison troops had no option but to wear their clothes and boots at night, and sleep under wagons and tarpaulins, often disturbed by false alarms. But even worse was to follow: annoyance and frustration were soon overtaken by sickness. By the beginning of February, many of the Helpmekaar force succumbed and most became stricken with enteric fever or typhoid. The medical officers were mystified by the speed with which diseases spread and it was believed, mistakenly, that the sodden and rotting mealie bags were responsible. Captain Walter Parke Jones wrote:

> 'I cannot account for it all as the place used to be so healthy. Of course being crowded together in a fort with rotting supplies and other stores and difficulties about sanitary arrangements has something to do with the question'.

When fever inevitably broke out at Helpmekaar during February, the news quickly reached the War Office. Although it was usual for more men to die through sickness when campaigning than to be killed fighting, the rate of sickness was so severe that the army Intelligence Branch at the War Office later voiced its own opinion as to the cause:

> 'Immediately after Isandhlwana this important place strategically was secured for defence by extemporizing with sacks of mealies to build revetments. The garrison of 1,000 Europeans and Natives were crowded together without tents or shelter except for a few tarpaulins, exposed to cold and rain. Some slept on wet mealie bags, others on the damp ground, disturbed by frequent alarms and subjected to noxious exhalation. The military authorities were informed of the danger from decomposing grain and mealies, and of the unsanitary conditions, but failed to take action, because it was considered vital for the military position. Thus men soon succumbed to the malaise, lost their appetite and the young men especially were attacked by fever, diarrhoea and dysentery'.[6]

Psychological disturbances, largely bred by the disaster of Isandlwana, began to proliferate through all ranks, a condition made worse by inactivity, boredom and ill-founded rumours. All those associated with Isandlwana were haunted by it, and continually harked back to 22 January. Some of the officers began to display an unnatural lack of interest in their duties while the men became lethargic and sullen, no doubt due to the disaster and general malaise that followed. At Rorke's Drift, Glyn was dysfunctional due to depression having lost his regiment at Isandlwana. At Helpmekaar, Colonel Harness, his friend

Colonel Cecil Russell and Lieutenant Curling, had all lost interest in their commands, though Curling could blame fever for his bout of apathy. The collapse of Russell could have had more serious consequences, as he was responsible for mounted patrols, which were sporadic and ill planned. His inertia was criticized by Clery, who realized that the absence of mounted forays, which Russell should have commanded, allowed the Zulus to roam at will. Among the troops, speculation on the progress of the war and possible future tactics occupied much time at Helpmekaar. It took several weeks, an improvement in the weather, and the news of a new military commander before morale began to improve. Even then, conditions remained far from satisfactory. A letter dated 5 March from an unnamed Colonial soldier to his family was reported in *The Natal Witness*. It reads:

> 'Here we are, Foot, Artillery, Engineers, Police, and Carbineers (about 500 strong), living in tents during the day, and turning into the fort at night. With the exception of a stink of rotten mealies, and the rain continually swilling through and through, the fort is not so bad, being so strong and well built that the men here now could hold it against the whole of the Zulu army. It is not healthy though, for the hospitals are always full, and we have had eight or ten deaths here. Hay of the Carbineers died last night; one of the N.M.P. shot himself last week, and several Engineers have died. What with guards, videttes (*sic*) &c., the duties are very heavy'.[7]

By the beginning of March, Chelmsford's preparations for the second invasion of Zululand were well underway and the previous invasion route through Rorke's Drift was changed for the easier passage to the north. In any event, Chelmsford did not intend to march his rejuvenated army past Isandlwana, which was still strewn with the debris of the wrecked camp and, worse, the unburied bodies of the 24th Regiment. This change of plan accordingly reduced the strategic importance of the Helpmekaar garrison, whose role was transferred to Dundee, 20 miles to the north. By the middle of April, only two companies of the 1/24th remained at Helpmekaar before they also joined the new advance into Zululand. Helpmekaar then became a shell with a small guard to watch over several sheds of unwanted supplies. These were eventually sold off at a public auction on 25 October when the garrison closed.

On a lighter note, two supply wagons were approaching Helpmekaar when they received reports of the British defeat at Isandlwana and the Zulu attack at Rorke's Drift. One was carrying Martini-Henry rifles and ammunition under escort by Colonel Bray and men of the 4th (King's Own Royal) Regiment. In their attempt to retrace their route the wagon with rifles and ammunition got stuck so, as a precaution, the escort off-loaded the rifles and buried them to prevent them being lost to marauding Zulus. The escort marked the hiding place and retraced their tracks. On their return several days later and, after several heavy rainstorms, they could not find the location. The rifles were never recovered. Another wagon under escort was near Greytown and on receipt of the same information, they unloaded two extremely heavy boxes marked 'Horseshoes' and deposited them in the town store. Following the Zulu War, a mounted troop arrived outside the store. The troop captain entered the store and reclaimed the two boxes, which the storeowner had meanwhile used as steps to reach his upper shelves. He reluctantly relinquished the two useful boxes and signed the necessary papers. As the two boxes were being carried out of his store, he noticed that the requisition paper stated 'two boxes of Gold sovereigns marked '*HORSESHOES*'.

Whilst at Helpmekaar, Major Dartnell collated the personal financial losses incurred by his unit, its surviving officers and men, in terms of lost possessions and equipment at Isandlwana. His unit's bill was submitted in August and included the loss of horses and personal effects. An unusual number of solid silver pocket watches were claimed by Dartnell's troopers. The bill was paid in full.

Helpmekaar was later used as a military garrison during both the Boer War and the Zulu uprising of 1906.

References

1. *Fields of Battle – Isandlwana*, Greaves, Adrian, Cassells, 2001.
2. *The Sun Turned Black*, Knight, I., Watermans, 1995.
3. *Fields of Battle – Isandlwana.*
4. Later in the war, when rumours that Spalding had deserted his men began to spread, Chelmsford intervened on Spalding's behalf. He wrote a memo to the Adjutant General in which he exonerated Spalding; Chelmsford believed that Spalding was acting correctly when he left Rorke's Drift to trace the overdue replacements. Chelmsford wrote that it was 'in consequence of the non-arrival of this detachment that caused Major Spalding to go to Helpmekaar to hasten its departure'. He went on, 'I refer to this latter point in justice to Major Spalding as I have heard that remarks have been made relative to his absence from this post at the time' (Chelmsford's letter dated 19 May 1879).
5. *The Natal Carbineers,* Rev John Stalker, Petermaritzburg, 1912.
6. *War Office: Précis of Information*, 1879.
7. The seriously sick who could be moved were sent to Fort Pine or Landsman's Drift; ten died and were buried at Helpmekaar cemetery, including Corporal/acting Quartermaster Chaddock; Trooper Smith ex-Royal Navy who committed suicide, and Troopers Nagle, Hayes, Bennett and Ingram. Other participants were badly affected by what they experienced, both physically and mentally; one of the NMP shot himself. In an age when mental trauma was misunderstood, there was little sympathy or understanding for those who broke under the strain of filthy conditions and from witnessing the savagery of fighting

Zulus. In an institution like the army, it was expected that emotions should be kept on a tight rein, especially amongst the senior officers; the 'stiff-upper lip' syndrome prevailed. It is well documented that Chelmsford underwent a period of severe depression in the aftermath of Isandlwana – see WO 32/7709 – and requested that he be replaced. Colonel Glyn suffered a breakdown at Rorke's Drift but eventually recovered sufficiently to take a limited part in the second invasion of Zululand. Colonel Hassard, Officer Commanding Royal Engineers, had such a severe nervous breakdown that he was replaced. Colonel Pearson, the defender of Eshowe, was invalided home suffering from mental and physical exhaustion. By the end of September 1879 the last detachments of the British Army had left Zululand with their baggage. Durban became chock-a-block, with the bars doing a roaring trade. In the general confusion one event put the finishing touch to the war.

Lieutenant General Sir William Butler wrote that just before one crowded transport was due to sail for England, the captain received an order to delay sailing; six soldiers found to be insane during the course of the war (including Rorke's Drift defender Private Wall) were about to be embarked under escort for consignment to a home lunatic asylum. The captain, nervous at losing high tide, waited impatiently. Presently a boat containing the six additional passengers arrived alongside. On the transport a mass of men of different units, many already demobilised, lined the sides, having a last look at Durban. The lunatics, still in their uniforms, scrambled up the ladder and immediately vanished into the crowd to the consternation of the escort and ship's captain.

The shore escort wanted to depart before the ship sailed and rapidly gave such descriptive details as they could remember before rowing back to shore. On board, the ship's officers held an emergency conference with the military. For fear of starting a general panic, news of the occurrence was kept a close secret. A select group of observers was enrolled, from men known to the officers or wearing decorations, and these were sworn to secrecy and detailed to watch different portions of the ship. All the way to Cape Town the observations continued. Any man sitting in isolation or in the throes of seasickness found himself under suspicion. At frequent intervals a passenger would be tapped on the shoulder and led to an inspection by a panel consisting of the ship's doctor, captain and an army officer. By the time the ship reached Cape Town there were twenty-six men in detention.

Accordingly, an urgent request was sent from Cape Town for someone to come from Natal who could positively identify the lunatics. An asylum orderly was hastily despatched to the Cape only to discover that none of the men detained were the missing lunatics. On the contrary, six of the men detained had been engaged on the search for the lunatics and had been the most conscientious in reporting others as madmen. The lunatics were never found.

Chapter 18

Account by Lieutenant Colonel F. Bourne OBE, DCM

From His Radio Interview with the BBC in 1936

In December 1936, Lieutenant Colonel Bourne made a BBC radio broadcast concerning the Battle of Rorke's Drift for a series entitled 'I was there'. It generated enough interest for 350 people to write to Bourne. It says something of the man that he replied to every one of them. Regrettably, the BBC scrapped the recording during the 1950s, stating it was not of sufficient interest. The following is a transcript of the broadcast:

'In December 1872, when I was 18 years old, I enlisted in the 24th Regiment and received the princely pay of 6d. a day, of which 3½d. was deducted for messing and washing, leaving 1s. 5½d. a week – for luxuries. I went to bed every night hungry but quite happy, and it made a man of me.

'The Regiment had just come home from India after fifteen years. Now the 'A' Company of any Regiment in those days was always called the Grenadier Company and was supposed to have the biggest men. I think the Sergeant Major must have been a wee bit humorous, for he posted me to our 'A' Company although I stood only five foot six inches and was painfully thin.

'After five years of home service, in February 1878 the Regiment received sudden orders to proceed to the Cape of Good Hope to take part in the Kaffir War. This was my first experience of active service, and shortly after, my Colonel promoted me Colour-Sergeant of 'B' Company – 100 strong. I was only twenty-three, very nervous, sensitive, and afraid of my new responsibilities. Several men of the Company were of my own age, others older, and some old enough to be my father, but after a few months I felt more secure and thought I was getting along quite well. I also found myself 'unpaid private secretary' to several men who could barely read and write, and I deciphered and answered their letters home, feeling quite happy in our relations. One day I heard a man named Wall ask my batman 'if the kid was in', a day or two later I asked Partridge casually who 'the kid' was, and received the answer, 'why, you are, of course.' My stock slumped at once. I think it does us all good to have our swollen heads reduced. But we were a very happy family. You can't live in tents, and on Mother Earth, for two years on Active Service without knowing your men intimately.

'The Kaffir War ended in June 1878 and we were moved to Pietermaritzburg, Natal, to assist in raising the curtain on the Zulu drama. On January 11 we crossed the Buffalo River at Rorke's Drift – into the Zulu country. Our Commander-in-Chief was Lord Chelmsford. Our strength was four thousand five hundred men – including thirteen companies of my Regiment, the 24th, now the South Wales Borderers. Our company was left behind at Rorke's Drift, to guard the hospital, stores, and the pontoons at the Drift on the Buffalo River. This was my company, and at the time I was bitterly disappointed. We saw the main column under Lord Chelmsford engage the enemy at once, and I watched the action, along with my four sergeants, from a little hill by Rorke's Drift. Then we saw them move on again, and they disappeared.

'And now I must tell you what happened to them during the next ten days.

'They made their camp under a hill called Isandlwana, about ten miles away. Then a day later, on the twenty-first, Lord Chelmsford learned that the enemy was in force ahead of the camp, and he moved out on the morning of the twenty-second with nearly half his force to attack them. But as he advanced they disappeared, and in his absence his camp was attacked and overwhelmed by fourteen thousand Zulus. So swift was the disaster that the few survivors who got away could give no reliable account of it, but the evidence of the dead who were afterwards found and buried where they lay told the unvarying tale of groups of men fighting back-to back until the last cartridge was fired. After the war, Zulu witnesses all told the same story. 'At first we could make no headway against the soldiers, but suddenly they ceased to fire, then we came round them and killed them with our assegais.' According to one account, the last survivor was a drummer boy who flung his sword at a Zulu. This was the last occasion that Band or Drummer Boys were taken on active service, as it was also the last occasion that the Colours were carried into action.[1] Lieutenants Melvill and Coghill lost their lives that day trying to save the colours. Fully twelve hundred men were killed. And by half past one no white man was alive in Isandhlwana camp.

'Of course, back at Rorke's Drift we knew nothing of this disaster, although my sergeants and I on our hill above it could hear the guns and see the puffs of smoke. But an hour later, at two o'clock, a few refugees arrived and warned us what to expect. One man whispered to me 'Not a fighting chance for you, young feller.' Up to that time we had done nothing to put our small post in a defensive position, as our force in front was nearly five thousand strong and had six guns, and the last thing that we expected was that we should be the saviours of the remainder of that force. The strength of our small garrison at the Drift was two combatant and six departmental officers, and one hundred and thirty-three non-commissioned officers and men, thirty-six of whom were sick, leaving about one hundred fighting men. Remember that twelve hundred men had just been massacred at Isandlwana.

'Can you then be surprised that, flushed with their success, the Zulus were making for our small post confident that we should be easy victims to their savagery? Having had the warning – but only two hours in advance, as it turned out – we set to work to loophole the two buildings and to connect the front of the hospital with a stone cattle kraal by sacks of Indian corn and oats, and to draw up two Boer transport wagons to join the front of the Commissariat Stores with the back of the hospital. These proved excellent barricades, but by no means impregnable.

'The native has often been credited with deep cunning, but luckily for us if the Zulu possessed any he did not use it, for as the sacks connecting the hospital had to be laid on a slope of the ground he could safely have crept along, cut the sacks open with his assegais, the corn would have rolled out and he could have walked in and I should not now be telling the story. When Lieutenant Chard of the Royal Engineers joined us he approved of what we had done, but considered that our inner space was too big, and suggested a line of biscuit boxes. This was done and proved of great value when the enemy set the hospital on fire.

'I was instructed to post men as look-out, in the hospital, at the most vulnerable points, and to take out and command a line of skirmishers. Shortly after 3.30 an officer commanding a troop of Natal Light Horse arrived, having got away from Isandlwana, and asked Lieutenant Chard for instructions. He was ordered to send detachments to observe the drift and pontoons, and to place outposts in the direction of the enemy to check his advance.

'About 4.15 the sound of firing was heard behind the hill on our front; the officer returned and reported the enemy close upon us. He also reported that his 100 men would not obey his orders and had ridden off. About the same time another detachment of 100 men belonging to the Natal Native Contingent bolted, including their officer himself. I am glad to say that he was brought back some days later, court-marshalled and dismissed from the service. The desertion of these detachments of 200 men appeared at first sight to be a great loss, with only a hundred of us left, but the feeling afterwards was that we could not have trusted them, and also that our defences were too small to accommodate them anyhow.

'We knew now that whatever might happen, we had to fight it out alone, and about 4.30 the enemy, from 500 to 600 strong, came in sight round the hill to our south, and driving in my thin red line of skirmishers, made a rush at our south wall. They were met, and held, by a steady and deliberate fire for a short time, then, being reinforced by some hundreds, they made desperate and repeated attempts to break through our temporary defences but were repulsed time and again. To show their fearlessness and their contempt for the red coats and small numbers, they tried to leap the parapet, and at times seized our bayonets, only to be shot down. Looking back, one cannot but admire their fanatical bravery.

'About 7 o'clock they succeeded, after many attempts, in setting fire to the hospital. The small numbers we were able to spare defended it room-by-room, bringing out all the sick who could be moved before they retired. Privates Hook, R. Jones, W. Jones and J. Williams were the last to leave holding the door with the bayonet when all their ammunition was expended. The Victoria Cross was awarded to these men, and they fully deserved it.

'The Zulus had collected the rifles from the men they had killed at Isandhlwana, and had captured the ammunition from the mules which had stampeded and threw their loads; so our own arms were used against us. In fact, this was the cause of every one of our casualties, killed and wounded, and we should have suffered many more if the enemy had known how to use a rifle. There was hardly a man even wounded by an assegai – their principal weapon.

'The attack lasted from 4.30 pm on the twenty-second to 4.00 am on the twenty-third – twelve exciting hours – and when daybreak occurred the enemy was out of sight. About 7 o'clock they appeared again to the south-west. But help was at hand; Lord Chelmsford with the other half of his original force was only an hour's march away. On the previous afternoon he had learned of the destruction of his camp at Isandhlwana. A certain Commandant Lonsdale had chanced to ride back to the camp and had been fired at by Zulus wearing our men's uniform. He escaped by a miracle and was able to report the news to Lord Chelmsford.

'Lord Chelmsford at once addressed his men and said: "Whilst we were skirmishing ahead the Zulus have taken our camp; there must be ten thousand in our rear, and twenty thousand in front. We must win back our camp tonight and cut our way back to Rorke's Drift tomorrow." 'All right, sir, we'll do it.'

'They got back to camp that night, but they found a grim and silent scene as they cautiously approached. The next day they resumed their march and appeared at Rorke's Drift, and our enemy retired.

'In his dispatch afterwards, Lord Chelmsford said: "To our intense relief the waving of hats was seen from the hastily erected entrenchments, and information soon reached me that the garrison ... had for twelve hours made the most gallant resistance I have ever heard of against the determined attack of some 3,000 Zulus, 350 of whose dead bodies surrounded the post." Our losses were 17 killed and 9 wounded, their 351 killed that we buried. Their wounded must have been between 400 and 500, which they removed under cover of the night.

'There are two things which I think have made Rorke's Drift stand out so vividly after all these years. The first, that it took place on the same day as the terrible massacre at Isandlwana, and the second, that Natal was saved from being overrun by a savage and victorious foe.

'Seven V.C.s were awarded to this one company of the regiment which is now the South Wales Borderers. I have told you the names of four of the men who won the V.C.; the other three were Lieutenant Bromhead, Corporal Allen and Private F. Hitch. The Victoria Cross was also awarded to Lieutenant Chard, Royal Engineers, Surgeon Reynolds, and Corporal Schiess, but not one, I regret to say, of those VCs is alive today.

'Lieutenants Chard and Bromhead and the men received the thanks of Parliament, the officers being promoted to the rank of Major. I was awarded the Distinguished Conduct Medal with an annuity of £10 – the same as awarded to the Victoria Cross – and awarded a commission, but as I was the youngest of eight sons, and the family exchequer was empty, I had to refuse it that time.

'Now just one word for the men who fought that night; I was moving about amongst them all the time, and not for one moment did they flinch. Their courage and their bravery cannot be expressed in words: for me they were an example all my soldiering days.

'The following year, Queen Victoria received at Windsor Castle a Colour Party of the Regiment, and decorated the Queen's Colours with a silver wreath of immortelles in memory of Lieutenants Melvill and Coghill, "for their devotion in trying to save the Colours of the twenty-second of January (that was at Isandlwana) and for the noble defence of Rorke's Drift." So if you ever have the great privilege of seeing the Colours of the South Wales Borderers uncased you will see the wreath. The original wreath presented by Her Majesty is now in the Regimental Chapel of Brecon Cathedral'.

(Article; Courtesy *AZWHS* Journal No. 4, December, 1998)

Reference

1. This was at Majuba Hill on 27.2.81.

Chapter 19

Who was Sister Janet?

'From David Rattray
'Fugitives' Drift Lodge
'South Africa
'January 2006

'The Anglo-Zulu War of 1879 caused many British soldiers and Zulu warriors' terrible wounds, and disease was rife. Hospital care was in its infancy, especially in the British Army, and so it is remarkable that in the midst of this terrible war a nineteen-year-old English nurse, Sister Janet Wells, was sent from London to take charge of the isolated British Army hospital at Utrecht. Already a decorated veteran of the 1878 Balkan War, she was highly experienced in treating war wounds. In her first two months at Utrecht she and Surgeon Major J. Fitzmaurice treated over 3,200 patients, both British soldiers and Zulus, many from the battles of Hlobane, Khambula and Ulundi.

'She performed numerous operations, tended the sick and wounded, and brought an air of discipline, tempered by her charm and femininity, into a chaotic and desperate situation. Towards the end of the war she was sent to Rorke's Drift where she administered to the remaining garrison. She walked the battlefields of Rorke's Drift and Isandlwana where she collected flowers for her scrapbooks – already containing many sketches and photographs, which survive to this day.

'After the war she returned to her home and family in London, just in time for her twentieth birthday. Recognition by Queen Victoria followed, who decorated her with the Royal Red Cross, the nursing equivalent of the Victoria Cross. A previous recipient was Florence Nightingale.

'Hers is an astonishing story, of bravery and determination, which I commend to everyone who loves an adventure; it will especially fascinate students of the Anglo Zulu War – to whom this true account will come, I am sure, as something of a surprise.

'David Rattray
'Zululand'

A week after the news of the defeat at Isandlwana had been received by a stunned Whitehall, General Sir Garnet Wolseley replaced Chelmsford as the commander in South Africa. Wolseley's methods, ideas and energy flew in the face of the military establishment as personified by the reactionary Commander-in-Chief, the Duke of Cambridge. One of the subjects that first concerned Wolseley on his arrival in South Africa was the well-being and health of his men; he was shocked at the number of soldiers unable to perform their duties because of sickness, wounds or injuries. Major General R.E. Barnsley of the Army Medical Department wrote of this period:

> 'Our great commanders had never learned that disease has always been more destructive than the most devastating engines of war which the mind of man conceived. None realised that the preservation of the troops was the final responsibility, not of medical officers, but of commanding officers'.[1]

Unlike most of his contemporaries, Wolseley was prepared to change his mind and accept medical help from outside the military establishment and for this his wife, Lady Louise, must be acknowledged. Her first approach was made to the British Aid Society, loosely allied to the Red Cross, who sent help in the form of medical and nursing teams to various war zones. Although these requests were made by a participating country, the British Aid Society was always prepared to care for any injured person. They had twice previously sent teams to the Turko-Russian Wars but this time they declined to send medical staff, although they were prepared to send aid in the form of supplies and 'comforts' to the army's hospitals in Natal.

The British Aid Society had been slow in deciding whether or not to become involved in the Serb-Turkish war of 1876, then, the Turkophile Duke decided to form a charitable fund for the relief of Turkish sick and wounded. With so many influential members, funds were readily raised and volunteers were plentiful. When the Russo-Turkish War began in 1877, they were able to respond without delay, and quickly sent volunteers, medicines and an ambulance to help the Turkish medical services. At the same time the British Aid Society had been asked to send a team of doctors, nurses and supplies to aid the Russian medical services at Sistova in the same war.

When news of the British defeat at Isandlwana and the plight of the sick and wounded British soldiers reached the Duke of Sutherland, he reconvened the British Aid Society as the new Stafford House Committee which met on 30 May 1879 under Baroness Burdett-Coutts, who passed a resolution that deplored the lack of care provided for the wounded in Zululand. It was minuted:

> 'As from the commencement of the outbreak of the war in Zululand no effort had been made on the part of any existing Society, or by any association of private individuals, to afford aid from England to our sick and wounded soldiers, suffering in the above war'.

On 4 June the London-based Stafford House Committee decided to dispatch trained nurses, including Sister Janet Wells, with a supply of medical comforts for the use at military hospitals. It was intended that the support would 'avoid collision or friction with the army medical staff'. The Army Medical Department immediately took the concept of female civilian nurses as a criticism of their capability and, predictably, such offers of help were refused.

When Wolseley took over his South Africa command in July 1879, he discovered the desperate shortage of medical personnel in Natal. The large number of sick and wounded soldiers from the invasion of Zululand highlighted the need for urgent additional help. Moving with great speed, the committee was meanwhile able to advise Wolseley that a party, including the young Sister Janet Wells, had already departed from London on 12 June bound for South Africa, under the overall command of Chief Commissioner Surgeon General (retired) James Tyrell Ross.

At first sight, Sister Janet Wells appeared to be rather young, at twenty years of age, to be chosen to lead a party of six nurses to South Africa, but she had already found acclaim and been awarded the Russian Red Cross for her nursing activities in the recent Turko-Russian war. Born in 1859[2] she was the second child of five daughters and three sons to Elizabeth and Benjamin Wells of Shepherds Bush in west London. Her father was a very talented musician and a professor of music and in his youth he had impressively performed in concert for the Duke of Wellington and was encouraged by Felix Mendelssohn. He became one of the foremost flautists of his generation and often played for the rich and famous, becoming a firm favourite of the Royal Family, often playing duets with Prince Albert at Windsor Castle.

Her journals and diaries reveal that, in spite of the shortage of time to prepare for such an epic journey, Janet managed to collect and pack the necessary items she knew from experience would be invaluable to her in the months ahead. The nurses were issued with a uniform by Stafford House, as well as an instrument case containing two subcutaneous injection syringes, two clinical thermometers, dressing and artery forceps, probes, directors and scissors. These nurses were expected to do much more than make beds, wash, and care for the bodily needs of their patients. They were not the usual concept of 'angels of mercy' handing out comforts and tucking in the odd sheet.

Janet's party under Chief Commissioner Ross set sail on board the *Dublin Castle* from Dartmouth on 13 June 1879. After a stormy voyage the *Dublin Castle* docked in Cape Town, where Commissioner Ross called on Lady Frere in her capacity as the Cape Town representative of the Stafford House Committee. He discovered the military were still reluctant to accept civilian nurses and that everyday supplies were running dangerously low. Before they left Cape Town, Ross organized an ongoing supply including cows, goats, and poultry, and particularly milk and eggs, considered necessary for the wounded and sick. The Castle Line's owner, Donald Currie, very generously volunteered to transport the nurses and supplies free of charge.

They arrived in Durban on 14 July 1879. The nurses were split into pairs with the exception of Sister Janet, who was considered to have the most experience. Janet was delighted to be sent to the remote border settlement of Utrecht accompanied by Ross, where the hospital supported Sir Evelyn Wood's northern column – although the prospect of a long and difficult journey across 220 miles of uninhabited African bush was somewhat daunting. The only means of getting the nurses to their various destinations was by the daily mail cart, drawn by two horses. Nearing their destination, Janet was thrown from the cart and suffered a dislocated shoulder. Ross was very impressed by her stoicism; once he had reduced the dislocation they continued their journey.

Sister Janet and Commissioner Ross were warmly welcomed by the British forces at Utrecht and Janet was lodged with the only British family resident. She was warned that malaria was rife in the area and that many soldiers suffered and even died of the disease without knowing they were carrying the parasite. She would soon come face to face with the side effects that included fever, rupture of the spleen, anaemia, and an impaired immune system which would leave her patients open to the endemic diseases such as typhus, influenza, dysentery, malnutrition, and black water fever. Her concerned hosts also warned her of the local gossip that syphilis caused more soldiers to seek medical help than any other ailment apart from battle wounds. There was no cure for syphilis and the end effect of the so called 'merry' disease was understood by the soldiers to be an inevitable death sentence. Tuberculosis was also prevalent among the soldiers; Janet had previously seen the ravages and effects of this disease in the slums in London and knew the disease was as old as humanity and for which there was also no cure. The germ thrived when hosts, both human and cattle, lived in cramped and squalid conditions and was spread by coughing and spitting, drinking contaminated milk, and for the cattle, ingesting polluted water, grass, animal feed and contact with polluted soil. Ironically, many of the soldiers had joined the Army to escape the poverty and squalor at home, but, frequently being forced to shelter in hastily prepared and cramped conditions, the disease soon became rife throughout the army in South Africa.

The hospital at Utrecht consisted of a substantial wooden single storey building situated just inside the main defensive laager of marquee and bell tents under the command of the hospital's doctor, Surgeon Major J. Fitzmaurice. There were already eighty-eight patients in the hospital and another twenty-nine were due to arrive from Ulundi that afternoon. Janet wrote that she was 'immediately immersed in much busy work'. She quickly settled in and by the end of the week had proved she was both talented and highly trained; the doctor was delighted to leave the running of the hospital in her capable hands. She wrote, 'It was a delightful pleasure to nurse the English soldiers'.

The defeat of the Zulus at the Battle of Ulundi found the hospital brim full of soldiers suffering from battle wounds and general sickness. Each day brought more casualties that were grievously injured, or seriously ill from a variety of medical conditions. There were many soldiers who had been in the hospital for some time. These men had been fighting in the hot summer months of the rainy season, so they had to endure both rainstorms and blistering heat; dehydration and heat exhaustion also badly affected the unsuitably clothed men. Heavy serge jackets and trousers in dark colours were unsuitable for such high temperatures.

Blisters caused by marching in heavy steel-shod boots affected just about every soldier, except of course the officers, who had their uniforms and boots specially made for them at considerable personal expense. Such wounds frequently became infected and Janet and her orderlies regularly de-roofed and cleansed and dressed the suppurating sores with salt. They often said that if they had a shilling for every pair of feet treated for blisters they would be able to retire to a mansion by the sea. The soldiers were highly amused by Janet's remedy for the rotting fungal disease (athletes' foot) that seriously affected their feet, a scourge for soldiers in any hot climate. She instructed them to urinate in their boots each evening, and then let the boots dry out overnight. Janet knew the urea in the urine would kill off the fungus; to the soldiers it was a miraculous cure.

Janet had not only to look after the camp hospital, but was also required to ride out to the outlying camps to attend the sick and wounded. After the final Battle of Ulundi, sporadic outbreaks of guerrilla fighting continued with bands of rebellious warriors often sniping at patrols causing several injuries.

With the war over, Wolseley visited Utrecht on 11 September while en route from Ulundi to Pretoria. A special parade was assembled to which Sister Janet, on the basis of her reputation, was specially invited. Brevet Major (Gonville) Bromhead and Private (Robert) Jones were called forward from the ranks and a letter from the Secretary of War to the General Commanding in South Africa was read out, describing the two acts for which Her Majesty the Queen was pleased to order the Victoria Cross to be awarded to these two men for their action in the defence of Rorke's Drift. Sister Janet wrote that she later tried to engage Lieutenant Bromhead in conversation but, like so many before her, she found it difficult to gain any response from him. She described him as 'rather a dull fellow'.

The fighting over, the hospital at Utrecht was ordered to be dismantled and moved to Durban via nearby Newcastle, although fifty-four sick had to remain until they had recovered enough to travel. Janet was able to leave with the last of the sick by 12 September. She was showered with thanks and received a glowing testimonial dated 13 September from the previously sceptical Surgeon Major Fitzmaurice.

Sister Janet's work was not yet complete. Rorke's Drift was on her route back to Durban and because no doctor had visited the British garrison there for many weeks, she volunteered to visit the outpost, scene of the now famous battle. She set off on the 65-mile journey, stopping overnight at Helpmekaar; she followed the precipitous trail to the isolated Mission sited on a rock outcrop under the lea of the Oskarsberg hill and facing the Buffalo River; she wrote the location was 'picturesque'. The two soldiers guarding the camp perimeter were astonished to see the young English nurse approach the camp. She was quickly directed to the replacement fort, Fort Melvill, where the officer in charge, Lieutenant Rowden of the 99th Regiment, welcomed her and accompanied her on a short walk from the fort towards the river where he had thoughtfully arranged to have a Zulu style hut built for her out of sight of the military accommodation. Janet was thrilled and wrote a glowing description and painted the scene of Rorke's Drift with her hut which she called 'our Mess hut'.

She learned that the site of the famed defence had been abandoned due to its unsanitary conditions caused by the mud from the torrential rains following the battle and overflowing excrement from both animals and the men who had remained there. Fort Melvill was named after Lieutenant Teignmouth Melvill of the 1/24th Regiment, who had ridden out of the massacred camp at Isandlwana with the Queen's Colour. With the war now over, the garrison had been reduced to a small rear-guard that was preparing to re-join their regiment at Pinetown, near Durban. The area was to be looked after by a retired trader, Mr. Croft, until the eventual return of the Reverend Witt, who was busy trying to make money in London suing the British government for the destruction of his house and by lecturing on the battle (although he had not been present).

Within a few days of arriving at Rorke's Drift, Sister Janet had managed to examine all thirty-five British soldiers stationed at the outpost. Most were in good health, although the majority were suffering from abrasions and sores. The ubiquitous stomach problem that had bugged the whole invasion force from its outset was still the garrison's main medical problem. One of her first acts was to demand that the fort's daily drinking water was collected upstream from the river and then boiled. Under her direction the camp's cooking utensils and cutlery were sterilized by boiling after each meal and within days the men's health improved. A laundry was set up to wash the soldiers' bed linen, underclothes and shirts. The eight sick men suffering from 'fever' were confined to two tents outside the small fort and so as not to spread the infection further she demanded a complete tidy up of the fort area and arranged for all litter to be burned.

With the fort now less of a health hazard and the men taking a modicum of pride in their appearance, Janet asked for an escort to visit the nearby battle locations. She wanted to be shown over the battlefield at Rorke's Drift by Lieutenant Rowden as she was keen to see the ruin that had been Surgeon Reynold's makeshift hospital.

Janet was also taken by horse to the top of the Oskarsberg where she could see the Buffalo River far below and across the valley to Isandlwana ten miles to the east. Coming down on the far side of the hill, her guide showed her the caves and Bushmen's paintings. These prehistoric paintings can be seen today; they are skilfully drawn with the vivid colours of the animals still evident; these included deer, buffalo, lion and elephant, mostly being hunted by the dwarf-like figures of the bushmen. Her guide then took her to the bank of the Buffalo River, and by hitching up her long skirts, she was able to wade across the flowing river to the far bank. On the far side she saw the recently constructed second British cemetery just 100 yards from the river. This cemetery was for the soldiers who had died of fever during the Zululand invasion and, according to the wisdom of the time, had to be buried away from the fort. The next day Janet was taken to Fugitives' Drift, about five miles from Rorke's Drift, where the bodies of Lieutenants Melvill and Coghill and the two soldiers found with them were buried high on the steep slope above the now gently flowing Buffalo River. She collected flowers and grasses from around their graves and pressed them in her bible and scrapbook, now in the possession of the *AZWHS.*

A few days later, accompanied by an escort and a guide, Janet set out to visit the Isandlwana battlefield. The camp presented a forlorn and woeful sight. All the 1,500 bodies on the British side had only recently been buried under some 300 large stone cairns, some ten feet high, but the ground was still scattered with the whitening bones of slain horses and oxen. After pointing out the main features of the battlefield, her escort left Janet to walk round the remains of the campsite but to be wary of wild dogs.[3] She noticed scraps of paper littering the area that had been caught in bushes or which lay among the rock outcrops that are such a feature of the area. She collected a number of these papers as souvenirs, some of which seemed so poignant; they included a frontispiece from Dickens's *The Pickwick Papers*, complete with Boz's drawing of Pickwick meeting Sam Weller, and part of a letter signed 'from your own Madgie'. She also picked up two pages of Romans and Corinthians torn from a pocket Bible. She found a page ripped from a pay book which belonged to Private Thomas Vedler of C Company, 2/24th Regiment, who had died along with Captain Younghusband and all his comrades as they made a valiant last stand on the slope of the mountain. These were put into an impressive album, now held by the *AZWHS*.

A few days later news reached the small Rorke's Drift garrison that they were to abandon the fort and join their regiment at nearby Dundee. Janet was ordered to report directly to Durban where she would embark for passage back to England. She was given a local guide, who claimed to know the way and would drive the cart provided for her and her soldier escort. On 17 October she bade farewell to the few remaining soldiers and set off on the 200-mile journey to Durban. Fortunately the guide did know the way and she reached Pietermaritzburg on 20 October and after spending the night in a hotel (sheer luxury, she said) they set off again the next morning and arrived in Durban on 22 October 1879.

Janet boarded the *Dublin Castle*, the same ship that had brought her to Africa. The ship stopped at Cape Town for the Stafford House team to reunite for the long journey home and for Janet to be received by King Cetshwayo, who was then being held at the castle prior to being sent to England to meet Queen Victoria. The Zulu King had heard of her kind treatment of his wounded warriors at Utrecht and Rorke's Drift and requested her assistance for a personal health problem. This was quickly resolved and as a mark of his gratitude and in recognition of her work with wounded Zulus, he presented her with his matching necklaces and bracelets, which survive to this day.

Surgeon General of Natal J.A. Woolfryes, who had been severely criticised by General Wolseley, wrote a very dismissive and derogatory report about the Stafford House Nurses whilst praising the Netley Army nurses who had remained at Durban's base hospital. The Netley nurses received their campaign medals on 19 October 1880 while the Stafford House nurses and doctors had to wait nearly four years until 15 July 1884 when their medals arrived by post. There was a great deal of criticism of this petty behaviour on the part of the military; consequently, Janet, her nurses, doctors and Commander Ross received many complimentary accolades from all quarters.

In 1882 Janet Wells became Mrs George King and the following year received the profession's highest accolade when Queen Victoria awarded her the Royal

Red Cross in recognition of exceptional service in the field of military nursing.[4] A previous recipient had been Florence Nightingale.

Sister Janet's diaries, papers, paintings and letters are currently held by the *AZWHS*. From these it is estimated that more than 3,200 sick and wounded soldiers passed through Janet's hands at the Utrecht and Rorke's Drift hospitals.

References

1. All references are from *Sister Janet*, Stossel, K., Pen & Sword, 2006.
2. Records give two dates for her birthday. This is the date recorded on her passport.
3. *Reminiscences of the Zulu War*, John Maxwell, University of Cape Town, 1979.

   The column's pet dogs at Isandlwana were also victims. Many ran away, terrified no doubt by the sound of battle, and later returned to the destroyed camp to find their masters dead. With no one to feed them, they survived by eating the carrion left on the field. Such luckless dogs were destined to share their masters' fortunes throughout the war. According to Lieutenant Maxwell of the NNC, their end was a sorry one.

   'About half a mile from the camp [Rorke's Drift] I was attacked by a pack of dogs about 20, consisting of various breed, Newfoundlands, pointers, setters, terriers etc a few with collars. These were the dogs that had belonged to the camp at Isandhlwana and having lost their masters, and been in the fighting, had become wild and although I tried, by calling them and whistling, could not quiet them, they followed still barking and howling some 3 or 400 yards, when they left me. These were shot at different times with very few exceptions afterwards'.

4. The Royal Red Cross, known as the 'Nurses VC', remains a highly valued decoration by the military nursing services. Until 1976 the RRC was conferred exclusively to women.

Two views of Isandlwana – both from Sister Janet's Scrapbook.

Appendix 1

The Main Requirements of the British Ultimatum to King Cetshwayo

a. The surrender of Chief Sihayo's brother and two sons (for crossing the river border into Natal, abducting and then murdering two of Sihayo's adulterous wives) to the Natal Government plus a fine of 500 cattle for not complying with the original order for their surrender, made in August 1878.

b. A fine of 100 cattle for having hustled and insulted two British surveyors, Deighton and Smith, at the Middle Drift border crossing.

c. The surrender to the Transvaal Courts of the Swazi Chief, Mbilini, (for cattle raiding in the (now) British territory).

d. That the King should observe promises made by him at his coronation to the British Government.

The promises …

1. Indiscriminate executions should cease.
2. No Zulu should be condemned without open trial and the public examination of witnesses, for and against, and there should be a right of appeal to the King.
3. No Zulu's life should be taken without the previous knowledge and consent of the King, after a trial and after the right of appeal to the King.
4. That for minor crimes, the loss of property should be substituted for the death penalty.
5. A number of prominent Zulus were to be surrendered for trial (no names were specified).
6. The Zulu army was to disband and every Zulu was to be free to marry.
7. A British resident official was to oversee Zulu affairs.
8. Missionaries were to be re-admitted to Zululand without let or hindrance. Any dispute involving a European was to be dealt with under British jurisdiction.

Having respectfully listened to the ultimatum, the Zulus requested an extension of the deadline but this was refused. By the middle of the afternoon, John Shepstone closed the meeting and ferried the Zulu chiefs back across the Tugela to take the terms of the ultimatum to King Cetshwayo. A local white trader, John Dunn, obtained a copy of the ultimatum and, being on good terms with Cetshwayo, sent him a copy directly – not that Cetshwayo nor his chiefs could have read it.

Cetshwayo was perplexed; he had been awarded the Disputed Territory but was ordered to comply with impossible demands deliberately worded to confuse him. His requests for clarification were rejected and a succession of attempts at reconciliation were ignored.

Appendix 2

Sergeant T. Cooper, 24th Regiment

The biographical records of those soldiers that had fought in the South Africa campaign of 1877–1879 record that, aged sixteen years, Thomas Cooper attested to the 24th Regiment of Foot on 7 November 1866. At a time when attestation forms merely requested a recruit's age, not his date of birth, and the accuracy of any information provided was only assessed by the recruiter, Cooper had been liberal with the truth. Born in 1850 he swore his age at 18 years. Having completed his first term Cooper re-enlisted as a corporal on 23 December 1873 and was promoted to the rank of Sergeant on 13 August 1874. Before his posting to southern Africa, Cooper had served with the 1st Battalion on garrison duty in Malta and then Gibraltar.

Serving with F Company since its arrival at the Cape of Good Hope on 2 January 1875, Cooper was to become well acquainted with the South African landscape and was one of the battalion's most seasoned campaigners. F Company arrived at Isandlwana on the night of 20 January, camping with the rearguard of the Centre Column at the Manzimyama River on the wagon track that approached Isandlwana from the rear. Cooper eventually marched into Isandlwana camp the following morning.

Chelmsford departed Rorke's Drift in the early hours of 22 January to reinforce Major Dartnell's reconnaissance of the Mangeni Valley. The 1st Battalion with Sergeant Cooper, under the command of Lieutenant Colonel Pulleine, was left to defend the camp and await further orders from Chelmsford.

It was breakfast time when the men of the 1st Battalion were initially called to arms in response to the first sightings of Zulus along the Itusi and Nqutu Ridge to the north of the camp. The men fell in on the slope in front of the 2/24th and NNC tents and remained there until late morning when they were stood down. Cooper and F Company returned to their own battalion tents to commence lunch but were ordered to keep their valise equipment on. Soon after, the '*alarm*' and '*fall in*' bugle calls again sounded, this time in response to the sighting of the main Zulu advance from the north. F Company was sent to reinforce the earlier deployment of E Company, about 1,000 yards to the north of the camp, on the Tahelane Ridge. After the twenty-minute march out of camp and the ascent of the spur, Cooper and his comrades came into action at a position between the main section of E Company and a small detachment to its extreme left, against the uNokhenke and uKhandempemvu Regiments of the Zulu right horn.

Like the fate of so many on that day, no record exists of Cooper's death and it was previously assumed he perished somewhere between the northern base of Isandlwana hill and the Manzimyama stream. Given the length of time that the fallen soldiers' bodies lay in the open it was impossible to identify all but a few, unless where personal items were found. One of these few was Lieutenant Edgar Oliphant Anstey. His remains were recognised by burial parties amongst the last clumps of dead along the Manzimyama River, two miles from the site of the British camp. Anstey had served with Cooper and the discovery of his body so far from the tented area gives credence to the possibility that more men from F Company, including Cooper, could have made it as far, and perhaps even further if they were able to catch a loose horse.

Cooper is included in the Casualty Roll of the 1st Battalion for Isandlwana. This is perfectly understandable, as Cooper was a 24th Sergeant with his unit at Isandlwana and was never seen alive again; logically he had to be recorded as an Isandlwana casualty wherever he was killed.

Appendix 3

Chelmsford's Report Reaches London

Courtesy of the AZWHS and Dr Wayne Bartlett, PhD Thesis 2013

Given the extended time it took for information to travel from South Africa to England it was some time before the full details of Isandlwana, fought on 22 January 1879, were available to Parliament. In fact, when the news was first received in London on 11 February 1879, Parliament was not yet in session for the year – it was scheduled to open proceedings two days later.

The 11 February 1879 may have been one of the most extraordinary of political days in the whole Victorian era. A message from Colonel Stanley to the Queen gives some details of what happened in what was a momentous few hours. News of the disaster at Isandlwana was received by Stanley at around 4.30 am and intense activity followed throughout the remainder of the day, culminating in the decision to send significant reinforcements to South Africa.

The Queen was at Osborne House, her elegant home on the Isle of Wight. The day before had been her wedding anniversary, which would have been a day of sad reflection for her. Before any news was received about Isandlwana, the Anglo-Zulu War had barely registered on public consciousness outside of political circles. This was about to change with a vengeance. Victoria was very soon fully informed (as far as the limited details went) on what had happened at Isandlwana. Her journal entry for 11 February is interesting.[1] It reveals that fingers were already being pointed at Colonel Durnford, even though there had been no formal enquiry and the details emerging in the panic-stricken hours after the battle, with the British Army retreating hastily from Zululand and Natal expecting an invasion at any moment, were sketchy to say the least. Many people – including some leading members of the British Army and troops in the field – blamed Chelmsford for what had happened or would come to do so. Colonials in particular resented the accusations against Durnford that appeared so quickly after the event.

In his speech in the House of Lords on 13 February Disraeli also endeavoured to deflect criticism of Isandlwana by dwelling on the bravery of the 24th Regiment at Rorke's Drift. He started by referring to the defeat:

> 'It is a military disaster – a terrible military disaster – but no more. It is not a military defeat arising from the failing energies or resources of the country. It is from accidental and, at this moment, not clearly understood circumstances that the calamity has arisen'.

It was noticeable that Disraeli was quick to take advantage of the public relations opportunities offered by Rorke's Drift and he told his audience that:

> 'We must not forget the exhibition of heroic valour by those who have been spared. At this moment, I am sure, the recollection of those 80 (*sic*) men, who, for 12 hours in a forlorn hope, kept at bay 4,000 of the enemy, and ultimately repulsed them, will prove that the stamina and valour of the English soldiery have not diminished'.[2]

There was nothing to be gained by defending Frere. The subsequent award of 11 Victoria Crosses was to be staggered at intervals over seven months in an attempt to manage public opinion. The art of spin was already alive and well.

References

1. RA VIC/MAIN/O/33/101.
2. Quoted in Saul David, *Zulu*, London, 2004.

Appendix 4

Rorke's Drift Awards

On 27 March, Mr Osborne Morgan asked in the House of Commons whether or not those individuals singled out for heroism in Chard's report concerning Rorke's Drift would be rewarded for their actions. Replying, Colonel Lindsay (in the place of the absent Secretary of State for War) said that he presumed that:

> 'The learned Member alludes to the decorations which are given to soldiers who distinguish themselves by Her Majesty, and which are valued as coming from the Queen. It takes a considerable time to allot these, according to fairness and precision ....'

But in fact the awards would not be too long in coming.

The recommendations for decorations came from Chelmsford himself, rather than Colonel Glyn, notionally the commanding officer of those responsible for the defence of Rorke's Drift – this was a breach of normal conventions. This perhaps evidences two things: the increasingly poor relationship between Chelmsford and Glyn, and the desire (one might speculate desperation) of Chelmsford to exaggerate the significance of the battle, something in which he would be ably assisted by Sir Bartle Frere.

On 6 May 1879, eight men were gazetted with Victoria Crosses for their roles at Rorke's Drift: these included Chard and Bromhead. The timing was auspicious as it coincided with the second invasion of Zululand with what was the largest British field force since the Crimean War and as such gave an invaluable fillip to morale. The public responded enthusiastically to the awards and more followed later in the year. A total of eleven Victoria Crosses given for the action at Rorke's Drift was extraordinary recognition of this fact.

Victoria appreciated that the role of public opinion had become ever more important in sustaining support for adventures such as the Anglo-Zulu War, and the generous distribution of medals was a way in which it could be kept on board. In this, she was perhaps reflecting the views of the (by now) late Emperor Napoleon III, who had said that:

> 'At the stage of civilisation in which we are the success of armies, however brilliant they may be, is only transitory. In reality it is public opinion that wins the last victory'.[1]

General Sir Garnet Wolseley let it be known that he thought the awards for the defence of Rorke's Drift were 'monstrous' on the grounds that the men were like 'rats in a trap' and had no option but to fight.

Both Chard and Bromhead received the Victoria Cross and both were quickly promoted to the rank of Major. Chard retired as a Lieutenant Colonel: in 1896 he was diagnosed as having cancer of the tongue and he was forced to retire. Queen Victoria was kept informed of his condition, which deteriorated and led to his death in November 1897.

An interesting postscript concerning Chard's Victoria Cross occurred in 1999. Stanley Baker, who played Chard in the celebrated film *Zulu*, acquired Chard's pair of medals in an auction in 1972. Although the campaign medal was genuine, the Victoria Cross was catalogued as a copy and, as a consequence, Baker paid the comparatively modest sum of £2,700 for the pair. On Stanley Baker's death, the Cross changed hands three times until it ended up, lodged for safety, with Spinks medal dealers who decided to check the nature of Chard's 'copy' medal. Its metallic characteristics were tested by the Royal Armouries. The test results were compared with those of the bronze ingot, kept at the Central Ordnance Depot, from which all Victoria Crosses are cast. The tests revealed that the 'copy' had come from this same block and there was no doubt that it was the genuine article. No price can be put on this authenticated VC belonging to such a famous recipient.

Reference

1. Quoted in Figes, p. 311.

Award of Rorke's Drift Victoria Crosses

The Victoria Cross

The Victoria Cross is Britain's highest honour for bravery in battle, awarded for acts performed in terrifying and bloody circumstances. In the past, the Victoria Cross could bring its own problems for, all too often, the qualities that made a man a hero in battle could elude him in times of peace. Of the 1,354 men who have won the VC, 19 committed suicide, a far higher proportion than the national average, although almost all were Victorian. About the same number have died in suspicious circumstances. Others fell on hard times and died in abject poverty, having sold their hard earned Cross for a pittance. In contrast, most officer recipients prospered, as did many other ranks who were held in high esteem by their neighbours.

Gazetted	Name	Date awarded	Where awarded	By whom
2 May 1879	Chard	16 July 1879	St. Paul's, Zululand	Lt. Gen. Wolseley
17 June 1879	Reynolds	16 July 1879	St Paul's, Zululand	Lt. Gen. Wolseley
2 May 1879	Hook	3 August 1879	Rorke's Drift	Lt. Gen. Wolseley
2 May 1879	Hitch	12 August 1879	Netley Hospital	Queen Victoria
2 May 1879	Bromhead	11 Sept. 1879	Utrecht	Lt. Gen. Wolseley
2 May 1879	Jones, R.	11 Sept 1879	Utrecht	Lt. Gen. Wolseley
2 May 1879	Allen	9 Dec. 1879	Windsor Castle	Queen Victoria
2 May 1879	Jones, W.	13 Jan. 1880	Windsor Castle	Queen Victoria
17 1879	Dalton	16 Jan. 1879	Fort Napier	Maj. Gen. Clifford
29 Nov 1879	Schiess	3 Feb. 1880	Pietermaritzburg	Lt. Gen. Wolseley
2 May 1879	Williams	1 March 1880	Gibraltar	Maj. Gen. Anderson

Appendix 5

Rorke's Drift Today

After the Zulu war, returning farm owners along the border with Zululand found their farmhouses had been plundered or had fallen into serious disrepair after troops had pulled out timbers for firewood and any remaining thatch had rotted away. The rough tracks that had served the farmers well had been destroyed by the many hundreds of army wagons leaving deep ruts from taking stores to and from the front line. Every tree had been chopped down for firewood, wild animals had been hunted out and, worst for the farming community, the army cattle and horses had eaten out all the pasture lands and grasses on the open countryside. The damage caused all those years ago can still be seen today.

After the war's end, visitors to view Rorke's Drift soon began to arrive, albeit in low numbers, and included the Empress Eugenie whose entourage passed through en route to the site of her son's death to the north of the drift. The local magistrate, Henry Francis Fynn, took it upon himself to accommodate such visitors and would take them via Helpmekaar to Rorke's Drift. In 1882 a visitor described Helpmekaar as:

> 'Quiet, with three or four houses, a few shanties, an 'hotel' and a Post Office Agency. The fort was still there. Unlike Isandlwana where relics could still be found, at Rorke's Drift nothing of the old fortification could be found other than Witt's house which was being restored. Outhouses stood around, hard by was the Chapel, belonging to the Mission, but of the defences, not a trace'.[1]

Unlike the remainder of Zululand, peace quickly returned to the rural community of Rorke's Drift. Otto Witt returned later that year to rebuild the two burnt-out and gutted ruins of his Mission, and the location thereafter slipped off the map of public awareness. The public perception of the defeated Zulus quickly transformed from one of warrior status to civilised garden boys and servants. There developed a growing tendency for Europeans, epitomised by authors such H. Rider Haggard, to view the 'old' Zulu order in terms of a romantic and proud nation which simply rose above itself and which needed putting in its correct place, and to supply compliant workers for the growing industries of South Africa. This overlooked the reality of the previously proud Zulus, now defeated, being obliged to learn and adopt European ways and having to accept the less attractive necessities of those in command of commerce and employment. With their best agricultural land taken from them by incoming European settlers, hunger forced tens of thousands of Zulus to seek low-paid domestic employment or work in the fast-growing sugar cane industry. The effect on both individuals and family life was severe, with Zulu workers being forced into committing themselves to work far from their homes for weeks and months without leave to visit their families.

Thankfully for the isolated Rorke's Drift community, the area was too far from the basic road network and of no use to any commercial enterprise. Even when the Boer war broke out, the nearest the combatants reached was Dundee with a small outpost at Helpmekaar, but with South Africa becoming famous for its mineral wealth in the 1880s, it was not too long before gold fever spread from the Transvaal to the steep and rocky Buffalo River gorges near Rorke's and Fugitives' drifts. The search for gold had originally started a few miles south of the drifts, and in one lucky period some 800 ounces of gold were recovered, and then the seam ran out. The prospectors left but one keen ex-sailor from HMS *Boadicea*, known as Barclay, stayed on convinced he would make his fortune. He took several mining options in the area including Fugitives' Drift where he prospected for several months. From the pump house at the drift, which today supplies water to the nearby Fugitives' Drift Lodge, the original workings built by Barclay can still be seen, as can the mineshaft built into the base of the cliff overlooking the river, known to the local Zulus as 'Albert's shaft'. Local folklore suggests Barclay never found any gold and worse, it is not known what happened to him.

Diamond fever had a similar affect when it reached the Rorke's Drift area, but only as a result of a simple human error. In 1920 Mr Ekron, the farmer who owned Petroscar Farm near the fugitives' graves, found two rough diamonds in a small pool next to the river. He took them for verification to a Mr Meyer at Dundee who, without telling Ekron, swiftly purchased the land surrounding the pool. Local folklore remembers him paying twelve times the current value for the land. Stone sifting equipment was transported to the site and washing began. For months work progressed but nothing was found. Ekron occasionally passed by and one day came across Meyer watching the sluicing operation. Ekron, by accident or design, mentioned that this was the very place where his ostriches once gathered to drink. Meyer knew Ekron had once owned a flock that had been reared for their feathers, but the venture failed and he asked Ekron where the ostriches had come from, to which Ekron replied, 'from the diamond fields at Kimberley where they had been used as "guard dogs" to prevent thieves scavenging loose diamonds'. On realising the diamonds found by Ekron had originally been passed by one of his ostriches, the Meyer diamond venture then closed down.[2]

The community remained small and eked out a living off the harsh countryside on both sides of the river, the only event of any significance to the people was when a trader crossed the river to trade in Zululand. Later, the occasional motor vehicle would arrive to make the crossing, for which the local community would assemble to watch and help if necessary. The two world wars had no effect on the community and so their lives at the river crossing remained mainly uneventful.

In the late 1950s the Rorke's Drift farmland of 5,000 acres was proclaimed 'White Land', thus making all the local Zulus living on the farm illegal squatters, though no serious attempt was made to remove them. In 1961 a committee was formed in Stockholm, the Evangelical Lutheran Church Art and Craft Group, for the advancement of African art and craft, which was established in 1962 by Peder and Ulla Gowenius in the midst of the Apartheid Era. This would have a significant impact on the development of South African art and craft in the 1960s and 1970s. In 1963 the Art and Craft Centre moved to Rorke's Drift and, on the strength of a loan from the Church of Sweden Mission, rebuilt and occupied some existing disused buildings. An exhibition in Stockholm in late 1963 enabled further funds to be generated for extensions to the existing buildings. The centre remains in operation, though on a limited scale.

Following the 1964 release of the film *Zulu*, together with the publication of Donald Morris' book *The Washing of the Spears*, interest in Rorke's Drift began to grow. Tourists and researchers began to make their way to the remote site, but not in any number to affect the community. It was the advent of the first centenary anniversary that focused the world's attention on the remote Mission. Events of commemoration were arranged and for a whole week visitors from across South Africa, Britain and the USA visited the site to learn more of the battle that had now become so well publicised.

They then departed and once again the community was left on its own. Following the 100th anniversary of the battle, a small school was built and the Lutheran Church assumed responsibility for the administration of the local area. Without any facilities, visitors to Rorke's Drift had to either camp or take accommodation in Dundee, 30 miles distant. This situation remained unaltered until the adjacent land, between Rorke's Drift and Fugitives' Drift, known then as West Kirby Farm, was purchased as a holiday retreat by Peter Rattray, a Johannesburg lawyer. Rattray's immediate neighbours were the Potgieter family who lived in what is today Fugitives' Drift Lodge. George Bunting, an accredited authority on the Zulu people, lived at the adjacent Umzinyathi House. In due course, both properties were sold to Peter Rattray.

Peter's son, David, and his wife Nicky, took over the running of the estate in 1989. Within a year, spartan accommodation was offered to visitors, one being the author. In 1990 the first tourist coach, with guests from the UK travelling with Holt's Battlefield Tours, arrived. Their arrival was auspicious, as they had been booked into a hotel at Ulundi which unexpectedly went 'on strike'. The tourists learned of the strike on a baking hot mid-afternoon at a police road check with the nearest town some 30 miles distant. An urgent phone call to Fugitives' Drift Lodge, just 30 miles away, was answered by David, who invited the stranded tourists to his new, and fortunately empty, lodge. Within an hour, David and Nicky had galvanised their staff into preparing accommodation for the twenty-four otherwise stranded visitors. Over the next three days David conducted the group around the battlefields of Rorke's Drift and Isandlwana, including an excursion along the Fugitives' Trail. Such was the quality of the accommodation, guiding and location on the battlefield that Holts booked all their subsequent Zulu War tours to stay at the new Rattray Lodge, which helped establish the lodge firmly in the eyes of the tourist industry.

At modern-day Rorke's Drift, still an isolated and impoverished rural community, there are two deeply rooted factors which strongly influence the local culture: they are education and religion. With modern technology impinging on education, it has been established that there are vast difficulties which teachers experience on a daily basis when dealing with learners from this village community. Their traditional and cultural orientations do not successfully accommodate the modern school curriculum, which is highly westernised and heavily influenced by computer science. Parents, who are frequently illiterate, still raise their children in traditional ways enforcing their classical values; as a result, the younger community finds it difficult to cope with a formal education that is invariably provided in a language that is foreign to them, namely English. Without doubt, the strong traditional mother-child relationship continues to play a major role in a child's development and this understandable influence can contribute to on-going difficulties facing these rural children in school.

The areas of local life that exacerbate problems among the young Zulus of Rorke's Drift are, among other things, poor financial background, no lighting at home in winter months and evenings, insufficient resources at school using old and few books, insufficient school facilities with school hours often in shifts, a challenging environment usually involving long walks to and from school, and sustained apartheid legacies which result in insecurity and shyness of white people. There is also a lack of career guidance in rural schools and little or no employment without leaving home, which is damaging to the local community and traditional family life; malnutrition through poverty, ignorant uneducated parents, the banning of corporal punishment so that there are no meaningful sanctions, the high rate of unemployed parents and frequently single parenting all combine to make growing up in rural Zululand a challenge. On the other hand, experience has shown that the children are not slow to approach visitors for help with their homework!

Religion plays an integral role in the development of Zulu teenagers at Rorke's Drift. The local Lutheran church has a strong influence across the life of the community and the church elders are well regarded and highly respected. To the local people religion can mean fundamental beliefs as well as superstitions and, naturally, most children, even approaching adulthood, remain highly superstitious even if they are devout Christians. Long-term local culture places a high value on marital issues such as weddings and initiation ceremonies which cover the graduation from childhood to adulthood for girls, known as *umemulo* – a ceremonial function performed by the father to announce publicly that his daughter is ready for marriage. This ceremony, in western terms, is equivalent to the European eighteenth birthday party or the debutantes' ball of past times.

Local industry is, by the very nature of the above factors, limited. The local Arts and Crafts business is highly professional, but only employs a few Zulu women and girls, as does the nearby wire-work and bead business. The community men-folk see their role as farmers and community officials, which results in an absolute delineation of labour between the sexes. It is a situation that is unlikely to change in the near future.

References

1. Henderson, Sheila, *The Turbulent Frontier – Biggarsberg and Buffalo at the Crossroads*, Qualitas Publishers (Pty) Ltd, 1979.
2. These amusing accounts were among a number given to me in 2009 by David Rattray at Fugitives' Drift Lodge while conducting my research into Sister Janet Wells' time spent at Rorke's Drift.

Appendix 6

Testing the Chard Reports

All charts and diagrams are copyright and courtesy of Dr David Holmes, The College of New Jersey, USA and *AZWHS Journal 32*, December 2012.

The key questions that the Stylometric[1] investigated were:

1. Are there any stylistic differences between the first and second Chard Reports?
2. Are there similarities in style between the first Chard Report and Clery's writings?

So, can stylometry help resolve the authorship of the two reports? Stylometry is a body of techniques used for the statistical analysis of literary style. These techniques date back to 1851, when the English logician Augustus de Morgan suggested in a letter to a friend that questions of authorship might be settled by determining if one text 'does not deal in longer words' than another. Since then, stylometrists such as Dr David Holmes and his team have searched for a reliable way of quantifying the style of a text which may be unique to an author. Growing computer power and the ready availability of machine-readable versions of many literary works have created a plethora of new techniques to examine authorship. Most researchers now believe that common words are the most valuable in characterizing an author's stylometric signature. They study the so-called non-contextual function words – prepositions, conjunctions, articles and adverbs – the 'humble servants' of speech, words that every writer employs subconsciously in a pattern as distinctive as a fingerprint.

Analysis by Dr David Holmes

Analyses with large sets (between fifty and a hundred) of these words have met with astonishing success. Essentially they pick a certain number (N) of the most common words in the texts under investigation and compute the frequency of these words in each separate text sample, thereby converting each text into a multi-dimensional array of numbers. A set of statistical procedures, known as multivariate analyses, are then applied to the data to look for patterns.

One type of multivariate analysis is known as 'principal components analysis'. This aims to reduce the dimensionality of the problem by transforming the N variables to a smaller number, usually 2, of new variables. The first two new variables (or principal components) capture a large proportion of the variation in the original data and plotting the text samples in the space of these first two principal components enables the analyst to observe N-dimensional data in just two dimensions. Another type of analysis, known as 'cluster analysis', provides an objective way of identifying any groupings amongst the samples of text. These samples are plotted on a tree-diagram or dendrogram. Two samples that have a large degree of similarity in the values of their word-occurrence rates rapidly merge together in the manner of two branches on a tree.

A number of control texts are necessary for this analysis, in the same genre and era but by writers who do not feature as contenders to the disputed Chard Reports. Letters from men writing home during the Anglo-Zulu campaign, not just officers, but NCOs and private soldiers whose letters, in the custom of the time, were passed on for publication in local newspapers, are available in *The Red Soldier* (Frank Emory, 1977). Three men in particular, Captain Edward Robert Prevost Woodgate, Captain Walter Parke Jones and Lieutenant William Weallens provided letters of sufficient length to qualify as suitable control texts, with each batch of letters being split into two to facilitate internal comparison.

Another excellent source of textual material used by Dr Holmes is the book *The Curling Letters of the Zulu War* (Ed. Brian Best and Adrian Greaves, 2004). Lieutenant Henry Curling was one of only five officers who survived the slaughter at Isandlwana. A family man and prolific letter writer, his detailed accounts of the invasion of Zululand make gripping reading. Two textual samples were taken from this book to add to the control texts.

Major Francis Clery was an experienced report writer. His letters are part of the papers of Sir Archibald Alison, who was Chief of Intelligence in the British Army and are published in *Zululand at War 1879: The Conduct of the Anglo-Zulu War* (Sonia Clarke, 1984). Three textual samples were taken from this book.

The second report is reprinted there by kind permission of HM The Queen. The first report at 1,301 words is too small to be split, but the second report at 6,462 words was divided into four approximately-equal-sized samples. Regrettably, apart from a brief 312-word letter written in September 1879 to Sir John Stokes from *The Royal Engineer Journal*, it may surprise readers to learn that no usable authentic written material from Chard is known to exist.

The following charts and graphs are from Dr Holmes' research and are included for readers interested in the finer points of his analysis. These can be omitted by the reader unfamiliar with such methods as the results are considered in the text.

All these samples are listed in Table 1, the samples being either typed or scanned into machine-readable form. The choice of text size in stylometric studies is always problematic. Smaller units are too short to provide opportunities for stylistic habits to operate on the arrangement of internal constituents, while larger units are insufficiently frequent to provide enough examples for reliable statistical inference. Forsyth and Holmes (1996) found the median text block size in a selection of stylometric studies to be around 3,500 words. In their study of the *Book of Mormon*, Jockers et al. (2008) they claim that even the smallest chapters are of adequate size for stylometric analysis, finding no correlation between the correct assignment of an author and the length of text sample. In all the following analyses, the occurrence rates of words are measured as percentages of the total sample size. For this study, differences in sample size are not critical provided we adhere to a stylometrically-desirable minimum threshold of 1,000 words.

Table 1: Textual Samples

Author	Title	Sample	Sample size in words
Henry Curling	*Letters*	1	3112
		2	3035
Walter Parke Jones	*Letters*	1	1168
		2	1336
William Weallens	*Letters*	1	1396
		2	1564
Edward Woodgate	*Letters*	1	1380
		2	1379
Francis Clery	*Letters*	1	2559
		2	2324
		3	3047
First Chard Report		1	1301
Second Chard Report		1	1687
		2	1632
		3	1698
		4	1445

The pioneering work of Mosteller and Wallace (1964) on the use of function words in authorship attribution was continued by J. F. Burrows (1992). Since then multivariate statistical analyses involving large sets of non-contextual high-frequency function words have been employed in problems of attribution in a wide variety of authors and genres. See, for example, the investigation into the authorship of the so-called *Pickett Letters* of the American Civil War (Holmes et al., 2001) and the new look at the authorship of the *Book of Mormon* (Jockers et al., 2008). The 'Burrows' approach has become the first port-of-call for attributional problems and will be the technique adopted in this investigation.

The number of function words used (N) varies by application and genre but typically lies between 50 and 75, the implication being that these words should be among the most common in the language and that content words should be avoided. A value of N set at 60 is used as a rule-of-thumb heuristic throughout this analysis, being an appropriate value for these sized text samples. A list these sixty most common function words, taken from the corpus of texts, follows this article.

The control samples used included correspondence from Curling, Weallens, Jones, and Woodgate.

The first phase in this investigation is designed to test the validity of the proposed technique. For the purposes of this study, it is required that known texts can be shown to be internally consistent and separate from each other. The occurrence rates of the sixty words selected were computed for the individual textual samples from the letters of Lieutenants Curling and Weallens and Captains Jones and Woodgate. These were used as input to both a principal components analysis and a cluster analysis. The positions of the samples in the space of the first two principal components, which together explain 52.9 per cent of the variation in the original data, are shown in Figure 1. An alternative analysis of the controls may be provided by conducting a cluster analysis on the textual samples, using the sixty word rates as variables and Ward's method as the clustering algorithm. Figure 2 shows the resulting dendrogram.

The results with these two methods of analysis are mutually supportive, with samples forming clusters on the basis of authorship. Our writers are internally consistent as regards their usage of these sixty words, yet are distinguishable from each other.

Fig. 1. Principal Components Plot: Curling, Jones, Weallens and Woodgate.

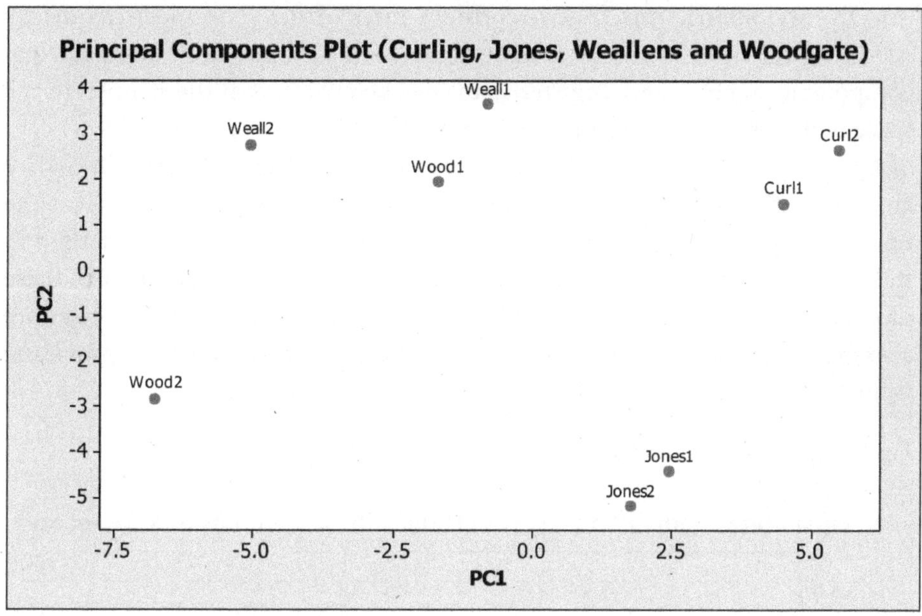

Fig. 2. Dendrogram: Curling, Jones, Weallens and Woodgate.

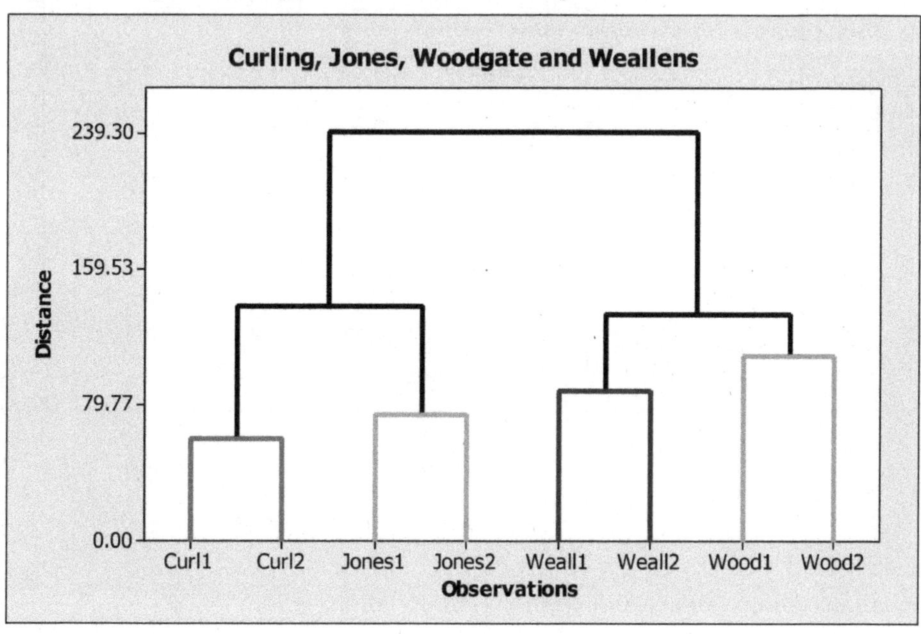

We now add the three textual samples from the letters of Major Francis Clery into the stylometric mix. The occurrence rates of the sixty most frequently occurring function words were once again used as input to both a principal components analysis and a cluster analysis. The positions of the samples in the space of the first two principal components, which together explain 45.6 per cent of the variation in the original data, are shown in Figure 3. An alternative analysis of the controls was provided by conducting a cluster analysis on the textual samples, using the sixty word rates as variables and Ward's method as the clustering algorithm. Figure 4 shows the resulting dendrogram. Both these plots show excellent internal consistency for the three Clery samples. They are also quite distinct from the samples taken from our three controls, providing validation for the 'Burrows' approach on works of known authors.

Fig. 3. Principal Components Plot: Clery, Curling, Jones, Weallens and Woodgate.

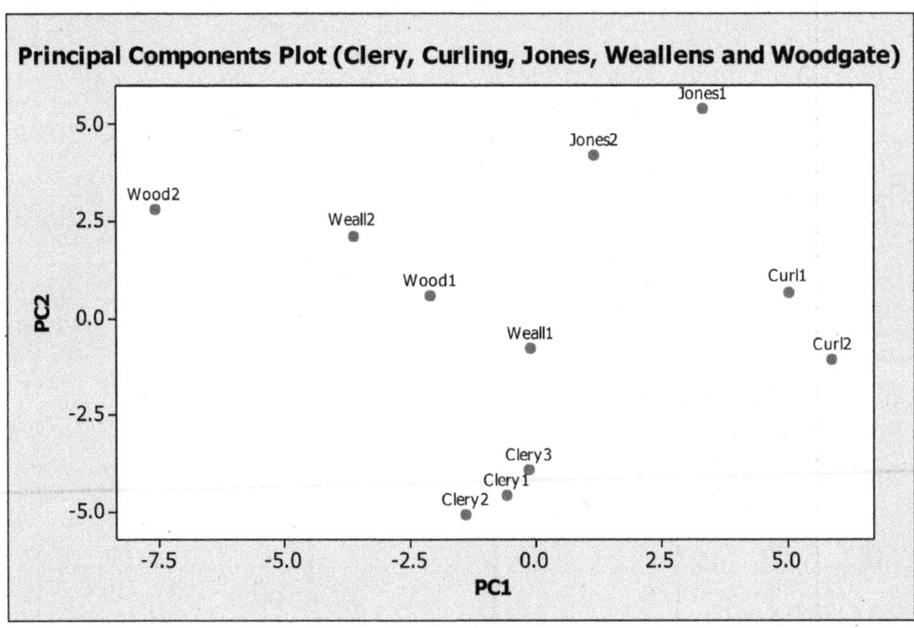

Fig. 4. Dendrogram: Clery, Curling, Jones, Weallens and Woodgate.

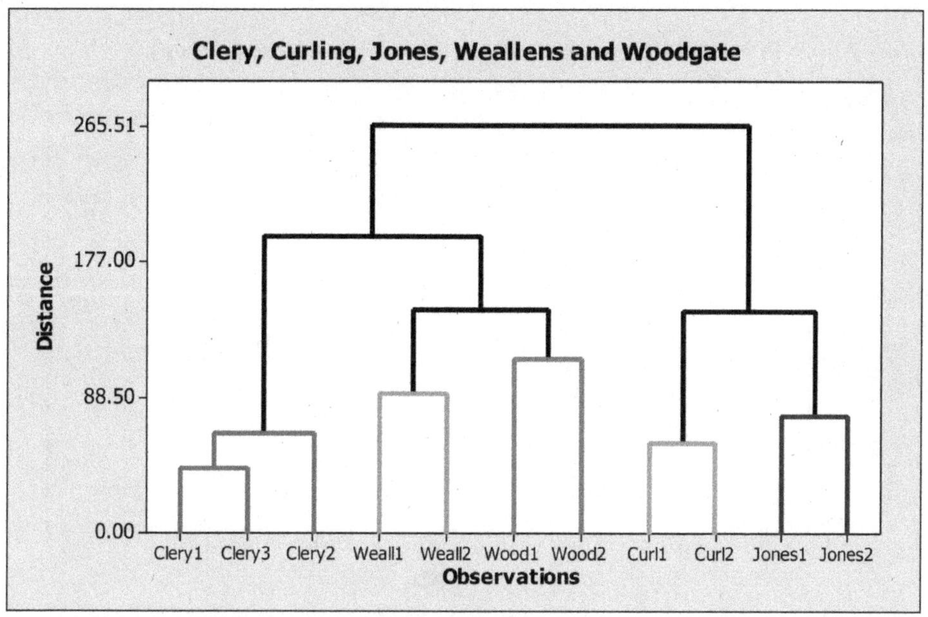

The Chard Reports and Clery

Having successfully established the internally consistent style in the letters of Major Francis Clery concerning the usage of the sixty function words it is now time to focus on both Chard Reports. Discarding Jones, Weallens and Woodgate, who have done their duty, we now take the first Chard Report and the four samples from the second Chard Report, and add them into the mix with the three Clery samples. Figures 5 and 6 show the principal components plot and the dendrogram, respectively, from similar multivariate statistical analyses on the sixty function words. The former plot explains 50.4 per cent of the variation in the original data.

Two important conclusions may be drawn from these clear and mutually supportive plots. First, there appears to be no difference in style between the first and second Chard Reports, suggesting single authorship. Secondly, the Chard samples cluster quite distinctly and separately from the samples of the writings of Clery. Our strong contender for authorship of at least the first Chard Report appears not to be a match. Might there be another contender amongst the British soldiers serving in the campaign?

Fig. 5. Principal Components Plot: Chard Reports and Clery.

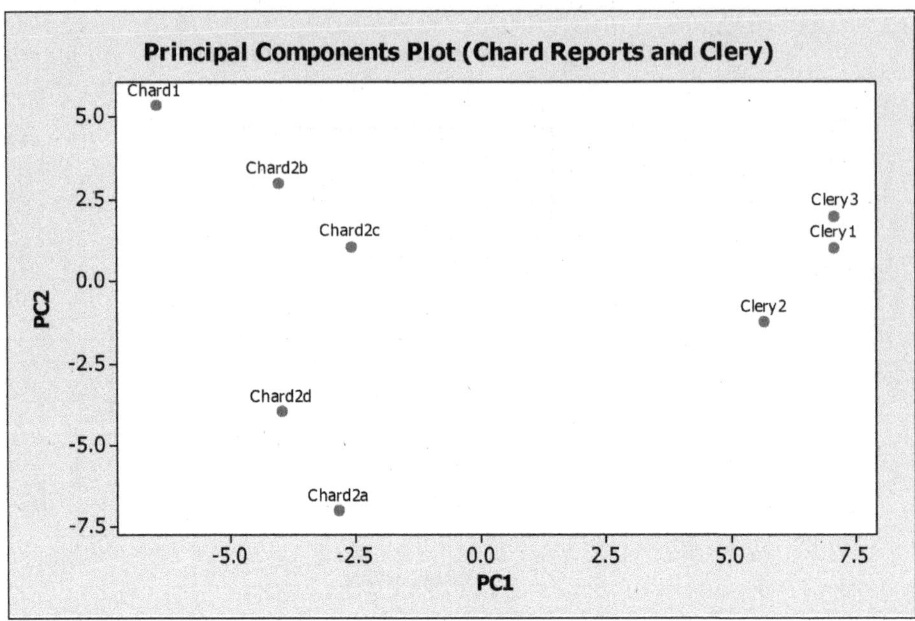

Fig. 6. Dendrogram: Chard Reports and Clery.

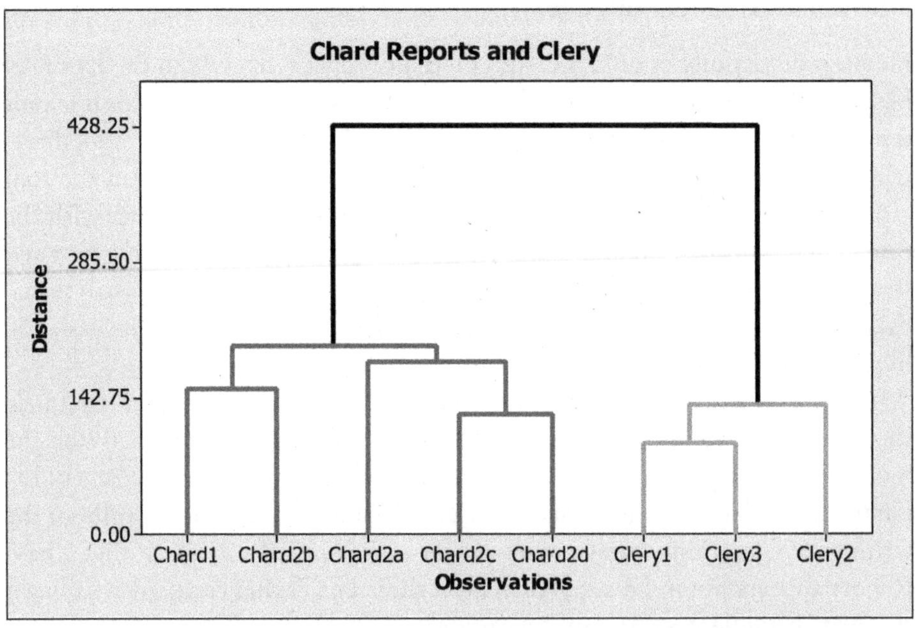

For many people, the outstanding character in the iconic 1964 film ***Zulu*** was Colour Sergeant Bourne, as portrayed by Nigel Green. The real Frank Bourne was born in 1854 and volunteered for the army in 1872. He was short and in his own words painfully thin, but upon arrival in South Africa rapidly ascended the promotion ladder. Bourne's first duties at Rorke's Drift on 22 January 1879 would have been to supervise the taking down of the bell tents to give a clear field of fire, to post lookouts on the higher ground and then to lead a skirmishing line to intercept the advancing Zulu force.

In penning his first report after the action, John Chard would certainly have elicited help from NCOs present at the defence of the post since he would not have seen everything nor known everyone's names. Frank Bourne was literate and acted as 'unpaid private secretary' to those soldiers who could barely read or write, deciphering and answering their letters home. Might Bourne be the author of the first Chard Report and might Chard have drawn on Bourne's notes for the second report?

Bourne died in May 1945 and it is believed that he was the last surviving member of the Rorke's Drift garrison. Yet in December 1936 he made a BBC radio broadcast concerning the battle for a series entitled '*I Was There*'. This 'Bourne Report' has 2,246 words and was divided into two approximately equal-sized samples for analysis. The Bourne Report samples were added to those from both Chard Reports and the Clery letters and the occurrence rates of the sixty most frequently occurring function words were once again used as input to both a principal components analysis and a cluster analysis. The positions of the samples in the space of the first two principal components, which together explain 49.7 per cent of the variation in the original data, are shown in Figure 7. Figure 8 shows the associated loadings plot from the principal components analysis, which helps to explain the groupings in the main plot. One can imagine superimposing this graph on top of the principal components plot. Figure 9 shows the dendrogram, again using Ward's method as the clustering algorithm.

Fig. 7. Principal Components Plot: Bourne, Chard Reports and Clery.

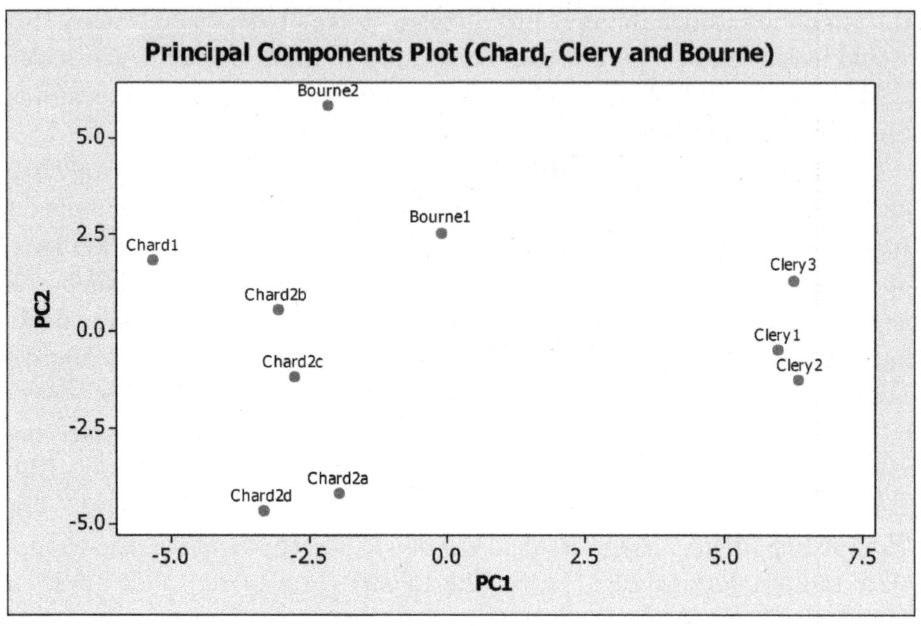

Fig. 8. Loadings Plot: Bourne, Chard Reports and Clery.

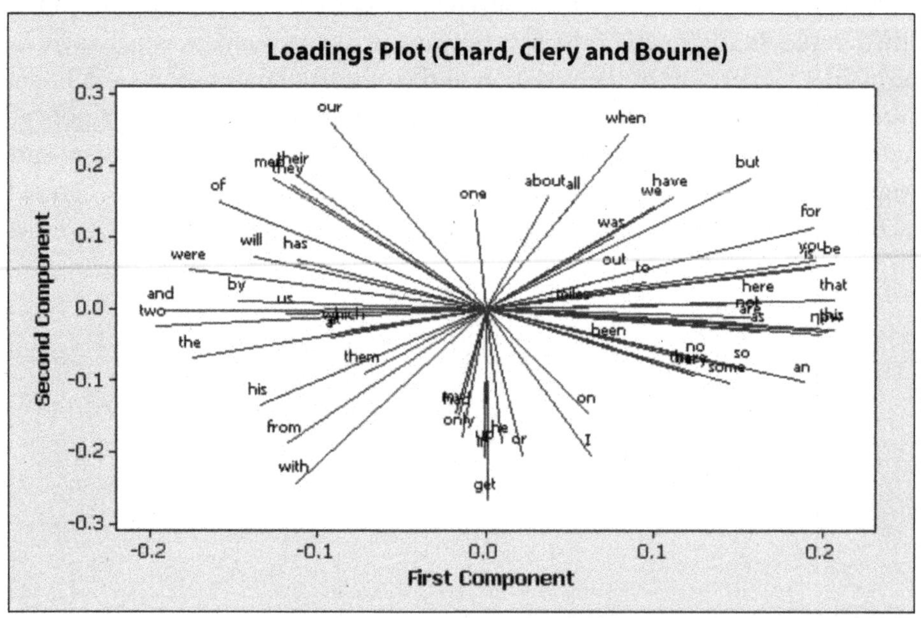

Fig. 9. Dendrogram: Bourne, Chard Reports and Clery.

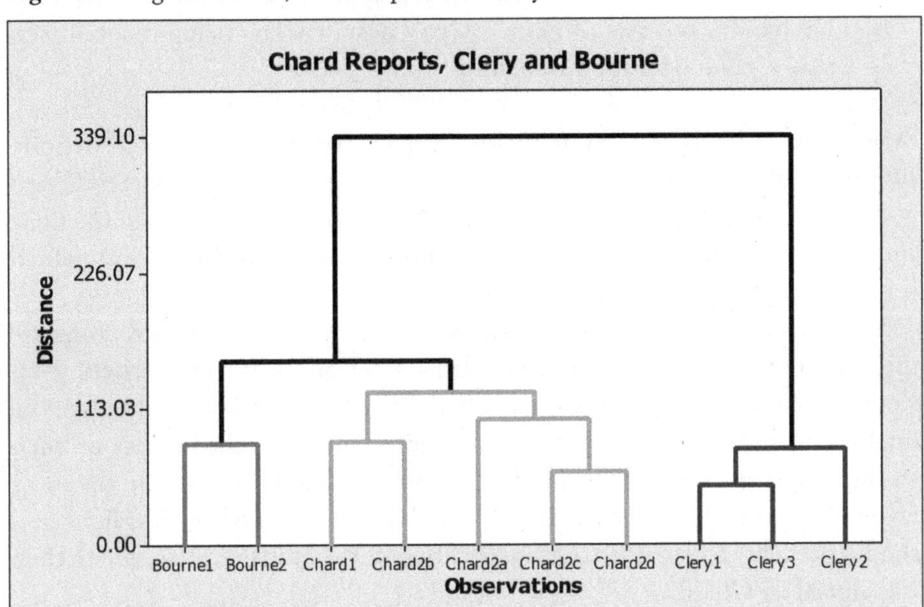

From Figures 7 and 9 we see that the two halves of the Bourne Report show excellent internal consistency but, although slightly closer in style to the Chard Reports than Clery's writings, cannot really be considered to be a stylometric match. Figure 8 shows how words on the right such as 'for', 'you', 'is', 'be' and 'that' have high usage by Clery, whereas words on the left such as 'were', 'and', 'the' and 'his' are words of high usage in the Chard Reports. Favoured words in the Bourne Report are words such as 'our' and 'their'.

The sixty most frequently occurring function words used in the analyses

the	and	to	of	a	we	in	I	is	it
have	on	as	was	at	are	with	that	not	they
all	be	for	were	he	very	from	but	had	our
there	about	so	this	will	one	men	been	which	them
out	now	by	get	my	up	no	two	or	when
miles	here	you	their	his	an	some	only	has	us

Neither do the reports appear to be by Frank Bourne. Bourne may well have added details but the slightly closer similarity here may reflect the fact that Bourne was very familiar with Chard's first report by the time he gave his own account. According to the researchers, they were left then with the following conclusions:

a. Both the first and second Chard Reports appear to be by the same hand.
b. That hand is not that of Francis Clery, despite Clery being mooted as a strong contender for authorship.

Stylometric analysis of the Chard Report has given us no clear and definite authorship of the report. There is the possibility that an original report by Chard was passed through several hands, with the corrections, additions, subtractions and stylistic improvements, all building and trimming the final report, which was then transcribed by a totally different hand.

Such an important document, which had in its power the potential to exonerate the senior officers from calamitous blame for Isandlwana by ratcheting-up victory at Rorke's Drift, would be likely to be reviewed and altered before the final submission. No senior officer would allow an unchecked report on such an important event to see the light of day until it had been put into the most favourable form. Thus the Chard report should be viewed in that light and should probably be regarded as a compilation of the available facts, which then was signed by Chard.

This research project now lies somewhat tantalizingly on hold, awaiting any future discovery by Anglo-Zulu War historians of new textual material from officers who were present at Rorke's Drift.

Reference

1. Dr David I. Holmes, The College of New Jersey, USA.

Appendix 7

Martini-Henry Rates of Fire at Rorke's Drift and Isandlwana

There were two types of fire employed by British infantry at Isandlwana and Rorke's Drift: volley fire and independent fire. Volley fire – in which a group of men, usually a section or a number of sections fire at the same time at a given target – was best used against an enemy en masse. Although the constraints of the manoeuvre mitigated against individual accuracy, volleys had a devastating psychological effect on the target, which was often as damaging as the actual casualties they caused. The sudden crash of the volley created the impression in the minds of those on the receiving end that it was more destructive than it actually was, and this in itself often caused attacks to falter, as happened to the first Zulu attack at Isandlwana. Independent fire – in which the soldier picked his own target and fired when ready – often caused more casualties, but among nervous soldiers could lead to a much higher rate of fire with a greater degree of wastage.

It is interesting to note that in the 1874 regulations, the soldier was required to load his rifle on the command 'ready', and on the command 'present' was to bring it to the aim, pause for a time equal to three beats of slow time – to steady himself – and then fire. No word 'fire' was given. If the situation changed during those crucial seconds, if the target was moving into cover for example, the soldier was still expected to fire, and the effectiveness of his shot could be greatly reduced. From July 1879 – presumably as a result of experiences in Zululand – Army Orders added the command 'fire', and this was incorporated into the 1882 edition of the *Field Exercise Manual*. This allowed those directing the fire to select the most opportune moment to actually fire, and to relieve individual soldiers of the obligation of firing by rote.

Throughout this period, the emphasis in British tactical doctrine was upon producing an effective rate of fire. By carefully pacing the rate of fire, commanders stood a far better chance of achieving their tactical objectives through a higher rate of hits. In the heat of battle, a natural nervousness encourages soldiers to fire as quickly as possible in the hope that this will discourage an enemy attack. Under such circumstances, aimed fire can soon be abandoned, and changes in the formation and distance of the target can be overlooked, so that the exact opposite of the desired effect can occur. By blazing away rapidly, the troops might cause fewer enemy casualties, and encourage rather than discourage attacks. Moreover, it has been noted on a number of occasions that the black powder charge of the Boxer cartridges employed with the Martini-Henry rifle produced a large quantity of dense white smoke when fired. This was particularly true when volley fire was used in close formations. As at Isandlwana, a windless day, one or two volleys were sufficient to obscure the target, and any subsequent volleys, if not properly controlled, had to be fired blind. One subsequent reason for slowing the rate of fire was to allow the smoke to clear. It also allowed officers to see the effect of their fire, and to change targets or adjust ranges if necessary.

The general principle embodied in British military practice therefore indicated that slow fire was more likely to be effective fire and there are no references in the training manuals of the late-1870s as to the rate of fire that was expected of infantry companies in the field. However, the *Musketry Instruction Manual* for 1887, when the Martini-Henry was still in use, indicates rates of fire for field practices that are deeply revealing. These rates were a reflection of what the rifle might achieve under ideal conditions. So, far from the eighteen or twenty rounds of modern myth, it was noted that:

> 'One minute will be allowed for each of five volleys, counting from the first command '*Ready*' ...It should distinctly be understood that the section commander is under no obligation to fire five volleys; on the contrary, it would be wiser to fire only four volleys if he thinks the results would be better'.

Rorke's Drift is the most famous example of the fire being effective without being unduly destructive. Here the defenders theoretically fired off nearly 20,000 rounds in ten hours, killing some 531 Zulus – an average rate of fire of rather less than 15 rounds per man per hour, with a kill ratio of 33:1. The circumstances here are of the greatest importance; after the initial attacks were met by volley firing, most of the fire would have been independent fire, at ranges so close that they effectively constituted hand-to-hand combat, or directed against an enemy concealed by natural cover. Moreover, much of that firing would have taken place with the bayonet fixed – which seriously affected accuracy – and in circumstances where careful aiming was difficult with all firing carried out in the dark, lit at best by the flames of the burning hospital. Under such circumstances, the low rate of kills-to-shots is not surprising, but the British fire could hardly be considered ineffective. On the contrary, it was particularly effective in its primary objective after dark, that of suppressing the enemy, and discouraging his attacks. Every time Zulu chants or shouts of command suggested that an attack was imminent, the defenders poured fire in that direction. Although the number of hits was undoubtedly minimal, it was often sufficient, by that stage of the battle, to prevent the attack from developing.

Index